Text
&
Image

Text
&
Image

Art and the Performance of Memory

Edited by
Richard Cándida Smith

Memory and Narrative Series

Transaction Publishers
New Brunswick (U.S.A.) and London (U.K.)

First paperback edition published in 2006 by Transaction Publishers, New Brunswick, New Jersey, by arrangement with Routledge.

This book is printed on acid-free paper that meets the American National Standard for Permanence of Paper for Printed Library Materials.

Library of Congress Catalog Number: 2005053806
ISBN: 1-4128-0485-X (paper)
Printed in the United States of America

Library of Congress Cataloging-in-Publication Data

Text and image : art and the performance of memory / Richard Cándida Smith, editor.—1st pbk. ed.
    p. cm.—(Memory and narrative series)
    Updated ed. of: Art and the performance of memory : sounds and gestures of recollection. 2002.
    Includes bibliographical references and index.
    ISBN 1-4128-0485-X (pbk.)
        1. Memory in art. 2. History in art. 3. Arts, Modern—20th century.
    I. Title: Art and the performance of memory. II. Cándida Smith, Richard.
    III. Art and the performance of memory. IV. Memory and narrative.

NX650.M45T49   2005
700'.458—dc22   2005053806

Eugene C. Smith, *Struggle for Memory*, 2001, oil on canvas, 24 × 36 inches.
Courtesy of the artist.

CONTENTS

CONTENTS

LIST OF ILLUSTRATIONS

NOTES ON CONTRIBUTORS

Ryan Snyder Ananat recently completed his Ph.D. in the Program in American Culture at the University of Michigan. His dissertation examines how new media technologies have worked to enable artistic improvisation. His next project will explore how advances in sound recording illuminate contemporaneous experiments in fiction writing.

Iain Borden is Reader in Architecture and Urban Culture at The Bartlett, University College London, where he is Director of Architectural History and Theory. He is author of *Architecture in Motion: Skateboarding and Urban Experience* (forthcoming) and, with Jane Rendell, coauthor of *DoubleDecker: Architecture through History, Politics and Poetics* (2001). He is also coeditor of *Architecture and the Sites of History: Interpreting Buildings and Cities* (1995), *Strangely Familiar: Narratives of Architecture in the City* (1996), *The Unknown City: Contesting Architecture and Social Space* (2000), *Gender Space Architecture: An Interdisciplinary Introduction* (2000), *The City Cultures Reader* (2000), and *InterSections: Architectural Histories and Critical Theories* (2000).

Richard Cándida Smith is Professor of History at the University of California, Berkeley, where he also serves as Director of the Regional Oral History Office, Bancroft Library. He is the author of *Utopia and Dissent: Art, Poetry, and Politics in California* (1995) and *Mallarmé's Children: Symbolism and the Renewal of Experience* (1999). He is past executive secretary and president of the Oral History Association (USA), and one of the principal editors of the Studies in Memory and Narrative series.

Jeff Friedman is Assistant Professor in the Dance Program at Mason Gross School of the Arts, Rutgers University in New Brunswick, New Jersey. He is also an active choreographer and performer, and Founding Director of LEGACY Oral History Project, which records and preserves the life-histories of San Francisco Bay Area dance community members at risk. He has performed *Muscle Memory* in residencies throughout the United States and in Europe. Jeff is also the author of a forthcoming essay titled "Fractious Action" on the theory and method of oral history-based performance for Altamira Press' *Oral History Research Handbook*.

Paul J. Karlstrom recently retired as West Coast Regional Director of the Archives of American Art, Smithsonian Institution. He has conducted numerous taped interviews and has produced video documentaries on modern and contemporary art. The author of various works on aspects of American art and culture, he is coauthor of *Turning the Tide: Early Los Angeles Modernists, 1920-1956* (1990) and the editor of *On the Edge of America: California Modernist*

Art, 1900-1950 (1996). He has contributed essays to *Diego Rivera: Art and Revolution* (1999) and *Over the Line: The Art and Life of Jacob Lawrence* (2000).

Lizzetta LeFalle-Collins is an independent scholar and curator. Her publication and curatorial highlights include *Sargent Johnson: African American Modernist, Personal Icons: the Art of Betye Saar, In the Spirit of Resistance: African American Modernists and the Mexican Muralist School,* and *Noah Purifoy: Outside and in the Open.* She was also selected as the official curator from the United States to present "The Poetics of Politics: Iconography and Spirituality" at the Twenty-second São Paulo International Bienal and the First Johannesburg Biennale. She has written on Jacob Lawrence and is currently developing an exhibition and catalog on the nineteenth-century lithographer and painter Grafton Tyler Brown and co-curating an exhibition *La Tercera Raiz (The Third Root): The African Presence in Mexico.*

Warren Linds is an Assistant Professor in the Department of Applied Human Sciences, Concordia University, Montreal, Canada. He has been engaged in popular theater facilitation and collaborative theater creation since 1985 and is interested in theater as a research methodology. His doctoral dissertation, "A Journey in Metaxis," explores the facilitation of theater for social change in communities and schools. He is a coeditor of *Unfolding Bodymind: Exploring Possibilities in Education* (2001).

Stephanie Marlin-Curiel is an instructor in drama at the Tisch School of the Arts, New York University; where she is completing a Ph.D. in the Department of Performance Studies. Her dissertation, "Theatre of Testimony: Performing Memory for a Post–Apartheid South Africa," was awarded a Dean's Dissertation Fellowship. Other articles from this work have appeared in *TDR: The Drama Review* and the *South African Theatre Journal.*

Ana Maria Mauad is an adjunct professor of the History Department and of the Post-Graduation Program of History and Science of Art at Universidade Federal Fluminense in Brazil. She also coordinates the Laboratory of Oral History and Iconography at her school. She specializes in historiography, theory, and method of history, and research on the use of images, particularly photographs, as historical sources.

Alejandra Medellín de la Piedra began acting for theater and professional television in 1984. She studied acting at the National School of Theater in Mexico City and theater at the University of British Columbia. She worked for five years at the Centro Nacional de Investigaci6n Teatral Rodolfo Usigli (National Center for Theater Research) in Mexico City, and she currently teaches in the theater program at the Universidad de las Américas in Puebla, Mexico, as well as at the National School of Theater. She has recently collaborated on a multidisciplinary project at the National Dance Research Center.

David Michalski is the author of *Cosmos and Damian: A World Trade Center Collage* (Lowell, MA: Bootstrap Press, 2005) and the editor of the online journal *Streetnotes* (http://www.xcp.bfn.org). He is a graduate student in

Cultural Studies at the University of California, Davis, where he is also a Humanities and Social Sciences Librarian.

Kadi Purru is from Tartu, Estonia, and studied theater at the Institute of Theatre, Music and Cinematography in St. Petersburg, Russia. In 1987, she moved with her family to Colombia, where she observed the work of the Teatro Experimental de Cali and taught theater history and Latin American theater at the Universidad de Valle. Since 1991 she has been living in Vancouver. Her dissertation, "Acknowledging Home(s) and Belonging(s): Border Writing" (University of British Columbia, 2003), is a performative journeying through the discursive landscapes of nation, ethnicity, diaspora, and "race." Her academic work co-emerges with her community theater work. She is currently tutoring post-colonial drama at Athabasca University and recently completed the community performance "Migrant Homes" based on the life-stories of the Canadian Estonians in Vancouver.

Jane Rendell is Reader in Architecture and Art and Director of Architectural Research at the Bartlett School of Architecture, University College London. An architectural designer and historian, art critic, and writer, she is author of *The Pursuit of Pleasure* (Continuum/Rutgers University Press, 2002), editor of "A Place Between," a special issue of the *Public Art Journal* (October 1999) and "Critical Architecture," a special issue of the *Journal of Architecture* (June 2005), and coeditor of *Strangely Familiar* (Routledge, 1995), *Gender Space Architecture* (Routledge, 1999), *Intersections* (Routledge, 2000) and *The Unknown City* (MIT Press, 2000). She is currently completing a new book on art and architecture and working on a project of site-writings.

Anne Rutherford teaches Cinema Studies at University of Western Sydney. Her publications include essays and interviews on affect and embodiment in cinema spectatorship and on documentary cinema and historiography. Her recent work includes a study of affect and mise-en-scène in the work of Lee Myung-se, forthcoming in *Seoul Searching: Culture and Identity in Contemporary Korean Cinema* (SUNY Press), and an essay on affect and mimetic visuality in the work of Indian documentarists Anjali Monteiro and K. P. Jayasankar. She has also made several short films.

Ivy Schroeder is Assistant Professor of Art and Design at Southern Illinois University. Her research focuses on contemporary American public sculpture and minimalist sculpture in the public sphere. Her areas of specialization are twentieth-century European and American art and architecture, contemporary American art, and art theory.

Elvan Zabunyan, historian of contemporary art and art critic, is Assistant Professor at the University of Rennes, France. She mainly works on contemporary feminist and postcolonial theories. She recently published *Black is a Color, A History of Contemporary African American Art* (Paris: Dis, 2004-2005). *Black is a Color* received the first prize for research from SAES/AFEA (Société des Anglicistes de l'enseignement supérieur/Association Française d'études américaines), 2005.

ACKNOWLEDGMENTS

Permission to reproduce an English translation of Antonio Machado granted by Harvard University from *Antonio Machado: Selected Poems*, translated by Alan Trueblood (Cambridge, MA: Harvard University Press), © 1982 by the President and Fellows of Harvard College.

The following authors have granted permission for their poems to be quoted in David Michalski's chapter: Robert Kroetsch, "The Ledger," from *Completed Fieldnotes* (Toronto: McClelland and Steward, Inc., 1998), 15; William Sylvester, "Wildlife Exhibit: Family Approved, A Collage from the Oral History Collections, State Historical Societies of Nebraska, Wyoming, and Idaho Arranged by William Sylvester with Some Words of his Own" (self-published, December 1978); David Michalski, "Making It (Up): A Collage Poem from Studs Terkel's *Working*," a poem written for the Oral History Association annual meeting in Buffalo, New York, October 1998; Mark A. Nowak, "Zwyczaj," *American Anthropologist* 100 (1998): 271–274.

Gordon and Breach/Harwood Academic Publishers has granted permission to reproduce excerpts of illustrative diagrams from Peggy Hackney, *Making Connections: Total Body Integration through Batenieff Fundamentals* (Amsterdam: Gordon and Breach Publishers, 1998), drawings by Mary Konrad Weeks, text by Peggy Hackney.

1

INTRODUCTION

Performing the archive

Richard Cándida Smith

> It is by lending his body to the world that the artist changes the world into paintings.
>
> > Maurice Merleau-Ponty, "Eye and Mind"[1]

> We are concerned here with nameless, nonacoustic languages, languages issuing from matter; here we should recall the material community of things in their communication.
>
> > Walter Benjamin, "On Language as Such and on the Language of Man"[2]

During an interview I conducted with the noted African American artist John Outterbridge, I noticed that John, in recalling his childhood in North Carolina, accompanied his vivid recollections of his mother making soap with a flurry of alternately subdued and expansive mime movements. As he spoke, his fingers paced out the dimensions of the kitchen and porch where she worked, carefully locating the stove, the counters where she placed her vats, and the storage area where she put the long, freshly prepared slats of soap to cool before cutting them into bars. For a few seconds, his fingers traced her steps in the old house where they had lived, then they merged back into his upper torso as his arms and shoulders expanded to imitate his mother's body going from task to task in a long and arduous process. The gestures became even broader as he described the smells and the emotions they stirred within him. A counterpoint emerged. His words centered on himself, once again in his mind's eye, a small boy watching, occasionally lending a hand when asked, but his body continued to recall the diligent craft of his mother. Intermittently, he evoked the aromatic experience with deep inhalations that relocated the boy into the body of a 57-year-old man. Words flowed as one part of a complex dance, another expression of which was a series of elegant, translucent sculptures inspired by the same memories.[3]

By making assemblages, tableaux, and sculpture, John Outterbridge had found the most effective way for *him* to express a continuing relation to the past. The

1

memory that inspired him was dispersed however across a number of expressive forms, each of which provided their own variations on a theme. We conducted the oral history interview in order to extract from him a verbal account of his life and concerns that might make it easier for others who knew nothing about him or his life to read his art. As objects, powerfully affective as they are, they nonetheless stand silent and therefore elusive. The words he and I recorded were to provide a set of clues for understanding their historical and personal context. My interview with John is one of thousands that scholars and journalists have conducted with artists. Interviews have become a primary, perhaps obligatory resource on the visual and performing arts.

Yet there is a conundrum that every interpreter of oral sources in the arts faces sooner or later. Visual and performing artists work in expressive forms and media that resist language. Interviews involve a translation from one level of experience to another. The process parallels what happens when a work first appears before the public. Words in the form of criticism, whether written or word of mouth, translate creative objects and gestures into a body of response that testifies to the impact a work has achieved. The need to throw immediate sensual experiences off into words underscores the ambiguous if necessary relation of word, gesture, and object in the consolidation of experience and memory.

The oral expressions that interviews document, however, contain more than words arranged into sentences arranged into narratives of varying lengths, an illusion that transcripts foster. Spoken expression is inseparable from emotion and gesture. A context of direct interaction with other people also suffused by emotions shapes what is said as well. Every interview occurs in a process of physical performance for an interlocutor. Body gestures provide wordless images that try to deepen a speaker's synthesis of a complex series of events into a readily comprehensible and expressible anecdote. Vocal gestures shape the delivery of words. Patterns of speaking, repetitions of words and phrases, variation in force, pitch, and tone contribute to an effort to convey meaning and not just information.

The mixture of interior and physical motion John Outterbridge displayed as he conjured himself into the mental space of his childhood forcefully reminded me of Frances Yates's descriptions in *The Art of Memory* of techniques that ancient Greek and Roman rhetoricians devised to assist the recall of lengthy memorized texts. One of the earliest writers on the subject, Simonides of Ceos, advised that memory training might best start by an adept imagining himself inside a building. Visualizing movement through this space provided a sequence to recollection. Each of the rooms should arise clearly in the mind's eye, decorated in a manner appropriate to the subject under recall. The texts themselves were to be marked by striking icons, the contemplation of which stimulated the hidden words to flood into the speaker's body.[4] The classic conception of memory relied upon a fusion of the senses. In and of itself, language was too slippery to hold onto with confidence. Vision provided, within this scheme, the most precise sensations, so words needed to be covered with forms that the eye could master. Images, however, did not appear unless the body first put itself in motion through space. A search for visual cues served as prelude to an effective performance making the recalled word present in every part of the body. Tongue, eye, feet, hands, hips, chest were all equally engaged in and equally necessary to the machinery of memory. As Plato suggested in one of his dialogs, the notation of words on paper had proved a useful tool for reminding people of things they had forgotten. For precisely that reason, however, writing invited amnesia as it disengaged humanity from a deep, embodied connection with past experience.[5]

Plato's well-known observation calls to mind a distinction that will be a running theme in the thirteen chapters constituting this new volume for Routledge Studies in Memory and Narrative. Memory exists in an ongoing process of performance and response. Traces of the past otherwise slip into the archive, an ever-present but usually ignored repository filled with the random survivals of antecedent social relationships stored in buildings, landscapes, libraries, museums, store windows, the electronic media, as well as in the everyday lives of the countless unknown people whose paths cross ours. One person's memory is another person's archive. The songs our fellow citizens sing, the gestures they make in talking to each other, the decorations they hang on their homes, the snapshots they bring to work provide clues to the histories they have endured – but only if we are willing to take as our own the memories they have endeavored to keep alive. The institutions surrounding the visual and performing arts orchestrate on a more formal level a retrieval from the historical archives upon which every society rests traces of a nation's past that the artists believe are necessary to confront if the public is to address present-day dilemmas and opportunities.

This volume considers the roles that the visual and performing arts have played in plucking fragments out of the historical archive and representing them to various publics as potential repertories for people to engage and perform as they confront the future. The contributors draw upon work based in art and architectural history, social and cultural history, and performance studies applied to topics drawn from North and South America, Europe, and Africa. The chapters share a common set of questions as they explore, firmly grounded in their distinctive disciplinary standpoints, the circuit of word, gesture, object in the formation and reproduction of knowledge, identity, and community. In engaging the relationship of verbal and physical expressive forms, the authors inquire in a variety of distinct historical and social contexts how verbal language conventions shape the reception of visual and performing art, while considering how performance of space, object, and/or gesture can upend the apparent content of verbal explanations.

What the authors consider is a process often taken for granted. What does a gesture, whether congealed in the movement of a hand, the rise in pitch of a voice, or in the shape of a fabricated object, contribute to meaning? The gesture itself lies beyond words, but without its presence, words stand devoid of context. Ludwig Wittgenstein maintained that every statement rested on unproven assumptions and illogical associations. Meaning arises from conditions external to though surrounding the statement. Only if a proposition generates a response that is capable of generating further responses, has one created a meaningful situation. Close analysis might likely reveal contradictions, but "to understand a proposition is to know what is the case, if it is true." The "case" meaning a sense of what one must do, for if there was nothing to do, there would be no meaning to a statement. Deficiencies in the formal expression of communication are overcome by reaching out to initiate an exchange process that he likened to a game. If players know the rules, they expect a range of possible responses and shape the statement accordingly. The rules of a language game provide prefigurative conceptions that allow configurations to be exchanged as if they were meaningful. Meaning does not lie in the text per se but in the relationship for which the text is one of many signs.[6]

Gestures are symbols of a reaction, that is to say, a response that affirms the factuality of a relation. Gestures, which would have no meaning if they did not invite respondents into a shared space, affirm an intersubjective experience which will also likely contain a verbal counterpart. An "I" speaks to a "you" about an "it" in order to get a reaction of one kind or another. This is true even if the intent is to repel or reject another person. During the moment that rejection is enunciated the speaker has invited another person into a connection that will be abruptly terminated as the other is forcibly excluded from shared space. Language in that case may often take the form of a special argot, understandable to those already initiated but confusing and threatening to everybody else. The gestural forms, both bodily and vocal, state unequivocally, "You cannot possibly understand me!"

For Merleau-Ponty, gesture emerged as a unifying effort that brought together impressions formed across the spectrum of the senses into a response. Gesture organized a system that included a subject-position by reaching back out to the sources of perception with a reaction. What he called the *postural schema* was the foundation of consciousness, for without it there was no sense of relationality. Consciousness and a sense of self emerged in intersubjective contact, which included as part of its arc, an interpretive performance of the other's actions.[7] Expressive gestures had a univocal meaning in an immediate context, but their presence "announced the constitution of a symbolic system capable of redesigning an infinite number of situations."[8]

The magic of the artist is an ability to reproduce a sense of shared space outside of immediate face-to-face encounters. Creative power to stimulate reactions brings to the surface patterns of habituated responses articulating rules needed for the given communication to occur successfully. Our bodies must be inseparable from the rules governing communicative exchange, or artists would lack the power to make something absent feel as if it were present. Conversely, the always present rules normally feel as if they were not there until work with particular power collages concept into a sensible pattern of gesture extending physically from one mind to others.[9] Words are gestures because they too are symbols of a reaction that continues in a chain of performances that art historian George Kubler once called "the shape of time."[10]

It is for these reasons that the expressive forms discussed in the following chapters – words, graphic and plastic objects, bodily and vocal gestures, spatial relationships – constitute a circuit through which enactive memory constantly circulates. There are "many ways for consciousness to be conscious," Merleau-Ponty observed, as

4

many ways as there can be perceptions.[11] To be accessible at all, art must be talked about, and thus verbal consciousness appears to be dominant. Criticism, whether published or word of mouth, is vital for public recognition of a work. On an everyday, personal level, spectators must talk about their reactions to an exhibition, a film, or a performance in order to organize a recollection of the experience worth retaining for the future. Nonetheless, no matter how much or in what contexts a work is discussed, its value in social exchange eludes all of its verbal approximations. A work finds and holds onto a public precisely because it offers an experience that slips away from words and the ready-to-hand categories they provide. We turn to the visual and performing arts because these modes of expression capture aspects of experience and feeling that elude words. Wittgenstein asserted, "What *can* be shown *cannot* be said."[12] But then we must use words to share processes that communicate on other levels. Verbal accounts act as currency, but they can be the whole story only in the archive.

So what do words add that are so important that the circuit disappears without their presence? On a utopian level, Francis Ponge thought that the semantic thickness of words restored and replenished the material thickness of things by "increasing the quantity of our qualities."[13] Every verbal account introduced new types of words that play against each other simultaneously as communities grasped to feel possibilities for connection. A verbal kaleidoscope revealed alternative modes of relating, some but not all incompatible. Gesture devolved into negotiation over preferred meanings and how unexpected responses might transform the nature of the contact. From this transfigured sense of connection would flow a future with room for broader ranges of difference. Ponge invokes a familiar, haunting dream of integration achieved through expressive gestures transcending the "here and now" with intimations of a previously unthinkable fullness of contact.

It is a dream that has motivated artists and poets for many generations, particularly those who want their work to support broader struggles for social justice. In a moving joint reflection, "Resonating Testimonies From/In the Space of Death: Performing Buenaventura's *La maestra*," Warren Linds, Alejandra Medellín, and Kadi Purru invite their readers to cross the proscenium arch and vicariously share their learning experience as theater professionals working on Enrique Buenaventura's dramatic expression of the violence afflicting his homeland, Colombia. Medellín, a Mexican stage director, Linds, a Canadian popular theater facilitator with a long history of support work for Latin American causes, and Purru, an Estonian theater critic and historian who moved to Colombia in 1987, where she had an opportunity to observe and participate in Buenaventura's theater-making process, enact for each other the relationship of memory and archive. What has been personal experience for one was until their collaboration background information for the other two. They must integrate their perspectives if they are to succeed in conveying to audiences the full horror of what Buenaventura depicts or find hope in a sense of connection with the characters the play has allowed them to touch. Their performative and interactive text explores a mode of learning the authors call *enactive knowledge*. Their challenge was not to get lost in the play as a world in and of itself, but to use it to reconnect back to the contemporary world and understand more deeply the cruelty embedded in its structures. Enactive presentations, if successful, actualize a space where the situations of others, normally vanishing into the patter of the media, become substantial. A moral connection forms that adds new responsibilities to relationships that already existed as a result of a long history of political and economic acts but which are as a result of dramatic performance understood in a new way.

The activities of the Truth and Reconciliation Commission (TRC) established in South Africa with the triumph of majority rule enacted on a national scale a full accounting of the human rights violations of the apartheid regime, as well as those of the liberation struggle. Public testimony from victims and victimizers allowed for a national ritual through which all social groups could recognize and accept the horrors of their collective history, form a new national consciousness based on a determination not ever again to tolerate racial injustice, and move forward to construct a new multiracial society. In "Truth and Consequences: Art in Response to the Truth and Reconciliation Commission," Stephanie Marlin-Curiel examines two recent art exhibitions in South Africa and several theater productions that have pushed against the juridical boundaries that structured performance of testimony and judgment in the TRC's hearings. Marlin-Curiel examines how visual and theater artists attempted a public performance of memories and feelings that the TRC's formal legal proceedings could not address. The work she analyzes has triggered considerable controversy in South Africa because the artists appropriated the experience of victims in order to probe for "truth" outside the definitions that the TRC had set. As this chapter demonstrates, some performances may have the goal of retiring memories to the archive where their inactivity gives them the appearance of being harmless. In this situation, are artists striving to keep alive the themes of truth, memory, and culpability endangering the nation by picking at wounds that might be better left alone to heal? Or are they facilitating healing by ensuring that collective memories form across a wider level of experience than a legal agendum might allow? The TRC, like parallel inquests into the Holocaust, have proven that words can be given to events that at first sight must seem to be beyond description. Without the semantic thickness that Ponge ascribed to verbal performance, the fullness of what humans have done to each other would be less sensible and more readily shoved aside.

The dialectic of verbal and non-verbal expressive gestures in the formation of thick understandings reappears as a central theme in Anne Rutherford's chapter, "Precarious Boundaries: Affect, Mise-en-scène, and the Senses." Taking as her case in point *Ulysses' Gaze*, Theo Angelopoulos's 1995 filmic trek through the Balkans during the height of the Bosnian war, Rutherford explores how sensual synthesis of multiple semiotic systems work to construct and/or deconstruct the feel of the past. Rutherford adopts a model of cinematic materiality that foregrounds the embodied aspects of spectatorship. She argues that corporeal reception generates a sensory awakening that she calls, following Walter Benjamin, *mimetic innervation*. These historically situated interior movements provide intuitive matrices necessary for an affective organization of "facts" into memories that one accepts as truth. She argues that a return to an understanding of film as embodied learning brings greater clarity to the dialectical relationship of sensory perception and ideological construction.

The ideas of Walter Benjamin inspire the next two chapters as well, which explore the city, everyday conversation, and new media technologies as spaces the occupation of which requires performances transfiguring archive into memory. Following the classic model of memory that Yates described, the authors associate the process of recollection with movement through space. Site provides a structure for the placement of memory cues. By modeling memory techniques on urban space, however, classic rhetoricians emphasized that their systems imposed order upon an otherwise unruly natural process for they imagined urban environment as an enclosure excluding the chaos of nature with logical form.[14]

Elvan Zabunyan, an art historian from France, adapts notions of the archive and site to movement through electronic space that the Net, the Web, and CD-ROMs have made such a common part of contemporary life. The flâneur of today is more likely to be trolling hyperlinks and chat rooms than promenading down the Boulevard Haussmann or Fifth Avenue and in the process experiencing a sense of self able to cross effortlessly barriers of both time and space. Can such a fragmented archive provide for integration as well as expansion? In "Stratum and Resonance: Displacement in the Work of Renée Green," Zabunyan considers what the performance and conceptual art of a contemporary African American artist tells us about memory in a world in which language, space, vision, and electronic records disperse the sites for the storage of memory cues. A viable link remains possible in the movement of the subject, whose ability to experience what has been obscured depends on her skill in locating and connecting the networks of clues enveloping her into a system of meaning. The system is only a proposition but its power can be seen in the narratives it allows as gestures of shared experience.

In "Cities Memory Voices Collage," poet and critic David Michalski links the experience of urban space to the development of new speech forms. He investigates the use by poets of oral history transcripts as source material for understanding the subjectivities that the modern urban archive puts in motion. He considers the use of poetry as an investigative method that can uncover what he calls the *interscripts*. Individual voices heard at random appear to be personal and individual, but the poet listens for patterns of sharing and repetition and assembles voices into an image of connection that reveals, however precariously, a situational totality. Through his focus on oral history as a research source that documents a full range of experience and not simply narrative accounts, Michalski offers insights into the relation of spoken language to visual sensation and spatial movement made possible in contemporary constructed environments.

The enactive knowledge that performance sparks connects memory to the present in a way that contrasts the congealed understandings of words with the fuller experience that embodied memory allows. The next chapters explore contrasts between voice and body and what might be learned from thinking about their relationship in the construction and expression of historical meaning. The authors ask how does attending to the distinction between categorical and embodied expression begin to open up for analysis fuller ranges of historical experience? How might the distinctions between voice, vision, and performance lead to more complex understandings of the past?

With "Eros in the Studio," art historian Paul J. Karlstrom compares the memories of artists' models with those of artists for whom they worked to understand more fully the process by which paintings, drawings, and art photographs articulate erotic desire. Karlstrom explores the differences in perspective between women who became models in the 1960s, the 1970s, and the 1990s to see how changing ideas about sexuality and gender reshaped both models' and artists' expectations. The author makes palpable the performance of power in artist–model relationships. He complicates the picture by paying attention to the ways in which the models felt they exercised power over the artist, as well as by examining how feminist artists in the 1970s developed an independent perspective on the presentation of sexuality through art. Karlstrom provocatively addresses the tensions involved in the displacement of desire into an image that must negotiate the tension between gesture and gaze.

In "*Muscle Memory*: Performing Embodied Knowledge," Jeff Friedman reconstructs the origins and goals of his oral history project documenting dancers and choreographers. He explores the relationship between verbal communication and gestural expression/exhibition in both oral history and professional dance. He brings to the study of oral sources concepts and methodologies rooted in dance scholarship and argues convincingly for their value in thinking more deeply about the importance of physicalized gesture to memory. He argues that oral history can bring into sharper focus the embodied knowledge, or *habitus*, that underlies and sustains all discourse. Friedman illustrates his points through reference to a performance piece he composed from oral history interviews with dancers, while bringing in other movement examples relevant to his argument. Friedman notes that every speech act is always a physical expression as well, a performance that inevitably places every speaker in a position analogous to that of the creative artist.

Ryan Snyder's ethnographic study "'Hope . . . teach, yaknowhati'msayin': Freestylin Knowledge through Detroit Hiphop" develops this perspective as a central aspect of a contemporary popular music form. Snyder explores freestylin, a form of vocal improvisation that is a cornerstone of hiphop. Snyder observed the club scene in Detroit and interviewed emergent artists to explore the distinctive form of knowledge that impromptu extemporization provides for both artists and fans. Snyder explores the parallels between interviewing and freestylin as expressions of the values of "diligent improvisation" explicitly treasured as providing an alternative to static and bureaucratic modes of knowledge. He argues that hiphop underscores the prevalence of the improvisatory and the oral as forms of knowing in contemporary societies. He focuses on the interview as a process having much in common with hiphop. He suggests that interviewing introduces into the academy both the opinions of the people and underlying popular epistemologies. He notes, however, that professional demands in both music and education tend to censor what can be learned through improvisation.

In my chapter grounded in intellectual history, "Les Gammes: Making Visible the Representative Modern Man," I review critical reception of Claude Monet to suggest how and why impressionist painting provided a ready screen upon which critics could project prototypical modern values of empirical science, self-negating morality, and craft virtue. By World War I, Monet had become one of the primary symbols of the French Republic and the values for which the nation fought, an association affirmed in his famous murals of water lilies enshrined at the Orangerie. Monet and the impressionists have continued to exert a powerful attraction for museum goers for well over a hundred years. Their work remains a mainstay of contemporary public culture in the occidental world. In examining the semantic registers refined in discussing Monet's achievement, I propose that the formal use of the painting medium had to be the focus of interest and discussion, more important than the content of imagery, because it was painterly technique that provided spectators with an attractive ideal self-image that they could use for constructing and reproducing a modern sense of middle-class identity able to balance the conflicting demands of rapid social change.

Social historian Ana Maria Mauad examines the construction of family identity and memory through the family photograph album in "Composite Past: Photography and Family Memories in Brazil (1850–1950)." She looks at styles and meanings ascribed to photographs by an upper-class Brazilian family in the nineteenth century when studio photographers created most images, and then examines the changes at the turn of the century as snapshot cameras became increasingly popular. She uses interviews to help understand genre conventions and the ways in which families have represented their own identity with the different visual languages that changing photographic technology made available to them. Mauad's chapter explores how photographs came to organize conversations about family history and events and provide a sense of continuity in a rapidly changing social environment.

Lizzetta LeFalle-Collins's "Memories of Mammy" examines popularized images of the mammy figure in the first part of the twentieth century, and then discusses how African American poets and artists adopted the mammy stereotype as a foundational figure for art of the "New Negro." She focuses on the sculptor Sargent Johnson (active 1930s–1940s), who subverted negative stereotypes by transforming them into positive archetypes articulating African American ideals of community and resistance. LeFalle-Collins examines how a single image can be performed very differently depending upon the cultural memories evoked/triggered and the historical resonances that artists learn to manipulate creatively.

Ivy Schroeder in "Official Art, Official Publics: Public Sculpture under the Federal Art-in-Architecture Program since 1972" surveys how tensions between aesthetic and civic ideologies played out in the design of art for federal buildings from the Nixon to the Clinton administrations. She discusses efforts to make public art more responsive to the concerns of the employees and patrons of federal buildings.

Schroeder uses her examples to detail how officially sanctioned art styles have involved negotiation between dominant ideas in the US art world about the relation of artist, critic, and public with images of the government–public/citizen relationship that administrations have wanted to promote.

In the concluding chapter, "Private Reflections/Public Matters: Public Art in the City," architectural historians Iain Borden and Jane Rendell present a brilliant collage of word and image that they invite readers to perform. The archives from which memory draws, they note, are inherently fragmented. They require the active participation of a reader before they can assume a coherent, meaning-laden form. The movement through the myriad cultural forms that urban life throws up calls into play an interplay of habit, chance, and desire that results in the activation of some traces, the ignoring of most, and the effacing of others. Drawing upon Walter Benjamin's conception of the *dialectical image*, an experience at once material and ideational, Borden and Rendell begin with a conceptual exploration of public art within the context of everyday city life. They explore the variety of spatial storytelling possibilities that use of a city provokes. They conclude with a provocative argument on the role of performance in daily life for creating structures of meaning out of the scattered and contradictory clues that public culture provides, shaped as it has been equally if not more through chance decisions of individuals as by the official strategies of public agencies. Their chapter emphasizes that any practice of intertextuality involves an exchange between and across media that occurs day in and day out as people engage each other at work, at home, and at play. Every recipient negotiates the play of forms and messages bombarding them by creating an inter-script that collages what they have seen into a point of view to be expressed in their own contributions to a contested, consequently shared culture.

One of the goals of this volume has been to think through the relation of content and medium in the circulation of expression without being confined by technical, formal, or institutional boundaries separating each medium. Enunciations disperse across forms occupying different social sites and directing themselves ostensibly to distinct sensual capacities. Each form involves discrete processes of production, distribution, reception, and interpretation, the shape of which will vary depending on who is involved and on the goals they seek. Their intersection reveals experiences and relationships that cannot be said with precision because the content eludes the formal communicative possibilities within any single given medium. Each individual statement keeps in motion propositions that may reaffirm, may expand, or may challenge the repertory available for "saying" this is who I am in relation to different people, objects, events, processes, for articulating a *reaction* that is the focal point of meaning. Whatever is put forward is tentative, waiting for the next relay in the circuit. Semiotic codes and the rules of communicative situations, what Wittgenstein called "language games," provide boundaries that, given political and social context, range from relatively flexible to relatively strict. Nonetheless, every communicative act is dependent upon performance, which introduces the possibility of improvisation and change. Semantic fields are inevitably altered with every addition, particularly when the effort to model relationships leaps across expressive forms.[15]

10

When and why gestures leap between forms is explored in the following chapters, along with a look at the theoretical and political implications of such movement.

In these examples of "storytelling," to use Benjamin's term for the steady transmission of past experiences in living social circuits, archive and memory intersect to reveal a range of tactical reactive possibilities for subjects that exist by and through acts of integrating, however temporarily, dispersed expressions of archived experience.[16] Each expressive form provides a site for memory that draws upon dispersed traces of the past that remain real only to the degree that their contents are incorporated into a repertory available to suggest options for future action. Archived traces have been retrieved as something that can be performed, but not at all times. The repertory provides an intermediary, replicatory layer that invites the personalization of performance. Repertories provide a recollection of a variety of experiences that once mattered and revivify them for the present.[17] First, however, someone has put into a circulation a proposition for a potentially new way of inhabiting the past, presented in a gestural expression the value of which is the way in which its form prefigures a memory yet to come.

Notes

1 Maurice Merleau-Ponty, "Eye and Mind," in *The Primacy of Perception: And Other Essays on Phenomenological Psychology, the Philosophy of Art, History and Politics* (Evanston, IL: Northwestern University Press, 1964), 162.

2 Walter Benjamin, "On Language as Such and on the Language of Man," in *Reflections: Essays, Aphorisms, Autobiographical Writings* (New York: Schocken, 1986), 330.

3 See John Outterbridge, "African-American Artists of Los Angeles: John W. Outterbridge," interviewed 1990 by Richard Cándida Smith, Oral History Program, University of California, Los Angeles, 2 vols, 1993.

4 Frances A. Yates, *The Art of Memory* (London: Pimlico Press, 1992), 17. Thanks to Robert Scott for bringing this example to my attention.

5 Plato, *Phaedrus*, 274c–275b; see also Augustine, *Confessions*, X. Herbert Marks has noted that prophecy in ancient Israel was both visual and rhetorical. The pre-exilic prophets heard the voice of God, and in an "overflow of divine presence," they received visions, or "mnemic images" that the struggle to describe verbally was central to a moral awakening. See Marks, "The Twelve Prophets," in *The Literary Guide to the Bible*, eds. Robert Alter and Frank Kermode (Cambridge, MA: Harvard University Press, 1987), 224–232.

6 See Ludwig Wittgenstein, *Tractatus Logico-Philosophicus*, 4.024; *Philosophical Investigations*, 217; *Blue Book*, 17. See also Paul Ricoeur, *Time and Narrative*, Volume 1, Chapter 3 (Chicago: University of Chicago Press, 1984) for more on the circuit of prefiguration, configuration, and refiguration.

7 Maurice Merleau-Ponty, "The Child's Relation with Others," in *The Primacy of Perception*, 117–118; "The Primacy of Perception," in *The Primacy of Perception*, 17.

8 Maurice Merleau-Ponty, "An Unpublished Text," in *The Primacy of Perception*, 7.

9 See ibid., 9.

10 See George Kubler, *The Shape of Time: Remarks on the History of Things* (New Haven, CT: Yale University Press, 1962).

11 Maurice Merleau-Ponty, *The Phenomenology of Perception* (London: Routledge and Kegan Paul, 1962), 124.

12 Wittgenstein. *Tractatus Logico-Philosophicus*, 4.1212.

13 Francis Ponge, "Introduction au galet," in Ponge, *Tome premier* (Paris: Editions Gallimard, 1965), 197.

14 Joseph Rykwert explored the ways in which urban form has signified separation from nature in *The Idea of a Town: The Anthropology of Urban Form in Rome, Italy, and the Ancient World* (Princeton, NJ: Princeton University Press, 1976).

15 For a discussion of the ways in which semantic performance limits semiotic determination see Paul Ricoeur, "Creativity in Language: Word, Polysemy, Metaphor," in *The Philosophy of Paul Ricoeur: An Anthology of his Work* (Boston, MA: Beacon Press, 1978), 120–133.

16 Walter Benjamin, "The Storyteller," in *Illuminations* (New York: Schocken, 1969), 83–110, see especially Sections V and VIII.

17 See Augustine, *The City of God*, XI, and *De Trinitate*, XV, 12, 21, for a discussion of the present as a focus of attention performing a relation to the past in order to anticipate the future.

2

RESONATING TESTIMONIES
FROM/IN THE SPACE
OF DEATH

Performing Buenaventura's *La maestra*

Warren Linds, Alejandra Medellín, and Kadi Purru

In early 1997, Alejandra Medellín, a director from Mexico, staged Colombian play-wright Enrique Buenaventura's *La maestra/The Schoolteacher* as a class project with students at the University of British Columbia, Canada. The performance of this one-act play, which forms part of the dramatic cycle *Documentos del Infierno/Documents from Hell*, became a place of encounters and translations of several languages, distant realities, different worlds. It became a meeting place for actors, educators, and theorists from Canada, Mexico, Estonia, and Malta as they crossed the disciplinary borders of theater and performance. The play became a shared space, where meaning-making was always being realized in the glimpses between us and our experiences, as resonances occurred and questions continually arise.

After the performance, three of us decided to continue with our journeys into the issues that our performative encounter raised. We took the opportunity of a Canadian theater research conference in June 1998 to carry on our exploration.[1] Alejandra Medellín, the director of the play, continued to explore the boundaries between theatrical fiction and the political crises of Mexico. Kadi Purru was interested in inquiring into the dissonances and resonances between her personal memories and encounters in Colombia with Teatro Experimental de Cali (TEC) and Enrique Buenaventura and then writing academically about it in Canada. Warren Linds wanted to integrate his own experiences in Canada–Central America solidarity work and popular theater in his own community in Saskatchewan with his interests in performance research and performative writing.

As we developed, revised, and rehearsed our script on the lawns of the University of Ottawa, new themes arose. This chapter in script form is our collaborative exploration/reflection after the performance and the research conference. These shared spaces have emerged from/through our experiences exploring *La maestra*. This has been a process of *inter-standing*, where, rather than arriving at grasping for conclusions as to what these performance/reflection processes have all been about, we begin to glimpse what lies between and *among* these experiences.[2] Through this engagement this process becomes not simply an account of what happened. Narrating the events of our lives contributes to an enactive reinterpreting and interpretative reenacting of what we have already lived through the play in relation to those effects that unfolded and are still unfolding. Such an enactive view recognizes performance in action and interaction as a place of learning and exploration.[3] The historical world of *La maestra*, the worlds of the play/performance and our reflections on all these unfold together. Resonances continue to occur and questions have not stopped surfacing even as we write this text. This chapter emerges from, and extends, our encounters with the play as it intertwines our performative script with extracts from *La maestra*, interweaving back and forth between our own and Buenventura's texts.

(Departures)

Black Curtains. A Rehearsal Room. Dust. Dirt. Broken Chairs. Audience. A Teacher's "Spot" in the Back Left Corner of the Room.

> I am dead. I was born here, in this town . . . in the little house made of red clay, with a straw roof. By the road, across from the school. The road is a slow moving river of red clay in winter, and a whirlwind of red dust in the summer. When the rains come you lose your sandals in the mud, the mules and horses get their bellies smeared with mud, the saddles and even the faces of the horsemen are spattered with mud . . . I was born from that mud, and now I have returned to it.[4]

ALEJANDRA: With these words opens *La maestra*, written by the Colombian playwright Enrique Buenaventura in 1968. I staged *La maestra* during my first year as a graduate student at the Theater Department of the University of British Columbia (UBC, Vancouver, Canada). I had arrived some months before from Mexico City, where I was born. Finally, I was *here* enrolled in a theater program in Canada.

América was behind me.
A-m-e-(′)-r-i-c-a.

Within the parenthesis lay, in suspense, marked by an accent – a different history, a different reality.

Estoy muerta. Nací aquí en este pueblo.

KADI: I am not dead. I was not born in
this town. I was born in the faraway
Estonian university town Tartu,

where I knew very little about
violence in Colombia and Latin
America . . .'

Estoy muerta. Nací aquí, en este pueblo.

ALEJANDRA: I am not dead. I was not born
in this town. I was born in México City
in 1971, three years after the police
repressed a student movement, killing
hundreds of people in Tlatelolco.

Estoy muerta. Nací aquí, en este pueblo.

WARREN: I am not dead. I was born in Regina,
Canada, and studying in Vancouver where in 1996
our meeting with *La maestra* took place.

I was born here, in this town.

En la casita de barro rojo	In the little house made of red clay
con techo de paja	with a straw roof.
que está al borde del camino	By the road,
frente al escuela.	across from the school.

El camino es un río lento de barro rojo . . .
The road is a slow moving river of red clay . . .

ALEJANDRA: I followed *La maestra* through this road, through this slow-moving
river of red clay.

Why did I choose to stage this play as part of my course work?

I was looking for answers. The differences between my own reality and this
foreign one, as well as the contrast between my artistic expectations and what
I actually found, made me experience, in a vivid way, how a given sociopolitical
context influences our perception, of the world and of what is important in art.
The staging of *La maestra* was not an exercise of nostalgia. Certainly, I was home-
sick, and directing a play originally written in my own language was familiar
for me. But more importantly, my staging of this play was motivated by a
question: "Who am I?" This apparently personal "I" was in fact the place where
my artistic, social, and political concerns converged. The question "Who am
I" could not be separated from the questions "Where did I come from," "What
is my relation to this context," "What are my reasons for doing theater?"

The Teacher, a young woman,
Is seated alone on an empty stage.

Her first lines are:
Estoy muerta. Nací aquí, en este pueblo.
The Teacher is talking from the cemetery.

My decision to stage *La maestra* was, for me, a public pronouncement. It spoke of my decision to conceive my theater practice as political and to swim, against the current, publicly disengaging myself from the mainstream practices of the Theater Department. I wanted to assert emphatically that, for us, who were not **here** but **there**, in *those towns*, political theater is not a fashion but a necessity. In a "Third World" country, theater cannot be an innocent act concerned only with fictitious characters, props, and rehearsals. Theater is political, whether it reproduces or counteracts the repressive environment that informs it. Although I was not born in Colombia, my voice, as La Maestra's voice, is also coming from the cemetery, because, in a way, I was also born **there** in that **town** and

the slow moving river of red clay took me . . .

is taking me to where I did not ask to go. As I walk, I realize that my journey has a precise itinerary: it goes from "La Esperanza," la Maestra's native community in Colombia , to "La Realidad," one of the towns founded by the Zapatista Army in the state of Chiapas, Mexico, after their uprising in January 1994.

KADI: The slow moving river of red clay took . . .

. . . is taking me back to Colombia . . . I have tried to forget about this country, about my life in Colombia, about my meetings with the Colombian theater group Teatro Experimental de Calí and Enrique Buenaventura . . . the immigrant, the traveler, the wanderer, the nomad (I do not know exactly who I am!) cannot afford to become fond of, attached to any place in the world. I have tried very hard to forget about the "turbulent" experiences of my Colombian past in order to live in the "tranquillity" of a Canadian present. I have tried to tell myself that Colombia is not **my** country, that I lived there for five years because I happened to marry a Colombian with whom I fell in love when studying theater in Leningrad.

But I have failed.
I have not forgotten.
It has not been possible.
I am connected to that country of "the slow moving river of red clay."
Connected through my blood.
My daughter ties me forever to **that** country.

16

Since the day I arrived in Canada, seven years ago, I have been living in constant anxiety and guilt. I know that my sensation of tranquillity here, in **this** country, is deceptive and very fragile. I am confronted with an enormous abyss that I cannot afford to overcome. It is this abyss between the social realities of Canada and Colombia, between the so-called "First" and "Third" Worlds, between **here** and **there** . . . I keep living with the memories of the past . . . *alucionada por este mundo Macondiano . . . borracha de fiestas tropicales caleñas . . . envenenada por las ideas de teatro de Enrique y Creación Colectiva . . . terrorizada y vomitando residuos de sustos y miedos de interminables bodas de sangre en Colombia . . . amarrada para siempre con lazos de amor y nostalgía por este país . . .*[5] When Alejandra arrived and decided to stage *La maestra* with students in UBC I learned that my present and past, here and there, are interwoven and intimately connected. I understood that I cannot and do not have the right to forget.

WARREN: The slow-moving river of red clay . . .

took me back and forth in my life's work from previous work facilitating popular theater work in my community to developing this *teàtro popular* at UBC. Connecting now not as facilitator but through the actions of One-Eyed Tobías, the character I played in *La maestra* who carries liquid from the spring for the teacher; water she wouldn't drink. Tobías – bringing hope, a wish for life that responds to my own forgotten images of death (camps) and of people standing by while millions were slaughtered. Now choosing to engage in solidarity work in Canada with *los compañeros* in Nicaragua and El Salvador (and later Guatemala and Grenada), and now exploring this work in a Canadian university as a community as we performed the play in darkened university theater spaces. Communities of actors and audiences explored this story of trauma in a safe space with the play-text as the basis of our relationships, a text of testimony, a recalling emerging differently for each of us in the telling. Our interplaying was a process of negotiating collective meaning, bringing us together in a shared experience with audiences wondering whether this play-script, written in the 1960s, was an artifact or a linking of memory between Colombia in *La Violencia* and more recent events in 1990s Latin America.

The slow-moving river of red clay is taking me back to my own educational work with/about Latin America.

Back   to questions of the role of popular theater in developing awareness, of my role as a Canadian popular theater worker.
Back   to questioning (again) where is there hope amidst so much pain, to questions I don't want to risk looking at.

TOGETHER:
Caminante, son tus huellas
 Wayfarer the only way is your footsteps,
 there is no other
el camino, nada má; caminante no hay camino,
 wayfarer there is no way;
se hace camino al andar.
 you make the way as you go.
Al andar se hace camino,
 as you go, you make the way,
y al volver la vista atrás
 stopping to look around
se ve la senda que nunca
 you see the path that your feet will never travel again.
se ha de volver a pisar;
Caminante, no hay camino,
 Wayfarer there is no way,
sino estelas en la mar,
 only tracks on ocean foam.[6]

WARREN: Our performance of *La maestra* in 1997 cannot be preserved, recalled, measured, or evaluated as it moved from moment to moment. All we have is *the me/mo-mento* of its movement. A mark of memory and of the momentary motion of remembering in the enactment of "the now of writing in the present."[7] The measurement of action is, in this case, this restaging (on the page) of an experience of performance. But even in looking at that performance our experiencing of it shifts. There is a leap of the quantum when it is observed.[8] The experience changes because it is marked – written and talked about. It becomes this performance with/in text. As we look back we see only tracks, traces of what we have done. Our research is a reliving of that experience, a performance in the present, where "something that once was, now is,"[9] not a commemoration or remembrance but, as Spanish poet Antonio Machado has written, "making our way as we go."

 The late Brazilian educator Paulo Freire wrote that "in the process of making the way, we have to be clear as to what underlies our process and the philosophies, worldviews and questions that emerge in that process."[10] Perhaps our (mis)understanding of our own making of the way will help others to see new questions to ask themselves

Resonances,   Identifications,
echoes,   reverberations,   recognitions,
          ripples . . .

(Journeys)

TOGETHER:
You can come with us,
>if you do not mind losing your shoes in the mud
>>and running the risk of ending up
>>with your feet, your hands and your face
>>all spattered with mud . . .

May 1997, at "home" in Vancouver. Kadi is crouched in the corner of the couch feeling disconnected. She turns to her journal, where she has written of her Colombian experiences. The glimpses, images, thoughts, and fragments of memories of Teatro Experimental de Calí slowly emerge as she tries to reconnect with her past and remember . . .

KADI: "La vida es dura . . ."

Enrique Buenaventura was always saying this to me as he smiled with an ever-present cigar hanging out from the corner of his mouth.

You walk three or four blocks southwards (or . . . westwards . . . I am not sure . . . I am bad with directions . . . but you have to walk toward *barrio* San Antonio, that's for sure) from the center of Calí, Colombia as I did the first time in 1987 coming from Estonia. Departing from the heart of Calí, where the constructions of the colonial era are slowly surrendering to the high buildings of the modern banks, you soon find yourself on old narrow streets with white, two-storied, somewhat crooked clay houses. Among the houses there is an iron fence, where, I am pretty sure, you will find the sign *Teatro Experimental de Calí*. Peeking through the bars of the gate you will be able to glimpse part of a surprisingly spacious patio sheltered by a wide crowned mighty mango tree with a long table and benches. In January 1987, when I visited the TEC for the first time, I also saw some papier-mâché "corpses" and a magnificent four-meter-tall puppet in a white wedding dress. I learned later that it was Mamá Grande from a production called *El encierro*. TEC was working on a theatrical adaptation of Gabriel García Márquez's story, "Los funerales de la Mamá Grande" ("Funerals of the Great Matriarch"). So it is here, I remember thinking, in this place, squeezed in between Spanish colonial architecture and North American industrial dictatorship, where Enrique has created his performance space of decolonizing of the Latin American self . . .

Enrique is glad but not surprised to meet me. He seems to have got used to the pilgrimage of countless travelers from the countries of "developed" theatrical traditions who come to refresh/rediscover/recolonize their languished inspiration from the abundant springs of Latin American creativity. Barba, Grotowski, Brook, which traveler from Europe has not tried to establish contact with indigenous cultures in order to reconnect with the lost ritualistic realms in hopes of saving western theater from its decline? I felt myself in an awkward position. I was also coming from "Europe," and yet, myself now a resident of Calí, I could perceive that Latin Americans look at the people arriving from Europe with caution and skepticism: what are they after now? And what do they have to offer in exchange: the obdurate heart and the soul sold to the God of Money? In Colombia in theater *couloirs* I heard an anecdotal story about Grotowski and the group of indigenous people who thought him an imposter of a witch, since to the ritual that Grotowski conducted the spirits did not arrive. So much blood and violence have been brought from Europe to Latin America that I do not wonder that Theater Gods from Europe are not always greeted with open arms. To establish a trusting relationship with the Teatro Experimental de Calí took me a long time and it was far from easy . . . I began going to the rehearsals every day and participating in different collective tasks.

Later I learned that Enrique considers it impossible to import art as art is closely related to the locality where the creative process takes place, getting its strength from the local soil and people. This seemed to be one of the reasons why Enrique decided not to pursue his success as a playwright in Paris but returned to Calí and to Colombia where he continues to live in circumstances which, as he has confessed, make him regret very much that he is unable to escape, where every day he has "to make an almost mystical effort not to run away."[11]

In an environment where social conflicts are extremely acute, where hunger accompanies the great number of people on an everyday basis, where obscure forces "clean" the city streets by killing homeless kids and throwing them into the river . . . who wouldn't criticize the existing "order," who wouldn't search the ways for resistance and who wouldn't desire to work for the more just society?! This is why Buenaventura's theater is so critical of the governing social system, this is why the principal characters of his theater belong to/come from the never-ending round dance of political and social machinations: President, Priest, Colonel, Sergeant, Prostitutes, Beggars, Teacher, and the perpetual companion of life – Death . . .

PERSONAJES
Presidente
Alfredo
Miguel
Esposa del Presidente
Marta
Rosa
Muerte Opulenta
Muerte de Cuello Blanco
Muerte Rata
Muerte Muerte[12]

One day at night, quite late, Enrique phoned. He invited us come meet the dancers from the city on the Pacific coast, Buenaventura. When we arrived at the TEC, the dancers were already resting, having made up their beds around the hall and stage of the theater. The members of the group did not seem to be very young, so I could not even imagine waking them up. However, a few minutes later, after we had entered with Enrique, I found myself in the midst of musical rhythms of *currulao* and dancing bodies. I saw Enrique moving softly and graciously in unison of the marimba and drumbeats. He seemed to enjoy enormously the African pulse of this dance from the Colombian Pacific coast.

I had heard stories about Enrique Buenaventura's life in Buenaventura on several occasions. He had told me how he participated in local carnivals and magic rituals; how he learned to love Pacific coast bailes and music; how he had caught malaria and almost died . . . When Enrique was speaking about death, whether in his "autobiographical" stories or in theater, he always did it through/with laughter. Death was a "popular" and always present character in every single play staged in the TEC. In *Pilot Project*, there are, for example, four Deaths: Opulent Death, White Collar Death, Rat Death, and Death Death.

The previous performance is over and the next one is about to start. White Collar Death is picking up the newspaper from the floor. Takes a look into it. The other Deaths are cleaning the stage and setting up the scenery.[13]

The "macabre" moments of laughter are also present in Enrique's story about his birth. This is how I remember it: "When Enrique's mother was in her sixth month of pregnancy, there was a fire in their house. As a result of this shock, Enrique's mother went into labor. Enrique was born but nobody knew what to do with this 'creature.' Nobody knew whether it was a baby or embryo. Finally, Enrique's aunt (or was it uncle? I don't remember) decided . . . just in case . . . to put the creature into her pocket."

On the stage of the Teatro Experimental de Calí, in the midst of frenetically but softly moving bodies, I am trying to imitate the steps of *currulao*. "Stop . . . it is a useless job, mona," I am hearing an elderly black woman say to me, "close your eyes . . . listen to the rhythms . . . let the music flow into your blood." Soon, I am feeling how I am starting to become part of *currulao*.

Winter 1998. Sitting in a living room, Warren's memories of performing La maestra *emerge as he wonders about how transformative drama might help us change the way we examine different, unknown, absent or other spaces within our own world, selves, or community.*

WARREN: Our development/performance of *La maestra* became an enactive interweaving of world, word, and wonderment. Building on concepts of embodied action, the enactive approach proposes that knowing does not develop solely in minds, but rather emerges through shared action and collaboration as self, other, and the environment co-emerge in a learning process. Knowledge and learning thus are not located in one of these elements but are *inter-standings* in the always shifting movements of experiencing.

In *The Embodied Mind*, Francisco Varela, Evan Thompson, and Eleanor Rosch provide three conceptions for the process of knowing which we might use to review the experiencing of performance: cognitivist, emergent, and enactive.[14] *Cognitivist* performance would be descriptive and disembodied with the text treated as an object with defined knowledge and as a description of a real world to which the author provides access. In this type of process, *La maestra* is a text of a play set in Colombia. Buenaventura provides us with access to this history through his text . . . the history of *La Violencia* in Colombia . . . over there. We interpret this text in performance; our research is based on what we think the author is trying to communicate. Our presentation of our research would be about what happened to us in our particular performance.

Emergent performance separates the subjective "I" from the objective "text" and describes the text as something arising from a particular historical process. The reader (the subjective "I") reads the text from their own biases and understandings. For example, we might investigate more of what we as actors and directors want to communicate in the performance. We work with the text, we also work with our interpretations of the history of violence in Latin America and we might engage in a dialog about these interpretations with you here.

We are seeking an *enactive* performance which is intertextual, never static, always moving in a dance between the constantly changing "I," the text, and the readers'/audience's world, viewing the text in a process of embodied and interactive reflection, intermingling the thoughts of the audience with the process of performance. We are reading the text not only through our own experiences but also with our experiences in reading the text and against other texts. This experience in reading the text also relates to the style and form of the text. How does it enable an interactive reading between reader and text, so we begin reading a text against our experiences and our ideas about the world and vice versa in what Salvio calls an "interpretive event"?[15] This may happen in the middle space where the tension between our own narratives and the text enacts possible worlds. We are no longer referring to what is past but to the now in the learning in the moment of the performing. We no longer look just for a meaning of the author but become comfortable being open to the meaning that emerges in the moment(s) of our interaction with the text. Understanding and interpretation then become not acts of "an individual conscious mind but enactments, performances,"[16] where we are open and willing to engage in a conversation, a process of learning. There is a co-evolving coemergence of drama (actors in performance), script (text), theater (space and words), and audience as active participants.

Other texts, other plays, making the play our own. Reading against the realities of Latin America and the realities of Canada's complicity in violence in other countries. Perhaps this only came out in the aftermath, in what happened at the results of the Asia Pacific Economic Cooperation (APEC) conference at UBC in Vancouver later in 1997, which was marked by protests against, among others, (now ex-) president Suharto of Indonesia for human rights violations and the invasion of East Timor.[17]

So, in the performance of *La maestra*, our quest was to weave an exploration of how a transformative drama process might help participants change the way they examine different, unknown, or absent other spaces within their own world, selves, or community. Rather than treating these spaces as objects to be grasped, or as something to understand only in light of our own experiences, we endeavored to *experience* these spaces of in-between. As we struggled to bring together different voices, worldviews, values systems, and beliefs so that they could have a conversation with one another, there was "always enough appreciation for difference so that the text can interrogate, rather than dissolve into, the performer."[18] This challenged our own preconceptions, "risking confusion and uncertainty,"[19] both about ourselves, our beliefs, knowledge, and ignorance, but also the other we sought to understand.

Characters with complex lives, complex desires, hopes, dreams and, yes, fears. And, as performers, exploring these. Lots of questions; few answers. Bearing witness, speaking Buenventura's words as testimonies. And, as characters in the living theater of the Teacher, listening to the words of the Teacher as witness to all she has seen/is seeing. In Buenaventura's words, "we and the audience are recreating a model reality, and only through that reality, in active proof of it, are we revealing ourselves to ourselves and to the public, just as we reveal the public to ourselves and itself."[20]

February 1997, a rehearsal room in the "Hut," UBC, Vancouver.

ALEJANDRA: Darkness increases outside the windows. Inside, I watch in silence. What unfolds in front of my eyes is in no way predictable but, at the same time, is an experience already framed by many hours of analysis and rehearsals. I am sitting on the edge of the stage, in the line which divides reality from fiction.

The actors, once they get ready, perform Buenaventura's *La maestra*. Kesten, Warren, Luisa, and Rita play the chorus in this scene. They are on the stage, trying to master the movement of two long pieces of red fabric that we are using to indicate the road. Steve, dressed as the Sergeant, is standing offstage as he waits for his cue. (Why are Sergeants always standing offstage, waiting for their cues?) Pryde, who plays the Teacher, is sitting on top of a set of stairs, the cemetery from where she watches over the town below. She is delivering her lines to an imaginary audience. I am listening to her, wondering how to give to these lines the force of a real, concrete action of resistance and rebellion . . .

They are afraid. Some time ago fear came to this town and hung suspended over it like a great storm cloud. The air reeks of fear, voices dissolve in the bitter spittle of fear, and the people swallow it. One day the cloud ripped open, and the thunderbolt fell upon us . . .

ALEJANDRA: Before turning my face towards the stage, I hear unexpected voices from the darkness –

> Estoy muerta. Nací aquí, en este pueblo.

A second voice adds itself to the crying . . .

> I am dead. I was born here, in this town.

A third voice is joining in . . .

> Estoy muerta. Nací aquí, en este pueblo.

Wait a minute! I am ready to exclaim, that is not the line you are supposed to say, we were at. . . .

But I stop, silenced by what I am seeing. I am paralyzed as I watch these women rising up from the floor, while repeating

> Estoy muerta. Nací aquí, en este pueblo.

. . . as they increase in number I wonder where are they coming from. Terrified, I realize that I am not in the rehearsal room anymore. I am somewhere else . . . I cannot move. I am a silent spectator. More than forty persons are walking around . . . women, children, men. And the line goes on, as a litany, but also as an accusation.

> Estoy muerto. Nací aquí, en este pueblo.

Here – I repeat to myself – in this town.
Which town . . . ?
I was doing theater and then. . . .
Oh, my God! My feet, my hands, my face are all spattered with . . .
No, it is not mud. What is happening? Why is all this blood running around as . . . as if these were real people, as if this were not fiction, as . . . I can hear their voices . . . dead . . . born here . . . in this town. Their voices . . . What is going on?

(SILENCE)

(LISTENINGS)

Hermann Bellinghausen, enviado, La Jornada. Mexico, D.F. 24 de diciembre de 1997:

Los hoy muertos y heridos se encontraban aquí, a orillas de Acteal, rezando. Estaban rezando. Así, de rodillas, los cogieron por la espalda desde los cerros circundantes los disparos de armas de alto poder. Y así se fueron muriendo hasta sumar 45. Segun los sobrevivientes, la balacera comenzó a las 10:30 de la mañana de ayer. "Y no teníamos ni con que defendernos," se lamenta con rabia Juan. Rosa Gómez estaba embarazada cuando cayó moribunda en la explanada de campamento. Sus asesinos llegaron hasta ella para rematarla. Y uno de ellos, "con un cuchillo – relata un testigo y hace un ademán de puñalada que inmediatamente reprime con un temblor – , le sacó su niño y lo tiró allí nomas."

ALEJANDRA MEDELLÍN, THE TRANSLATOR: "Those today dead or injured were here, at the edge of Acteal (Chenalho, Chiapas), praying. They were praying. There, while kneeling down, they were taken by surprise by the gunshots coming from the surrounding hills. They died, one by one, until they totaled 45. According to the survivors, the shooting began at 10:30 yesterday morning. 'And we did not have anything to defend us,' Juan laments in anger. Rosa Gómez was pregnant when she fell down on the terrace of the camp. Her assassins went to where she lay to finish their killing. And one of them, 'with a knife – relates a witness making a gesture to indicate the stab, a gesture he immediately suppresses with a trembling – removed her child from her and threw him to the ground.'"

THE TEACHER: They put my father against the mud wall behind the house. The sergeant gave the order, and the soldiers shot. Then the sergeant and the soldiers came into my room and, one after the other, they raped me. Then I wouldn't eat or drink again, and so I died, little by little. Little by little.

WARREN: In the middle of our rehearsals there is on the newswire on cable TV one Sunday morning the summary of a Toronto newspaper article . . . I go to the library and find it. It becomes part of what Alejandra calls her "Brechtian distancing moment" that used theatrical distancing to bring the text of Buenaventura written in 1960s Colombia home to 1990s Canada, home to this rehearsal hall; this space of death in the space of living.

Colombian historian Ricardo Peñaranda

La Violencia is the term that Colombians have adopted to describe the complex political and social phenomenon – a mixture of official terror, partisan confrontation, political banditry, pillage and peasant uprising – that the country endured for nearly twenty years between the 1940s and the 1960s. In trying to identify the consequences or the possible evolution of the phenomenon, it has become obvious that the Violence has projected itself into the present. It traverses every area of Colombian society and constitutes the matrix of the present social and political conflicts in our country.[21]

Performance of La maestra, University of British Columbia, February 1997

In 1997, UBC President David Strangway invited 18 Asian Pacific leaders to the university for the APEC conference in November. This gathering included men responsible for massive human rights violations, such as Indonesia's president Suharto and Chinese president Jiang Zemin.

Toronto Sun, February 9, 1997

At least 250 known modern-day war criminals, torturers, and former senior officials of murderous government regimes are free in Canada. The list ranges from former death squad members from Latin American countries to senior officials from Bosnian, Somali, Iraqi, and Afghan regimes, and the former Duvalier government of Haiti.

The Permanent Committee of Defence of Human Rights (Bogotá)

Between 1981 and 1986, 3,547 journalists, students, teachers, professors, union members, and members of opposition were assassinated in Colombia. In the country 149 Death Squads were operating and Listas Negras (Black Lists) of death threats were circulating, frightening thousands of Colombians. Since 1986, the situation in Colombia has been deteriorating.[22]

KADI: Calí, Colombia, January 1989

Patricia Ariza, president of
Corporación Colombiana de Teatro,
director and actress, of the theater
group La Candelaria, had been using a
bulletproof jacket and bodyguard escort
for years. Finally, in 1989, she was forced
to leave for Cuba. Coincidentally, I was
present when she came to say good-bye
to Enrique Buenaventura. Her farewell
visit was far from being sentimental.
Very soon I heard from my friends that
Patricia is back in Bogotá continuing
with her theatrical activities with La
Candelaria and the living beside
death . . .

WARREN: UBC, Vancouver, British Columbia, November 1997

Someone tells me she heard
a Royal Canadian Mounted
Police member of a riot squad
during protests at the APEC
conference that month say
*This isn't my doing I am Not to
Blame I'm just following orders.*

Toronto Sun, February 9, 1997

She fled here, looking for
sanctuary from the pain
and torture of her native
Ethiopia. From those
who had detained her in
prison, had beaten her,
scarring her for life. She
believed herself safe here.
Tried to bury her memories,
allowed herself to breathe
the air of the free. And
then she saw her torturer
in the subway. Stared into
the dark eyes which had
tormented her, haunted
her. Her heaven was his
as well. We had opened
our gates to the man who
had locked her in his.
For the Ethiopian woman
who saw her torturers in
a Metro Toronto subway,
that injustice turned her
heaven into a tarnished
hell. How could she live
in a country that would
welcome her nightmare as
easily as it had welcomed
her?

WARREN: We as a group of three had many discussions about how to perform these testimonies in place of all the absent others that could not testify for themselves. Our performance became an act of witnessing of **there** and **then** in the **here** and **now**. And yet, as I reread them again and again, as I hear them in my mind, feelings and sensations of numbness, of pain, and of anger re-emerge again and again.

How can we deal with these stories of trauma that we hear over and over and over and over again; happening over there on the stage/in another place, another time? There is a desire for conclusions, for certainty, for answers to my questions as to why all these things happen. This is a quest to understand, to put under control, to resolve the "problem" so that I may exclude these events and stop thinking about them in order to go on with my life here and now.

Perhaps we must listen to these stories and learn to accept the perpetual failure of in/sight; that every effort to understand also runs the risk of misunderstanding. Because our knowing of/about the world is fluid and always unfolding, there is a simultaneous unfolding of understanding and misunderstandings of the above events. The possibility for understanding difference lies in the active acceptance of the inevitability of misunderstanding.[23] Thus we may continually attempt to walk and live in suspension, allowing that mis/understanding to continue to sit in tension, leaving us not only open to, but also obligated to engage in, reflection, and further action.

Peggy Phelan suggests that the attempt to walk and live on this rackety bridge between self and other is where we may discover hope. We do have a desire for conclusions (and, for answers) to knowing not only why this violence persists but also how we can stop it. By accepting that we may never fully understand something, our encounters with that which we mis/understand become opportunities for questions and dialog rather than a betrayal of hope. To be in such a conversation there is always the "possibility" of an *inter-standing*, where we simultaneously risk confusion and, perhaps, glimpse what we can only begin to comprehend.

A resonance can emerge from exploring this tension through paying attention to our feelings as well as our thoughts as we listen to these testimonies.

How might this resonance be cultivated? Ethnographer Unni Wikan suggests we need not have the "same" stories but we need to "dip into the wellsprings" of ourselves to use as a bridge to others. This does not come by an act of will, though will helps. It also doesn't happen through just wanting to observe the world around us in a detached way. "Practical exposure to a world of 'urgency, necessity' is required" as we confront our own responses to such stories of violence.[24] Enacting such stories became an immersion in witnessing the past, a past that is only a brief image which flashes up at an instant "when it can be recognized and is never seen again."[25] At the same time, we are testifying in the here and now of the play which was not some historical account but something we lived and re-lived, repeating its words, acknowledging, remembering, and listening to what happened.[26] Such a witnessing establishes living memories, admitting the stories of the dead into our community and raising barely articulated questions about how we might respond. So we move beyond a preconception that these events so far from our experiences are stumbling blocks: that others are essentially different, to be understood only by means of thought, rather than paying attention to our own feeling-thoughts. We willingly try to engage with this other world on the stage, using our own experiences to try and convey "meanings that reside neither in words, 'facts', nor texts but are evoked" in the interplay of us with the text.[27] Experiencing, thinking, doubting, risking together. Making contact. Embracing the Other we are becoming in the play. Dissolving the boundaries while crossing them. as we live through the evocative intertwining of our own issues with the stories of others that we embrace as we tell.

Resonance, Re-sounding. A world of urgency, necessity; within the play of the Community confronted by the evil of violence; outside the play, as we are daily confronted by the violence of the world. I think of the reactions of some audience members to the play, who are surprised that this violence is still occurring in the world and at the list of actual disappeared people we used as the Sergeant continually denied being to blame, just following orders. One commented, "I thought the wars were over in Central America in the 1980s."

Then, eight months later, I heard a student say, "this doesn't happen here," as he relates how shocked he was at the violence of the police in the APEC demonstrations could be happening in Vancouver, Canada, in November 1997.

(The Space of Death)

May 1998, Vancouver, UBC, a dormitory. Alejandra is preparing a paper for a conference in Ottawa.

ALEJANDRA: I can hear her voice.

Estoy muerta. Nací aquí, en este pueblo.

I hear her voice constantly.

I am dead. I was born here, in this town.
. . . muerta . . . aquí, en este pueblo.

I hear her voice, slipping through the labyrinth of my ears, . . . her voice, slipping through the labyrinth of my fears. Who is she, you will wonder. This question does not have a simple answer. She is not only she, but someone else. She is someone I cannot name, yet she does have names. She is talking from nowhere, but this does not mean that I cannot show you on the map the place where her voice comes from. She is dead, but nevertheless she is speaking. She is the twenty-one women killed December 22, 1997, in the community of

Acteal, Chenalho, Chiapas, by a paramilitary group, armed and protected by the government of the state. She is also the fifteen children killed that day. She is the nine men assassinated in the massacre. I hear her voice again.

Estoy muerta. Nací aquí, en este pueblo.

This time she is Guadalupe Méndez López, killed in Ocosingo, Chiapas, January 12, 1998, during a peaceful demonstration. The same day, thousands were marching not only in Ocosingo, but in each state of Mexico and also in several cities around the world. The aim of the demonstrations was to pressure the Mexican government to recognize the San Andrés Larrainzar agreements and to protest the military repression in Chiapas. At the same time these people were asking for peace, Guadalupe, an indigenous woman, was killed by policemen who fired on Ocosingo's demonstrators.

And she was born there, in that town.

I, Alejandra, was also born there, in that town.
But she is dead, and I am alive.

Do not think that my life and her death are due to a stroke of luck. Do not assume these things happen by chance. Somehow there is a logic and if you watch us carefully, you will find out. Her face is a constant image in my mind, through her face I find out why she is dead and I am alive: because I am white and she is not.

She are dead.

But I am alive and I was also born there in that town.

April 1998, Vancouver, UBC, here *in* this *town. Kadi has finished her term paper on* La Maestra *for a graduate seminar. She struggles with the ongoing question: how does the "theorization" of the space of death help to stop violence?*

KADI: Michael Taussig in his book on popular traditions of healing in Colombia, observes that "the space of death is important in the creation of meaning and consciousness, nowhere more so than in societies where torture is endemic and where the culture of terror flourishes."[28] Critics have pointed out the frequent presence of dead narrators on the Latin American novel and dead characters in Latin American stage.[29] Little wonder the predilection of Latin American authors for the narratives of dead, since it was in the space of death where Indian, African, and white gave birth to a New World.[30]

    Buenaventura's character of La Maestra gains her strength to resist the violence in Colombia from the space of death where she becomes reunited with eternity and earth. Although ceasing to exist in the temporal world of history, La Maestra continues (returns!) to live in the realm of myth outside of time. She becomes one with red mud and dust covering the road passing by her village. As a matter of fact there is no way in Buenaventura's text to separate the two realms – temporal and atemporal – in the narration of La Maestra. Not only is her story connected with mythic consciousness, La Maestra's narration follows also the structure of myth enveloping the historical events into circular time in which past, present, and future intermingle.

The play begins with La Maestra's monolog evoking the image of the road, red dust, and mud, passing by mules, horses, and people. It is impossible to define the time described in this monolog – it does not have limits. *La maestra* pictures the life in its eternal movement and circulation: winter is followed by summer and rain by dry season, red dust becomes red mud and red mud becomes red dust, the people lose their sandals in the mud and find them in the dirt . . . The play ends with La Maestra's monolog resulting in the same image.

But this is not the description of simple repetitive closed circular time. There is a difference in the imagery of nature evoked by La Maestra. If in her opening monolog La Maestra describes nature in present tense, at the end she refers to the future:

> It will rain soon, and the red dirt will turn to mud. The road will be a slow moving river of red mud, and the sandals will come up the road again, and the mud-covered feet, and the horses and mules with their bellies full of mud, and even the faces and the hats will go up the road, splattered with mud.

Regardless of the fact that the red road undoubtedly symbolizes bloodshed and violence, the final image of the road introduces not a feeling of defeat and desperation, but hope. The future is promising because the life cycle continues . . . rain transforms a sterile red dust into a fertile red mud again. Furthermore, the symbol of red blood acquires a vitalizing life-providing connotation, a meaning it has in pre-Colombian indigenous cultures. Mythical consciousness gains its power connecting (and not separating) human beings with nature. La Maestra, telling the story of violence, identifies the political invasion with forces of nature:

> Some time ago fear came to this village and hung suspended over it like a great storm cloud . . . One day the cloud ripped open, and the thunderbolt fell upon us.

Perceiving the political intervention as a thunderbolt empowers La Maestra and provides her the force for resistance. A great storm cloud and thunderbolt may bring death and destruction but they will also bring rain, restituting life in the

31

sterile red soil. Michael Taussig has also suggested that the space of death is preeminently a space of transformation: through the experience of coming close to death there well may be a more vivid sense of life.[31]

(Questions)

On the edge of the stage, in between performers and audience, in between here and there, in between then and now:

ALEJANDRA: Darkness increases outside the windows. Inside, we watch in silence. What unfolds in front of our eyes is in no way predictable.

WARREN: I recognize that theater about the important issues of violence and human rights is not a magic wand that will transform society. But, can we go beyond simply talking about the issue or problem, as something "out there" in the space of death? An enactive approach to performance has shifted our emphasis from what is experienced (as in reflection on past experiences) to an embodied experiencing (a re-experiencing through the body in performance) where the world is brought forth by actors, audience, and our writing about this in the moments we are re-living it. This opens our capacities for perceiving possibilities. Can we learn to journey, both into the complexities of that space of violence and death, as well as into the space of living where we can address our involvement with both the problem and the possibilities of addressing it? How might such a pedagogy of hope, and of an obligation to respond, emerge from different aspects of our theater work in Canada?[32]

Stories such as La Maestra's have readily incorporated themselves into our felt experiences; their (e)motions echo and resonate with our own encountering of the world. In hearing and watching we cannot sit passively but re-live the story as the struggles of the characters infuse themselves with/in our own bodies. Can a theater of witness and memory provide a space within our communities in Canada where we can listen to each others' stories of hope, where the language of possibility can be explored?

ALEJANDRA: We are still here, on the edge of the stage. But everything has changed. The dividing line between theater and reality is not the safe place anymore that I had imagined.

KADI: The gap between my past in Colombia and my present in Canada, here and there, is widening while I am trying to make my road through academic investigation. How can we overcome this gap between our academic and personal lives, between our memories, feelings, impressions, doubts, passions, and academic thoughts? How can we tell the stories of Colombia, stories of the South, stories of injustice and suffering to First World audiences so that those stories not only move, touch, resonate but make a difference? So that they make the gap between those worlds disappear?

ALEJANDRA:

América/ America

I wonder
why an accent makes such a big difference

An accent:
A wall a fence a cop
Another language
A different universe

The difference hurts
The difference
Has changed my vision
Of my land my future my history my life

My land it is not even a country
It is a mobile space
My landscape,
That of the
Displaced
The marginal
The outsider

D e s p o i l e d
of my own continent
each time someone says "North America"
to refer to the United States and Canada

D i s p l a c e d
From my own center
When I hear the words
"Third World Countries"

M a r g i n a l i z e d
By this cult to the order
The clean the hygiene the organic

I wonder

What is the lace for my world
In this self-contained universe?
What to do with the violence,
The injustice, the war?

33

TOGETHER: When will we stop being passive spectators, when will we cross the boundary?

Acknowledgments

Our performative journey would not have taken place without the inspiration of Enrique Buenaventura's theatrical work and vision. We also appreciate the editorial insights of Lynn Fels and Jan Selman, who assisted us in struggling through writing these encounters. Neither could this chapter have been written without the fine work of all the cast in the non-profit, student production of Buenaventura's play. The performance was directed by Alejandra Medellín with Rita Amisano, Kesten Broughton, Pryde Foltz, Luisa Jojic, Warren Linds, Steve Noble, Kadi Purru, and Carmel Sammut.

Notes

1. Association of Canadian Theatre Research (ACTR), Ottawa, Ontario, Canada, June 1998. The title of this text was the title of our performance.
2. Mark Taylor and Esa Saarinen, *Imagologies* (New York: Routledge, 1994), vol. 1: 8.
3. See Lynn Fels, "In the Wind Clothes Dance on a Line: Performative Inquiry, a (Re)Search Methodology: Possibilities and Absences within a Moment of Imagining a Universe," Ph.D. dissertation, University of British Columbia, 1999. Fels has conceptualized and articulated *performative inquiry* which arises out of an enactive interpretation of cognition. Performative inquiry is a research methodology that recognizes "performance as a viable research venue which enables participants . . . to realize and explore co-evolving world(s) through creative action and interaction with each other, their shared, absent and/or imagined environments, and motivating (im)pulse of inquiry" (1). See also Lynn Fels and Karen Meyer, "On the Edge of Chaos: Co-evolving Worlds of Drama and Science," *Science Education* 19 (1997): 75–81.
4. Enrique Buenaventura, *The Schoolteacher*, translated by Gerardo Luzuriaga and Robert S. Rudder, in *The Orgy: Modern One-Act Plays from Latin America* (Berkeley, CA: University of California Press, 1974), 24. In both the performed play and the re-presentation of the text, Buenaventura's words are repeated as a constant refrain to convey collective memory.
5. I have been struggling with the translation of these Spanish lines into English; my *real* feelings seem to get lost in the process. Therefore, I am only able to provide the literal translation of these lines for those readers who feel confused and uncomfortable in the realm of the *other* tongue: . . . *hallucinated by this Macondian world . . . drunk with Cali's tropical fiestas . . . intoxicated by the theater ideas of Enrique Buenaventura and the method of Collective Creation . . . terrorized . . . vomiting the residue of fears (frights, despairs) of unending "blood weddings" in Colombia . . . tied for ever with bonds of love and nostalgia for this country.*
6. Original text reprinted by permission of Herederos de Antonio y de Manuel Machado, CB, as published in *Poesía y Prosa, Antonio Machado*, edición crítica de Oreste Macrí con la colaboración de Gaetano Chiappini (Madrid: Espasa-Calpe). English translation from *Antonio Machado: Selected Poems*, translated by Alan Trueblood (Cambridge, MA: Harvard University Press, 1982), 142–143. English translation reprinted by permission of the publishers from *Antonio Machado: Selected Poems*, translated by Alan Trueblood (Cambridge, MA: Harvard University Press), © 1982 by the President and Fellows of Harvard College.

7 Peggy Phelan, *Unmarked: The Politics of Performance* (New York: Routledge, 1993), 149.
8 Ibid., 171.
9 Peter Brook, *The Empty Space* (London: MacGibbon and Kee, 1968), 139.
10 Myles Horton and Paulo Freire, *We Make the Road by Walking: Conversations on Education and Social Change* (Philadelphia, PA: Temple University Press, 1990), 7.
11 Enrique Buenaventura, "Theatre and Culture," *Drama Review* 14 (2) (1970): 153.
12 Ibid., 151.
13 Enrique Buenaventura, *Proyecto piloto, Gestos* 11 (1991): 215. Translated by Kadi Purru.
14 Francisco J. Varela, Evan Thompson, and Eleanor Rosch, *The Embodied Mind: Cognitive Science and Human Experience* (Cambridge, MA: MIT Press, 1991).
15 Paula Salvio, "On Keying Pedagogy as an Interpretive Event," in *Action Research as a Living Practice*, eds. Terrance Carson and Dennis Sumara (New York: Peter Lang, 1997).
16 Thomas Schwandt, "On Understanding Understanding," *Qualitative Inquiry* 5 (4) (1999): 455.
17 The events surrounding the APEC Summit had an aftermath since we developed this script and wrote this chapter. In fall 1998, the Royal Canadian Mounted Police Public Complaints Commission began hearings in Vancouver into complaints of the rights of free speech being violated as demonstrators were pepper-sprayed, their signs torn down, and they were arrested and held without charge. There were also allegations that Prime Minister Jean Chrétien became personally involved in the security arrangements around the summit, including assuring Indonesian President Suharto that he would not be "embarrassed" while at the meeting. In winter 2001, the prime minister refused the Complaints Commissioner's request that he appear before the inquiry. The Commission's hearings continued despite this setback, and in July 2001, its final report found police actions during the demonstrations at the 1997 APEC summit "did not meet an acceptable and expected standard of competence and professionalism and proficiency" (CBC News Online, "The APEC Summit: The APEC Report's Recommendations," August 2001, http://cbc.ca/news/indepth/background/apec_recommendations.html). In addition to the involvement of the RCMP in quelling protests, several Indonesian government security people were deported for carrying weapons, amidst fears that they would shoot demonstrators if Suharto's motorcades were blocked.
18 Dwight Conquergood, "Performing as a Moral Act: Ethical Dimensions of the Ethnography of Performance," *Literature in Performance* 5 (2) (1985): 9.
19 Schwandt, "On Understanding Understanding," 458.
20 Buenaventura, "Theatre and Culture," 156.
21 Ricardo Peñaranda, "Conclusion: Surveying the Literature on the Violence," in *Violence in Colombia*, eds. Charles Begquist, Ricardo Peñaranda, and Gonzalo Sánchez (Wilmington, DE: Scholarly Resources, 1992), 294–295.
22 María Pianca, *Testimonios de teatro latinoamericano* (Buenos Aires: Grupo Editor Latinoamericano, 1991), 8.
23 Phelan, *Unmarked*, 174.
24 Unni Wikan, "Beyond the Words: The Power of Resonance," *American Ethnologist* 19 (1992): 471.
25 Walter Benjamin, "Theses on the Philosophy of History," in *Illuminations* (New York: Harcourt, Brace and World, 1968), 257.
26 Roger I. Simon and Claudia Eppert, "Pedagogy and the Witnessing of Testimony of Historical Trauma," *Canadian Journal of Education* 22 (1997): 175–191.
27 Wikan, "Beyond the Words," 463.
28 Michael Taussig, *Shamanism, Colonialism, and the Wild Man: A Study in Terror and Healing* (Chicago: University of Chicago Press, 1987), 4–5.

29 G. O. Schanzas, "El teatro hispanoamericano de post mortem," *Latin American Theater Review* 7 (1974): 5–14.
30 Taussig, *Shaminism*, 4–5.
31 Ibid.
32 John Caputo, *Against Ethics: Contribution to a Poetics of Obligation with Constant Reference to Deconstruction* (Bloomington, IN: Indiana University Press, 1993).

3

TRUTH AND CONSEQUENCES

Art in response to the Truth and Reconciliation Commission

Stephanie Marlin-Curiel

As citizens of the "new" South Africa, we cannot afford to invest in placebo cures to the past. We need to explore our consciences and our complicity with recent history, deconstructing the legacies of apartheid. This cannot only happen "officially" as it is currently through the Truth and Reconciliation Commission; it is an invested process which involves the individual and needs to be enacted on many levels as part of the process of establishing a way forward and recognizing that the future is complex, en-grained and marked with the traces of the past, the resonance of process.

Artists' Statement, Fernando Alvim,
Carlos Garaicoa, Gavin Younge, *memórias íntimas marcas*

Artistic and cultural concerns in many ways engage with, yet are distinct from the legal-political questions that will arise. Betrayal, sadism, mourning, loss, confession, memory, reparation, longing, these are the persistent themes of the arts. The Commission will be examining the legal and political implications of these same themes. Through the arts we can explore who we are, and why we do what we do to one another.

Fault Lines exhibition press release

These two statements reflect the motivations behind two particular South African art exhibitions created in response to the Truth and Reconciliation Commission. Their statements suggest that the TRC and artists' responses to it are distinct, yet interdependent, processes. *Fault Lines* was a series of exhibitions and readings around "the Truth and Reconciliation moment" that explored the embedded and complicated themes of truth, memory, history, culpability, and narrative.[1] *Memórias íntimas marcas* gathered responses specifically to the Angolan war experience, a story marginalized by the TRC's publicly performed emphasis on apartheid-related human rights violations taking place within South Africa.

37

Resulting from the extensive political negotiations, which produced the Promotion of National Unity and Reconciliation Act of 1995, the TRC is the central "performance" of South Africa's transition to democracy. The TRC publicly stages individual testimonies of both survivors and perpetrators of gross human rights violations under apartheid. Founded on the notion that "truth is the road to reconciliation," amnesty for perpetrators was considered a fair price to pay for that truth. That perpetrators would have to confess publicly to their roles in the apartheid machine that disappeared, killed, and tortured so many activists and civilians was the limit of retributive justice being offered to victims. The Commission instead offered restorative justice, defined as "the restoration of human and civil dignity to victims." Victims would regain human and civil dignity in being able to learn the truth about those whom they had lost, tell their stories in public in their own languages, and by receiving reparations. In reality, only a proportionate few were given the opportunity to testify in public, only meager and symbolic reparations have been awarded to a select number of victims, and many cases have been unresolved and bodies remain unrecovered. At the time of writing, the TRC is running overtime. The final report has been submitted, yet some of the most significant amnesty hearings continue and judgments yet to be rendered.

The submission of the final report has nevertheless invited post-TRC evaluation. As a historical document, the final report expresses both more and less than the TRC process. It includes only a limited selection of the testimonies that were submitted to the commission, but also includes additional research on the broader events that involved the system of apartheid and particularly on South African Defense Force (SADF) activities beyond South Africa's borders. The public hearings, by contrast, focused on gross human rights perpetrated against nameable individuals rather than mass casualties. Exceptions to this include such seminal historic events as the Soweto student uprising of 1976, the 1992 Bisho massacre, and the 1993 St. James Church massacre. The Commission failed to address the stories of daily humiliation and deprivation affecting ordinary people who did not enjoy white-skin privilege, or the suffering of those who were displaced from their homes during the forced removals. The human rights violations by SADF soldiers that took place in Angola are a faint scar on the newly constructed national collective memory, as compared with the seared imprints still fresh in the soldiers' memories.

As if watching perpetrators go free were not painful enough, the psychological and physical trauma of what so many have suffered and the inability of the commission to follow through with its promises means that there are many gaps both in investigation and in healing that ordinary citizens must undertake for themselves. As Sean Field at a recent TRC conference pointed out, the attempt at political closure by no means accomplished emotional closure.

Emotional closure at a national level is often addressed by erecting monuments and memorials. Such structures symbolize a public moral judgment on a particular event, endure as an assurance that histories of bravery and suffering will not soon be forgotten, and serve as a beacon for future generations. More successful as a symbolic ritual process of mourning and nation-building than as a judicial process, the South

African TRC functions potentially as monument or memorial, carrying an overall message of moral condemnation of perpetrators of gross human rights violations.

Its actual moral message, however, is much more ambiguous. Because of the political necessity to accommodate South Africa's white population and to appear evenhanded, the TRC has succeeded in condemning individual use of violence and torture on both sides of the struggle in lieu of condemning apartheid as a system. More importantly, the TRC has demonstrated the blurred lines between perpetrator and victim. For example, an ANC soldier fighting against apartheid may have perpetrated violence against his own people, while a white SADF soldier may, in turn, have been a victim of indoctrination and manipulation by a totalitarian system. Those who do not think they fit into either of these categories are most likely "beneficiaries" of the system – guilty of indifference toward exploitation and oppression. Everyone, then, is left to grapple with their own role in history, and their relationship to the nation and their fellow citizens. Everyone's story is complex; a number of truths *lie* within each person. The artistic responses to the TRC range from those functioning as memorials and monuments trying to extract a more coherent moral truth to those that seek to bring out truth in all its moral complexities and complicities. The potential conflict to be reconciled is that to be effective, a truth commission depends on a notion of truth, while art depends on disrupting and questioning truth.

To say that the TRC and art about the TRC are interdependent, as in the above quotations, suggests that the relationship is not unidirectional. The TRC does not merely provide the content of the art. Rather, the processes of truth-telling and its aesthetic realization through artistic practice are both necessary to carry out the "promotion of unity and reconciliation." In the opinion of these artists, art such as *memórias íntimas marcas* and the works exhibited at *Fault Lines* are not mere representations of the TRC or its subject matter, but instead are *performative* actions that constitute parallel and ongoing processes of truth and reconciliation. Rather than reflect the TRC, they actively critique, and/or provide an alternative to the TRC.

Truth in art and the art of truth

The *Fault Lines* exhibition took place at the Castle of Good Hope in Cape Town in June 1996, only three months after the TRC began to hear the testimonies of victims of gross human rights violations. *Fault Lines: Inquiries into Truth and Reconciliation* included not just the exhibition, but also poetry readings, a community arts initiative, and an academic conference. Significantly, the series of cultural events was launched on June 16, 1996, the twentieth anniversary of the Soweto student uprising, so as to resonate with an established event in public memory. *Fault Lines* was inspired by the idea of carving out a role for artists in the truth and reconciliation process. While the TRC was perceived to be addressing political and legal issues, artists were left to respond to issues such as "memory, loss and the past, reconciliation, guilt and revenge, confession, truth and history."[2] Thus, *Fault Lines* explored an alternative, but participatory, role for artists in the nation's transformation.

Confessions from artists themselves, however, were deemed patently inappropriate by the conference participants. Mark Behr, a South African writer now living in Norway, incurred huge disapproval for his surprise confession at the *Fault Lines* conference that he had been an apartheid police spy. He was specifically criticized for instilling his confession with so much self-pity and self-criticism so as to prejudge himself before others had the chance. He was further criticized for not giving sufficiently detailed information, for using the platform to promote his forthcoming book on spying and betrayal, rather than facing those whom he betrayed.[3] This last criticism is the one that I have most often heard. Behr's confession, then, tested the limits of the *Fault Lines* conference. *Fault Lines* was not intended for personal excavation or confession. Although some of its participants, and presumably some of its audience, had been detainees and victims of torture, this was not meant to be a forum for perpetrators' confessions and social amnesty applications. The *Fault Lines* exhibition was specifically not the TRC. Its voice was at the edges of the TRC, in the untold stories, in the truths of metaphor rather than facts, and in the histories still embedded in space and landscape – but not in individual histories.

In order to divert focus from the pervasiveness of the TRC material being circulated in the public sphere, the visual artists went to the Mayibuye Center at the University of the Western Cape to dig through the archives for images that had been smuggled overseas and been recently returned. These graphic images of broken bodies were as shocking, perhaps more so than the TRC testimonies. For many people, it was the first time seeing such images. Suddenly there was an archive. Private bodily pain and suffering became publicly accessible, the evidence of the nation's hidden history.

Penny Siopis's "Mostly Women and Children" responded not only to the photographs, but also to the history of the Castle site, challenging the historical inscriptions on the space itself. Her installation is located in the office, which she thinks of as the "grand Western and masculine imprint on Africa."[4] This orderly office space is strewn with the debris of catastrophe. The piece used four body casts found at the Museum of Cultural History in Pretoria. The casts were of African women adorned with "traditional" jewelry that she used as "traces, as icons of apartheid."[5] These black figures place in relief the museum of white history installed at the other end of the Castle.

Siopis laid the figures on their sides, their bodies in rigor mortis, at the edges of the room. Two artificial fires burned in the space. The work is a multilayered commentary on the domestication and preservation of African women cast as museum objects representing "tradition," while on the outside they are people whose lives are wasted in war. These images depict the silence of women's suffering, as well as the survival of women who appear at the TRC talking about the men they have lost. In her piece, they lie among primarily male-gendered objects: a Boy Scout uniform, an army uniform, military toys, devices and tear gas canisters. The title's indication that children, along with women, are often the wasted objects of war reflects both the tragedy and the heroism of the students of Soweto. The sight/site of these objects invokes both the past and the present, and questions the viewer's gaze. Do viewers empathize with or resist the image? Do they walk past, averting their gaze,

Figure 3.1 Clive van den Berg, *Men Loving*, 1996. Photograph by Mark Lewis.

or do they stop and indulge voyeuristically in the sight of helpless victims, war-torn bodies, and destruction? Siopis's work is one of many that examine the culpability of the viewer as a voyeur of violence, but it falls short of examining her own culpability.

Clive van den Berg "unearthed" the history literally buried by institutions, such as the Castle. In one of the rooms, van den Berg created a slope of real grass enveloping the bodies of two male lovers of different complexions, leaving only their heads visible (Figure 3.1). The other objects strewn on the grass are an open suitcase and a ship made from white paper. The caption reads:

> In 1735, two men were taken into the Bay off Cape Town when the ship was near Robben Island. They were made to walk the plank chained together. They had loved each other.

After a few lines of white space, the caption continues:

> Friday, May 8 we adopted a constitution which forbids discrimination on the basis of sexual preference. Perhaps now loving will be easier.[6]

The fact that there is a gap both in space and time between these two captions indicates that there is much unstated historical memory that lies in between. The different complexions of the two heads would suggest that as society and the legal system have accepted the sight of "mixed" couples so too might it accept same-sex couples. At the same time, the buried heads are a memorial to those who lost their lives in these struggles. On public holidays, we revere such victims as heroes who have sacrificed their lives. We say never again, but these ideals are soon forgotten, as soon as the grass dies.

Malcolm Payne's total assault on the senses, *Title in Progress* (Figure 3.2), creates an abrupt collision between the space of the Castle and the current historical moment of opening, rewriting, and closing the book on the past. Within the castle walls, Payne built another wall of bricks in the shape of books, faintly patterned with black and white images of bandaged hands and feet. Five of the bricks are video screens showing bandaged hands turning pages of blank books. Dichotomies intermittently float onto the pages, such as "us/them," "warm/cold," "mother/father," "black/white." A featureless rag doll in a metal chair mounted on a pedestal

Figure 3.2 Malcolm Payne, *Title in Progress*, 1996. Photograph by Mark Lewis.

watches all this. The chair jerks backward, repeatedly hitting the pedestal with a loud metallic crash before it rebounds forward again. A soundtrack accompanies the work with fragmented speech uttering lines such as "Don't press the button"; "Getting closer"; "the truth"; "Where's the text, Jack? . . . where's the fucking text?"[7] The image invokes torture and interrogation, fiercely juxtaposed against the benevolent information-gathering institution of the TRC, and the Castle site, which has been cleanly transformed from colonial slave and military fortress of the Dutch East India Company to tourist site and museum. The dichotomies suggest that discourse divides and wounds before yielding truth.

There were at least two artists in the show who did use their discoveries in the Mayibuye archive to reflect on their personal histories and indirect guilt. Interestingly, both used photographs screened onto white cloth and both combined these photographs with religious iconography. Lien Botha used images of mutilated bodies from the Angolan raids. These deaths, after all, were the direct result of the regime for which her father Pik Botha served as Foreign Affairs Minister during that time. As a gesture of ritual cleansing she combined the photos she found with religious images, as well as images of the corpse of her recently deceased mother. Her white cloths hung on a clothesline spanning the room.

Colin Richards also had several pieces on display that drew upon different aspects of his experience. I will focus only on those that were exhibited both as part of *Fault Lines* and as part of *memórias íntimas marcas*. As a medical illustrator Richards once had to label a set of autopsy photographs, which he eventually realized depicted the mutilated body of Steve Biko. In the work, Richards used only two non-identifiable images from the autopsy. The rest are of Biko's cell, reproduced onto cloths made from torn bed sheets from his own home. He arranged these cloths in the shape of "Veronica's veil" with which, according to the liturgy, she used to wipe the sweaty, bloodied face of Christ. Christ's visage became imprinted on the cloth as the first "authentic" image of the divine.[8] Around the space he had installed cherub heads and broken angel wings, ruins left over after vandalism that he regularly collects at a nearby cemetery. The "blue eyes" of one of the cherub heads signified the blue eyes of perpetrators that so many TRC witnesses recounted. For Richards, they also signified the blue eyes of a young white girl who was part of a refugee family on the Angolan border. He fed the girl against the orders of his general because the girl reminded him of his daughter. The piece reflects conflict and contradiction on every level. It draws on personal memories, as well as other people's memories, his past and his present, his culpability and his contributions, of truth revealed and concealed, the purity and degradation of death and Christianity, and the unrelenting unreliability of whiteness.

In another piece, Richards also grappled with his memories of serving in the SADF in Angola. Against an image of the Castle wall, he superimposed two images of found objects from his Angolan experience with that of a personal object he collected on a trip with his wife to Venice. While in Angola he had been made to strip and sort the clothes from a rotting pile of dead "enemy" soldiers. He tells of coming across a helmet lined with clotted blood, hair, flesh, and bone. He did not include this image, but rather that of some cartridges he had lifted from a soldier and managed to smuggle across the border. On the right-hand side is a "Pro Patria" medal he received for his service in Angola, a country that the South African army publicly denied ever having entered. Between these two army "souvenirs" is the souvenir from his trip to Venice, a metal flame torn from a Catholic relic.

As a group, Richards's collection encompasses both souvenirs and relics. The relics come from mortal, divine, and living bodies memorializing the death, life, degradation, and immor(t)ality in each. Each of these souvenirs is illicit: one smuggled, one the result of vandalism of a sacred symbol, and one a medal from a brutal regime that lied to its own soldiers and fellow citizens. Each is an instrument of power materialized as metal. Although one comes from a soldier defending himself, one from a font of moral religiosity, and one from an aggressor, as a group they are all just pieces of metal, only regaining significance in the personal memory of the artist.

All three of these objects negate themselves in their dual functions as both souvenirs and relics. This is because relics, according to Susan Stewart, are "anti-souvenirs." She writes:

> Because they are souvenirs of death, the relic, the hunting trophy and the scalp are at the same time the most intensely *potential* souvenirs and the most potent antisouvenir. They mark the horrible transformation of meaning into materiality more than they mark, as other souvenirs do, the transformation of materiality into meaning. If the function of the souvenir proper is to create a continuous and personal narrative of the past, the function of such souvenirs of death is to disrupt and disclaim that continuity. Souvenirs of the mortal body are not so much a nostalgic celebration of the past as they are an erasure of the significance of history . . . such souvenirs mark the end of sacred narrative and the interjection of the curse.[9]

Relics become antisouvenirs precisely because their meaning is eclipsed by their materiality. A meaning that may have exceeded the individual during life becomes reduced again to the level of the individual at death. The meaning of a relic of an unknown deceased is manifest in the one who remembers. Its materiality does not metonymically signify a greater meaning or a larger story that is readily apparent, as would that of the souvenir. Indeed, Richards has interjected the curses that he has had to live with, but I would disagree with Stewart that they stand for the erasure of the significance of history. The sites of disruption in temporal or spatial continuity are the very ones that reveal the significance of history. The souvenir connects the collector with something larger, a place or an event, a public history whose meaning has already been determined. A relic of an unknown person is that which is snatched from what has been excluded from public history. While the relic's meaning is private, it is publicly displayed; while the souvenir's meaning is public, it is privately collected.

Colin Richards's objects could be seen as both relics and souvenirs. This personal exploration of deep contradiction in his memories of Angola piqued the interest of Angolan artist Fernando Alvim. Colin Richards recounts:

> He phoned me and he said, "would you be prepared to contribute to this show [*memórias íntimas marcas*]?" And I thought it was a great show, this was much more my kind of show, much more focused, much more contradictory, much more messy, much more painful and much more real.[10]

Memórias (memory), *íntimas* (intimacy), *marcas* (traces) grew out of a pilgrimage to Angola by three artists: Fernando Alvim (Angolan), Carlos Garaicoa (Cuban), and Gavin Younge (South African). The three had met at the Johannesburg Biennale in 1995 and realized that they might have faced each other through opposite ends of a barrel had they themselves fought the war in Angola. The three artists experimented in creating a collective memory of the war in Angola, which none of them had directly experienced. They convened for twelve days at Cuito Cuanavale, site of a major battle in the Angolan conflict. In 1987, the SADF, backed by the United States, joined the UNITA (Union for the Total Independence of Angola) rebel movement in the fight against the ruling MPLA (People's Movement for the Liberation of Angola). The Angolan government forces were bolstered by Cuban troops and Soviet advisors. The SADF suffered an embarrassing defeat, which they proceeded to try to cover up.

Although the battle had taken place nine years hence, the landscape was still scarred. The tanks and landmines still remained where they stood at the end of battle. On the fourth day, their guide stumbled on one of the mines and was seriously injured. Carlos Garaicoa, who explored the landscape by digging holes in the banks of the Cuito River, miraculously escaped unharmed. Photographs of these holes appear in the exhibition.

Gavin Younge rode around on a bicycle videotaping the landscape. One of his works in the exhibition is a circle of bicycles with TV monitors in the baskets, showing footage of a blown out armory and children in rags. The title, *Forces Favourites*, refers to a military propagandist show that aired on South African Broadcasting Corporation (SABC) during the conflict.

According to Karl Maier, "the Battle of Cuito Cuanavale contributed to forcing South Africa to look inward and inevitably to begin a reform process that led to the unbanning of the African National Congress in 1990."[11] The exhibition similarly looked inward. It was a sensual, tangible, and personal excavation of physical and emotional trauma and devastation. Returning to the battle site created a collision between past and present, and a "common ground" on which the three artists could stand, with a luxurious freedom from the TRC labels of victim and perpetrator.

The exhibition opened at Cuito Cuanavale in April 1997. Like the Truth and Reconciliation Commission, it was itinerant. From Cuito Cuanavale, it moved to Luanda and then to the Castle in Cape Town where *Fault Lines* had been the year before. At the Cape Town site, the works of other artists such as Colin Richards were added. The exhibition curators invited audiences and artists alike to "become involved in the labor of remembrance" (brochure).

What had excited Richards about the show was the opportunity to write as part of his contribution. While artists more often take to image to communicate the

Figure 3.3 Lien Botha, *Salver 8/24.* © copyright Sussuta Boé. *Mémorias íntimas marcas* project. Concept by Fernando Alvim. Intellectual Property of Fernando Alvim. All rights reserved.

unspeakable, Richards needed to speak in the first person; he needed to testify. At the entrance to his installation was a text about an argument he had with his father about going to Angola. He told his father the military leaders had said the army was not in Angola, and that he would never sign a document agreeing to go there. However, once in the army, he was put on the truck and Angola was the first and final stop. He had been lied to and forced to betray his father, who died before he returned. Richards had a story to tell.

Lien Botha joined the exhibition for the Johannesburg and Pretoria shows. She exhibited a set of trays with painted images of prosthetic limbs (Figure 3.3). These trays were suspended against the walls at serving level in a disconcerting interplay of absence and presence. Visitors were forced to walk cautiously through two flanks of the trays as glasses randomly littered the floor, like landmines. Beneath the title, "*Salver 8/24*," she lays out a play on words beginning with the word salver (meaning serving tray) and salvo (meaning discharge of artillery), evoking all the meanings of saving, salvation, and healing in between.

Many of the images in the show, like Botha's, hinged on the surreal. At once literal, corporeal, and testimonial in their materiality and mimetic qualities, they were also dreamlike and fantastic, like the hauntings of belated trauma. Alvim exhibited images of a brain and heart pierced by mattress springs and a hospital bed with casts of dead babies on it. Younge contributed animal images using real skins that he sutured and stretched. These were intended to stand for the military vehicles to which the SADF habitually gave animal names. Other images and installations included graffiti, ruined "pock-marked" buildings, a collection of the components of a soldier's uniform, and several pieces of furniture enhanced with skin, nails, or paintings of birds. Not only did this exhibition deal with subject matter that took place beyond South Africa's borders, but the exhibition itself has since traveled beyond those borders. *Memórias íntimas marcas* is unique in its attempts through travel to engage with a history that is not just South African, but which involved multiple international players and to which the rest of the world bore witness.

The devastation of Angola and other frontline states, although fueled by the National Party's apartheid regime and included in the TRC's Final Report, was not heard in amnesty hearings. In reality, more gross human rights violations took place beyond South Africa's borders between 1960 and 1994 than within the country.[12] The media and the ANC government ignored this fact, however, and it was thus sidelined in public discourse. The ANC, whose human rights abuses against its own people in their training camps in Angola did come under scrutiny by the TRC, chose to avoid the whole subject of Angola as much as possible.

To stop another veil of silence from falling over this war and its victims, the exhibition performed dialog on several levels: first, among the artists who took part, second, with the postwar site of Cuito Cuanavale; third, with the exhibition audiences; and fourth, with the venues in which the exhibition is installed. The artists and others who had experienced the war in Angola wrote for a newsletter, *Marcas News*, and compiled a book written in French, Portuguese, and English.

The contents of the exhibition and the exhibitors changed in every venue. Each space endowed the exhibit with a different set of meanings. At the military hospital in Pretoria, apartheid's administrative headquarters, viewers were placed in the role of hospital visitor, presumably visiting soldiers whom they knew. At Johannesburg's Electric Workshop, the pieces were installed in intimate cubicles. According to South African art critic, Brenda Atkinson, this configuration reflected "an old African belief that if you experience tragedy or an insurmountable problem, you can put it in a box, and it will be resolved after two years."[13] The visitors entered into the boxed spaces, which meant that they were implicated in the "problem." Problems did not just belong to histories, governments, or even the soldiers that fought in Angola, but to everyone whose country was in any way affected. The cure, therefore, is not instant, but is initiated and put into effect over time.

Both *Fault Lines* and *memórias íntimas marcas* displayed a concern for the performative role of the viewer, and moving through thresholds of time and space. Also like *Fault Lines*, *memórias* began with an archive. For *Fault Lines*, this was the Mayibuye Center photographs and for *memórias*, it was the war-torn landscape of Angola itself. Most of the artists, therefore, worked with material evidence of events they never directly experienced.

The archive, in these cases, stands in for real events. Communally and simultaneously experienced, they are easily converted to collective memory. Is it possible to be traumatized by the aftermath of an event that one has not directly experienced? Dori Laub speaks of the hazards threatening one who listens to a survivor's testimony.[14] What about those who are not listening to such testimony directly, but are responding to photographs and desecrated landscapes where there are no survivors? If, as Cathy Caruth says, "the historical power of trauma is not just that the experience is repeated after its forgetting, but that it is only in and through its inherent forgetting that it is *first* experienced at all" (my emphasis),[15] then remembering forgotten events by way of discovering their evidence could be traumatizing. These artists' works function as "the belatedness of historical experience." The event "not experienced as it occurs is fully evident *only* in connection with another place and another time" (my emphasis).

As citizens of South Africa and other countries involved in these events, these artists are not disinterested parties. The visual artists in these exhibitions, who are predominantly white, seem to see their task as engaging with the past on as primary a level as possible. Yet, only secondary evidence is available to them. The task of the "translator," according to de Man, "is to read the textuality of the original event *without disposing of* the body, without reducing the original event to a false transparency of sense."[16] These works imply the intent of the artists to "get their hands dirty," and as such, to participate in a public manner in the truth and reconciliation process. With the exception of Colin Richards, however, the artists' own subject positions remain unexplored.

The TRC mandate to uncover the facts of the past and make recommendations to the government on how to legislate against such violations in the future demonstrates that this process does not end with facts. Taking responsibility for the facts is equally important. The institutional hearings, such as the business and media hearings, helped whites to see beyond the rubric of victims and perpetrators of gross human rights violations and recognize their own culpability. "English liberals," for example, have borne heavy criticism for denouncing apartheid from within the safety of their living rooms. After these hearings, they could no longer see themselves as just bystanders, but were forced to see themselves as beneficiaries and even perpetrators. Some artists had broken the cultural boycott in the 1980s by participating in state-sponsored exhibitions. Some served in the SADF. Others just did whatever was fashionable. In response to the 1995 Johannesburg Biennale Sander Gilman wrote: "The truth of the matter becomes the working through of the memories of trauma and of the abuse of power. It becomes a question of the 'now' as much as (perhaps even more than) the 'then.'"[17] In taking up the past in their work, artists must inevitably determine their own relationship to it in the present.

The TRC hovers in the gap between documentary and metaphor and between individual and collective memory. At the TRC, the live testimony of eyewitnesses gives testimony the legal weight of truth. Yet, the TRC also functions on a metaphoric level, as a means to heal the nation and as a ritual of transition between the past and the future. Despite the difficulties in verifying the truth of testimonies and confessions, the TRC is reluctant to abandon all efforts to do so. Factual truth will underpin important legislative and communal efforts to prevent the repetition of past injustices and to compensate victims for the psychological trauma, physical pain, and material losses they have suffered. But there is also a need to capture the imagination of South African citizens who may not have been as directly affected by apartheid.

The artist, however, does not seek to represent or collect a version of the truth. Instead, the work of art, likewise, is created and read as a performance of truth. An insight of Fabio B. DaSilva and Jim Faught is useful here. They write:

> the truthfulness of art is not ascertained by its complete depiction of faithfulness to a lived reality, but appears in its import for persons not in the abstract, but as they really exist.[18]

Its "import" is in its performativity, in the ability to perform self-reflection and share personal memory with another person or a public. Memory, though unreliable, nonetheless enables a witness to communicate an embodied reality and solicit an empathetic response to victims of violence. In as much as artists bear witness to memory, they take responsibility for carrying its force beyond the personal into the social.[19] Poet and Communist Party leader Jeremy Cronin wrote these lines in his poem, *Even the Dead*, presented at one of the *Fault Lines* readings:

> I am not sure what poetry is. I am not sure what the aesthetic is. Perhaps the aesthetic should be defined in opposition to anaesthetic.
> Art is the struggle to stay awake.
> Which makes amnesia the true target and proper subject of poetry.[20]

Performing the past

As a "nation-building" ritual engaged with the truth of the past, to participate in the TRC or its efforts at any level is to gain acceptance as a "new" South African. The TRC is a performance model consisting of testifying and bearing witness to testimony. According to Richard Schechner, performance is "twiced-behaved" or restored behavior. The TRC is a complex performance exhibiting the restoration of several behaviors: storytelling, testimony, courtroom behavior, church behavior, and – in its subject matter – apartheid violence itself, here restored in narrated form. The TRC does not restore facts, but previous performances and their consequences. For example, the TRC tries to help people to feel healed and inclined to forgive by often invoking religious symbolism, singing hymns, and by soliciting confession. Superimposed upon this, however, is the semblance of a legal hearing designed to bring about an amnesty judgment. This judgment, in turn, rests on loosely legislated concepts such as political motivation, full disclosure, and proportionality of act to aim, all of which are difficult to determine on a purely objective basis.

The cross-purposes of the TRC can be partially accounted for by the different goals and performances associated with the human rights violations hearings (otherwise referred to as victims' hearings) and the amnesty hearings. The TRC was born of a political compromise designed to avoid a violent overthrow of the National Party regime and instead helped to insure a relatively peaceful political transition to ANC rule. The amnesty hearings were part of this political negotiation. The victims' hearings, on the other hand, were not. Added on for the sake of nation-building, they allowed those previously silenced to be heard, to "restore the human and civil dignity of the victims," to rewrite public history and to create an opportunity for national *communitas* and catharsis.

In response to these cross-purposes, the notion of truth in the TRC legislation and literature evolved from the factual to the performative. Based upon the Promotion of National Unity and Reconciliation Act 1995, the TRC's mandate was to gather truth as fact, which would then be put to use:

> AND SINCE it is deemed necessary to establish the truth in relation to past
> events as well as the motives for and circumstances in which gross violations
> of human rights have occurred, and to make the findings known in order
> to prevent a repetition of such acts in future.

By the time the final report was submitted to President Nelson Mandela in October 1998, the notion of truth had expanded and slipped into its performative role. The report defines four types of truth at work in the TRC: factual or forensic truth; personal or narrative truth; social or "dialog" truth; and healing and restorative truth.

Factual and forensic truth is defined straightforwardly as based on factual and objective information and evidence. In defining personal or narrative truth, the final report makes explicit reference to South Africa's "oral tradition."[21] This definition of truth recognizes the potential for validation and healing of survivors who are allowed to tell their stories in their own language. Social or dialog truth refers to the alleged openness and participatory structure of the TRC. Conferences, public debates in the media, and NGO participation largely excluded non-organized or non-represented victims as well as those who did not suffer gross human rights violations according to the TRC definition. These "public" forums had minimal impact on the hearings, but did influence the final report and the future life of the reconciliation process. Healing and restorative truth refer to the repair of the relationship between the state and its citizens through reparations, legislation outlawing human rights abuses, and public acknowledgement that "a person's pain is real and worthy of attention."[22]

The TRC, at least philosophically, then, has substituted a truth based on fact with one located in the performance of democracy and healing. With the TRC performing "truth" in so many forms, artists have a range of "performative effects" to choose from in making art that attempts to contribute to societal transformation: the literal, the metaphorical, the testimonial, the confessional, the cathartic, the scientific, the interpretive, and the implicative. The TRC's primary performance, however, is testimony, the performance of personal memory. Those who did not themselves suffer gross human rights violations, however, do not have recourse to such memories. Their memories can only take them as far as the spectacle of testimony at the TRC that has ingrained itself on the public's imagination. Again, *the archive* (in performance) *stands in for the "real" event.* If the survivor's memory is the result of a belated visitation of the trauma itself, the public remembers only faces and voices of survivors of brutal violence telling their stories on television before the nation and the world.

Yet, if truth is in the telling, what happens when artists appropriate TRC stories, stories that they themselves have not lived? Or as Shoshana Felman writes: "What does it mean that testimony cannot be simply reported, or narrated by another in its role as testimony?"[23] The debate on whether the non-trauma survivor has a right to represent trauma hovers at the borders of the debate raging in South African art circles over the right of white artists to portray black subjects.[24] As with the non-black portrayers of black subjects, we might ask does the non-trauma survivor have the ability, or more importantly the authority, to create images of trauma? More to my point here, does their art have any testimonial or truth-value, important in dealing with this subject matter in this historical moment? Art inspired by TRC testimony inflames the same kind of sensitivities as art on the Holocaust; hence, the recent criticisms by several reviewers of Roberto Begnini's *Life is Beautiful* as being too much a fiction with no basis in fact. At the opposite end of the spectrum, Claude Lanzmann's approach in his *Shoah* was to create narrative solely through testimony. Lanzmann's opinion of Spielberg's *Schindler's List* is that its use of fiction transgresses the ethics of unrepresentability.[25]

Of course, the TRC has well demonstrated that the horrors of apartheid are not unspeakable. Perhaps, though, they are unspeakable under any other conditions but those of testimony. What does it mean to fictionalize atrocity through the addition of the imagination, aestheticize it through the use of metaphor, or narrativize it in order to make it comprehensible?

Three pieces of theater inspired by the TRC demonstrated the creative potential in navigating this ethical conundrum. The earliest theater works addressing the TRC were *Ubu and the Truth Commission* and *The Story I am About to Tell*. In each of these works a sharp distinction was drawn between "truth" and "theater." In *Ubu* puppets delivered TRC testimony as direct proxies. They were not people so they were not in danger of "inhabiting" these stories. The creators of *Ubu* were well aware that using puppets saved the audience from having to believe the testimony was the actor's own story. The words clearly did not belong to the puppet. William Kentridge provides the following explanation for his decision to use puppets as witnesses:

> What is our responsibility to the people whose stories we are using as raw fodder for the play? There seemed to be an awkwardness in getting an actor to play the witnesses – the audience being caught halfway between having to believe in the actor for the sake of the story, and also not believing in the actor for the sake of the actual witness who existed out there, but was not the actor. Using a puppet made this contradiction palpable. There is no attempt to make the audience think the wooden puppet or manipulator is the actual witness. The puppet becomes a medium through which the testimony can be heard.[26]

The puppet as theatrical device separates the body from speech. In fact, the puppets manage to do this in part by evoking the language translation of testimonies at the TRC. Audience members usually do not hear the testimonies directly unless they speak the language of the witness. Instead, they don earphones to be able to hear the testimony in the language of their choice. The puppet represents the displacement of the witness's voice in this process. The puppet is essentially an "empty vessel" like that of the translator. An actor, on the other hand, would attempt to convince the audience that the story was one of personal experience. The testimonies in *Ubu* were delivered in Truth Commission style. Not only did the puppetry metaphorically refer to translation, but also Pa Ubu's shower stall on stage doubled as a translation booth. The testimonies were delivered in the original language by the puppet manipulators and then translated by actors who stood in the booth and translated the testimonies just as at the TRC hearings. Mimicking the scenography of the TRC became an important means of grounding truth in the "original" scene of testimony.

By contrast, in *The Story I am About to Tell* three actual witnesses who testified at the TRC retell their stories on stage. These three witnesses were joined by three professional actors. Like *Ubu*, the play is divided into two modes, dramatic and "real." In the beginning of the play, one of the actors even introduces the players as three actors and three "real" people who have come together to make this play. The play itself dramatizes a debate about whether there is anything to be gained by going to the TRC. The debate begins in a *kombi* (minibus taxi) and almost erupts into blows when the scene abruptly shifts and the three witnesses deliver their testimonies. The argument which begins in the *kombi* resumes after the testimonies are spoken.

Both *Ubu* and *Story* exhibited the same concern over compromising the truth of the stories they were re-presenting in the context of the otherwise fictional space known as theater. In addition to their hesitations in using actors to deliver testimony, the playwrights also scripted the testimony scenes as separate from, rather than part of, the plot. Scenes of testimony suspend the stage action, and the audience recognizes the stage configuration as that belonging to the TRC. The "theater" resumes after the testimony. The imperative of *performing* the truth could only be fulfilled by *performing* the scene of testimony. Testimonial performance of the TRC stands in the public imagination as the most "authentic" and "authoritative" model of such performance.

While both *Ubu* and *Story* avoided the use of actors speaking TRC testimony, Nan Hamilton's *No. 4* braved the use of an actress in its testimonial scene. Staging an environmental "ritual" at the Old Fort, formerly a prison, "No. 4," she led audience members through a series of scenes and participatory events designed to break the bonds of the psychological imprisonment of the past. In the "Domestic Court" scene, testimony from the TRC was transcribed and then workshopped with the actress to generate associations from her own personal history. Without changing the script, she weaved these personal associations into her performance of this testimony. Because the intention of her testimony emerged from her own experience, her performance does not attempt to speak for the victim even if the words have been appropriated from someone else's testimony. According to Kali Tal, if the listener had suffered a similar experience, then the narration might trigger visceral memories from their own experience.[27] She would thus not be acting. She would be testifying through someone else's words, or to evoke Artaud, she would be "signaling through the flames."

Media and metaphor

The openness of the TRC enlisted the media as the means by which the general population would partake in the process. For many who did not attend the Commission, the news media in all forms became the performance that replaced the TRC event.

As Daniel Dayan and Elihu Katz observe:

> The conferral of media event status on a given occasion consists in pulling
> it away from the news and translating it in a fictional register. The result
> is a text which neutralizes the opposition between fiction and news.[28]

The media thus contributed directly to the metaphoric functions of the TRC. As a "media event," the TRC hopes to motivate its public to "respond cognitively and emotionally in predefined categories of approval, disapproval, arousal or passivity."[29]

Three artists responded specifically to the mediatized portrayals of the TRC. Judith Mason responded with works of mourning, honoring, and commemoration; Willemein de Williers felt her complacency awakened and reflected the violent effects that could be felt from these reports; and Sue Williamson created her own media event of the media event.

In an exhibition of Judith Mason's work, two news clippings containing quotes from the testimony of perpetrators during exhumations hang on the wall. The news clippings written by the well-known poet and journalist, Antjie Krog, tell the stories of Phila Portia Ndwandwe and Harold Sefola, whom Mason dubs "The Woman Who Kept Silent" and "The Man Who Sang." Their testimonies came not from their own mouths but from those of their murderers who recalled their bravery while digging up their corpses. Harold Sefola's murderer first shocked Sefola's friend to death with a generator right in front of him. Sefola began singing the Xhosa national anthem and kept singing for as long as he could while he, too, was inflicted with the shocks that killed him, his murderer recounts. Ndwandwe's corpse was recognized by the blue plastic bag that still hung around the pelvic bones of her skeleton. She had been kept naked for ten days while under interrogation. On the tenth day, she had constructed a pair of underpants from a blue plastic bag she found lying around. She never broke under interrogation. Her killers recall burying her in that blue plastic bag and surprising themselves with the sense of respect they showed by not stripping her naked again.

The focus of Mason's exhibition, *Requiem*, is on these two victims who could no longer speak for themselves but whose bravery is remembered and spoken about by their murderers. "The Woman Who Kept Silent" and "The Man Who Sang" reflect the absence of words. Mason's art, however, is not silent. She fills the void with the words of others, displacing the testimonies of the perpetrators as the only living memorial. She enlists quotations from politicians and literary figures, South African and international, and arduously pens them by hand onto strips of plastic that become sinews and filaments hanging off of a metal cage containing a piece of blue plastic. This piece, *Catafalque of The Woman Who Kept Silent*, hung from the ceiling as one of the exhibition's centerpieces (Figure 3.4). The other centerpiece was a gown constructed out of the same type of blue plastic bags that Ndwandwe had used to construct her "underwear" (Figure 3.5). Mason and her "domestic assistant" collected the bags used for the dress rather than buying them from a store.[30] On this gown, Mason penned a tribute in her own words:

> Sister, a plastic bag may not be the whole armor of god but you were wrestling with flesh and blood and against powers, against the rulers of darkness, against spiritual wickedness in sordid places. Your weapons were your silence and a piece of rubbish. Finding that bag and wearing it until you were disinterred was such a frugal, commonsensical housewifely thing to do. An ordinary act, yet having about it the wit of art. A feminist act

Figure 3.4 Judith Mason, *Catafalque for The Woman Who Kept Silent*, 1998. Photograph by Bob Adshade.

which, although it lacks the rhetoric of falling beneath horses' hooves is at least as fine. For at some level, you shamed your captors, and they did not compound their abuse of you by stripping you a second time. Yet they killed you. We only know your story because a sniggering man remembered how brave you were. Memorials to your courage are everywhere. They blow about the streets and drift on the tide and cling to thorn bushes. This dress is made from some of them. *Hamba Kahle, Umkhonto* ("Go safely, warrior").

Figure 3.5 Judith Mason, *Dress for The Woman Who Kept Silent (Nike)*, 1998. Photograph by Bob Adshade.

Judith Mason identifies with this woman through an imagined bond of feminist and mythological sisterhood, which she symbolizes by naming this gown after Nike, the Greek Goddess of Victory. She has created a formidable memorial. But where was Judith Mason during apartheid when she was needed? She was, as she says, "a cowardly old lefty . . . slipping around on the side-lines and surviving when [others] didn't."[31] She admits to a heavy case of "survivor guilt," and these works may clearly have to do with working through that guilt. Art is her medium, but to it she added words, upon words, upon words. She never appropriates testimonies, however, but instead offers a personalized response.

Another artist whose imagination was suddenly captured by the media coverage of the TRC was Willemein de Williers. When cooking soup one day in her kitchen, the newspaper she was reading interrupted and invaded her cooking reveries. She realized that she too had remained in a safe space while atrocities were being committed by her own government. The kitchen had always seemed to her an especially safe place, full of womb-like shapes: cups, bowls, spoons. In a ceramic soup bowl she placed shards of pottery with handwritten excerpts from the newspaper. Sentences were broken so only a few words could be made out. Violence, she discovered, could reach her even in her kitchen. The kitchen itself could easily turn lethal, full of pointed objects: knives and forks. De Williers created sets of teacups caged in by forks. On the teacups handwritten excerpts from the news clippings are juxtaposed with a shopping list. The writing is blurry, scratched through, difficult to read. It is like a ghostly presence enveloped her kitchen.

Sue Williamson presents a third interpretation of the TRC inspired by its media coverage. Her exhibition *Truth Games* retains grossly fragmented and dissected text from the TRC hearings. These fragments are arranged on sliding panels with photographic images. Viewers can manipulate these, demonstrating the multiple versions of truth being produced at the TRC and the people's lives and deaths caught in between. Herself a journalist, Williamson also implicates herself in the manipulation of these words and images. She takes advantage of the possibilities of working with media in these works as she arranges photographs of victim and perpetrator to achieve a certain point of contact or lack of contact between them. Placed opposite each other, victim and perpetrator appear to glance past or toward each other, lending new interpretations to the events and their participants (Figure 3.6). With the sliding panels, Williamson offers this interpretative prerogative to the viewer.

Such multiple or layered versions of the truth are, according to Andre Brink, the hallmark of "post-apartheid narrative." Yet, while Brink sees post-apartheid narrative as a kind of inevitability resulting from the unreliability of memory, Williamson's work goes further in demonstrating the active role of the viewer/receiver in the creation of truth. Brink steps back in with an ethical agenda when he says that given the existence of "multiple versions of history," "the imperative of choice is even more urgent, and certainly more richly textured and more rewarding."[32]

There is a troubling contradiction in Brink's emphasis on the importance of choice between multiple versions of history and his insistence on the existence of presumably immutable historical facts. The contradiction arises because Brink sees the TRC as an essentially fact-finding enterprise as opposed to fiction, which is an enterprise of the imagination.[33] But we have already seen the fictional, metaphoric processes in the mediatization of the TRC, without which the TRC would not be a completely "public" process. As Njabulo Ndebele insists, if the TRC is to have any meaning, the journey into metaphor is inevitable. Ndebele has called the TRC an example of a people reinventing themselves through narrative:

> The narrative of apartheid, which can now be told, has reached that part
> of the plot where vital facts leading to the emergence of understanding are

Figure 3.6. Sue Williamson, *Tony Yengeni – "Wet Bag" Torture – Jeff Benzien*, from *Truth Games*, 1998. Photograph by Wayne Oosthuizen.

in the process of being revealed . . . it is going to be the search for meanings that may trigger off more narratives. If and when that happens, the imagination, having been rescued by time, will be the chief beneficiary. The resulting narratives have less and less to do with facts themselves and with their recall than with the revelation of meaning through the imaginative combination of those facts. At that point, facts will be the building blocks of metaphor.[34]

In other words, Ndebele seems to be saying that at the moment of making meaning through narrative, the facts immediately disappear into the recesses of metaphor.

The metaphorical process is already evident in the way the TRC selects particular testimonies, briefs witnesses, and then poses specific questions so that it can construct certain narratives, certain truths. For example, with the testimony of Ellen Kuzwayo, author of *Call Me Woman*, the Commissioners posed a host of questions about the instrumental role of community organization that led to the Soweto uprising in 1976. As an emblem of the struggle, Kuzwayo was considered an authoritative source who could speak on behalf of the community. Belinda Bozzoli makes a similar point in analyzing how at the hearings in Alexandra, famous for the bus boycotts and rent strikes, the testimonies were shaped to reinforce the historical identity of the community.[35] Other testimonies were used to conjure the images of mutilated bodies, and others invoked to be read as the pathetic images of mothers and lost children.

The media have often remarked upon the TRC's theatrical qualities. In talking to artists about why there is not more art about the Truth Commission, the frequent response is that the Truth Commission is already so dramatic, and thereby defies further dramatization. The expressions of the absolutely extraordinary at the TRC are a present-day updated version of Njabulo Ndebele's words about the "rediscovery of the ordinary":[36] the everyday lives of blacks under apartheid, just like these stories of outrageous torture and killing, are already beyond what the imagination could dream up.

But there must also be a limit to metaphor. While metaphorical imagining is necessary to receive the witness's testimony for spectator-listeners who have not shared the same experience, there is the danger that this process will entail imagining oneself as the other in the role of perpetrator or victim rather leading to a self-revelation.[37]

Performing the future

Antjie Krog writes that "an unwritten TRC assumption is that *simple illiterate people tell the truth; well-dressed powerful people do not.*"[38] Since it is expected that such "well-dressed powerful people" will not tell the truth, the authority to speak is unchallenged by the audience. There is no cause to question whether or not a person has the *authority to tell* a lie since it holds the lowest moral value. The truth, however, holds too much moral capital to allow just anyone to stake a claim to it. This is especially the case when moral capital has the potential to turn into real capital or when the moral high ground is being claimed by those seeking amnesty, who are perceived as less deserving.

According to Michel Foucault, an author is merely a means by which a piece of writing or artwork can be ascribed value and enter into circulation.[39] The same may be said of the label of truth as we have seen it to be contingent upon the possibility of assigning an author -- but an authentic author, one who claims to have had experience of the non-aesthetic version of their aesthetic object. Since the TRC "authorizes" the truth of the testimonies, it potentially becomes the author when the public sphere exchanges in "testimonies from the TRC." The TRC or the witnesses may be accepted as author, but what of the non-TRC witness, the non-survivor of trauma? Is there a story – is there a truth – to be told in not surviving trauma, or of surviving, as Dori Laub would say, the trauma of listening?[40] Can this type of testimony be accorded equal moral value to the survivor's testimony?

As Hayden White notes, a struggle for truth, a contest of memory is part of the inherent drama of historical events. As a moral principle is so often the guidepost of any narration, the narrator must be thought to hold moral authority.[41] In South Africa, where artists and citizens are dealing with the enigma of reconciliation and restorative justice in place of retributive justice, ethics and historical truth are vital to the cause of transformation. The TRC seeks to write and then close the book on the past. It creates a moral narrative of the transition from an unjust to a just society, where the previously silenced now speak. The protagonists of the TRC's moral narrative are the survivors, the ones who speak the truth, the possessors of memory. Perhaps at the end of the process the TRC will succeed in creating moral equality for all, a blank slate. At this stage, however, relinquishing of moral authority, and of the truth of memory, to non-survivors, even artists, amounts to a relinquishing of authorship.

The South African public is not cajoled by metaphor. The public discourse on the TRC is critical of its lack of authenticity and ability to enact material change. Metaphoric or symbolic reparations are insufficient and truth does not substitute for justice. Even the art-going public have registered protest over what seems to some a denial of memory and truth in art. Nan Hamilton's *No. 4* and Judith Mason's *Requiem* received criticism on different grounds from the *memórias íntimas marcas* exhibition. About *memórias*, a person wrote to the *Mail and Guardian* accusing Gavin Younge of making representations that were untrue to his own experience:

> It seems all too strange that a white liberal like Gavin Younge has been chosen to represent the South African component of an exhibition dealing with an aspect of the "liberation struggle" of which he has only second-hand knowledge, or for that matter, contact. Younge was never involved in the struggle, conscripted and forced to fight in Angola, and has no personal and first-hand knowledge of the human drama . . . Seems like the same old white liberals are getting up a second head of steam at the expense of the majority who continue to be marginalized on the cultural front.[42]

Judith Mason, whose exhibition opened at a gallery in Wynberg outside of Cape Town, received hate letters from right-wing Afrikaners. They were horrified that she was giving so much credibility and empathy to the motives of the Truth Commission, which they deemed was nothing more than a witch-hunt.[43] Although she was English, her letter-writers seemed to feel that her identity as a white South African should have dictated her response. To her critics, she was clearly speaking for the wrong side. They could accept this kind of reverence perhaps coming from a black person but not from a white. Nan Hamilton, on the other hand, was criticized for not telling the stories of people who had been held in the Johannesburg Fort, where the piece was performed.[44] The Fort, as a place of history that had its own story to tell, was being denied its own authorship. In their critics' eyes, neither Mason nor Hamilton could be the authors of the stories they were telling. The audience experienced a confusion over authorship since the Fort competed too much with the non-Fort related histories being told there. Mason could also be criticized for allowing her sympathy for the victims she memorializes in requiem to redeem the stories of their deaths. A similar criticism has been made of Antjie Krog, in her book *Country of My Skull* (1998), where her own suffering and distress over reporting on the victims' hearings seemed to overshadow that of the victims themselves.[45]

Conclusion

I have argued that the TRC is caught between its multiple missions of uncovering facts in order to refute the lies of the previous government, giving comfort to survivors who have no explanations for the fate of their missing loved ones, and to learning concretely from the past to safeguard the future. I have further argued that the TRC functions as metaphor, the vehicle by which individual memory becomes the collective memory that "builds the nation." The metaphoric level manifests on the micro scale between the traumatized survivor and the non-traumatized listener, as well as on the macro scale of the mediatized TRC performance. Testimony is the "authentic" voice of the newly legitimized individual citizen, as much as it becomes a metaphoric and collective representation of suffering. The TRC, therefore, must function on both a real and a metaphoric level. I would argue that art that seeks to supplement the TRC process is caught in the same bind. It must also satisfy on both a real and a metaphoric level. By real, I do not refer to an idea of truth as fact, but a truth of the performance and the performative.

Notes

1 De Kok, Ingrid, "Fault Lines Initiative: Initiatives into Truth and Reconciliation," *West Coast Line: A Journal of Contemporary Writing and Criticism*, Number Twenty, 30(2) (1996): 107–110.
2 Ibid., 108.
3 Borain, Nic, "The Smell of Rotten Apples," *Mail and Guardian*, July 12–18, 1996.
4 Siopis, Penny, Interview with author, Johannesburg, January 26, 2000.
5 Ibid.
6 Williamson, Sue and Jamal, Ashraf, *Art in South Africa: The Future Present* (Cape Town and Johannesburg: David Philip, 1996), 52.
7 Ibid., 126.
8 Richards, Colin, Interview with author, Johannesburg, January 27, 2000.
9 Stewart, Susan, *On Longing: Narratives of the Miniature, the Gigantic, the Souvenir, the Collection* (Durham, NC: Duke University Press, 1993), 140.
10 Richards, interview.
11 Maier, Karl, *Angola: Promises and Lies* (London: Serif, 1996), 33.
12 Daniel, John, "The Truth about the Region," *Southern Africa Report* (August) (2000): 3–7, p. 3.
13 Atkinson, Brenda, "Dealings in the Past," *Mail and Guardian*, July 3–9, 1998.
14 Laub, Dori, "Bearing Witness, or the Vicissitudes of Listening," in *Testimony: Crises of Witnessing in Literature, Psychoanalysis, and History*, by Shoshanna Felman and Dori Lamb (New York: Routledge, 1992), 72–73.
15 Caruth, Cathy, Introduction, in *Trauma: Explorations in Memory*, ed. C. Caruth (Baltimore, MD, and London: Johns Hopkins University Press, 1995), 8.
16 Felman, Shoshana, "After the Apocalypse: Paul de Man and the Fall to Silence," in *Testimony: Crises of Witnessing*, 158.
17 Gilman, Sander, "Truth Seeking, Memory and Art: Comments Following Four Weeks of Life in the New South Africa," *The Official Internet Archive of Africus '95, The Johannesburg Biennale*. http://sunsite.wits.ac.za/biennale/essays/gilman.htm
18 DaSilva, Fabio, and Faught, Jim, "Nostalgia: A Sphere and Process of Contemporary Ideology," *Qualitative Sociology* 51(1) (1992): 47–61, p. 58.

19 Felman, Shoshana, "The Return of the Voice," in *Testimony: Crises of Witnessing*, 204.
20 Cronin, Jeremy, "Even the Dead," *West Coast Line: A Journal of Contemporary Writing and Criticism*, Number Twenty, 30(2) (1996): 24–29, p. 25.
21 Truth and Reconciliation Commission, Promotion of Unity and National Reconciliation Act, No. 34, 1995. http://www.truth.org.za/legal/act9534.htm, Truth and Reconciliation Commission Website CD-ROM, 1998, 1: 5: 36.
22 Ibid., 1: 5: 45.
23 Felman, "Return of the Voice," 205.
24 Atkinson, Brenda and Breitz, Candice (eds), *Grey Areas: Representation, Identity and Politics in Contemporary South African Art* (Johannesburg: Chalkam Hill Press, 1999).
25 Kearney, Richard, "Narrative and the Ethics of Remembrance," in *Questioning Ethics: Contemporary Debates in Philosophy*, eds R. Kearney and M. Dooley (London: Routledge, 1999), 28.
26 Taylor, Jane, *Ubu and the Truth Commission* (Cape Town: Cape Town University Press, 1998), xi.
27 Tal, Kalí, *Worlds of Hurt: Reading the Literatures of Trauma* (Cambridge: Cambridge University Press, 1996), 16.
28 Dayan, Daniel, and Katz, Elihu, *Media Events: The Live Broadcasting of History* (Cambridge, MA: Harvard University Press, 1992), 114.
29 Ibid., 93.
30 Mason, Judith, Interview with author, Cape Town, July 14, 1998.
31 Pienaar, Peet, "Grand Gestures: Peet Pienaar Speaks to Fellow-Artist Judith Mason," *Mail and Guardian*, July 17–23, 1997: 7.
32 Brink, Andre, "Stories of History: Reimagining the Past in Post-Apartheid Narrative," in *Negotiating the Past: The Making of Memory in South Africa*, eds S. Nutall and C. Coetzee (Cape Town: Oxford University Press, 1998), 41.
33 Ibid., 30.
34 Ndebele, Njabulo, "Memory, Metaphor and the Triumph of Narrative," in *Negotiating the Past: The Making of Memory in South Africa*, eds S. Nutall and C. Coetzee (Cape Town: Oxford University Press, 1998), 27.
35 Bozzoli, Belinda, "Public Ritual and Private Transition: The Truth Commission in Alexandra Township, South Africa 1996," *African Studies* 37 (2) (1998): 167–195.
36 Ndebele, Njabulo, *Rediscovery of the Ordinary: Essays on Literature and Culture* (Johannesburg: Congress of South African Writers, 1991).
37 Tal, *Worlds of Hurt*, 16.
38 Krog, Antjie, *Country of My Skull* (Johannesburg: Random House, 1998), 13.
39 Foucault, Michel, "What is an Author?," in *The Foucault Reader*, ed. Paul Rabinow (New York: Pantheon, 1984), 109.
40 Laub, "Bearing Witness," 57–58.
41 White, Hayden, *The Content of the Form: Narrative Discourse and Historical Representation* (Baltimore, MD, and London: Johns Hopkins University Press, 1987), 21.
42 Sampson, John, "The Wrong Front," letter, *Mail and Guardian*, August 15–21, 1997.
43 Mason, interview.
44 Hamilton, Nan, Interview with author, Johannesburg, March 10, 1999.
45 Braude, Claudia, "Elusive Truths," *Mail and Guardian*, June 12–18, 1998.

4

PRECARIOUS BOUNDARIES

Affect, mise-en-scène, and the senses in Theodorus Angelopoulos's Balkans epic

Anne Rutherford

> I sat in a / small / developing lab /
> endless nights / listening to the golden fluids /
> there are times / that the golden fluids /
> sound like a song / you see /
> like a song / you know /
> It / it / sounds like a song / like / like a song

Breathless, panting with exertion, film archivist Ivo Levy gasps this story into life haltingly, beat-by-beat, as he runs, bent down with the weight of heavy water canisters, across a Sarajevo bridge. Alert, hounded by the omnipresent snipers and shells, Levy recounts this experience to the Greek filmmaker, A, with an urgency that mirrors the desperate encounters that run all the way through Theo Angelopoulos's *Ulysses' Gaze* – fleeting connections driven more by need than by desire, more by pressure than by choice. A, played by Harvey Keitel, has traveled across seven countries and into the war-zone in search of the film reels in Levy's lab: three undeveloped reels, perhaps the first film of Greek cinema. While the narrative of A's quest enacts the repeated rituals of borders and divisions across the rugged terrain of southeastern Europe, it is crossings and connections that drive it forward the bridge rather than the boundary is its pertinent motif.[1]

"Yugoslavia is full of rivers," says the journalist who directs A to Sarajevo. Rivers are the conduit that bring A to Levy and the "golden fluids" in his lab, and fluids mark the affective poles of the film: frozen in ice, driven in rain and snow, suspended in mist, swirling in the river currents, and singing in the developing lab. It is also an economy of fluids that defines Angelopoulos's shooting style: frozen moments, fluid mobile camera, and the porousness of sensation as sound bleeds across image and image melts away into the fog (Figure 4.1).

How then can we understand how this film has been described in the rhetoric of barriers, distance, disconnection?[2] Individual elements in the film may be seen in this way, if viewed in isolation, clinically: camera distance, for example – the preponderance of long shots; or the slight disjunction between character and performance Keitel does not so much speak his lines, as they speak through him.

Figure 4.1 Theo Angelopoulos, *Ulysses' Gaze*, 1995. Having spoken of three undeveloped reels that comprise the first Greek film ever made, filmmaker Yannakis Manakis collapses and dies as a blue ship sets sail in Salonika harbor and a journey begins. Still courtesy of the film's producers, the Greek Film Center.

The film, however, orchestrates these elements, mobilizes their energies, toward a riveting affective engagement with history, desire, identity, love, and their entwinement together. *Ulysses' Gaze* produces an affective agitation that can be understood only by examining Angelopoulos's work with his spectator, and it is a sense of fluidity that pervades this work also – a sense that the subjectivity of the spectator is not a boundary, but a permeable membrane – that the images, soundscapes, and sequences of the film can permeate the "skin" of the spectator.

Affect and the senses/materiality and corporeality/a particular type of experience

The "connectedness" of this affective engagement is central to Angelopoulos's own description of his process of filming, which he characterizes above all as a process of bringing into play the full sensory registers of his own experience, in order that he can evoke this awakening in his audience. The narrative of the film traces the journey of A, in his search for three lost film reels of the Manakis brothers, the first Greek filmmakers, who filmed "all the ambiguities, the contrasts, the conflicts in this area of the world" (as A says). A's journey brings him face-to-face with the traumatic contemporary conflicts reshaping the post-communist Balkans, culminating in besieged Sarajevo.[3] Although Angelopoulos repeatedly requested permission to film on location in Sarajevo itself, while the Bosnian war was still raging, refusal led him to shoot in the rubble of Mostar, Vukovar, and the Krijena area. In discussing his preference for shooting on location, Angelopoulos has said:

> I believe something special happens on location, in the real place, and I do not mean just the ability to photograph the decor, the landscape. But it is more that when I am in the place I have set the film, all five of my senses are working. I become more *completely aware*. I therefore feel I am living the experiences I want to film.[4]

While many critics have attempted to explain how it is that Angelopoulos can draw his audience into an intense, visceral engagement with the unfolding crisis of the Balkans, citing his constant blurring of the boundaries between history and fiction, or history and myth, this one quote, perhaps more than any other, can assist to unravel both the principles which inform his filmmaking, and the extraordinary affect which his films can produce. Indeed, in this statement, Angelopoulos reveals the particular quality of the cinematic intelligence, which finds its way onto his screen. This could be encapsulated as an understanding of the sensory intensification of experience as the vehicle by which an affective charge is translated from filmmaker to audience, and of the role of the material elements of the film as the means to produce this. Angelopoulos clearly understands these material elements – landscape, decor, etc. – as energetic units, as potential units or sparks of experiential energy.

This relationship between the objects or elements of the material world and their capacity to generate a sensory awakening – so pivotal to understanding the affective work of Angelopoulos's film – is often overlooked in the critical literature. Indeed, the theoretical frameworks which could address this sensory/material aesthetic derive from "the roads not taken" in the development of film theory as a discipline and are only now being reinscribed into contemporary debates, with the consideration of the embodied aspects of cinema spectatorship.[5] Central to these contemporary debates has been the work of scholars such as Miriam Hansen, whose detailed excavation of the writings of Siegfried Kracauer has given the question of cinematic materiality a historical framework.[6] Hansen highlights Kracauer's focus on the "physical, tactile dimension of film spectatorship" (WS, 458), which, she claims, offers "a theory of a particular type of film experience."[7] To Kracauer, she argues, "film addresses its viewer as a corporeal, material being . . . it stimulates the material layers of the human being . . . it seizes the human body with skin and hair" (WS, 458).

While Kracauer's theoretical work has repeatedly been dismissed by film theorists as "naïve realism," Hansen argues that his early work opens up a "notion of the material dimension [which] is far more comprehensive than the term 'physical reality,'" and "[his] concept of realism . . . is bound up with the problematic of the subject (rather than simply film's referential relation to the material world)" (TOF, xvi).[8] Cinematic reception is crucial to this understanding. Hansen discerns what she calls a "centrifugal tendency" in Kracauer's film theory – the physiological impact of the film induces "a movement away from the filmic text and into cinema – [into] . . . the social, public space of reception" (TOF, xxxiii); on the level of reception the "material dimension assumes a life of its own and triggers in the viewer associations, memories of the senses" (TOF, xxviii). Whereas conventional notions of realism focus on questions of authenticity or verisimilitude, Kracauer writes of the experiential potential of the close-up, for example, to "blast the prison of conventional reality": a familiar pair of hands in close-up "will change into unknown organisms quivering with a life of their own."[9]

The sensory/material focus in Angelopoulos's work situates his project as pivotal to these attempts to reinscribe the question of cinematic materiality at the center of contemporary theories of cinema, and to rethink notions of cinematic realism. While working with the actual locations of present and historical events, Angelopoulos does not envisage these "material realities" as outside the experience of them: location is privileged not for verisimilitude, but for the sensory associations and memories it can evoke. Angelopoulos's description of location shooting mirrors Kracauer's "seizure" almost word for word: "When I begin a new film and I begin to travel around looking for locations with Giorgos Arvanitis, my friend and cinematographer, I often start to feel *a tingling in my skin, the hairs of my arm standing up*" (my italics).[10]

Angelopoulos's vigilance to the senses, his search for the production contexts and locations that will arouse this vigilance, are intrinsically linked to both the corporeal, material focus of what Kracauer calls "psychophysical correspondences," and to Walter Benjamin's related concept of "mimetic innervation." The mimetic here is "a mode of cognition involving sensuous, somatic, and tactile forms of perception [which] transcends the traditional subject–object dichotomy" (NOW, 5): the concept emphasizes the "palpable sensuous connection between the very body of the perceiver and the perceived."[11] Innervation is understood as a mode of perception that "reconnects with the discarded powers . . . of mimetic practices that involve the body" (NOW, 6), as a "mimetic reception of the external world . . . that is empowering."[12] As Hansen reads this focus in Benjamin on the corporeal, material aspects of this mimetic innervation, it is a two-way process, encompassing both a movement away from the sensorium into the world and an "ingestion or incorporation" of the world.[13] As such, the concept envisages "the precarious boundary or rind of the bodily ego [as] a bit less of a carapace or armor and a bit more of a matrix or medium – a porous interface between the organism and the world that would allow for a greater mobility and circulation of psychic energies" (NOW, 5). This concept of mimetic innervation is the crucial term to understanding the central role the senses play in the way Angelopoulos draws his spectator into the complex and traumatic history of the Balkans.

Mise-en-scène

Through his description of the elements of a location as not just objects to be photographed, but as catalysts to a sensory awakening, by "redeeming" the material elements – landscape and decor – from an "object" status, Angelopoulos extends this sensory understanding of "corporeal material nature" explicitly to what has traditionally been defined as mise-en-scène: the "elements" of mise-en-scène become experiential entities, potential sites for mimetic innervation. By envisaging mise-en-scène within the terms of this "porous interface" between spectator and the material, the materialities of cinematic experience are understood as intrinsically linked with the affective power of cinema. The focus on reception applies pressure to the notion of the "material world," challenging the empiricist thinking about mise-en-scène which has underpinned conventional notions of cinematic realism.

Mise-en-scène is the critical link in the relationship between the material dimensions of cinema and its affect. The chrysalis of this understanding, kept in hibernation for so long through the decades of ideology-based and psychoanalytic film theory, begins to mature and reveal its potential with the re-emergence of interest in the material and the corporeal aspects of spectatorship, particularly with the more rigorous studies of Benjamin and Kracauer and the paradigm shift this work has effected. The relevance of this latter work to the understanding of mise-en-scène, however, has been almost suffocated by the critical entropy imposed on the term in contemporary Anglo-American film studies: it has evolved in its most common, contemporary usage as one of the most sterile of analytical terms, degenerated in film teaching and theory into an empirical term used to describe the elements of the profilmic (that which existed in front of the camera at the time of shooting). One need not look very far to find endless inventories of the so-called elements of mise-en-scène, divorced from their context in the energetic work of the film. Again and again, English-language texts start doggedly from a literal translation of the French: "mise-en-scène means literally 'what is put onto the stage,'" and proceed to apply this mechanically from stage to screen: "costume, décor, lighting, camera movement, setting and the behavior of figures" are enumerated as if this technical scrutiny of each term, divorced from its synthesis in the film, or from the reception of the ensemble for an audience, provides productive analytical tools.[14]

Mise-en-scène has been described as the "grand undefined term" of film theory.[15] Adapted from the stage, its understanding has been persistently shackled by this heritage in the stasis of the proscenium arch. While objects can be "put onto the stage" in theater and be expected to maintain their integrity as solid objects, no such assumption can be made in cinema. How can the common theatrical understanding of mise-en-scène make sense in cinema? An object does not maintain its status as an object once it is in the frame: color or a set are not merely background – they are by definition part of the ensemble of experience of the spectator, constituted in and through the temporal experience of a scene/a shot. As Kracauer writes, cinema does not just reproduce the material world, but "brings the whole material world into play" (WS, 447).

There is of course no such thing as "put onto the stage" in cinema, only what is put into the scene. This is not just what has been "put" into the frame (in the past tense: by definition the result of an action already completed, rather than a present moment in play), but what is put into the moment of experience, how the spectator is drawn into the scene at the moment of its unfolding.[16] This double-edged materiality is what a theory of mise-en-scène must address: how are the elements of the material world both material and energetic at the same time? And what is the relationship between sensory experience and affective experience? Once we understand the concept of mimetic innervation, this mimetic appropriation of the material world that, in the moment of contact, generates an "affectively charged, excentric perception," as Hansen describes it (NOW, 10), how then do we rethink the materiality of mise-en-scène within this relationship?

Our understanding of mise-en-scène is, of course, constituted in the definition of the term, and only a definition *in process*, that is, of the operation of mise-en-scène *in situ*, can provide a productive understanding. The early writings of the critics and filmmakers of *Cahiers du cinéma* in the 1950s and 1960s avoid a literal transposition of the concept from stage to screen, and provide the beginnings of a dynamic understanding of mise-en-scène. In Fereydoun Hoveyda, it is inseparable from the process of its conceptualization, part of "the intellectual operation which has set to work an initial emotion and a general idea."[17] In Alexandre Astruc, mise-en-scène is also understood as a conceptual process, as "interrogation and dialogue," and, when he explains this on a more material level, "mise-en-scène [is] a certain way of extending states of mind into movements of the body. It is a song, a rhythm, a dance."[18] Despite being limited by the auteurist emphasis on mise-en-scène as an expressive tool for the genius of the director, these writings contain the germ of an understanding of mise-en-scène as energetic process, rather than empirical object or technique. Astruc in particular, in his later work, formulates mise-en-scène as an energetic engagement with the spectator: "What pleases me [in a film] is the mise-en-scène: to make the spectator feel the moment of disequilibrium where everything suddenly falls apart,"[19] and "[the] mise-en-scène is a look which forces people to act, which has a power over what it looks at."[20]

In his writing on melodrama in the 1970s, Thomas Elsaesser extends this understanding of mise-en-scène as energetic, through his exploration of the emotional effects of what he calls "melos."[21] The "dynamic use of spatial and musical categories" characterizes what he describes as a "subtle and yet precise formal language" brought into play in the "orchestration of emotional effects" (287). Constrained by the structuralist model of language which saturated film theory in the 1970s, Elsaesser does, nevertheless, insist on melos as a material, affective counterpoint to the linear meaning-producing structures of language, and thereby keeps alive the understanding of mise-en-scène as an energetic field.[22]

Despite the recognition in the early formulations that mise-en-scène comes into being in the interface with the spectator, we still find, omnipresent in film theory, the clinical dismembering of the so-called elements of mise-en-scène which renders the use of the concept as an analytical term defunct. Angelopoulos leaves this sterile empirical understanding for dead when he describes and works with the appropriation of location, landscape, and decor by the filmmaker in the terms of sensory intensities. These corporeal, material intensities which cycle between filmmaker, film, and audience could perhaps best be described in murky, indistinct terms like sympathetic vibration, as redolent as they are with indefinables like intuition, feeling, resonance, or intensity. From Angelopoulos's description of the central role of his own sensory experience, we have an understanding that what is paramount here is that he produce an image which, for him, generates a sensory awakening, an innervation. The implication is that an experience which resonates so provocatively for him will also resonate for the spectator. Angelopoulos himself has signaled the importance to his work of this "vibration" with the spectator: "I need to see the eyes of the others. Only in the regard of the viewer do I recognize what I have made."[23]

This idea of sympathetic vibration or resonance is the core of the mimetic capacity – "the capacity to relate to the external world through patterns of similitude, affinity, reciprocity and interplay" (NOW, 5). This affinity is not the meeting of one identity with another, in a recognition of the referent. Recognition and memory are freed from the exclusive logic of the literal, and reactivated in the logic of the visceral. It is a "sympathetic vibration" that puts me into action as a spectator, that "puts me into the scene." It is a staging of my full mimetic potential that evokes the connection. Circumscribed of course by cultural memory and tradition, and assuming that this resonance will be layered – some layers more universally recognized than others – this mimetic capacity holds the key to understanding the role of the corporeal, the material in the affective work of images.[24]

The modernist grid

It is precisely the lack of an adequate understanding of the relationship between affect and mise-en-scène that hampers some of the critical work on Angelopoulos, particularly that which locates his work within a modernist canon. David Bordwell, for example, argues that detachment and distanciation provide the key underpinnings of a form of "de-dramatization" which assimilates Angelopoulos to a modernist aesthetic.[25] He claims that techniques used to "drain away drama from charged situations" characterize Angelopoulos's films, and dissects the visual techniques of Angelopoulos to establish stylistic similarities with modernist directors such as Michelangelo Antonioni. Founding his analysis on the principles of visual composition in Angelopoulos's films, Bordwell finds "empty spaces" (17), "dead intervals" (22), the "suspension of dramatic progression . . . detached contemplation and dry, understated emotion" (18). However, it is only through an understanding of mise-en-scène which severs visual technique from the performative unfolding of a film across time, that Bordwell's study of the techniques of Angelopoulos's cinematography could yield nothing but an inventory of devices of visual style, conceived as akin to static pictorial design.[26] The only way Angelopoulos's/ Arvanitis's shots could be seen as dead or inert, is to rob them of this temporal amplification which is at the core of Angelopoulos's cinematography – all of the elements he deploys are fused together, pressured, transformed by time.

Even on the level of shot construction, Angelopoulos's image and sound are conceived in terms of dynamic energies which escalate with the pressure of time: tensions between static, monolithic city structures and the movement of figures that run in diagonals across them; between vault-like interior spaces or vast desolate landscapes, the groups and individuals dwarfed by them and the relentless, exuberant movement of the camera; between vision withheld and the knowledge that breaks through the shot with the sound.

At the border with Albania, A's taxi picks up a frail old lady left stranded in the snow, traveling to meet the sister she has not seen for forty-seven years, since the civil war. In the center of Korytsa, they leave her in the icy town square, and as the car drives off into the silent snow, she is dumped by the narrative, incidental to A's journey. As the camera pulls back, abandoning her, a vast empty expanse of gray road and white sky engulfs her tiny lost figure. Even as she becomes just another incidental casualty of Balkans dislocation, the desolation of the square lingers in an overwhelming sense of vulnerability, bewilderment, and disorientation. As A returns to "snow and silence," her memory echoes across the subsequent shots.

As A crosses the border into Albania, the camera tracks across vast fields of static human figures, mute, immobile against the icy landscape, waiting or watching: Albanian illegals, "rifiugati" as the taxi driver calls them. The shot slides in one long take from closely framed naturalistic dialogue and action of A and the taxi to the epic panoramas of ritualized stasis and motion. As the spectator is transported across these physical divides, Eleni Karaindrou's haunting music, a monotone, accompanies the choreography of the camera in a hypnotic harmonic register. Static, mute figures give way to the movement of people trekking through the snow and then the constant motion of nameless figures walking the streets cloaked in ice and snow. Icy hillside, sky, streetscape, and figures blend into one palpable rhythm of moving figures, the sensuous caress of the fluid camera and the hypnotic music.

The solidity of human figures and buildings have only a tenuous claim on the shot, as the coordinates of the space become indistinct, the horizon suspended somewhere between the hazy white sky and the white, snow-covered hillside. Time becomes indeterminate, as the camera tracks through the streets in slow motion while figures walk briskly by. As eerie as this sequence is, to talk of it simply as mood, understood in a cognitive sense, would miss the intense corporeality of its affective charge. Even as the viewer is left to puzzle over the significance of the figures in the snow, this is not an absence, an empty space – as the camera glides in long shot past the silent figures dwarfed against the desolate landscape, the spectator absorbs the epic dimensions of this historical moment mimetically – a whole history of displacement and dislocation inscribed in one shot as a visual, temporal, and aural rhythm.

Bordwell marginalizes this affective engagement with an image: effects not affects are his focus. It is only by detaching, in the analytical moment, the frame, the light, and the mobility of camera from their inscription across the bodies of the spectator, that these techniques can be seen as formalist devices, universalized across genres and cultures, working toward a universal goal of distanciation. To focus on these stylistic similarities is to miss their differences, for modernism is not just a set of techniques, but their deployment in a particular context toward particular ends. As Fredric Jameson writes, "'style' can so often look like a relatively simple recipe: . . . when we enumerate a certain number of the classic features of Angelopoulos's style, we risk . . . reducing the unique pleasures of his work among an enlightened public to a formula."[27]

While the paradigm of modernism may shed light on Angelopoulos's earlier films, in the case of *Ulysses' Gaze*, even though the film does draw on some elements of a modernist idiom, this analytical grid obscures at least as much as it reveals. While a grid suggests that the stylistic elements of a film can be mapped according to fixed coordinates, and with mathematical precision, it is imprecision which marks the rhetorical tropes of *Ulysses' Gaze*, and the indeterminate, shifting dynamics of spectatorship which must be explored to arrive at any productive understanding of the film. *Ulysses' Gaze* is full of scenes which are open-ended, whose meaning cannot be pinned down.

The chaotic, unpredictable flux of history in the Balkans throws up moments which resonate according to the memory, the experience, the chance location of the viewer upon that flux. Angelopoulos works these indeterminate moments to draw his spectator into an engagement with the uncertainty and ambivalence of this history – nowhere is this more profound than in the camera's extended eulogy to Lenin. As the demolished statue of Lenin is transported down the river in fragments, his finger still pointing the way forward from his severed arm, throngs of watching people drop to their knees, making the sign of the cross. While the figures on the bank running to keep up with the barge are mute, numbers in a crowd, the statue of Lenin, his face in close-up, becomes articulate. His face maintains a composure, heroically moving forward to dominate the frame; his slightly furrowed brow looks clear over the horizon. Even the concrete ear of Lenin is granted the right to take over center frame in close-up, holding the viewer in its sway.

71

Even as Lenin's statue evokes awe, nostalgia or fascination, other lines, traces, cross each other, sometimes as distant echoes, shock waves reverberating from the same source across different terrains. Lenin's grandiose passage is in stark contrast to the ravages of history unfolding in its wake; his concrete cerebrum maintains a solidity against its scaffold that is not permitted the concrete rubble of Sarajevo. This Lenin only barely masks the many others that shadow his passing, those dismembered, brought down in triumph, smashed with sledge-hammers across the breadth of former communist Europe. His trajectory is layered, saturated, steeped in monumental significance and ambiguity: condensed into the resonances of a few long takes is the momentous history of the aspirations and allegiances, the demise and contradictions of the whole of communist Europe, gliding by in a solemn obituary.

Without doubt there are sequences, particularly in the first half of *Ulysses' Gaze*, which work to disable a more conventional "psychological" viewing. However, relinquishing the modernist grid reveals a much more complex set of strategies for engaging the full affective potential of the viewer. There is dislocation in *Ulysses' Gaze*, to be sure – the awkwardness between Keitel and the lines which "recite him," as mentioned previously. A woman who has lost her husband/lover to the shelling is driven to Keitel's body. Her embrace, however, is not with Keitel, but with the lover whose name she calls repeatedly, inscribing it over the substitute flesh of Keitel – "Vania, Vania, Vania." This fissure between actor and character, the mismatch between body and identity, between need and realization are not the estrangement of modernist distanciation. These interactions are not suspended in a field of abstract disjuncture, but driven to forge new links across the gaps, links that resonate with stifled cries, inarticulate sobbing, or the wailing wrenched not from Keitel's throat but from somewhere in his entrails. How can we think of this visceral unleashing as a modernist distanciation?

Angelopoulos has said that he "hopes to create a new kind of audience, 'not just a consumer who uses only his emotions, but a person who uses his mind.'"[28] To reduce this to simply an "alienation effect" is to ignore the affective part of the equation. This is not an either/or that Angelopoulos offers, but a more complete affective and intellectual synthesis. As Andrew Horton claims, "the mixing of theatricality and reality in his films often leads us into a deeper, fuller, emotional bond with the film" (CC, 14–15).

Hansen has pointed out the ways in which the "tradition of narrative film conflicts with a materialist aesthetics of film because it imposes the closed structure of 'a finite, ordered cosmos' upon the heterogeneous, heteronomous, open-ended flow of life" (TOF, xxxi). Applied to *Ulysses' Gaze*, the modernist grid simply posits a binary opposition to classical narrative, one in which any gaps in the narrative flow are seen as either a lack or a radical disjuncture: both models impose the primacy of the cognitive interpretation of a film over a materialist aesthetics. Kracauer's attention to the material experience of reception offers a much more productive understanding of Angelopoulos: his understanding sidelines this rigid opposition, in favor of "loosely composed, 'porous,' 'permeable,' open-ended narratives . . .

that leave 'gaps into which environmental life may stream'" (TOF, xxxiii).[29] Just as Kracauer's analysis moves "away from the filmic text and into the cinema . . . the space of reception" (TOF, xxviii), the analysis of *Ulysses' Gaze* must acknowledge "the gaps and fissures in the filmic text that allow for moments of contingency and indeterminacy" (TOF, xxxiii), that lead "into the slippery realm of experience, the heterogeneity of social space, the unpredictable dynamics of public life" (TOF, xxxiv).

Diffraction of the drama

Angelopoulos clearly conceives of his film in terms of drama: in response to a suggestion that *Ulysses' Gaze* ends on a depressing note, he evokes Aristotle: "I would say simply what Aristotle said about tragedy, that a drama or, in this case, a film should evoke pity and fear in an audience, and then create a catharsis by which these emotions are released" (LM, 105). It is not necessarily a "draining away of drama" that Angelopoulos achieves in *Ulysses' Gaze*, but a diffraction of the drama through several means. If one were to draw a flow chart, a score of *Ulysses' Gaze*, the melodies, the rhythms that run through it would emerge as dramatically counterpointed one to the other – sound, color, landscape, figures, and narrative are orchestrated through time in elaborate relationships, patterns, divergences. It is here that Sergei Eisenstein's conception of the elements of a film as a score really comes into its own – it is the polyphony, the complex orchestration of these divergent instruments that Angelopoulos is working with in his search for the sensory amplification of experience.

While it is vision that propels the narrative of the film – Keitel's desperation to "see that gaze," the gaze revealed in the Manakis brothers' undeveloped film reels, propels his journey across the Balkans – vision, the gaze itself, is constantly undercut, prefigured, or superseded by sound. At times, the emotional registers of the film are largely carried by the aural density – a cacophony of industrial noise, engine hum, mechanical winches, and fog horns that accompanies the installment of Lenin's head scrupulously into place in its collar-bone on the barge; a ritualized confrontation between shuffling feet and running boots as the police run between demonstrating religious fanatics and umbrella-wielding movie-spectators in a dark street; the amplified interrogations of border guards reverberating through the dark night across the restless, rootless space of the frontier.

It is vision that collapses finally in Sarajevo. At the moment in the film that appears to be its culmination – Levy has discovered the formula to develop the three film reels, to recover the "lost gaze" that has been the object of A's quest – footsteps and the music of the youth orchestra signal the welcome relief of the fog that descends on Sarajevo, shielding its citizens from the omnipresent threat of snipers. As Levy, A, and Levy's family walk through the city in a joyous respite, vision yields to the sounds in the fog – the nursery rhymes of children wafting through the mist; a motor that warns of a soldier's approach; a mother's desperate pleading; shots, one after another, dull, final; and the aching wailing of Keitel. It is as if the whole film has led, inexorably, to the collapse of vision and its substitution with this visceral cry.

The narrative of *Ulysses' Gaze* is a quest, a journey: reflecting the Ur-story of Ulysses, A is propelled toward his goal which momentarily finds resolution before its success disintegrates, fragments with the brutal killing in the fog. Set against this striving to reach a goal is another trajectory which moves inexorably downwards, toward decline, devastation. Just as A's Greek taxi driver talks of Greek civilization as a 3000-year fall from glory, the film itself is like a relentless collapse in slow-motion: as A travels across Europe toward Bosnia, solid buildings give way to rubble, window panes to blackened holes, the remnants of civil society to barbarism, hope to anguish, faith to despair.

Just as the landscapes follow a trajectory of their own, the journey is enacted as a tightly controlled progression through the cold, retracting end of the color spectrum. Angelopoulos and his cinematographer, Giorgos Arvanitis, work in a palette of muted browns, blues, and grays. Fawn and slate, with an occasional tinge of a dark, muddy purple-brown, give almost the only respite from black, white, and gray. Only in Sarajevo does a hot orange-red emerge with the fires in the deserted streets, and the red of the developing lamp in the lab, only to be blanketed, smothered in the relentless white spread of the fog.

It is this structure of "images which resonate, reverberate and ricochet off each other [in a] honeycomb of meaning" that epitomizes Gerald O'Grady's description of Angelopoulos's layering or mosaic-like "tessellations" of "significance," the structuring of material elements into the "making and merging of multiple metaphors."[30] O'Grady lays the understanding of temporality into this spatial structure of tessellation, claiming that "Angelopoulos's many angles of incidence reflect more and more light at each successive moment of his films, and even more enlightenment when one reflects on them" (56). The echoes, the layering of metaphors and memory traces, circle back as each new scene harvests the resonances of the layers set down before.

It is this "enlightenment" that leads Andrew Horton to nominate Angelopoulos's films as a "cinema of contemplation" (LM, 1). And yet, a "cinema of contemplation" or "meditation," as Horton refers to it elsewhere, cannot do justice to this multilayered experience which *in-corporates* – makes corporeal or material – our experience, both intellectual and emotional, of the histories and stories which unfold. Contemplation here is a disembodied term. That one is left contemplating a film like *Ulysses' Gaze* is not in question, but one is also left with inarticulate sensation, traces of sounds, spaces, fragments, that permeate and linger in the corporeal memory. It is, above all, a cinema of embodied affect.

How do we understand the "tessellation" of images – and sounds, rhythms, and colors – that ricochet off each other? What is the mechanism of their collisions? Kracauer refers to a similar dynamic when he claims that film "brings the material world into play," arguing that cinema has an "affinity with the pulsations of material life" (WS, 451). Kracauer gives this pulsation a topographical metaphor when he claims that film "comes into its own when it grasps the material dimension"

– he writes that film "pushes downwards," into the "lower levels" (WS, 447).[31] If one were to apply the same topographical metaphor to the model of contemplation that informs Horton's and Bordwell's readings of Angelopoulos, film would be seen to strive upward, toward the "higher" levels of intellect. This is the blind spot in much of the critical writing on Angelopoulos: it is a reluctance to conceptualize spectator-ship as material, spectators as embodied, and affect as simultaneously intellectual, emotional, and corporeal, that mandates this recourse to contemplation as the defining motif to explain Angelopoulos's films.

The implications of this characterization of Angelopoulos's work as a contem-plative cinema extend into the consideration of history, and the assumed strategies for staging historical questions for the spectator. Bordwell, for example, argues that the techniques of "dedramatization," by which he characterizes the "minimalist," modernist shooting style in Angelopoulos's films, "block empathy." This leads, in his reading of the films, to a critical detachment which in turn leads us "to consider the larger historical forces at work."[32] The rhetorical moves which underpin this argument are standard in the critical literature on modernist film: empathy is withheld by refusing the psychological techniques of close-up, character identi-fication, etc.; attention is deflected away from absorption in emotional pathos, and onto detached intellectual contemplation; the familiar is "made strange" and the lethargic viewer is jolted into critical awareness.

None of these rhetorical moves can be adequately applied to *Ulysses' Gaze*. The affective power of the film is neither equivalent to, nor dependent on, empathy. Affective intensity is not deflected onto intellectual contemplation, but diffracted, dispersed across all of the available sensory registers; it is not detachment that ensues, but a more embodied engagement. Angelopoulos refuses to remove history from its material, lived experience: his spectator does not need a break or rupture from the senses to grasp this history: not simply an object of cognitive or contem-plative awareness, it is enacted on the sensorium.

In Kracauer, as Hansen argues, the concept of embodied spectatorship is inseparable from an understanding that, by its assault on the senses, film "dissociates rather than integrates the spectatorial self" (TOF, xxvii). Both Kracauer and Benjamin draw on the concept of distraction to argue that film "still contains the possibility of losing oneself, albeit intermittently, of abandoning one's waking self to the dreamlike, discontinuous sequence of sense impressions."[33] Any account of Angelopoulos's historical project must acknowledge this potential "dissolution" of the contemplative subject: in its affiliation with Benjamin's "mimetic innervation," Angelopoulos's work with the affective potential of the embodied sensory/material experiences of cinema is, as Hansen writes of Benjamin's concept, "anything but the critically distanced, testing look of the Brechtian observer."[34]

Temporality

The emphasis on the work of the senses, on a sensory awakening, links Angelopoulos's project to a broad body of work which questions the role of the

senses in modernity and attempts to grasp the experience of the sensory moment.[35]
Leo Charney has outlined the concern of philosophers of modernity with the
ephemerality of the moment as a characteristic of modernity, its contradictory status
as both present, "immediate [and] tangible sensation" and simultaneously "fleeting,
tentative and unstable." Through this category of the moment, Charney has charted
the links between the concern of early filmmaker and theorist, Jean Epstein, with
the "fleeting fragments of [sensual] experience that the viewer cannot describe
verbally or rationalise cognitively" (285), and the "category of the sensual moment"
which informed the Russian Formalist Viktor Shklovsky's understanding of defamil-
iarization: both explore the "possibility of experiencing a moment . . . feeling the
presence of the moment, fully inhabiting it" (279) as a means "to seize fleeting
moments of sensation" from their evanescence (293).

While Angelopoulos's work with the senses, in *Ulysses' Gaze*, is inseparable
from his work with the material experience of temporality, this is informed by an
entirely different understanding of the relationship between temporality and sensory
experience. The spectator is not jolted into fleeting moments of awareness and
sensation, and time here is not the passing of this intense, fleeting experience of
the ephemeral moment, not its undoing, but the intensification of the experience
through duration. The passing of time does not carry us away from sensation but
into it; time does not disperse the awareness but deepens it. Rather than punctuation
or interruption to "passages of [otherwise] lost time" (IM), in *Ulysses' Gaze*, sensory
experience is a dilation of time, like a slow-release time-bomb. In *Ulysses' Gaze*,
Angelopoulos's shots set up a resonance which bit by bit infiltrates through layer
after layer: osmosis not rupture. By stealth the shots shift registers for the viewer;
like sound, the image sets up a rhythm, a vibration which spreads across the film.
The amazement that these shots can awaken is not a piercing of the alienated
sensorium, the epiphany of a single moment breaking through the flow, but
the amplification of the experience of that flow itself. In Charney's account,
"Epstein conceived of film as a chain of moments, a collage of fragments" (285). In
Angelopoulos, time is an accumulation, a layering: more like laying tracks one over
the other, than a collage of disparate moments.

To come back to Sarajevo, Ivo Levy and the bridge: there is no moment in this
shot that could encapsulate it: it is only on the maturation of the shot, its denoue-
ment, that one can say, "that was the shot." There is no single moment of visual
pyrotechnics which propels the shot into sensory awareness: the movement of
the figures and the "song" of the fluids, as Levy recites it, give the shot a rhythm, a
pace, breathe it into life. The bridge itself is like a suspension bridge, a scaffold on
which the song is suspended, unfolding into significance with the passage of time.
The action is played against the base line of the bridge like a foundation: the running
figures cut a diagonal arc across its monolith, the two articulated against the flat
white sky which leads nowhere, more like a screen than a space. The bridge does
not stay still. It quivers, pulsates, amplifies, as Levy's recitation is inscribed across
its span with the beat of his gasping breath. The dynamic energies and tensions of
the shot shift as it unfolds, its momentum generating the "centrifugal force" that

projects the viewer onto the screen of history, of memory: the incongruity of this gasp of life struggling to preserve itself in the face of despair and futility is inscribed across the viewer's sensorium.

Shock, physiology, corporeality/ embodiment and reception

Kracauer's discussion of the corporeality of cinematic reception, while cryptic, is framed within what he calls the physiological dimension: "such kinesthetic responses as muscular reflexes, motor impulses, or the like" (TOF, 158). Within this model, shock plays a central role in accessing this material dimension. Kracauer posits corporeality within the terms available from physiology, and incorporates his understanding of "psychophysical correspondences" into this physiological model. However, the phenomenological tradition makes a clear demarcation between the physiological concept of the body, or *Körper*, and a separate understanding of the lived body, or *Leib*.[36] While the physiological model delimits physiological stimulus, such as movement or shock, as the "trigger" of a corporeal response, the concept of the lived body does not prescribe the understanding of corporeality in this way: it is more amenable to understandings of affect, and the relationship between sensory and affective experience, and also more compatible with understandings of memory as embodied. This model also allows for a different understanding of the means to access the material, corporeal aspects of cinematic experience. Not necessarily tied to the physiological concept of shock, an understanding of corporeality as *Leib* distances this question from traditional distinctions between montage, aligned to shock, and mise-en-scène, aligned to duration. While Angelopoulos's work with temporality relies extensively on the materiality of duration and the unity of space that come with the long take, other techniques, working with a comparable grasp of embodied spectatorship, could also engage the viewer in a similarly sensory-affective register.

Ulysses' Gaze's corporeal address does not rely on shock, with its foundation in sensational effects to elicit a "physiological" response. The root impulse of the film, its source, is not journalism, as it is for other films that attempt to show the realities of war: *Welcome to Sarajevo*, for example, that sprays its opening credits across the screen like a volley of rapid bullet fire and confronts the spectator with the horrors of severed limbs and bleeding flesh. The cringe, the retraction from the shock of these images of devastation, the withdrawal into the defensive "stimulus shield" that characterizes Benjamin's understanding of this shock experience, is the antithesis of the experience for the spectator of the shooting in the fog in *Ulysses' Gaze*. While vision is snuffed out, occluded by the fog, the spectator strains to grasp more of the shot, is actively transported into the shot, scanning the white screen for clues with all the senses awakened. The terrible knowledge that reaches the spectator with the sound, as Levy and his entire family are shot, does not reach a hardened, toughened shell, but an anxious, alert sensory web, open, searching for significance. It is not just the immediacy of the present moment that Angelopoulos targets with this sensory heightening, but the potential of an experience to go beyond that moment, to connect with other layers of embodied experience and memory, and thereby, through this embodied experience, to access the significance of history.

In Benjamin, the "antidote – and counterconcept – to technologically multiplied shock and its anaesthetizing economy" (NOW, 5) is the capacity for mimetic innervation, the "possibility of undoing the alienation of the senses" (NOW, 2). Benjamin's understanding of experience (*Erfahrung*), of the "fullness of experience," rather than being tied to the "present" moment, is intrinsically linked to the question of memory, "the faculty that connects sense perceptions of the present with those of the past" (NOW, 2). It is memory, the *mémoire involontaire*, or involuntary remembrance, which brings a "painful shock of rejuvenation . . . when the past is reflected in the dewy fresh 'instant.'"[37] The past evoked by this involuntary memory, as Benjamin sees it, is "somewhere beyond the reach of the intellect, and unmistakably present in some material object (or in the sensation which such an object arouses in us)."[38] The sensory evocation of this involuntary memory is the key to understanding the affective power of Angelopoulos's exploration of Balkans history.

History, memory and the sensorium

Horton has written that "few filmmakers anywhere have been so concerned and involved with history from such a variety of angles" as Angelopoulos, and cites Nikos Kolovos who writes that "[Angelopoulos's] films are meditations on history, not historical films per se" (CC, 56).[39] The quest which drives the journey of A across the Balkans is itself a dialog with the entire history of cinema: A searches for a "vanished gaze," a "gaze struggling to emerge from the dark – a kind of birth," "a captive gaze from the early days of the century set free at last at the close of the century."[40] (This lost gaze is given a mnemonic presence by the mesmeric repetition of a few shots from the earliest known Greek film, the Manakis brothers' *The Weavers* of 1905.) Just as the narrative enacts the search for a lost historical moment, the film takes place across a transhistoric field. Its scope is a century of Balkan conflicts, and beyond. Just as the Manakis brothers filmed "all the ambiguities, the contrasts, the conflicts in this area of the world," the polemical complexities of Balkan history are inscribed across *Ulysses' Gaze*. These conflicts themselves are cast into a broader frame: when two journalists in Belgrade argue over whether the Serbs or the Albanians arrived first, "the conclusion is it's Hegel's fault for influencing Marx." Sarajevo, in Angelopoulos's own words, is "a symbol for all of Yugoslavia" (LM, 103), and as the birthplace of World War I, a symbol for all of Europe.

Fredric Jameson credits Angelopoulos with the reinvention of a historical cinema, at a time when "such approaches to cinema were becoming ever scarcer," and with a redrafting of the terms of realism.[41] Jameson speculates "that it is the commitment to matter in his cinema which successfully neutralizes or at least suspends the fictive, while it is the commitment to perception and its temporalities which neutralizes or suspends the documentary" (88). Jameson links the impact of Angelopoulos's historical cinema to his work with temporality: "perhaps it is this distended temporality itself which allows for this realism of the interstices, between the scripted sequence of narrative events" (82).

Jameson claims that these elements in *Ulysses' Gaze* "demand us to invent a new kind of reception or reading . . . an enlargement of our perception of narrative time" (84). And yet, while posing the question of what this new form of reception might entail, Jameson deflects the answer onto the content and narrative structure of the film. The core of Angelopoulos's achievement in reclaiming a space for a historical cinema, as he sees it, is a spatiality that clearly demarcates it from modernist work.[42] Jameson's argument seeks to establish an affinity between new narrative structures and transformed social and political realities. Recurrent scenes in *Ulysses' Gaze* at frontiers, border posts, transit stops, etc., lay the groundwork for what he calls a "transnational spatiality," and a new form of "narrative spatiality," which he defines as a "regional epic" (91ff).[43] However, Jameson's argument leaps almost entirely over the question of how reception is refigured in Angelopoulos's historical cinema. Some of the answers to this question can be drawn from Angelopoulos's transformations of narrative form, but narrative structure itself must be understood within the framework of its reception if it is to provide any insight into the historical impact of *Ulysses' Gaze*, or the new formal situations that it explores.

Angelopoulos's work with history does indeed draw on a reinvention of narrative form, but this transformation cannot be defined solely by the transnational locations of its action. The narrative of *Ulysses' Gaze* takes place across many layers. The contemporary narrative of A and his journey across the Balkans is framed at the beginning and end of the film with lines, recitations that bear only tangential relevance to the contemporary journey, but cast it within the frame of the ancient epics, of Angelopoulos's earlier films, of the Greek poets, of other myths and other stories: "the three reels, the journey," "how many borders must we cross to reach home?,"[44] "between one embrace and the next, between lovers' calls, I will tell you about the journey, all the night long and in all the nights to come . . . the whole human adventure, the story that never ends." Echoes of *The Odyssey* recur throughout the film: "The sun dipped into the sea as if abandoning the scene. I felt I was sinking into darkness;" "let's drink to the sea, the inexhaustible sea, the beginning and the end." The script unfolds within this expanded narrative field, slides almost effortlessly between the turmoils of the contemporary narrative, the ebbs and flows of the epic frame and the resonances of the other narrative layers.[45] Traditional cause-and-effect logic gives way repeatedly: A is at times almost somnambulist, as if an action can be motivated by one layer or the other of this expanded narrative field: "my footsteps, somehow they led me here." The voice-over slips as effortlessly from past to present in the contemporary narrative, as one scene is haunted by the traces of another: as A crosses the border into Albania, the scene shifts registers, is washed by the oneiric mood, the memory, of another scene: "We entered Albania with snow and silence. Your image, still damp, unchanged since the day I left it, emerges once again from the night. Am I leaving?"

Read with one eye on the epic frame and the other layers, these moments of slippage emerge not as devices of distanciation but as devices of connection – the affinity that is evoked here is not necessarily on the level of form, between narrative structures and global realities, but on the level of reception: a mimetic affinity, a resonance between the quotidian narrative of the film and memory traces of other stories or histories, echoes of other journeys, other quests, other traumas.

It is in this way that O'Grady's "tessellations of significance" weave their way through the recurrent icons and motifs of the film into the corporeal memory. But how does the viewer navigate from one level to another, what is the mechanism that allows the viewer to slide across the layers as if narrative and mythic time and space, past and present are permeable membranes of a single field? Benjamin's concept of "mimetic innervation," with its emphasis on the role of involuntary memory, is the closest we can come to encapsulating this process. Angelopoulos's exploration of Balkans history is inseparable from this evocation of involuntary memory: more than simply a blurring of history and fiction or history and myth, it is his blurring of history and memory, his interweaving of one temporality with the other, that gives the historical frame of *Ulysses' Gaze* a profound affective charge. It is his ability to draw, from the materiality of the mise-en-scène, a spark, a trigger – to generate a sensory experience that evokes a mimetic affinity with other embodied experience, an affective resonance. At the core of this fusion between history and memory, between memory and the senses, and between sensory experience and affect is a profound understanding of cinematic experience as simultaneously corporeal and affective and of mise-en-scène as the material core of embodied cinematic experience.

Acknowledgments

I would like to thank Sinead Roarty and Laleen Jayamanne, who both offered very generous assistance with detailed critical readings and editorial suggestions on this chapter.

Notes

1 *Ulysses' Gaze* (*To Vlemma Tou Odyssea*), 1995, Color, 180 minutes. Directed by Theo Angelopoulos; screenplay by Theo Angelopoulos with Tonino Guerra and Petros Markaris; cinematography by Giorgos Arvanitis and Andreas Sinanos; art direction by Giorgos Patsas and Miodrac Mile Nicolic; editing by Yannis Tistsopoulos; music by Eleni Karaindrou; produced by Theo Angelopoulos, the Greek Film Center, Mega Channel, Paradis Films, La Générale d'Images, La Sept Cinéma, with the participation of Canal+, Basicinematografica, Istituto Luce, RAI, Channel 4. Cast: Harvey Keitel, Erland Josephson, Maia Morgenstern, Thanassis Vengos, Giorgos Michalakopoulos, Dora Volanaki, Mania Papadimitriou, Angel Iavanof, Ljuba Tadic, Gert Llanaj.

2 This rhetoric is particularly pervasive in the work which frames *Ulysses' Gaze* as a modernist text; see, for example, David Bordwell, "Modernism, Minimalism, and Melancholy: Angelopoulos and Visual Style," in *The Last Modernist: The Films of Theo Angelopoulos*, ed. Andrew Horton (Trowbridge: Flicks Books, 1997), 106 (henceforth LM).

3 The war in Bosnia erupted with the break-up of former Yugoslavia in the wake of the collapse of communist governments across eastern Europe at the end of the 1980s.

Following the declaration of independent republics by Slovenia and Croatia, support for independence by Muslims and Croats in multiethnic Bosnia-Herzegovina was rejected by Bosnian Serbs, who laid siege to the Bosnian capital, Sarajevo. As negotiations between Serbs, Muslims, and Croats failed to agree on the terms of a future republic, and NATO, the United Nations, and the European Union failed to broker a settlement, war also broke out between Muslims and Croats. The war raged for several years, characterized by "ethnic cleansing," reports of atrocities against civilians and a refugee crisis with vast numbers of displaced people from the former Yugoslavia. Greece was also entangled in the regional instability, with its opposition to the declaration of an independent Macedonian republic.

4 Andrew Horton, *The Films of Theo Angelopoulos: A Cinema of Contemplation* (Princeton, NJ: Princeton University Press, 1997) (henceforth CC), 199, from an interview with Angelopoulos, July 1995.

5 Miriam Hansen, "the metaphor of the many roads not taken in early film history, that Tom Gunning uses, Benjamin's phrase of a ' – forgotten future' – there are so many starts, beginnings, directions that history has discarded and that still contain utopian possibilities. That forward look backward," in "'The Future of Cinema Studies in the Age of Global Media': Aesthetics, Spectatorship and Public Spheres," interview with Laleen Jayamanne and Anne Rutherford, *UTS Review* 5(1) (1999): 100.

6 Miriam Hansen, "'With Skin and Hair': Kracauer's Theory of Film, Marseille 1940," *Critical Inquiry* 19 (1993): 437–469 (henceforth WS).

7 Miriam Hansen, Introduction to *Theory of Film* by Siegfried Kracauer (Princeton, NJ: Princeton University Press, 1997), x (henceforth TOF).

8 Hansen has highlighted the long-standing critical misunderstanding of Kracauer's concept of the "redemption of physical reality" (TOF, ix). Tracing the complexity of Kracauer's proposition of a materialist film theory from its development in his Marseilles notebooks in the 1940s, Hansen points out that Kracauer's early "notion of the material dimension is far more comprehensive than the term 'physical reality'" which predominates in Kracauer's 1960s published work, *Theory of Film* (TOF, xvi). Through his focus on the ways that the photographic (and cinematic) image is grasped as a material entity which is engaged directly by the material, corporeal capacities of the spectator, Kracauer argues for the "redemption of physical reality" – the redemption of our understanding of the image from its supposed referent to the real, and its conceptualization in relation to the subject. Hansen points out that Kracauer's material world is "not merely an object of representation, but crucially includes the subject and the subject's relation to the Other" (452).

9 Kracauer, *Theory of Film*, 48.

10 Horton, "'What do our souls seek?': An Interview with Theo Angelopoulos," in LM, 106.

11 Michael Taussig, *Mimesis and Alterity: A Particular History of the Senses* (New York: Routledge, 1993), 21. As Taussig elaborates the concept of mimesis, it has two parts: the first, the idea of imitation or copy, as in the capacity to mimic, and the second, the idea of contact, this much more complex visceral experience of a relation, a porousness between one's self, one's own body and the objects or images of the world. It is this second aspect of mimesis that is most useful to this discussion. This understanding of mimesis has an affinity with the contemporary rethinking of perception by perceptual psychologist, James Gibson, whose model of "ecological perception" describes the ways in which the beholder "inhabits the spectacle," as Sue Cataldi describes it. See Cataldi, *Emotion, Depth, and Flesh: A Study of Sensitive Space: Reflections on Merleau-Ponty's Philosophy of Embodiment* (Albany, NY: State University of New York Press, 1993). Cataldi relates Gibson's understanding of perception to Merleau-Ponty's "flesh ontology" to develop a theory of affective experience and its relation to perception. For an extended discussion of these arguments as they relate to film theory, see Anne Rutherford, "Cinema and Embodied

Affect," in the forthcoming anthology of conference papers, *Cinema and the Senses* (Sydney: Power Institute, Centre for Art and Visual Culture).

12 Hansen explains innervation as "broadly, a neurophysiological process that mediates between internal and external, psychic and motoric, human and mechanical registers" (4). Crucially, in Benjamin this is understood as a two-way process, i.e. "not only a conversion of mental, affective energy into somatic, motoric form" (5), but also the possibility of the reverse. The concept of innervation is linked here to his concept of the "optical unconscious" as the condition of possibility for this innervation to be brought into play. Miriam Bratu Hansen, "Benjamin and Cinema: Not a One-Way Street," *Critical Inquiry*, 25 (1999): 10 (henceforth NOW). Hansen points out the associations between Benjamin's "innervation" and the mimetic "psychophysical correspondences" which Kracauer explores (TOF, xxvix). See also Hansen's discussion of the relationship between Benjamin's understanding of innervation and Eisenstein's revision of William James's "axiom that 'emotion follows upon the bodily expression'" (NOW, 5).

13 It encompasses both "a decentering and extension of the human sensorium beyond the limits of the individual body/ subject into the world . . . and an introjection, ingestion or incorporation of the object or device" (NOW, 10).

14 See, for example, David Bordwell and Kristin Thompson, *Film Art: An Introduction* (New York: McGraw-Hill, 1997), 119.

15 Brian Henderson, "The Long Take," in *Movies and Methods* vol. 1, ed. Bill Nichols (Berkeley, CA: University of California Press, 1976), 315.

16 This argument is developed more fully in "Cinema and Embodied Affect," my paper presented at *Cinema and the Senses*, University of New South Wales, November 1998.

17 Fereydoun Hoveyda, "Sunspots," in *Cahiers du Cinema vol. 2: 1960–1968 – New Wave, New Cinema, Revaluating Hollywood*, ed. Jim Hillier (Cambridge, MA: Harvard University Press, 1986), originally published as "Les Taches du Soleil," *Cahiers du Cinema* 110 (August 1960).

18 Alexandre Astruc, "What is Mise-en-scène?," in *Cahiers du Cinema: The 1950s*, ed. Jim Hillier (London: Routledge and Kegan Paul, 1985), 267, originally published as "Qu'est-ce que la mise-en-scène?," *Cahiers du Cinema* 100 (October 1959).

19 Alexandre Astruc interviewed in Claude-Marie Trémois, "Les jeunes réalisateurs français ont-ils quelque chose à dire? – Alexandre Astruc," originally published in *Radio-Cinéma-Télévision* 40 (January 18, 1959), quoted in *Alexandre Astruc* by Raymond Bellour (Paris: Editions Seghers, 1963), 95, cited in Lutz Bacher, *The Mobile Mise en Scene: A Critical Analysis of the Theory and Practice of Long-Take Camera Movement in the Narrative Film* (New York: Arno Press, 1978), 231.

20 Astruc, in Jacques Rivette and Eric Rohmer, "Entretien avec Alexandre Astruc," *Cahiers du Cinéma* 116 (February 1961), 11, quoted in Lutz Bacher, *Mobile Mise en Scene*, 232.

21 Thomas Elsaesser, "Tales of Sound and Fury: Observations on the Family Melodrama," in *Film Genre Reader*, ed. B. K. Grant (Austin, TX: University of Texas Press, 1986).

22 In his discussion of the theories of mobile mise-en-scène, Lutz Bacher makes a distinction between "long-take theories" and "mise-en-scène theories." The former, which derive largely from André Bazin's ideas of ontological realism, focus on the long-take as a means to preserve the unity of time and space, whereas the latter emphasize the expressive possibilities of mise-en-scène. However, regardless of the motivations which determine the découpage, the breakdown of shots in production, this distinction blurs when the focus shifts to reception. Even in Roberto Rossellini, on whose practice, with Jean Renoir's, "Bazin's theories were primarily founded," as Bacher writes, the long-take sequences are experienced as a sensory amplification across time (Bacher, *Mobile Mise en Scene*, 197). As Jacques Rivette has written: "Think of any Rossellini film: each scene, each episode will recur in your memory not as a succession of shots and compositions . . . but as a vast melodic phrase, a continuous arabesque, a single implacable line which leads

people ineluctably towards the as yet unknown, embracing in its trajectory a palpitant and *definitive* universe" (Jacques Rivette, "Letter on Rossellini," in Hillier, *Cahiers du Cinema: The 1950s*, 194. First published in *Cahiers du Cinéma* 46 (April 1955)).

23 "Theo Angelopoulos in Conversation with Gideon Bachmann," *Film Comment* 34(4) (July–August 1998): 50.

24 Horton writes, for example, that "there is much in each of his Angelopoulos's ten features made since 1970 that is quite 'Greek', and thus only partially grasped by a non-Hellenic audience" (LM, 2).

25 David Bordwell, "Modernism, Minimalism and Melancholy," in LM.

26 It is no coincidence that Bordwell's analysis focuses on the principles of visual composition which he argues determine the "perceptual dynamics of the shot" (LM, 19). The core of Bordwell's argument resides here in the dissection of ways in which the planes, perspectives, and spatial transformations in the shot work to cue viewer expectations. The experience of the viewer is here reduced to an "act of apprehension" (LM, 23), the mechanism by which the attention of the eyes is shifted to a particular point in the shot (more accurately, in the frame). This is precisely the slippage between two divergent concepts of "physical reality" that Hansen points out, in the critical rejection of Kracauer – one which relies on an empiricist understanding of physical reality as an "out-there" object, observed by the intact gaze of the observer; and fails to grasp the centrality of the corporeal, the material to the moment of perception.

27 Fredric Jameson, "Theo Angelopoulos: The Past as History, the Future as Form" (LM, 81) (henceforth PH).

28 Samantha Stenzel, "An Interview with Thodoros Angelopoulos," *Athenian* (June 1981), 34–35, quoted in Horton (CC, 46). Perhaps Gideon Bachmann is seeking clarification of this synthesis when he asks Angelopoulos in an interview: "Is filmmaking, then, for you, a form of poetry, in the sense of the 'cinema di poesia' of Pasolini, as juxtaposed to the 'cinema di prosa' of Antonioni?" Angelopoulos's answer: "That is too large a question" ("Theo Angelopoulos in Conversation with Gideon Bachmann," *Film Comment* 34(4) (1998).

29 Hansen quotes Kracauer (TOF, 255–256).

30 Gerald O'Grady, "Tessellations and Honeycombs," in LM. In O'Grady's elegant and evocative essay, the metaphors of the bee-hive and the compound eyes of insects encapsulate this composite and complementary structuring of material elements into the "making and merging of multiple metaphors." While O'Grady writes of meaning and metaphor, he layers this understanding itself, folds it into the material experience of the film. Where he describes the complex "commingling" of metaphors in the opening scene of *The Beekeeper*, it is the materiality of the shot that he sees inscribed into the memory of the spectator: "it is the long take of the image, the long white table, almost co-extensive with the white rectangle of the frame, which enters our own memories" (LM, 52).

31 "It does not aim upward, toward intention, but pushes toward the bottom" (WS, 447).

32 Bordwell (LM, 23). Bordwell here discusses the earlier films, but characterizes *Ulysses' Gaze* and the more recent films as merely an updating of these techniques.

33 Miriam Hansen, "Benjamin, Cinema and Experience: 'The Blue Flower in the Land of Technology,'" *New German Critique* 40 (1987): 219 (henceforth BCE).

34 NOW, 10. While elsewhere Hansen acknowledges some allegiance in Benjamin's writings to a Brechtian idea of estrangement, she traces an ambivalence, arguing that Benjamin's understanding of shock goes beyond "formal discontinuity and distortion" (BCE, 185).

35 Leo Charney, "In a Moment: Film and the Philosophy of Modernity," in *Cinema and the Invention of Modern Life*, eds. Leo Charney and Vanessa Schwartz (Berkeley, CA: University of California Press, 1995) (henceforth IM).

36 For an elaboration of this distinction, see Thomas Ots, "The Silenced Body – the Expressive Leib: On the Dialectic of Mind and Life in Chinese Cathartic Healing," in

Embodiment and Experience: The Existential Ground of Culture and Self, ed. Thomas Csordas (Cambridge, MA: MIT Press, 1990). For an extended discussion of the limitations of the physiological model, see my "Cinema and Embodied Affect," 2ff. I argue here that physiology derives its core concept of the physical body from anatomy, and outline a distinction between this concept of *Körper* and the concept of *Leib*, intrinsically a concept of affective embodiment, "the living body, my body with feelings, sensations, perceptions and emotions."

37 Walter Benjamin, "The Image of Proust," in *Illuminations* (New York: Schocken, 1969), 213. Involuntary memory or remembrance "is incompatible with conscious remembering (*Erinnerung*) which tends to historicize, to fixate the image of memory in an already interpreted narrative event" (Hansen, BCE, 200). As Hansen traces the intersection between the concept of involuntary memory and Benjamin's idea of the "optical unconscious": "like the images of involuntary memory . . . the optical unconscious does not just actualize a lost prior vision: rather it makes us see 'images that we have never seen before we remember them'" (NOW, 13, citing Benjamin's "Little History of Photography").

38 B Walter Benjamin, "On Some Motifs in Baudelaire," in *Illuminations*, 160.

39 In Horton's account, it is the construction of temporality that engenders a historical reading in the viewer: "Angelopoulos's combination of long shots with nonchronological time forces the viewer to be actively engaged in the process of 'reading' the images that flow before him or her, both for their narrative significance and for their historical significance" (CC, 58). He is writing here of *The Travelling Players*, but would no doubt apply a similar argument to similarly structured sequences in Bucharest in *Ulysses' Gaze*.

40 This cinematic quest mirrors in many ways the film historical project that has informed the work of scholars such as Hansen in the detailed historical excavations of the work of Benjamin and Kracauer.

41 Jameson (PH, 88).

42 Rather than framing *Ulysses' Gaze* as modernist, Jameson sees it as a hybrid work, comprising scenes which "recall older moments of a late modernism from which something new is seeking convulsive emergence" (PH, 92). He discerns in the film elements which "leap ahead to a new formal situation utterly unforeseen in the earlier period, and anticipatory of realities not yet adequately confronted anywhere in the art beginning to emerge in our New World Order" (89).

43 He points out that the Greek focus of the earlier films, which "stubbornly [cleave]" to questions of national culture and history, opens out in *Ulysses' Gaze* onto a pan-Balkan contemporary stage. As appealing as this supposed affinity may be, I would argue that Jameson's adoption of the "new world market" as the overarching model for contemporary cultural production assumes too great an isomorphism between global or regional political realities and narrative forms.

44 Quoted from Angelopoulos's previous film, *The Suspended Step of the Stork*.

45 Angelopoulos makes clear in an interview with Horton that Odysseus, *The Odyssey*, and other ancient myths are "reference point[s]," "figurative match[es]" rather than direct models for his film (LM, 99). Angelopoulos describes another layer in the film as drawing on the poems of Greek poet Seferis: "we Greeks are a dying race" (LM, 97). Horton confirms that Angelopoulos's method "shares such a broad canvas with his ancient predecessors. Like these early historians, he makes use of stories, myths, known events, and figures, and presents them so as to force us to go beyond the events themselves to ask ourselves about their importance and meaning" (CC, 60).

5

STRATUM AND RESONANCE

Displacement in the work of Renée Green

Elvan Zabunyan

How does memory of "real time" given formal shape in a sound or visual image facilitate grasping the movement connecting things from the past, acts or deeds situated in the present, and an unfolding future? The question requires closely examining different forms of contemporary representation as well as the way in which historians pose the notion of a present within which they recount a past story about art with social, cultural, and political implications for the future. The historian's account itself is an active "fragment" of a movement always in transformation. The question, finally, leads to a stress on the present that reconsiders the parameters appropriate to genealogy, to the archive, and to historical research and then fluidly joins the elements of personal life to a repertoire of artistic, literary, cinematic, and philosophical allusions.

The whole process might rely in a significant manner on the insights of a theorist such as Walter Benjamin, whose ideas have fostered new methods for the analysis of history, memory, translation, and interpretation. For Benjamin, a resonating web of citations provided allegorical expressions of a past reactivated in the present only in the form of a *transmissible* narration directed towards subsequent generations. Benjamin argued, "The storyteller takes what he tells from experience – his own or that reported by others. And he in turn makes it the experience of those who are listening to his tale."[1]

By quoting Benjamin, one becomes an integral part of a system of references. Benjaminian reflection applied to the domain of visual art allows for a fresh understanding of the spectator. Reading a work of art, no less than the process of creation that permitted its emergence, is not a process of standing apart. The spectator is never just a simple viewer. The art experience requires interior movement. The trick of the artist's trade is to convert a passer-by into a go-between by transmitting clues to the work that engage the imagination. The specific relationship that the spectator/viewer establishes with a work directly addressing notions of memory, documentation, and the archive emerges in the course of encounters *with* the represented form, the broadcast sound, the projected image.

For Renée Green, the artist upon whom we will repose the argument, the spectator is not on the other side of the artwork. The spectator stands on the same side as the artist, that is to say, the spectator's movement through space is not a reversed mirror image of the artist's relation to the work, with the viewer replacing the artist in order to conclude an analysis. Green underlined this position in discussing her film video *Some Chance Operations* (1999):

> There is a reference to Walter Benjamin's writing on narrative and the ways in which narratives function in the sense of the listener's desire to retain the story of the storyteller by concentrating and listening to how the story is structured to be able to try to remember it. I think that in some sense that's one of the things that I could imagine occurring for a viewer.[2]

Memory is direct: one remembers in order to transmit. Renée Green calls for a supplementary intervention from the spectator, who is both the witness of numerous articulations of the artist's work and equally the person through whom the memory of these articulations will be conveyed in a polyvalent manner. Thus, she insists on the multiplicity of the "repertoires" that she draws upon in the creation of her work. "How can one travel and live simultaneously in the heart of these many repertoires," she asks of herself.[3]

This idea of a repertoire, which she associates with music, is for her a means for considering the different elements of her artistic practice as so many notes on a musical score. A score that the spectator in turn must perform and interpret. In an interview with Green, Russell Ferguson observed that in order to understand her installations, spectators needed to spend time moving through the space in order to piece together the whole from the different elements presented. He underlined the idea that a multiplicity of displacements made it possible to detach oneself from a single viewpoint, not only physically but also through metaphor and the perspectives it offered for viewing the world. Renée Green agreed: "My idea was that the process of actually physically piecing things together would lead people to act out, even in an unconscious way, certain ideas having to do with power, movement, and the way places and positions are designed."[4] Displacement is situated equally at the level of reference. The point of departure for her repertoire is reading. "I read to make," she has said. "The material comes from a number of places, and I try to incorporate some of those shifts of location in the reconstituted pieces."[5]

The whole of the work is thus composed from fragments taken from reading, from interviews, from conversations, from lectures, from teaching, from writing, from photography, from films, and from traveling. These last three are at the heart of her artistic investigation into displacement – mental (the dream), virtual (internet), real (geographic exploration) – of location. In *Some Chance Operations* and subsequently in her exhibition *Between and Including* mounted at the Vienna Secession in 1999, Green played with the possibility of relating architecture (as "storage of thoughts") to the alphabet. She selected twenty-six locations as presumed spaces of memory but also as probabilities of reassembled structures according to an aleatory formula

Figure 5.1 Renée Green, *Between and Including*, 1999. View of the exhibition at the Secession, Vienna. Images from CD produced by Green. Courtesy of the artist.

governed by chance (Figure 5.1). She observed, "I have been thinking about earlier systems of memory that had to do with architecture and locating certain spaces architecturally in assisting ideas or memorizing different things in relationship to these."[6]

This question of reunited locations linked to the parallel idea of displacement from one point to another has been an essential concept in the development of "site specific" contemporary art. To pose the specificity of a site is, by extension, to reference the possibility of quitting the site. By crossing the frontiers – whether real or fictive – that materialize the change of perception effected by moving from one place to another, one simultaneously creates a physical link between the two places in question. This is why, carefully underlining her genealogical artistic process, Green creates formal contacts with artistic milestones and insists on their historical importance. The work of Robert Smithson and his dialectical proposition of "sites/ non-sites" prompts Green's sustained attention when after a long stay in Europe she interrogates her own standing as an "American artist." Since 1996 with *Partially Buried in Three Parts*, she has integrated these self-interrogations into the heart of her work.[7]

In January 1998, in conversation with Eduardo Carrava, Green stated:

> I was trying to think why I did turn to Smithson. That's why I mentioned genealogy, because it partly had to do with returning to the United States, trying to work in the United States, thinking about how nationality is figured into . . . can be figured into artistic production. And Smithson was an interesting example because it seemed as he uses a lot of American mythology in terms of his work, and . . . vast open spaces that have do with frontiers . . . At the time, these things seemed kind of important in terms of trying to figure out how one returns to place . . . what is a place?

Responding to the issue of the "site specific," Carrava responded by affirming that all sites become specific through relationship to other sites: "they have singular relations to everything else that is taking place, which is what specifies that site. But that site is never specific to that locale."[8]

World Tour, a show presented at the Los Angeles Museum of Contemporary Art in 1993, had four separate sections, each of which referenced a different city – Clisson, Cologne, New York, and Los Angeles. Green had already exhibited in the first three locations. The last section explored her reactions to the locale of the new show. Each section was a fragment, integrated into the whole as memories of her own past reactivated in the present installation. "It [the installation] is perceived in different ways in each place, and I try to incorporate some of those shifts of location in the reconstituted piece," she emphasized.[9] She demands a "global reading" of the exhibition. The movement of the spectator may facilitate making links between different elements in the show, but visual documentation fragments the installation anew.

Green insists that spatial identity is plural. "I'd prefer to think in terms of places of interaction," she has stressed.[10] "Places of interaction" are equally forms of "disorientation." No longer to know where one is in a given space is both a physical and a mental experience. In *Inventory of the Clues (Inventaire des indices)*, mounted at Anvers in 1993, Green visually underscored a feeling of disorientation by inscribing large circular sentences on the white floor of the museum. Viewers could read a sentence, translated into several languages, that evoked the feeling of knowing where one was while having no idea where the place was located. This installation permitted Green to move back and forth between the disorientation she herself usually feels on arriving at a new place for the first time and the disorientation of the spectator locating himself through confrontation with her work. The sentences inscribed on the floor, which create a sensation of vertigo as spectators read them, are complemented with the visual punctuation provided by numerous snapshot images taken during her explorations of the town of Anvers. These appear like the list of an inventory, but contrary to the usual function of such a record, her inventory provides an open-ended list of clues composed from her personal subjective choices. She places the clues in the exhibition space with little or no supplementary information for the spectator. In the logic of Green's work, the clues are hers and the public can, if it wants, attempt its own interpretations of her work.

Underlying the idea of displacement is the concept of change, utilized by the artist, on the one hand, as inherent to different means of communications and, on the other hand, as intrinsic to the structure of meetings, conversations, and interviews. In April 1997, Green conceived *Flow* for FRI-ART, the contemporary art center at Freiburg. She assembled as much information as she could about Switzerland available to tourists coming from the United States. She examined the specific research methods she used to locate the information she wanted. She sent out a message on the internet, she visited the Swiss Cultural Institute in New York City, she studied books in the institute's library as well as the nature of exhibitions presented there. At the same time, she conducted a parallel research project to recover more personal responses to Switzerland and discovered "Stranger in the Village," an essay written by James Baldwin during a visit to the country, published in 1955 in *Notes of a Native Son*. In discussing her project, she stated:

> The project is called *Flow* and deals with a certain exchange of cultural material. One aspect involved postcards. I was sending postcards to the director of the space every day. It was a way to cope with the anxiety of having to produce an exhibition and about things that were happening in everyday life here . . . I was also trying to imagine the various technologies for sending and receiving, and how they are really in a process of change. I wanted to think about earlier ways of communication, like the sending of postcards or the manual typing of a letter in conjunction with thinking about using the Internet.[11]

Renée Green's project united investigation of national culture with research into the town where she had come to work. Urban culture permits her to pose questions about the relationship a person establishes with a place after arriving. How can she interact with residents of a city she does not know? How can she develop a program for seeing one country while being from another? Robert Frank's book *The Americans* was Green's first contact with Switzerland, and his example provided clues on how to answer her questions. Frank, a photographer, emigrated from Switzerland to live and work in the United States after World War II. "That book is constantly referred to as one which emblematically depicts a particular time in American history in a way in which no Americans supposedly were able to do so," Green observed.[12] In this sense, she asked herself if, putting herself in continuity with Frank, she might conceptualize an iconic vision of a place that is not her own home.

She insists on diversifying questions concerning identity, following the orientation she has chosen for constructing a visual work. For *Flow*, Green collected elements expressing impressions she had formed of Swiss culture and formally deployed them in a variety of representational media. The work process she developed for this installation carried out her intent to constitute an archive through the collection of icons. If, in their own way, these archives involved a form of genealogical research, Green underlined the particular connection she found between history – social and political history as well as the history of art – and contemporary culture. Her conception of history is "as an activity reflecting lived lives which relates to something that is very present. It is not something distant."[13] The past itself permits her to research the traces of buried memory (Figure 5.2).

Figure 5.2 Renée Green, *Between and Including*, 1999. View of the exhibition at the Secession, Vienna. Images from CD produced by Green. Courtesy of the artist.

Her Vienna exhibition, *Between and Including*, brought together variations on recurrent themes with new interpretations of previous installations. The encounter effected in the course of the show was structured but paradoxically labyrinthine. Discussing the design of the show, Green noted that the labyrinth functions in the exhibition as an architectural structure, within which it is possible physically to plant references ("things to remember"). At the same time, she emphasized that

> in the process it becomes so dense that it also reflects an inability to remember, or to hold on to everything at once, and in that sense we become lost. I'm suggesting that this loss is connection to the notion of oblivion, which reflects an incapacity to hold on to everything at once. Memories emerge and fade and are triggered.[14]

The theme of the archive plays an essential role for Green as the aspect of memory that acts to keep it "alive." The archive makes up for "absence" by preserving a form. Sound recording preserves a memory of voices past, and images invoke "vanished" objects (Figure 5.3).

Pursuing the theme of how archives unite presence and loss, Green asked in two subsequent projects she undertook what happens when absence and forgetfulness merge and the resulting amnesia is "unearthed" in the course of developing an artistic interpretation. Green modeled *Partially Buried in Three Parts* (1996, 1997, 1998) after Robert Smithson's lost work *Partially Buried Woodshed*, created in 1970 during the student demonstrations at Kent State University protesting Nixon's invasion of Cambodia. On May 4, 1970, National Guardsmen killed four students on campus. Smithson inscribed the date on the woodshed he had constructed, and

Figure 5.3 Renée Green, *Between and Including*, 1999. View of the exhibition at the Secession, Vienna. Images from CD produced by Green. Courtesy of the artist.

his work assumed entirely new dimensions of meaning. Today nothing remains of Smithson's piece other than a single photograph. This sole piece of evidence served as Green's point of departure, allowing her to ask, "How do we retain access to memory and history?"[15]

Green locates the creative process emerging through repeated readings of surviving traces. The process is a form of genealogical excavation, and she links her approach to Michel Foucault's concept of "archaeological territories," proposed in 1969 in his book, *The Archaeology of Knowledge*. The artist's aims are realized through a reconstitution of a memory that itself must be pieced together. Foucauldian archaeology leads to reconstructions of the past that may seem risky given how widely evidence of events under consideration has scattered across space and time. Discovered clues are no longer present as obvious outcomes of earlier acts. Instead, genealogical traces link together in a network; they are knowable through an intersection of "memory sites" with "specific sites."

Building on these propositions, Green created a equivalence between her interest in art history (with the reference to Smithson), her personal history, and American history more generally by addressing the question of how nearly thirty years later one might understand the 1970s. She made a film, in which, as the principal character, she investigated different locations of this memory for which she intended to construct a continuity. She interviewed protagonists from the period at the exact location where Smithson had constructed his work but where not a single physical trace remained. This absence of evidence heightened the painful emotional feelings Green recalled experiencing the day the students at Kent State University were killed. Her mother, a classical singer, was enrolled that very semester in a contemporary music course at Kent State. The day of the demonstrations, Renée was only 11 years old, and she waited at home anxiously for her mother to return from school. Extracted from memory, her subjective feeling stands against her creative act. Through a personal anecdote, Green presented an artistic perspective questioning the very notion of absence – or the mental image that it incites. How to fill up an absence? Green responded to the question indirectly with a montage that supported the construction of a fragmentary narrative. The film draws upon documentary clips while a subjective approach to editing introduces an element of fiction.

When she presented *Partially Buried* at the Pat Hearn Gallery in 1996, Green projected slides of documents from the period alongside the film. Her voice-over introduction spoke of her "return to a place tied to childhood and to a work on a place important to the artist for the place it holds in the genealogy of American art." The importance of Smithson's work for Green is apparent as well in her treatment of *Site/Non Site*, a work where she identifies "site" with "open boundaries" and "non site" with "closed boundaries." This duality is important for Green's artistic practice, notably in her movement between place and memory, between real and mental sites. "The function of personal memory is the protection of impressions," she says at the conclusion of the film and continues, "Commemoration aims to destroy them, memory is essentially conservative, commemoration destructive."[16]

With this last point, Green highlights the precise role that the creative process has in examining the destructive side of memory. Art does not reconstitute memory intact but reveals it in its fragmentation. That is why, parallel to the film at the exhibition, she published a "piece" of the scenario and several images extracted from the film in the journal *October* in 1997. This primarily theoretical extraction serves as a documentary presentation of the larger project while providing a parallel, complementary reading of the original artwork created for the gallery situation.

Green's subsequent projects have continued her engagement with Robert Smithson. His 1968 essay, "A Museum of Language in the Vicinity of Art," begins by declaring,

> In the illusory babels of language, an artist might advance specifically to get lost, and to intoxicate himself in dizzying syntaxes, seeking odd intersections of meaning, strange corridors of history, unexpected echoes, unknown humors, or voids of knowledge . . . but this quest is risky, full of bottomless fictions and endless architectures and counter-architectures.[17]

Smithson's allegorical extensions bear an interesting relation to Green's work, particularly since through continuing exploration, she herself recovers the meaning of the different languages she has appropriated. In his essay on Smithson, theorist and critic Craig Owens emphasized that, "What the fissures in Smithson's 'earth-words' disclose is the disjunctive, atomizing principle which, according to Walter Benjamin, defines allegory. In allegory, language is broken up, dispersed, in order to acquire a new and intensified meaning in its fragmentation."[18] This last point is close to Green's conception of creative process as constructing a work out of the potential fractures of a palimpsest that she has imagined as infinitely resonant.

After having finished *Partially Buried in Three Parts*, Green continued with work based in poetic resurrection. She researched the lost archives of the Neapolitan film producer and actress Elvira Notari. Between 1906 and 1930, this prolific figure made over sixty films, but only three have survived. Green *literally* effected a renaissance of a lost body of work that she tenderly adopted as her own. As with *Partially Buried*, Green composed *Some Chance Operations* in several complementary and successive stages. The 1998 installation in Milan and the film-video at the beginning of the following year underscored, through the paradoxically ephemeral character of the notion of the archive, the evanescent figure of this forgotten filmmaker. Michael Eng, in his correspondence with Green, presents an essential perspective on the possibility of interpreting a work through the focus of its potential disappearance:

> We could discuss Benjamin's claim that the drive to order and unify just creates more disruption and difference, just promotes the workings of chance rather than masters it. So instead of preserving memory, all the archive does is make forgetting possible. It does not satisfy the desire to remember, it guarantees that there will be forgetting. Even stronger, it's

not only that forgetting is a part of memory but more that memory is forgetting, and the archive is the ultimate example of their identification.[19]

Through montage that privileges the dissolve, the opening and the conclusion of the film *Some Chance Operations* presents the spectator with images extracted from *È Picerella* (1921), one of Notari's three salvaged films. Drawn into a quasi-mental voyage, the spectator watches clips from Notari's film intercut with other visual inserts, including sequences where the camera follows Green from behind retracing Notari's steps, sometimes superimposed upon the Italian actress's expressive face. In a very significant gesture, a monotonous male narrator's off-screen voice recalls Robert Smithson's narration for his 1970 film *Spiral Jetty*. Likewise, always in reference to Smithson's work, fade-ins of filmic or photographic documents are conceived as a discontinuous narration through which the notion of disappearance and effacement assumes its fullest sense, as if the superimposition of direction serves to obscure connections and to wear out, visually, the film stock. Shot in Naples, Vienna, and New York, *Some Chance Operations* minimizes geographic and cultural difference by juxtaposing evidence of the complex character of spatial memory. To recollect a moment from the past puts into motion a veritable roundtrip across time and space. In one scene people living in Vienna tell personal memories of Italy and Naples. In another scene, there is as well a montage of famous films such as *Journey to Italy* by Roberto Rossellini (1953). For the most part, personal testimony is presented straightforwardly in the original language of the witness. With the logic of geographic displacement, language difference underlines the question of translation and the degree to which the function of language as a medium of communication is an essential theme in Green's work. The idea of translation at the same time leads to the notion of interpretation and the crossing of territories, whether they be those of art or of language.

Green's presence in the film involves physical displacement when she appears on screen, mental displacement when she edits the images, and finally visual displace-ment as she guides viewers through her "discovery." Her goal of reawakening previous moments is an artistic determination explicitly posed as part of her own sense of the present. Gilles Deleuze has remarked:

> It is true that the memory-machine does not consist in recollecting but in reliving a precise moment of the past. However, what is possible for the animal, the mouse, is impossible for the man. For the man the past moment is like a shining point which belongs to a sheet and cannot be detached from it . . . So that the hero will only be able to relive [the past] by crossing these sheets again, and by, from that moment, crossing many others.[20]

With this example, Deleuze reminds us of the essential mobility of a cinemato-graphic hero lost within the twenty-four frames per second. Nonetheless, he indicates as well that this renewed crossing of many, overlapping sheets of time is a journey at once horizontal and vertical, a journey that burrows into genealogical

94

STRATUM AND RESONANCE

strata (rather than geological) with a perspective that follows at the same time the earth's movement.

Deleuze's observation calls to mind the end of the film *Spiral Jetty* as Smithson stumbles when he moves closer to the artwork he is filming and trips against a rose-colored boulder. It calls to mind as well Renée Green searching for the exact, weed-covered location on the Kent State campus of *Partially Buried Woodshed*, or in her later work, rediscovering and retracing Elvira Notari's steps in the streets of Naples. The memory on which Green works is, as Jean-Luc Godard might say, a "time recovered." Nonetheless, time resumes its flow only through the mediation of a sound or an image recovered from an archive. *Some Chance Operations* appears in addition as a film that one could almost "listen to through the eyes" or "hear through the images." The artistic experience that Green's work engages is a form of experimental research into the perception of sound and image. Image and voice function as indices of a direct, immediate memory, even though the image may be at the limit of the visible or the sound a bare murmur. In this sense, Green constantly reworks notions of presence and absence, of appearance and disappearance.

Speaking of "Between and Including," Lynne Tillman argues that moving through the exhibition "is like the process of memory itself as well as becoming part of a history in which your own history is inscribed too."[21] The observation encouraged another question, posed this time by Joe Wood: Where does Green situate the location of the "personal archive"? Is she trying to assemble an "archive of the self"? The artist accepts the methodological inevitability of distortion (Figure 5.4). As a result, she cannot have a unilateral point of view about herself: "The methodology for how it was done is not that obviously defined, you know it is partly subjective, its purpose is to circulate and not primarily be stored, as in an archival situation."[22]

Nonetheless, she places herself in a system of archives that permits her to begin an interior self-examination. She is her own subject in the sense that the elaboration of her identity relies upon parameters that could all as well pertain to works of fiction. This does not mean that she "invents" her character; instead she "invents" a fiction in which she is inscribed as an artist. This fiction is a history that becomes the very thread of her artistic process. At the same time, she puts her status as an artist at a distance in order to have an external perspective on herself. Jan Avgikos has written that Green appears "as a fiction of herself within her work."[23]

Reference to a fictive history affirms the importance of narrative form for Green's work, but not as a continuous storyline. As with her identity as an artist, plot occupies multiple positions. It is at once both the form of the fiction and its contents. On the cover for her book *Certain Miscellanies: Some Documents*, Green offers a "character profile" as a kind of joke that draws the reader into the labyrinth of identity:

> The character is often visibly detectable as a female with brown skin and dreadlocks. She was born in the U.S. and speaks English as her native tongue, but she studied French and in brief exchanges can seem to be from some French-speaking place. Where she might be from is very dependent upon the language she speaks. She's been asked at various times and in

95

various places whether she's from Martinique, Puerto Rico, Guyana, Jamaica, some island near Venezuela, Paris, London, and New York. She's been told by a Senegalese that she resembles a girl he knew in Senegal and by a Mexican that she looks just like his cousin. She is from the Metropolis, in her case New York.[24]

Figure 5.4 Renée Green, *Between and Including*, 1999. View of the exhibition at the Secession, Vienna. Images from CD produced by Green. Courtesy of the artist.

Green introduces her genuine identity in a deliberate narrative tone, but not in the form of clearly recognizable autobiographical elements. Instead she presents herself in a fictive form that hints at its links to reality. The overlapping accounts of her origins open up a multiplicity of interpretations that the artist uses to construct a character that is both specific and fluid. Fluid as well because, despite visible signs of African ancestry, she can escape identification with any specific place. The cover reinforces her mobility with a photograph of the artist taken from behind as she is walking. A determined gait combines with the slightly out of focus quality of the image, reproduced from a film still, to reinforce a feeling of movement away from anything that might pin the artist down.

Green conceived the book design as a displacement built into the structure of her work. Even more, the book is constituted as a multidimensional, visual narration where image, color, text all confront each another in response to the title. *Miscellanies*, the primary sense of which is "mixture," can signify both a collection of different objects or an anthology of texts. The word suggests a grouping lacking a defined and limited common trait or subject. Green plays on all these senses of the word, as well as posing the concepts against the subtitle's key term *document*. The book appears as an object "parallel" to the artwork. In fact, as a "document" of the artist's work process it forms an integral part of the artwork.

The artist prefers to locate personal archives in the context of historical experience. Thus, when Green was invited to exhibit at the Ateliers de Clisson in 1992, she undertook an investigation into the city of Nantes in the eighteenth century when it was a center of the slave trade. Parallel to her research in existing archival sources, she looked for traces of this period of the city's history in the contemporary urban space. She photographed stuffed animals in the Museum of Natural History, exotic plants in the botanical garden, and a local restaurant called The Slave. These legacies of the city's past demonstrate how eighteenth-century slavery continues to exist as cultural fiction supporting the local tourist industry. The photographs became part of *Mise-en-Scène*, an exhibition for which she created a museum of fictional decorative arts. For the show, she had special Jouy linen made in which the usual floral motifs were replaced by scenes showing a slave and his master on a woodsy background. Period chairs presented in the installation were reupholstered with the same material.

Green's approach to artistic space revealed with relative clarity the aesthetic and social connection that she has with the Belgian artist Marcel Broodthaers. Indeed, in his last installation, *Daumier's Angelus* (1974), Broodthaers said of his process:

> I have tried to present objects and scenes arranged according to a series of dates between 1964 and this year in order to create rooms true to the time [*esprit décor*]. That is to say to restore a real function to the object or the painting, the décor not being an end in itself.[25]

Broodthaers was, like Green, a historian of his own work. In this spirit, he proposed a precise analytic approach when he said:

> I believe that my exhibitions depended and depend still on recollections
> of the period for which I took upon myself the creative situation in a heroic
> and solitary form. Otherwise said – In other times: Read, look. Today:
> Permit me to introduce you.[26]

Even if Green's body of work is located in the cultural realities of previous generations, representative documents from her installations do not evoke the minutiae of
Broodthaersian mise-en-scènes, for which the notion of decor had special meaning.
Green's position is situated in a more affirmative subjectivity, one arrived at and
confirmed through the continuing process of work. Some elements of *Mise-en-Scène*
presented at Clisson reappeared in "World Tour: Souvenirs" presented later that
year in New York City at a private gallery. Each exhibition functions as a fragment
of a larger, ongoing artistic project, each unfinished fragment finding in the artist's
personal life a unifying frame of reference. In effect, to the degree that she conceives
her work as a totality in process, every piece of information recorded on any subject
is added to preceding references. The whole can be considered a database stored in
a computer memory drive as well as in the artist's personal memory.

Every representational form that Green creates, regardless of medium, functions
like a text file fully linked to the rest of the artist's work. In *Miscellaneous: Continued*
(1995), Green provided spectators with a computer they could use to access the
archives documenting the organization of the preceding exhibit, *Miscellaneous*.
The CD-ROM provided was organized around a list of key words (such as Africa,
America, Black Culture, diaspora, crime, culture, memory, police, prison) and
proper names (notably Theodor Adorno, James Brown, Angela Davis, Ralph
Ellison, Melvin Van Peebles, Gil Scott-Heron). The majority of the key words
referenced elements of African American culture, which were integrated, given
the operation of the CD-ROM, in open-ended extensions.

However, Green does not limit herself to virtual documentation. She may directly
reference works in an exhibition in order that some function as messages responding
to other parts of the show. They then illustrate her idea of "research." As the owner
of an impressive book collection, Green believes the concept of the bibliography is
fundamental to what she does. Bibliography permits multiple references of any
subject, and it allows for including peripheral readings that reinforce the argument.
Green thus in each of her installations provides a list of background readings and
signifies the relevance of each with several key words. These defining concepts
underline the content of the overall work while creating meaningful connections
between individual pieces within the show. These connections are always those that
Green has constructed. Her personal choice thus provides a structured order for the
spectators' reading.

Whatever the medium might be that the artist might chose to use in an exhibition,
there is always the need to leave a trace. Sooner or later, they will begin to disappear.
By placing the concept of the archive at the center of her work, she has created
systems for the organization of documents that wind up by archiving each other
according to a fluid schema. While it would be inaccurate to speak of *Between and*

Including as a retrospective exhibition, it is no longer possible to use a closed set of categories to identify the constitutive elements in her body of work. The title of her recent Vienna show is significant because it suggests that there is always a possibility of making a space "between" come alive, that there is always the possibility of adding new, parallel forms to the ones that already exist. Exploring the infinite field of research, Green escapes from the limits of the traditional disciplines. She glides over words, images, sounds, and the accumulations of memory traces that she has recovered to bounce into new spaces for language, vision, and sound. She has not yet forgotten that the work of art, whenever it is connected to memory, always keeps the past alive in the present.

(translated by Richard Cándida Smith)

Notes

1 Walter Benjamin, "The Storyteller," translated by Harry Zohn, in *Illuminations* (New York: Schocken, 1969), 87.

2 Renée Green in a public conversation with Lynne Tillman and Joe Wood, February 10, 1999, at the Secession, quoted in exhibition catalogue *Between and Including* (Vienna: Secession, 1999; exhibition catalogue), 10.

3 She insists elsewhere on this subject: "My production functions in different registers, so working as a writer, or as a teacher, or as a person who programs films and organizes symposia or who produces videos and books, all of this is incorporated into what I consider to be my practice" (text of a lecture at the Academy of Fine Arts in Copenhagen, March 1995, unpublished).

4 Russell Ferguson, "Various Identities: A Conversation with Renée Green," in *World Tour* (Los Angeles: Museum of Contemporary Art, 1994), E56.

5 "Insights," Renée Green interviewed by Donna Harkavy, in *Bequest* (Worcester, MA: Worcester Art Museum, 1991), 6.

6 Unpublished extract from a conversation between Renée Green, Lynne Tillman, and Joe Wood at the Secession, February 10, 1999.

7 It is especially in the second part of *Übertragen / Transfer* that she engages in a study of the United States during the 1970s constructed from the point of view of the German community living in the country. She questions Kwame Anthony Appiah's notion of the "cosmopolitan patriot" while underlining the idea that a person's roots move with them from one geographic territory to another. Appiah cites Gertrude Stein's statement that "America is my country and Paris is my hometown."

8 Unpublished conversation communicated by Green to the author.

9 Ferguson, "Various Identities," E56.

10 Mark Kremer, "Interview with Renée Green," *Archis* (February 1994), 71.

11 Pauline Boudry, "Entretien avec Renée Green," in "Environ 27 ans (peut-être plus . . .), pratiques artistiques et féminismes," *Cahiers des Beaux-Arts* (Geneva) 113 (February 1997), 66.

12 Ibid., 67.

13 Ibid., 69.

14 Renée Green, correspondence with Michael Eng, April 1999, to appear in the catalogue accompanying her exhibition *Between and Including* at the Vienna Secession. Document communicated to the author by the artist.

15 Quoted from the text of Green's talk during her May 1998 exhibition at the Emil Fontana Gallery in Milan, "Some Chance Operations: Known Only from Photographs" (two pages, unpublished).

16 The last installment of *Partially Buried*, entitled *Partially Buried Continued*, attempts to recapitulate with precision the stages of the process through which a formal memory comes into being. Presented at the Kwanju Biennale in South Korea, Green engages in parallel examination of photographs taken by her father while he was a soldier in the Korean War, photographs taken by the artist Theresa Hak Kyung Cha in 1980, and images recorded by Green during her first trip to Kwanju in 1997 to prepare for the exhibition. Once again, she poses questions concerning genealogical research by interrogating different archives as sources that are at one and the same time personal and artistic.

17 Robert Smithson, "A Museum of Language in the Vicinity of Art," reprinted in *The Collected Writings* (Berkeley, CA: University of California Press, 1996), 78–94.

18 Craig Owen, "Earthwords," reprinted in *Beyond Recognition* (Berkeley, CA: University of California Press, 1992), 43.

19 Michael Eng, correspondence with Renée Green, April 1999 (unpublished).

20 Gilles Deleuze, *Cinema 2: The Time-Image*, translated by Hugh Tomlinson and Robert Galeta (Minneapolis, MN: University of Minnesota Press, 1989), 117.

21 Public conversation between Renée Green, Lynne Tillman, and Joe Wood, February 10, 1999, at the Vienna Secession.

22 Ibid.

23 Jan Avigkos, "How to Read Fiction," in *World Tour*, B4.

24 Renée Green, *Certain Miscellanies: Some Documents* (Berlin/Amsterdam: DAAD, De Appel, 1996).

25 Marcel Broodthaers, quoted in *L'Angélus de Daumier* (Paris: Centre National d'Art Contemporain, 1974).

26 Irmeline Lebeer, "Entretien avec Marcel Broodthaers," in *Marcel Broodthaers* (Brussels: Société des Expositions du Palais des Beaux-Arts, 1974), 156.

6

CITIES MEMORY VOICES
COLLAGE

David Michalski

WESTERBECK: Winograd seemed to be happiest when he confronted a wall of
humanity surging down the street. He threw himself into it.

MEYEROWITZ: Yes! It's like going into the sea and letting the waves break over you.
You feel the power of the sea. On the street each successive wave brings a whole
new cast of characters. You take wave after wave, you bathe in it. There is
something exciting about being in the crowd, in all that chance and change –
it's tough out there – but if you can keep paying attention something will reveal
itself – just a split second – and then there's a crazy cockeyed picture![1]

A city is replete with courses and routes intertwining and tangled where people
pass and rub the structures and paths of others. When walking focused on the haptic
sensations brought on by the friction of this state of motion within motion, the
city becomes fluid, and landmarks and people write themselves upon us. This text,
written by the streets has many authors and registers both competing and complementary values. It is an *interscript* rich with texture, each distinct voice entering from
different angles and passing in and out of perception, a scrapbook marked by the
moments of passage. The individual in this metaphor is a kiosk for the traffic. Leaflets
and bulletins are posted only to be buried by more information, sticking just as long
as the glue holds, eventually flying away. The wanderer, experiencing the city as
such a hedonist, engages in a phenomenological exploration, collecting syncopated
patterns of fragments which collect as new perceptions brush against the body. The
journalist or drifting tourist explores as well, collecting mementos, or jotting down
events on the pages of his or her field notebooks or postcards. This is the method of
the street photographer too. Diane Arbus, Manuel Alvarez Bravo, Roy DeCarava,
and their ilk engage in this enterprise, confronting both spontaneity and multiplicity
to "respond to errant details, chance juxtapositions, odd non sequiturs, peculiarities
of scale, the quirkiness of the street."[2] Theirs is a genre wedded to wandering;
la dérive; the methodology the Parisian situationists, drifting through city streets to
collect the specific effects of the geographical environment, consciously organized
or not, on the emotions and behavior of individuals.[3] The goal is to make the city

new, to move contrary to routine, to step out of step, and see the familiar as strange, so that the city may be seen with new eyes. One becomes the stranger, observing people's gestures and characters, turning them into typographical characters, letters, in which each person's story or image contributes to the spelling of the *interscript*.[4]

To explain what I mean by *interscript*, I like to use the metaphor of Union Square. Each day I pass through the Union Square train station in Manhattan, transferring from a west bound train to a north bound train. I know the route quite precisely. I have found the shortest distance between the train cars on which I prefer to ride. I have made this connection thousands of times. I can see a map in my head. I turn left after detraining, and walk to the second staircase. I walk up one flight. Make a jog right, go up the next stair case. Pass the turnstiles, I take a left. Up the stairs. Walk to the right. Then finally, down the stairs on the left. If any one asked me, I would tell them I know Union Square very well, "like the back of my hand."

Yet, a while ago I had to make a connection from the north bound train to the west bound train, a connection I had never made before. Suddenly I was disorientated. I saw the same pillars and staircases but from a different angle. I saw different people as I turned my body to follow this new direction. The changes were of course subtle, but the experience was new. For a slight moment, the station I had become weary of, became fresh, dangerous, and exciting.

My knowledge of Union Square had been formed by my singular path. By changing my routine I had collected another view of the station. If I were to collect the stories and observations of other commuters, all going through the station at their own pace and discretion, I would thereby compound my picture, each additional path adding to the meaning the station has for me. As map layered upon map, I would begin to see a *collected memory* of Union Square.

This new map however should not be confused with a super map or *collective* memory. In the course of walking through streets, and engaging such a collection method, one does not simply collect the forces imprinting themselves on the geography. Instead, each curator of stories is both a contributor and composer.

Georg Simmel wrote in *The Stranger*,

> If wandering is the liberation from every given point of space, and thus the conceptual opposite to fixation at such point, the sociological form of the "stranger" presents a unity, as it were, of these two characteristics.[5]

For Simmel, the conception of the sociologist as the stranger, describes an individual who is simultaneously inside and outside the group or phenomena being studied, one who is detached, yet participatory. The craft compels the sociologist to negotiate objectivity and enter into the debate defining the identity of the place. Through my collection of Union Square stories, not only would the status of the place change, but my own subjectivity would be effected as well. Likewise, the work of ethnographers or writers of culture is one of projection and representation. The ethnographer becomes the medium through which situations are displayed.

The more observation actually means meeting, talking, and interacting with participants, the more a researcher will be affected by such an experience.

The pressure of our weight and the trajectory of our movements draws attention to the influence of our own actions. Our wandering produces what Michel de Certeau calls *lignes d'erre,*

> indirect or errant trajectories obeying their own logic. In the techno-cratically constructed, written, and functionalized space [of the city, these trajectories] form unforeseeable sentences, partly unreadable paths across space. Although they are composed of established languages . . . and although they remain subordinated to prescribed syntactical forms . . . the trajectories trace out ruses of other interests and desires that are neither determined nor captured by the systems in which they develop.[6]

For Certeau, these trajectories correspond to "ways of operating" or tactics people use in everyday life to negotiate the interlocking systems of the city. The city is written through this interaction in a kind of daily social poiesis. We perform roles, interpret events, and participate in the interplay which writes the city large. The city itself takes the form of the *interscript*, at once a foreign and familiar terrain, an amalgamate of geographical and personal maps which we engage and write through our own motion.

While we inherit language, architecture and culture from the ages, our contemporary use of them entails a disassembly, reworking and reassembly of fragments based on the situational demands and emotional needs of our time and place (Figure 6.1). The city is both exterior and interior, existing in the dialogue between the self and the environment. It exists as a conversation which we may enter and turn.

Since Plato, memory has been likened to marks etched upon wax tablets. A notion revived in cybernetic models of the brain where memories are stored in bundled packages of data existing within our neural nets. Memories are construed as copies of sensory experience, existing in the mind. For many years neuropsychologists have sought the elusive trace of memory or *Engram* in the tissue of the brain without positive results. These metaphors neglect the everyday creation of memory technology in scrapbooks, libraries, and photo albums, which point to a distributed system of recollection. Such concepts of memory negate compositional power and intentionality by obfuscating memory's link to remembering.

> Storage models of discursive recollection must necessarily both decontex-tualise and reify elements of what is manifested in an account of some witnessed past of affairs, treating such elements as enduring properties of persons' brains rather than as contextually variable features of a telling's construction.[7]

When memory is reconceptualized as an act of living consciousness, the objects of memory can be seen as linked to larger accounts and stories.

Figure 6.1 Debra Steckler, Untitled collage on paper from *Flashcards*, 9 × 5.6 cm, 1996. Courtesy of the artist.

This is why many oral historians and ethnographers will painstakingly transcribe verbatim long interviews and advocate close listening. They know what they are getting down is important – the sound of thoughts forged where words get meaning, through argument, performance, and engagement. Similarly, the ethnographic object is not an isolated fragment but rather an entry point into a discussion of the researcher's ethnographic experience, a conversation piece. Their notebooks and photo albums are not the culmination of distilled artifacts, but instead an extension of cognition holding stable the inseparable continuum between perception, retention, and the articulation of events. Both referential and evocative, these notebooks contribute to the cognitive environment, a human ecosystem made up of physicality and mental activity, a collected or collage consciousness. They are memory technology representing the intersection of mind and matter.[8]

Robert Ezra Park's essay, "Natural History of the Newspaper," relates the newspaper as just such a memory technology,

> The press, as it exists, is not, as our moralists sometimes seem to assume, the willful product of any little group of living men. On the contrary, it is the outcome of an historical process in which many individuals participated without foreseeing what the ultimate product of their labors would be.[9]

The motive of the editors is to reproduce life on the streets, a life frequented by the juxtaposition of forces intermingled, telling us about ourselves. The paper, even today, begets the form of the collage, as articles recreate the friction of our passage through the human environment. It is a medium judged by the accuracy of its representation of present experience. Park traces the history of the newspapers to bulletins of gossip, hearsay, and reproduced correspondence, organized and posted in town squares to relate the conditions of daily life.[10] From this beginning the newspaper has evolved to become the record of public memory as well as a fundamental source for historians. Yet in its daily practice, it is mired in controversy and contested facts. The archived newspaper is not so much history, as it exists in master narratives or under a single conceptual paradigm as it is a variety of present situations.

Walter Benjamin's twenty-year *Passagen-Werk* attempted to develop an alternative way of writing history,[11] one in which artifacts and quotations were allowed to speak for themselves. He saw the progress of history as a growing pile of debris made up of multiple present experiences. In the objects of history, he recognized a synthesis of the collected material histories of objects and the mental imagery that define objects in the eyes of the viewer. For Benjamin, a collection of artifacts is capable of rendering history without narration or theoretical framework because objects hold both the process of their development and their conceptual essence.[12]

> The method becomes a dialectical (dialogic) relationship with that world, which in turn, is represented not as an all-encompassing totality but rather in terms of specific material and experiential constructions.[13]

In the writing and layout of newspapers, Benjamin saw the beginnings of a new historicity. Newspapers were seen not only as documents of city life, but as artifacts making up city lives. He likened the morning paper to daily nourishment. Editors cater to the impatient readers who choose what they want to read.[14] In doing so, each reader constructs his or her own version of the day's events, similarly to the way each library patron, if polled upon their exit from the stacks, would construct a different story of the collection. Through their discriminating assimilation of facts the readers collaborate with reporters and editors, assembling the day's events. Here Benjamin insists, "a dialectical moment lies concealed: the decline of writing in the press turns out to be a formula for the restoration in a different one."[15] The breadth of juxtaposed antinomies in subject matter and opinion are reconciled through the piece meal construction of interpretations. Journalistic reporting, with its reliance on fact, photograph, and direct quotation, became a model for the *Passagen-Werk*. Upon surveying Benjamin's files after his death, in an attempt to make sense of the never-completed project, Theodor Adorno wrote to Max Horkhiemer of the problems he was having trying to build a general thesis from the work.

> The most significant is the extraordinary restraint in the formulation of theoretical thoughts in comparison to the enormous treasure of excerpts. This is explained in part by the . . . idea that is formulated in one place, of the work as pure "montage," that is, created from the juxtaposition of

quotations so that the theory springs out of it without having to be inserted
as interpretation.[16]

Walter Benjamin's endeavor to write a philosophical history, in which the events,
and occurrences would be used to build systems of thought, was directly influenced
by visual collage. Historical events were to be collected in a visual rather than linear
logic. History, he wrote, "decomposes into images, not into narratives."[17] The goal
of his project was to foreground "a consciousness of the present which explodes the
continuum of history."[18] By blasting objects from their ideological, or teleological
shells congealed around them, Benjamin allows for the re-collection of the
unearthed materials. This is not done to clear objects of their time-worn characteristics, or reduce their features through the application of murky relativity. Objects,
words, and pictures were not reduced to a system of signs without meaning. He
intended to release the objects of history from the mainline of progress.

> This was something that could be realized only indirectly, through
> "cunning": it was not the great men and celebrated events of traditional
> historiography but rather the "refuse" and "detritus" of history, the half-
> concealed, variegated traces of the daily life of the "collective," that
> was to be the object of study, and with the aid of methods more akin
> – above all on their dependence on chance – . . . to the methods of the
> nineteenth-century ragpicker, than to those of the modern historian.[19]

The reader of his history becomes a wanderer among ruins, choosing, embellishing,
and elaborating upon the objects. By untying the stars from their constellations,
women and men, no longer the puppets of fate, are free to creatively remember them
in a manner apropos to their lives.

> For Benjamin, the view of history as a continuum is fundamentally
> dangerous because it reinforces the ideology of mechanistic progress,
> which is dangerous no matter into whose hands it falls.[20]

Benjamin's display of fragments in the *Passagen-Werk* was meant to break up the
linear nature of history by exhibiting consciousness as a kind of assemblage.

The word *collage* comes from the French *coller*, "to paste" (Figure 6.2). It is an art
form with diverse origins. The idea of fastening pieces together, of mixing theme
and variation, to stir the imagination and evoke the presence of objects, is as old as
culture itself.[21] In scrapbooks, and grangerized texts in Europe, and in performance
or storytelling objects in Africa and America, collage is principally tied to memory.
In nineteenth-century America, some African Americans practiced the making
of memory jars, ceramic containers covered with plaster and stuck with shells,
glass, coins, and objects from people's daily life.[22] These were placed on graves
of the deceased. I see the bricolaged outside of these jars representing the physical
or material side of memory, while the inside speaks to memories immaterial or

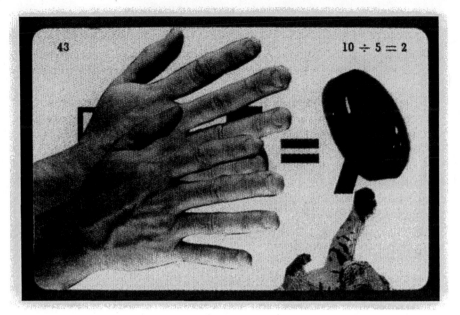

Figure 6.2 Debra Steckler, Untitled collage on paper from *Flashcards*, 9 × 5.6cm, 1996. Courtesy of the artist.

spiritual or mental side. Here the exterior serves to literally *jar* or re-mind the contents of the vessel.

As a memory technology, such a collage serves as both a launching point and crossroads. From the ordered juxtaposition of distinct pieces, stories extend like mathematical singularities outward, while simultaneously pulling distinct forms onto its imaginary stage. The dual character collage, a zone where objects exist alternatively as objects and referents, provides a way of understanding how memory plays off of our physical and social environments.

In the early twentieth century, the cubists utilized collage as a way to represent a reality absent in nineteenth-century impressionist and landscape paintings. The cubists wished to represent memory as a landscape independent of time and space, where percepts persist and reassert themselves in new territories. The surrealists used collage to represent a reality above the real, a reality deemed more accurate than linear representation in that it allowed unseen emotions and thought to cohabitat with the rational world. Likewise, the futurists justified this interpenetration of imagery as a proper representation of consciousness as it is felt. The Italian artist and poet F. T. Marinetti in his "Manifesto of Futurism" of 1914 asks,

> How often have we not seen upon the cheek of the person with whom we were talking the horse which passes at the end of the street?

> The motor-bus rushes into houses it passes and in their turn the houses throw themselves upon the motor-bus and are blended with it.[23]

The history of collage in the visual arts parallels its use in experimental prose and poetry where it was seen as an apt response to the problems of social description and the expression of memory. Appollinaire's collage poems "Les Fenêtres" and "Lundi Rue Christine" arose from his participation in the cubist experiment. They

> both make use of snippets of spoken language, assembled from what seem to be unrelated and disconnected conversations being held in some public place. The intention seems to be to face the reader with a mass of unintegrated details, not unlike the profusion of planes that, at first sight, obscure the overall design and organization of a cubist painting.[24]

In the visual arts, texture is rendered through the application of materials. In writing, texture is a function of voice.

> Those pancakes were divine
> The water's running
> Dress black as her nails
> It's impossible
> Here sir
> The malachite ring
> The ground is covered with sawdust
> Then it's true
> The redheaded waitress eloped with the bookseller
> Apollinaire, "Monday in Christine Street"[25]

This poem displays the street in a painterly fashion. Out of the mouths of bystanders and pedestrians come a palette of colors and variety of surface qualities, but what shapes these lines is the traffic. A variety of perspectives are displayed by letting distinct voices cross each other. Dubbed by Apollinaire a "conversation poem,"[26] it marks the beginning of a great body of interdisciplinary work; work which applies observer accounts, interviews and found language to poetry, to construct socially descriptive and ethnographic poems.

The art of social description thrives in interdisciplinary environments, where distinct genres and systems of knowledge intermingle. In the United States, the Black Mountain College nurtured a renaissance across the arts and sciences. There, photographers like Aaron Siskind and Harry Callahan, painters such as Robert Rauschenberg, and poets such as Charles Olson extended their fields of inquiry so that they might inform each other. Rauschenberg developed, through his study of art history, a technique which is "both aleatory and associative in its mixing of intimacy and veracity."[27] In works such as *Random Order*, where he mixes text and photography to elevate the scrapbook to artistic documentary, Rauschenberg saw his art as the creation of memory technology. He saw his art as "a public act of collective memory,"[28] where an "elaborate disjuncture of . . . imagery . . . fabricated from daily residue"[29] "sets up a relationship between the external source of the image and the internal space of its reception."[30] Rauschenberg's work surfaces stood for the mind itself. Of special interest to this chapter is his assemblage *Interview*, which displays an elaborate association of imagery and myriad subdivisions and compartments to render the complexity of conversation.

From a different perspective, the Black Mountain poet Charles Olson also contributed to formation of voice collages. In *The Maximus Poems*,[31] collage and first-person quotes are used to compose his mytho-historical city of Gloucester. Combining Whitman's attention to the ordinary and an allegorical understanding of the commonplace, Olson opens the events of this New England city to cosmological metaphors. The space of the poem becomes the chthonic stage where a variety of present times may coexist. In "Letter, May 2, 1959,"[32] the Englishmen setting sail to Gloucester in the seventeenth century are contemporaneous with seafaring Greeks in the time of Ramses II. Elsewhere in the *Maximus Poems*, Olson pores over particulars of New England historical documents, conjoining ship logs with Pilgrim diaries, to assemble the mythic construction of Gloucester as Columbia. Although Olson's *interscript* is exposed to criticism of being wildly conjectural, the influence of his inclusive mode of knowing, fostered by his open epistemology, cannot be overstated. Paul Metcalf, a student of Olson at the Black Mountain College, went on to develop the collage history style in works like *The Island, Waters of Potowmack*, and *Willie's Throw*,[33] a multi-voice composition of one of baseball's most memorable moments. By writing historical and ethnographic documentaries in the form of poems, he relates how diverse narratives intertwine in the construction of both history and our own subjectivity.

In the manner that photography effected the art of painting, the tape recorder revolutionized the art of writing. Writers like Bernadette Mayer[34] and William Burroughs[35] employed recording machines to explore the nature of memory and collected consciousness. The street photographer Robert Frank, eminently aware of the camera's ability to capture interacting forces producing a picture, experimented as well with a tape recorder and typewriter to capture and reproduce the assembly of sounds making up our lived environment. In a space of one hour on July 26, 1990, he recorded twenty-seven voices between 3:45 and 4:45 p.m. He then transcribed the voices in his book *One Hour*.[36] With acute attention to the ordinary, Frank is able to transform the pedestrian into the poetic. The consciousness recorded belongs to none of his participants, but it is an energy traveling through each. Frank allows this energy to flow unbridled by narration or summation. He focuses and frames the event, but like his photography, he lets the contrasts and differences develop.

Transcribing speech historicizes a language event. Oral interviews, aside from their value in contributing to a people's history, display the pattern of thinking through memories, through events and communities. Beyond the creation of authentic individual records, speech documents are descriptive of neighborhoods and occupations through the special way people use language. The formal or casual tones one uses to describe events are indicative of societal structures. Every phrase is a language event relating the history of the verbal gesture, conveying identity configurations, style, clan, community, and culture. When we speak, the words we use are inherited from the vast reserves of time and cultural interplay. The language world we live in is built by the slow culmination of choices. It is our social inheritance. The everyday construction of language events, in the bricolage of words, clichés, and semantic units, mirrors the construction of consciousness and community identity. In oral testimony each gesture in combination with others relates a specific descriptiveness unrivaled by other means of cultural transmission in their ability to conjure explanation through practice. It is the perspective told from being in the world. This is what draws the practitioners of oral history to first-person accounts, its uniqueness and its thoroughness. They begin to appreciate oral history for its maximalist tendencies, the inclusiveness it affords the social environment. Emile Durkheim saw language as the gateway to the "group mind."[37] He was not referring to a collective unconscious, but rather a conceptual entity (i.e. society), to which people contribute, and from which people are effected. Orality and found signs are not only indicative of the contours of this social environment, but also the plenum in which our identities are shaped, understood, and articulated.

By placing voices in the documentary poem, the poet evokes both the speaker and the speech situation. For a moment the speaker enters the poem. For a moment the poet sublimates his or her authority to the speaker. I say for a moment, because in the voice collage each speaker does not completely enter the poem, they are only participating in the artist's picture of their world. The voices are excised from longer quotations, longer quotations that are themselves cut from more complete memories, memories excised and assembled from the cloth of living. The voices are instead conscripted by the poet so that they might re-enact the enduring qualities which so captured the poet's intimacy.

In visual collage the artist develops an intimacy with the texture he or she includes. These fragments hold meaning in two realms. The ticket pasted to a collage by Kurt Schwitters, a letter in a Joseph Cornell memory box, or even a select piece of fabric sewn into a quilt synecdochically present the greater world to the world of the artwork. Such artifacts are mnemonic inserts linking the poem to lived experience. They are metaphorical bridges. The oral clips gesture towards the speaker. The speaker leaves footprints while walking through the poem. The collage opens art to the common stuff of daily life,[38] providing a stage on which the voices of history may interact.

Robert Kroetsch in his book, *Completed Fieldnotes*,[39] has a poem entitled "The Ledger" which serves to catch the documents of everyday life. Kroetsch's "Ledger" serves as a ledger, a place where accounts are inscribed. Here financial statements and calculations regarding the provisions purchased by his Canadian farming family sit side by side with observer accounts, eyewitness statements, and calculations about the nature of writing, heritage, and history (see Box 6.1).

When Kroetsch assembles a dialog with his past, he, like Benjamin, constructs an archaeological site. This is his way of writing his autobiography.[40] Words foreign to the poet are appropriated to become his own. The poet reacts to what was said, and what was done. The phrases become soaked in contemplation. The artifacts,

Box 6.1 Robert Kroetsch, "The Ledger"

---

page 119: John O. Miller, brickmaker in Mildmay

1888

Aug 17: two cedar shingles	12.50	Aug 17: by Brick 2500	
		at 50 cents	12.50

(I'll be damned. It balances.)

yes:no
no:yes

"a specimen of the self-made men who have made Canada what it is, and of which no section has brought forth more or better representatives than the county of Bruce. Mr. Miller was never an office seeker, but devoted himself strictly and energetically to the pursuit of his private business, and on his death was the owner of a very large and valuable property"

shaping the trees
pushing up daisies.

Have another glass, John.
Ja, ja. What the hell.

What's the matter, John?
My bones ache.

Take a day off, John.
No time.

A horizontal piece of timber
supporting the putlogs
in a scaffolding, or the like.

---

like ethnographic objects develop deep layers of meaning. In our own intimate relations this is borne out. What did she mean by so and so? What was he referring to? When my father said . . . what was this allusion to? In French there is a term for this afterthought, *l'esprit de l'escalier*, the spirit of the stairs. It refers to the lingering effects of the voice, how words are replayed in the minds of recipients, and how the haunting nature of meaning plays on a phrase. In poetry the reader controls the timing of the document. Every pattern of feeling or thought can develop its own texture. The voice montages become thicker. The textures collide and blend within the drama of juxtaposition.

Box 6.2 William Sylvester, "Wildlife Exhibit: Family Approved"

Our beds had ropes. Dad made the beds. He drilled
holes along
the sides and ends; then he'd pull a rope through a hole
run the rope
across the bedstead to the other side until
all the holes
got used up. He'd draw them up when the
ropes got saggy.
That was a better bed than most people had.
We had a mule
Could single foot trot pace and run she weighed about
eleven hundred
pounds like sitting in a rocking chair. I slept in
all kinds of beds.
Some were hard and some were soft.
I'm a concrete worker.

      He said, "Statues? Then you mean
      Greek
      Statues." I said, "What about the Egyptians?"
      He said: "We move to the Renaissance."
      I said:
      "How about Jackson Pollock?" He said,
      "My child
      Does better than that." I said, "You're so
      middle class."

And now
I'll tell you how all that hickory stick
stuff started
and what it meant to us kids in those days.

William Sylvester illustrates how a poem may become just such a dramatic exhibition. Aptly titled "Wildlife Exhibit: Family Approved,"[41] it is arranged by the author from oral testimony culled from the State Historical Societies of Nebraska, Wyoming, and Idaho. Inserted also are some of his own words (see Box 6.2).

The poetics of this juxtaposition are tools the poet uses to explore and communicate the social. In an essay concerning Richard Kroetsch's work, Manina Jones relates Shirley Neuman's insights.[42] Neuman refers to the effect of borrowing, and juxtaposing quotes in *Completed Fieldnotes*, as the creation of the intertext. The "intertext," she explains, "is the space shared by, the relations between, different poetic texts in the frame of the larger 'Collected Poem.'" The "poem" exists in the lacunae and intersections between the different texts it holds in its space. She uses the term "intertext" where I would substitute *interscript*, due to the implication of action in the latter. In either case, juxtaposition is used to bring out contrast, and inform the elements of the poem through conflict and augmentation.

The voice collage poem allows for the multivalent understanding of ourselves and events. It fosters a hermeneutic reading of phenomena, where multiple subjectivities jostle to determine reality. In his poem, "I-57,"[43] Paul Metcalf explained,

> The voices are heard in my head, though often in the air, or in different parts of the room, each different, speaking or singing in different tone and measure . . . my thoughts flowing regularly from left to right, guided by these voices.[44]

While at first glance, a man guided by inner conversations may seem to have a severe personality disorder, in actuality this statement displays an acute awareness and cogent depiction of the socially constructed self. "The mental process . . . has evolved in the social process in which it is a part. And it belongs to the different organisms that lie inside of this larger social process."[45] Consciousness is not to be regarded as a static substance. William James likened consciousness to a

> bird that alights on one branch and then flies to another, continually moving from one point to another point. The transitive phases of experience are those answering to relations; the substantive phases are those that answer to what we call the things we perceive.[46]

The voice collage poet flies from participant to participant utilizing their perceptions to gain a multiple perspectives on events.

For the Oral History Association annual meeting in Buffalo, New York, in the autumn of 1998, I read a poem built of quotations from Studs Terkel's oral history classic, *Working*.[47] The construct is largely excerpted from Terkel's chapter, "Making It," and is called "Making It (Up)" (see Box 6.3).[48] I wished to illustrate how oral history collages might be composed to produce new understanding of the data collected, one closer to agit-cinema, than individual narratives.

The voices in this presentation blur to create a singular phrenotropic environment. The aim was not to access the subconscious, but to develop a multiple consciousness. By stretching and highlighting particular parts of the evidence Terkel collected, the poem attempts, in the manner of scientific computer simulations, to display events from alternative points of perception.

In Charles Reznikoff's book, *Holocaust*,[49] excerpts of testimony are taken from the Nuremberg trial and the Eichmann trial in Jerusalem. Here the evidence compounds. The *interscript* relays the force of the successive waves of evidence. The voices of several eyewitnesses are more effective in relating trauma and crimes than a single narrator. Kamau Brathwaite utilizes the voice collage poem in *Trench Town Rock* to display corroborating tales of a police assault.[50] Likewise, Juliana Spahr shows how multiple accounts can build credence and sympathetic understanding in her book *Response*.[51]

Box 6.3 David Michalski, "Making It (Up): A Collage Poem from Studs Terkel's *Working*"

If you're in the business
you're in the fucking business!

> Actually, my career choice in advertising.
> which I drifted into
> is connected with the fantasy of power

You're a hustler, but because you're witty and glib.

> but the limits are very frustrating.
> I feel I want to do more.
> but I feel restraints within the system and myself.

I'm gambling, I'm gambling on a person's outside.
I know nothing about their character.
I gamble on what other people have told me.

> I try to ignite symbols in your head so we can
> come to a point of agreement on language.

> I have an active fantasy life.
> – not during the work day because it's coming at me
> so fast.

I know it's part of my job, I do it.
If I made the big stand my friend made
I'd lose my job. Can't do it.

> Many of my fantasies
> have to do with control in society.
> Very elaborate technological-type fantasies:
> a benign totalitarianism controlled by me.

I'm expected to write whatever assignment I'm given.

> I needed a job
> I saw this ad in the paper:
> Equal Opportunity. Salary plus commission.

> The way, you see, is by being very confident
> Advertising is full of very confident people.

I called and spoke ever so nicely.
The gentleman was pleased
with the tone of my voice

> Coming into a meeting is a little like
> swimming in a river full of piranha fish.

and I went down for the interview
My mind raced as I was on the train coming down.

In an ethnographic collage I assembled from interviews with workers at the World Trade Center in New York,[52] the *interscript* speaks to the multiple perspectives employees have of their purpose and experience. In one section, I run two contradictory interviews in parallel vertical columns down the page. One is an interview with a New York born African American broker, who tells stories of the racial environment of his firm. The other is an interview with a Senegalese worker who relates stories about the relative equality in opportunity available in New York. The graphic display I use forces the reader to simultaneously process both accounts. Each voice becomes the other's footnote, amending truths through contradiction. The interviews depicted in this manner do not cancel each other. Instead a fuller and deeper picture comes into play.

In each of these cases, poets utilize the grammar of exhibitions to displace and display voices in poems. The aim of each is to communicate what cannot be said through single narrators. The poets try to formulate a picture of a collected consciousness, a fiction bent on developing a picture from multiple perspectives. The result is a situational totality, a concrescence of experience.

The value of the voice collage rests on this perilous foundation. For the imaginary conversation to work it must construct from its parts an intelligible representation of culture. It must provide a view of the process of history or the making of culture. If this fiction disappears from the poems, they will disintegrate, becoming in the words of Douglas Crimp,

> a heap of meaningless and valueless fragments of objects which are incapable of substituting themselves either metonymically for the original objects or metaphorically for their representations.[53]

In each case the artist risks misrepresenting individuals in the name of poly-optical displays. These assemblages are never wholly representative of individuals but are instead works of interpretation. Like the fable of five blind men explaining an elephant, the voice collage poet creates the useful fiction of pan-subjectivity to interpret events and scenes.

To temper the necessary inaccuracies in representation which occur in collage, poets frequently employ methodological footnotes which shed light on their process of selection and assembly. New methods of referencing, through the use of graphic design and hypertext programming have brought new opportunities to the poet. Such creative, nonobstructive references add weight to poems by tying the collage more tightly to the world.

Some advocates of voice collage also work to prepare the reader for what they are receiving. By displaying theory, methodology, and motive, in the composition, the voice collage poet can generate a more empathetic treatment of their work. Juliana Spahr's *Response*, and the work of the poet and documentarian Mark Nowak, deal directly with the predicament of representation.[54] Elements of reflexivity and power relations are included in their assemblages to question how truth is manufactured. Nowak inserts snippets addressing the problems of relativity and objectivity

Box 6.4 Mark Nowak, "Zywczaj"

"As a result, the task of
the ethnographer
truth . . ."

". . . at that time they thought
butter was no good
        so we started frying 'em
in margarine."

". . . but to reveal the multiple truths
apparent in others lives."

"Talking to Mrs. Nogas,
"it becomes clear that being
"a meat packer
        "and Assistant Pastor's mother
"are not mutually exclusive activities."

". . . the ethnographer's presence
in a setting
inevitably has implications
for what is taking place."
        "A lot of people
don't like don't put onions in theirs,
and we put onions in ours.

        "there are discussions
"and opinions
"on everything

"from current fashions
"to unions."

That's the way we are used to 'em
but you know we like onions anyway."

within his display of field notes. The inclusion of quotes concerning ethnographic
praxis and the collection process opens the composition itself to debate. In doing
so, Nowak's voice collage becomes less of a closed summation of lives and more of
an expository document (see Box 6.4).[55]

The art critic, Donald Kuspit, contends the completeness of a collage is
illusionary,

> The concrescence is in effect, never finished . . . This is the poetry of
> becoming – the poetry of relativity – and it is what collage is all about:

the tentativeness of every unity of being because of the persistence of becoming, even when absoluteness seems achieved.[56]

In today's cultural systems collage has become omnipresent, jolted and embraced by the new media and technologies. This is why it is crucial that the poetics of assembly be reviewed. In my research I found the use of oral history in poetry to be a rare, but persistent form of inquiry, occupying a space between the boundaries of history and fiction, existing in the crevices between journalism and art, and most often being employed in the writings of a fickle avant-garde. The voice collage however holds tremendous potential as a tool for teaching us how to think not only as the other but as many others. The voice collage challenges us to develop a multivalent understanding of our lives.

In the recent installations by new assemblage artists such as Jason Rhodes, Karsten Bott, and Gregory Green, one can feel a mounting anxiety and powerlessness in the face of overburdened archives crammed with a seemingly endless variety of objects and perspectives. Karsten Bott's *One of Each*,[57] a vast collage installed at the P.S. 1 Contemporary Art Center in New York in 1998, duplicates the uneasiness about the future felt by one staring into an attic bursting with objects accumulated over thirty years of living. The weight of history is made literally unbearable as everyday artifacts crowd the floor. One gets the sense that there is too much stuff, too many variables, too many separate stories vying for our singular attention. The work is indicative of our plight as we fully engage the information age. No longer is it possible, in light of our awakening to a multicultural world, comprising thousands of cultures and billions of people, to reduce our differences, our history, or our futures to convenient scenarios. No longer is it possible to collapse and ignore what we already know through our increased perception. We must find a way to split our attention. By recognizing the multivalent and eccentric nature of our own consciousness we may be able to affirm multiple truths and think beyond contradictions. In the carefully executed voice collage one can begin to grasp the multiple nature of our universe as an *interscript* of many verses. It is a challenge formulated most beautifully by Marcel Proust in *A la recherche du temps perdu*:

> The real voyage of discovery . . .
> consists not in seeking new landscapes,
> but in having new eyes,
> in seeing the universe with the eyes of another,
> of a hundred others,
> in seeing the hundred universes that each of them sees.[58]

Notes

1 Colin Westbeck and Joel Meyerowitz, *Bystander: A History of Street Photography* (Boston, MA: Little Brown, 1994), 2.
2 Ibid., 34.

3 Elisabeth Sussman (ed.), *On the Passage of a Few People through a Rather Brief Moment in Time: The Situationist International 1957–1972* (Cambridge, MA: MIT Press, 1989).

4 Taro Amano, "The Doubleness of Character or the Doubleness of Photography," *Parkett* 34 (1998/99): 134.

5 Georg Simmel, *The Sociology of Georg Simmel* (New York: Free Press, 1950), 402.

6 Michel de Certeau, *The Practice of Everyday Life* (Berkeley, CA: University of California Press, 1984), xviii.

7 John Coulter, "Cognition: 'Cognition' in an Ethnomethodological Mode," in *Ethnomethodology and the Human Sciences*, ed. Graham Button (Cambridge: Cambridge University Press, 1991), 187–188.

8 Henri Bergson, *Matter and Memory* (New York: Zone, 1991), 179.

9 Robert Ezra Park, "Natural History of the Newspaper," *American Journal of Sociology* 29 (1923): 80.

10 Ibid.: 83.

11 See Susan Buck-Morss, *The Dialectics of Seeing: Walter Benjamin and the Arcades Project* (Cambridge, MA: MIT Press, 1989). The *Passagen-Werk* was never completed nor fully assembled. Susan Buck-Morss's exposition of the material contained in Benjamin's files and notes is the most comprehensive available in a single volume and makes an excellent launching point into a work which Benjamin characterized as Copernican.

12 Ibid., 71–77.

13 Michael P. Steinberg, "The Collector as Allegorist: Goods, Gods, and the Objects of History," in *Walter Benjamin and the Demands of History*, ed. Michael P. Steinberg (Ithaca, NY: Cornell University Press, 1996), 91.

14 Walter Benjamin, *Selected Writings Volume 2: 1927–1934* (Cambridge, MA: Harvard University Press, 1999), 741.

15 Ibid.

16 Buck-Morss, *Dialectics of Seeing*, 73. Buck-Morss is quoting a letter from Adorno to Horkheimer from May 1949.

17 Ibid., 220.

18 Steinberg, "Collector as Allegorist," 91.

19 Eiland Howard and Kevin McLaughlin, "Translator's Foreword," in Walter Benjamin, *The Arcades Project* (Cambridge, MA: Harvard University Press, 1999), ix.

20 Steinberg, "Collector as Allegorist," 92.

21 William Seitz, *Assemblage* (New York: Modern Museum of Art, 1959), 1.

22 M. Berns, *Dear Robert, I'll See You at the Crossroads: A Project by Renée Stout* (Santa Barbara, CA: University Art Museum, University of California, Santa Barbara, 1995).

23 F.T. Marinetti quoted in Robin Lydenburg, "Engendering Collage: Collaboration and Desire in Dada and Surrealism," in *Collage: Critical Views*, ed. Katherine Hoffman (Ann Arbor, MI: UMI Research Press, 1988), 273.

24 S. I. Lockerbie, "Introduction," in Guillaume Apollinaire, *Calligrammes: Poems of Peace and War (1913–1916)* (Berkeley, CA: University of California Press, 1980), 5.

25 Guillaume Apollinaire, *Alcools et Calligrames* (Paris: Imprimerie Nationale Editions, 1991), 198. Translated from the French by the author.

26 Lockerbie, "Introduction," 4.

27 Rosalind Krauss, "Perpetual Inventory," in *Robert Rauschenberg: A Retrospective*, Walter Hopps and Susan Davidson, curators (New York: Harry N. Abrams, 1997), 214.

28 Ibid., 218.

29 Ibid., 220.

30 Ibid.

31 Charles Olson, *The Maximus Poems* (New York: Jargon/Corinth, 1960).

32 Ibid., 145.

33 See Paul Metcalf, *Paul Metcalf: Collected Works*, vols 1–3 (Minneapolis, MN: Coffee House, 1997).

34 Bernadette Mayer, *Memory* (Plainfield, VT: North Atlantic, 1975).

35 William S. Burroughs, *The Ticket that Exploded* (New York: Grove Press, 1967).

36 Robert Frank, *One Hour* (New York: Hanuman, 1992).

37 John Lee, "Language and Culture: The Linguistic Analysis of Culture," in *Ethnomethodology and the Human Sciences*, 199.

38 Harold Rosenberg, "Collage: Philosophy of Put Togethers," in *Collage: Critical Views* 6.

39 Robert Kroetsch, *Completed Fieldnotes* (Toronto: McClelland and Steward, 1998), 15.

40 Shirley Neuman and Robert Wilson, *Labyrinths of Voice: Conversations with Robert Kroetsch*, Volume 3, Western Canadian Documents Series (Edmonton, Alta: NeWest Press, 1982), 206.

41 William Sylvester, "Wildlife Exhibit: Family Approved, a Collage from the Oral History Collections, State Historical Societies of Nebraska, Wyoming, and Idaho Arranged by William Sylvester with Some Words of his Own" (self-published, December 1978). Accessed via the Poetry and Rare Books Collection at the State University of New York at Buffalo.

42 Manina Jones, *That Art of Difference: "Documentary-Collage" and English-Canadian Writing* (Toronto: University of Toronto Press, 1988), 52.

43 Paul Metcalf, "I-57," in *Paul Metcalf: Collected Works, Volume Two, 1976–1986* (Minneapolis, MN: Coffee House, 1997).

44 Ibid., 5.

45 George Herbert Mead, *Movements of Thought in the Nineteeth Century* (Chicago: University of Chicago Press, 1936), 381.

46 Ibid., 387.

47 Studs Terkel, *Working: People Talk about What They Do All Day and How They Feel about What They Do* (New York: Pantheon, 1974).

48 David Michalski, "Making It (Up): A Collage Poem from Studs Terkel's *Working*," an experimental poem written for the Oral History Association annual meeting in Buffalo, New York, October 1998. This poem consists of five voices cut from Studs Terkel's *Working*. Each voice is differentiated from the others by its placement within a vertical column. From left to right their names, occupations, and the page from which they were excised are: (1) Barbara Herrick, Advertising Writer/Producer, p. 66. (2) Richard Mann, Installment Dealer, p. 88. (3) Enid Du Bois, Telephone Solicitor, p. 94. (4) Jack Hunter, Professor of Communications, p. 39. (5) John Fortune, Copy Chief, p. 73.

49 Charles Reznikoff, *Holocaust* (Los Angeles: Black Sparrow Press, 1975).

50 Kamau Brathwaite, *Trench Town Rock* (Providence, RI: Lost Roads, 1994).

51 Juliana Spahr, *Response* (Los Angeles: Sun & Moon Press, 1996).

52 David Michalski, *Alleged Metropole* (unpublished manuscript, 1999), 64.

53 Douglas Crimp, *On the Museum's Ruins* (Cambridge, MA: MIT Press, 1993), 53.

54 See James Clifford and George Marcus, *Writing Culture* (Berkeley, CA: University of California, 1986).

55 Mark A. Nowak, "Zwyczaj," *American Anthropologist* 100 (1998), 271–274. Regarding his source elements Nowak provides this note at the end of his poem, "Note: Boldface quotations in *Zwyczaj* are taken from transcriptions of ethnographic interviews conducted by the author with Ellen Nowak in May, 1995. All non-boldface quotes are taken from one of two sources: Elizabeth Goldstein and Gail Green's 'Pierogi and Babka-Making at St. Mary's' [*New York Folklore* 4 (1978): 71–79]; or a section on 'Ethnographic Participation,' in *Writing Ethnographic Fieldnotes* [eds.] Robert M. Emerson, Rachel I. Fretz, and Linda L. Shaw (Chicago: University of Chicago Press, 1995)."

56 Donald Kuspit, "Collage: The Organizing Principle in Art in the Age of the Relativity of Art," in *Relativism in the Arts*, ed. Betty Craig (Athens, GA: University of Georgia Press, 1983), 127.

57 See Ingrid Schaffner and Matthias Winzen (eds.), *Deep Storage: Collecting, Storing, and Archiving in Art* (New York: Prestel, 1998), 83.

58 Marcel Proust, *A la recherche du temps perdu: La prisonière* (Paris: Flammarion, 1984), 360. Translation by the author.

7

EROS IN THE STUDIO

Paul J. Karlstrom

What can one say about artists and models without resorting to a series of clichés? A great deal, as it turns out. When my friend Sam Clayberger invited me to write an introductory essay for a portfolio devoted to his erotic drawings, I was both pleased and puzzled. Pleased because I know how central the nude female figure is to Sam's work and to his ideas about life as well as about art. I was flattered that he seemed to think I understood him well enough to place the drawings within the context of his studio practice and his relationship to his models. The puzzling aspect had to do with the fact that I could recall few of his works that I would characterize as unequivocally erotic. In their generalized, linear simplicity, the drawings seemed to me to lack the potential for sexual arousal that would seem a prerequisite of erotica. Nonetheless, I accepted the assignment with pleasure, although with a measure of trepidation. When I began, I was scarcely aware of the implications of the study and the complicated layers of human experience, and individual motivation, that awaited me just beneath the surface of this deceptively simple story set in an artist's studio.[1]

My wife, Ann, and I have known Sam and his wife, Pat, since the mid-1960s, when we were in our early twenties and they were in their late thirties. Ann was among those young women, all non-professionals, who have been flattered by Sam's invitation to pose and agreed to do something they had never done before and probably had never imagined they would: remove their clothes and stand (or sit or lie) completely naked before a man they barely knew as he examined their bodies for extended periods of time and from various angles. The intimacy of the studio situation was underscored by the fact that they were generally alone (Sam seldom allows an observer in these private sessions), the two of them involved in a shared enterprise. In contemporary terminology his models willingly submitted to the "male gaze," allowing themselves to be objects of the artist's desire.

So, my own friendship with the artist really began when Ann stepped into the private world of the Mt. Washington studio and he closed the door behind them, offering her a cup of coffee, a kimono, and some reassuring conversation before asking her to remove all of her clothing so they could get down to the work at hand. That was the beginning of a long social relationship that had at its center her visits to his various studios, either for private posing or eventually for the small workshops

Figure 7.1 Paul J. Karlstrom, "Artist Sam Clayberger and model Ann Karlstrom," 1999.
Photo: the author.

he conducted. She obviously enjoyed the "work" enough to return again and again
over a period of almost eight years, with two nostalgic sessions during the 1990s –
the most recently in the summer of 1999 at age 55 (Figure 7.1). Posing had become
an activity that contributed positively to her mature self-conception and personal
identity.

As a cultural historian interested in art and in human behavior, I looked forward
to this project as an opportunity to examine and understand the nature of the studio
dynamic involving (male) artists and (female) models, using this one situation as
the basis for the study. What interested me most is just how the women involved
view this "collaboration," how they respond to the underplayed but nonetheless
inevitable eroticism present in the encounter. However, my task is complicated –
and here is where the "trepidation" comes in – by my own personal experience of
Sam's studio and the fact that my wife was one of his favorite models. What might
I learn about their relationship within the protected studio realm in which they play
separate but complementary parts? To what extent did his "seduction" (my wife's
term) and her response figure in their interaction over almost a decade of posing?
And how do I keep my own considerable interest and speculative curiosity in
the background, allowing the story to unfold from the accounts of those actually
involved: the artist and his models? To that end I focused my attention on five
models, three of whom I knew personally (subsequently I met a fourth, Kelly), and
their recollections of posing for Sam. This was accomplished in the form of a fairly
elaborate, and pointed, model questionnaire. Sam was then interviewed about each
of them, before and after reading their responses. Although not scientific in terms

of the sample, this approach amplifies our understanding of the theme by giving the typically silent participant, the model, her voice. How erotic did *they* find the studio experience? And what do they think of their contribution to works that the artist sees as sexually provocative and therefore categorizes as part of his own erotica?

Art supposedly transforms a frankly sexual situation, at least in its potential, into a creative interaction in which the sexual is presumably neutralized. Artist and model are partners in this elevated activity. Whatever natural attraction or fantasies are present are sublimated or ignored, deemed inappropriate for the serious business of art making. Indeed, the models with whom I have spoken almost invariably use the term "muse" to describe their role and the primary reason for posing. The women discussed in Sam's essay, all amateurs, required this protective and idealistic concept to first step over the studio threshold. Nonetheless, virtually all of them end up participating in what I describe as the studio *dance*, a series of steps involving physical placement and psychological negotiations in which inhibitions and modesty are progressively discarded leading to a very specific intimacy between artist and model. In most cases this grows from a relationship of trust, the reassurance that the artist will not transgress by violating the vulnerability of her nudity. And in many cases, the liberating nature of this experience and newly discovered confidence in her body – a sense of her erotic self – can lead to a conscious display of a repressed sensuality and sexual self-awareness. At these moments, both partners willingly join the sexual metaphor of the dance of the studio, and the seduction implied by such a ritual.

The models

Participating in the model survey were five models, including three amateurs who posed in the late 1960s and early 1970s. Each of these was in her early twenties, married, and from relatively conservative backgrounds. Two were products of fairly religious Protestant families. All would be described as essentially conventional young women with middle-class values and goals. They had no experience as artist models and probably had never been entirely undressed in the presence of a man other than their husbands, or perhaps (they were after all products of the 1950s) a boyfriend or two. Each, to some degree, associated nudity with liberal sexual views and, perhaps above all, personal freedom in the sense of bohemian behavior. And, without actively seeking a sexual encounter, each was interested in testing their attractiveness and in some cases exploring their powers to arouse. The differences appeared in how they did so and in how they responded to Sam's attentions. Ann, Anita, and Sandi – and two more recent models, Kristina and Kelly – wrote thoughtful and candid answers to the survey questions and generously agreed to be quoted in those cases where their experiences might illuminate the theme of this chapter. Here are their stories.

Ann Karlstrom was 22 when Sam asked her to pose. A 1965 Stanford University graduate, she was out of college less than a year, recently married and working as an escrow officer trainee at Lytton Savings and Loan. Her company was located across the street from Jay Ward where Sam worked as an animator in addition to teaching at Otis Art Institute. Artist and model met at the Lytton Center for the Visual Arts, one of the first corporate exhibition spaces, where Sam was helping to install an exhibition. Ann remembers that she was flattered and, after discussing the proposal briefly with me, agreed: "I liked Sam; and I was curious about the experience. I assumed Sam liked painting pretty young women and he seemed to like me." So, it would appear that from the beginning there was the understanding of a physical attraction. Ann's recognition of Sam's affection for her, that he felt she was special and sexually attractive, emerges throughout her survey responses:

> There were no issues that had to be resolved. I knew he had an affection for me (and I'm sure he knew I liked him as well) – and he showed it a couple of times, but not in any way that made me uneasy or made me feel something else was expected of me.

Ann initially declined to specify the way in which Sam's affection for her was expressed in the studio, so it left open what physical contact may have been involved (see p. 152, note 5). But the important point is that, throughout the years of posing for him, Sam made this model – and presumably most of the others – feel relaxed and comfortable, with their solitary nudity, in his highly appreciative presence. Such was not the case with at least a few models, one of whom we will hear from in a moment.

When asked about the first session, Ann had difficulty in recalling her feelings of anticipation, other than that she was a little nervous. She doesn't remember "any more erotic energy generated than would be expected when you have a nude woman in a room with a heterosexual man," adding that she was "probably too self-conscious to fully appreciate the situation." However, some years later, she realized that in some of these sessions Sam was encouraging poses of a more directly sexual nature. She continued to be available for posing, presumably accepting that interest and objective as a part of the experience. According to Ann,

> I sensed Sam enjoyed looking at women's bodies. I'm vain enough to enjoy the attention. I figure if a man asks you to pose in the nude, you are automatically an object of desire. But I never felt that the *main* issue was sexual. And I liked the idea of being part of something created that might be good as art.

As for the critical "open" pose, Ann does not recall such being specifically requested. But she acknowledges that there were "subtle suggestions that led to some because he gave me two drawings that are of slightly open poses." Ann also does not remark on what assuming those poses may say about her response to what she recognized as his sexual desire for her. So, it appears that, for Ann, Eros in the studio was acceptable as long as it did not need to be acknowledged. If she happened to naturally fall into an open pose, something she came to understand as Sam's erotic objective, she no doubt felt exempted from complicity. Somehow it simply *happened* to her. Ann appears to have been a mistress of "spin," turning the situation into that which made her comfortable while allowing her to indulge her vanity and "innocently" participate in the exhibitionistic eroticism of the studio dance.

Other models, among them Anita and Kristina, were more forthcoming in their descriptions of the dance. Both seemed to have understood immediately what Sam sought and how their separate fantasies and desires could be simultaneously realized by a collaborative response. **Anne (Anita) Nickerson** was introduced to Sam's studio by her friend Ann. She acknowledges that she was interested in expanding her experience, deeply aware of a world of sensation from which she had been excluded. Another recent Stanford graduate, she too was recently married shortly after graduation and was living in the Los Angeles area. The two young women and their husbands spent occasional evenings together. Intrigued by her friend's no doubt slightly boastful account of her exciting bohemian nude modeling experience (and perhaps my accounts of the studio), Anita asked if the artist – Sam – would like to draw her. Sam remembers that Ann told him that Anita wanted to pose, but that she was very proper and probably would not make a good model. Nothing could have been further from the mark. Sam fondly recalls Anita as among the most abandoned and exhibitionistic of all his models, adopting fully open poses with absolutely no encouragement or direction.

In her survey responses Anita describes the studio experience for her as an exciting journey of self-discovery and adventure. Her awareness of and attention to the issue of "self" betray her present professional concerns as a psychotherapist. In fact she now believes that an important factor in her response to the studio experience, including dealing with the sexual aspects and initial apprehension about body matters, was – as she wrote – "a too-great capacity to separate my 'self' from my body." She remembers the specific moment she recognized that she was, for Sam, an object of desire. After describing a silent but nonetheless unambiguous overture during an open pose, she recounts that he returned to painting and, in her words, "I probably separated my 'self' from my body a bit more." This capacity would surely explain her ability, from the beginning, to adopt extremely revealing poses, almost as if the body displayed belonged to somebody else. Despite being aware of Sam's attraction to her as a woman, Anita appears to have felt very comfortable with him in the studio, enjoying their interaction. She recalls that even after the described incident he was very gentle and "polite," accepting her limits in a way that created an environment of trust that made possible what she remembers as a "relationship of equals" involved in a "mutual endeavor." Although recognizing that some poses were more erotic than others, she seems to have made little distinction between them: "My sense was that Sam and I were mutually determining the poses, with me slowly moving and very slowly changing part of the positions until Sam thought the pose was just right."

The excitement of creative collaboration and the belief that she "inspired Sam to paint" appear to have become, certainly as viewed through the lens of memory,

Anita's main motivation and chief source of pleasure from the posing sessions. She recalls that

> Sam's attention was enjoyable . . . [He] told me, and I had no reason to doubt him, that he had been able to accomplish more in a given time frame with me than with previous models, rather as if I induced a little "painterly frenzy" in him.

The erotic charge in that remark should not go unnoticed for it points to another channel for the energy that Sam was seeking to stimulate in his studio.

The models' desire to please, to be successful in their task, must never be discounted. In fact it may explain the reason even reluctant models may eventually open up in response to Sam's encouragement to "relax." His interests and objectives in this regard generally became clear, and refusal to cooperate may – for some models – have seemed unattractively prudish, something to be overcome in the bohemian art spirit of the studio. After all, one's perspective could change quite dramatically in such circumstances, voluntarily standing naked before a clothed man whose job it was to arrange you in the most interesting configurations the two of you could come up with. And some of these poses could unavoidably be seen as sexually provocative. This dynamic no doubt explains Ann's partly open poses. In contrast, Anita seemed to naturally relish the heady sense of liberation her enthusiastic displays of self (for her, in the very beginning, the body, not the *true* self) afforded her. She reports that this collaboration began with two sessions with Ann and continued solo for about six months afterwards. She acknowledges that "my first thoughts were that it was my body that inspired Sam. I now believe that it was my self that provided the inspiration, of which my body is one part." Reflecting upon her own motives and interests within the framework of Sam's studio, she recognizes that, as she became more comfortable with the situation, awareness of her own sexuality developed and evolved, leading her to increasingly explicit poses.

Describing her reasons for posing, and that one experience involving two women, she writes,

> I'm sure my reasons for posing were only partly known at the time. The simplest answer is "ego," both in the common sense of pride and focusing on oneself and the more profound sense of *integration of self* [my emphasis]. Add some thrill into the mix! Add some exploration of self and boundaries, too. When I look at the photograph of myself sitting on the floor with Ann in the chair behind, I have a powerful tactile sensation, as if I'm inside that young figure pressing outward with my hands toward the outer skin of her body, feeling in every direction to know where her form ends and "I" begin.

The pose itself (Figure 7.2), the basis for an elaborate watercolor, was in fact subtle in its eroticism. But it was perhaps all the more potent for that subtlety (Figure 7.3).

Figure 7.2 Paul J. Karlstrom, "Models Ann Karlstrom and Anita Nickerson in Sam Clayberger's studio," *c.*1969. Photo: the author.

Figure 7.3 Sam Clayberger, *Two Seated Models (Ann and Anita)*, *c.*1969, watercolor on paper, 22 × 28 inches (sight). Collection of the author. Photo: the author.

Sam suggested that the two friends create a composition in and around the studio easy chair. Ann sat down with Anita, at Sam's suggestion, seated on the floor in front of her. He asked Ann to spread her legs so her partner could nestle closer. Ann did so and Anita, her legs widely spread as well, leaned back towards her friend's crotch. Sam then instructed Anita to put her arm on Ann's thigh, bringing them into further contact. Anita's medium-length dark hair touched her shoulder exactly at the level of Ann's equally dark pubis, providing textural, coloristic, compositional, and metaphorical correspondences that vitiated a complex and compositionally effective image.

The drawings and painting of **Kristina Faragher** were done twenty years later. She came of age in the late 1970s, and her understanding of herself as a woman was shaped by the resurgence of feminism that accompanied and critiqued the sexual revolutions of the 1960s. She is an artist, currently enrolled in the prestigious graduate program at Claremont College, and therefore more involved from the beginning in the world of artists and models. Her survey answers suggest a sexual worldview of a different generation. And they suggest that she welcomed the erotic energy provided by Sam's studio. In fact, Sam described in a taped recent interview that Kristina is the model with whom he was at the highest risk of having an actual love affair. But apparently they both survived temptation while continuing to appreciate and enjoy the life-enriching experience of the eroticized studio. Kristina was 28 when in 1989 Sam first asked her to pose. And she agreed because, as she writes in her survey, "I was compelled to discover all the aspects of my craft, including being an 'object' instead of 'artist.'" She readily acknowledges that she found the first session "totally erotic, a wonderful experience." For her, "sexual tension is the yin-yang of life." She further describes the poses as "passionately motivated, a dance between artist and model."

Of the models in this small sampling, she was the only one who admitted that she knowingly posed for explicitly erotic drawings and/or paintings. She takes pride in what she describes as "contributing to the creative process." As did Anita, she sees this process as collaborative: "As an artist my body talks about art, so it was natural for me to pose." She raises an interesting question when she asks rhetorically, "Who is the artist – artist, model, or both?" This speaks to the issues of participation and, even, who is in charge in terms of generating creative energy. Perhaps more than the other respondents, Kristina seems to have understood the nature and quality of Sam's appreciation of women. "He is *fascinated* by women and who they are," she wrote, "[and] his drawings/paintings are media for the visual experience to express character." Furthermore, "There is *always* an erotic dynamic between artist and model." Her concluding statement indicates the degree of her response to the eroticized studio and the pleasure she derived from the experience. Ten years after her first session, Kristina writes in almost transcendent terms of her own studio encounter with Eros.

> Posing for Sam was/is an exquisite experience. It feels like a spiritual thing
> at times. It is intensely intimate – Sam's sessions are about art as his life is
> about art. The female body/sexuality is art when appreciated by an

artist. The model makes the expression possible by sharing her body with the artist – in a way it is as intimate as a sexual encounter. They say sex is mainly a function of the brain!

Sandi Meyer, judging from her survey responses, was the model most uncomfortable with the sexual ambience of the studio and therefore with the posing experience itself. She was 25, a housewife and young mother living in the San Fernando Valley, when she met Sam at a dinner party at our small home in Santa Monica. Sam found her attractive and, predictably, invited her to pose. She agreed, according to her account, "so that I could break out of the puritan world that I had been held in for so long . . . I was so strictly brought up, sex was never mentioned at home, that the prospect of posing [represented] sheer freedom." Furthermore, she never felt that her body was "anything special, so it was flattering to be asked." An undergraduate art major at California State College (now University), Northridge, Sandi had worked from the live model numerous times, and was curious – as was the case with Kristina and Kelly – what it would be like to be on the other side of the easel. Still, despite her apparent interest in sexual self-discovery, she was increasingly uncomfortable with the focused attention she received from Sam: "I tried to be relaxed, but was very aware of another man looking at me, not as a statue but visually caressing my body" [and] "I did enjoy the attention as long as it did not involve physical contact."

Sandi also resisted, as did Ann, requests (which in her case she recalls as quite direct) for open poses. She also remembers, contrary to Sam's assertion that it was his practice to allow the models to determine the poses, that he "always set up the poses and, unless they were open, I generally did comply." Both she and Ann seemed to equate open poses with sex, probably wary of appearing to thereby invite unwelcome contact. Interestingly, none of the other three models seem to have made that direct connection, instead enjoying the opportunity to openly express their female sexual identity through displays of genitalia.

As seems to have been the case with several of Sam's models, Sandi experienced a one-time overture. It occurred while she was seated during a break, sipping a glass of burgundy. She was nude, because according to her the blue wool robe made available to her was rough and scratched her skin (she speculates that this was an intentional strategy to encourage models to move around the studio naked). This unexpected episode marked for her the beginning of the end of what had been regular Saturday posing dates that extended over a three-month period. Sandi recalls with convincing detail how Sam took her breast in his mouth and "gently flicked my nipple with his tongue" (see note 7). There is no indication of how long she permitted this liberty (she speculates that she may have "pulled back" in surprise) nor does it seem to have provided reason for her to terminate the session. It did, according to her survey account, make her uncomfortable. Nonetheless, she describes the experience of modeling as a positive one, something she can "look back to now and enjoy." Notwithstanding the sexual tension for which she was not ready, she concludes with "I am glad that I posed."

Finally, there is **Kelly O'Neill**, who at age 31 first posed in 1999, thirty years after Ann and Anita began working with Sam. He discovered her clerking in the nutrition/vitamin department at Whole Foods Market in Glendale and asked her to pose after telling her that he "loves painting redheads." She had done some modeling and agreed after checking with another of Sam's models who was given as a reference. From the beginning Kelly appears to have been clear on the nature of Sam's interests and of her own motivations. And she was entirely comfortable with this new relationship and the studio dynamic. After only one session she was able to write about their interaction with admirable self-possessed understanding. For her, posing nude is "a very asexual experience (or has been thus far)." Not unlike Ann recalling her feelings from years ago, Kelly confesses that she would be "too self-conscious if there were any sexual chemistry felt on my part." She recognized that Sam enjoys looking at naked (nude, she added parenthetically) women, and that his appreciation of her body "bordered on lustiness." But her intention was not to arouse him: "My main reason for posing is to feel that my body can be seen as an aesthetically pleasing *object*."

She agreed to his request for an open pose because "I figured it was about time I tried one." In general, he "asked for slight modifications [in poses] that seemed more visually stimulated than sexually." She acknowledges that at a future session she might agree to pose for explicitly erotic drawings, but that for her even that activity would not be sexual in nature.[2] Kelly understands that Sam is physically attracted to her, as he is to many of his models. But despite a "a mild suggestion that I think he knew I would negate," she intends to pose for Sam "as long as the friendship/working relationship continues as is." After only one session her appraisal of Sam and his studio was realistic and positive:

> Sam knows how to draw the female figure and makes no bones about enjoying women – my experience is what I make it, as long as he's open and not aggressive. It's neither a purely scholastic arena nor a sexual one – friendly, mutual respect is how it feels thus far.

Like Kristina, Kelly is an art student pursuing her own studies of which nude modeling seems to have become an elective component chosen to enhance her education, contributing to her understanding of artistic practice.

The artist

In many, sometimes surprising, ways Sam's memories of the models and their sessions are quite divergent. Memory, of course, has a mind of its own as it selects the events and actions we remember and those we do not. For example, Sam had forgotten the overtures – certainly the form they took – that some of his models recall quite vividly (see notes 5 and 7). However, both he and his models agree that all their interactions, their relationship in the studio and out, were distinguished by mutual affection. In discussing these women Sam acknowledged the contributions they made to his art. By his own account, his main interest, and the reason for his preference for amateurs, was observing "real" people dealing with their nudity and discovering things about themselves, including unrecognized or unacknowledged dimensions of their sexuality.

Responses to the situation can range in quality and kind from the demure to the aggressively erotic, as exemplified by Ann and Anita. The complexity of the studio dynamic is best seen in the frequent disjunction between an artist's perception of his models and the women's own motives. This becomes apparent in the artist's appreciative description of Ann, apparently among the least erotically responsive of his models. Sam is candid about his initial attraction to this, his first amateur model: "I just looked at her and thought up the idea of posing." In addition to her physical appearance, he was attracted to her intelligence – which he credits as an aspect of her beauty – and to her sense of humor. As with his other favorites, the ability to converse easily was important. He described Ann as nervous at first then quite relaxed, self-aware but with little evident sense of sexuality. The sexual urge on his part remained but her lack of response (he named her the Ice Princess) forced him to sublimate it into the creative experience. Sam recalls her two or three open poses, naturally assumed, as both unexpected and serendipitous: he drew quickly in the fear that she would recognize her vulnerability and make the necessary adjustments. Her ladylike sense of correctness and clearly understood and communicated limits appealed to him, and he hoped that this – along with the womanliness that excited him – would come through in the drawings.

This creative process is not at all uncommon and has played a central role for many twentieth-century male American artists. In my1981 interview with well-known figurative painter Nathan Oliveira, he spoke of the sexual energy of models and the difficulty for him of dealing with that energy directly in his art:

> As an artist you are reflecting the sexuality of certain models. You're aware of it, you're responding to it. They know it and they're trying to give to you. There's a good deal of energy in the nude model. If one is in the frame of mind to look at the woman sexually and create fantasy about the ideal . . . that model then becomes the vehicle for realizing it. [And] there has to be energy, a certain desirability about this symbol – sexual or otherwise. [But] I'm more able to paint those things [human qualities] away from the model. When I'm directly in contact with her she is dominating the situation.[3]

Oliveira solved this dilemma, the need for the energy and the difficulty of channeling into art, by working from drawings of live models that he later translated into paintings at a safe remove in the seclusion of his studio. For him, and other Bay Area figurative artists such as Richard Diebenkorn, the erotic power of the nude model is most potently evident in drawings and watercolors done at the group sessions they regularly attended. Even abstract expressionist artists such as Frank Lobdell availed themselves of the studio opportunity to deploy the male gaze.[4]

As for Sam Clayberger, he described his models in terms that spread them across the erotic landscape, from tentative (reluctant) to engaged (enthusiastically abandoned). Anita, Kelly, and especially Kristina are in the latter camp. Ann and Sandi are in the former. Sam described Sandi as a "still-life" with a lovely body but personally uncomfortable, knees pressed firmly and resolutely together. Kristina was among the first to pose for Sam's sketchbook for which he asked models to adopt the poses they thought most erotic (Figure 7.4). Many, of course, were the classic open poses in which legs were spread as wide as possible to provide the most complete view of genitalia. Sam did not choose the poses. In this project, the models were entirely in charge in terms of defining the erotic. And what of the male gaze, the subject–object relationship that for many has defined the treatment of the female nude in western art, when the model determines the pose? Does her free will, her choice, transform the sexual use of her body to something else entirely, something about her as an entire person in whom the body and the "self" are integrated and thereby empowered? This is a key question, one that we will briefly consider in a moment.

But first, what is to be learned from these revelations and, especially, the responses to a survey questionnaire? I suppose they provide a means to deduce the extent of the model's participation in what the artist describes and, to varying degrees, each of the models has acknowledged as an erotic studio exchange. These poses could

Figure 7.4 Sam Clayberger, *Kristina* (from erotic sketchbook), 1995, pen, ink wash, and charcoal. Courtesy of the artist.

very well be seen as signals of availability, of opening up literally and metaphorically to the desire of a lover. To establish that possibility is, at the very least, to understand the model's self-aware exhibitionism and possibly even reciprocal desire. For Ann, part of the attraction of posing was the anticipated effect of/response to the sight of her nude body. There is in this self-awareness a kind of power or control, or at least affective agency. So, in that respect the stage is set for Eros to enter the studio, whether or not his presence is evident in the results.

Indeed, the recognition and acknowledgment of Eros in the studio, and the need to "domesticate" him – to render his presence acceptable – recurs as an element in the stories of most of the models interviewed. Many view this aspect of the amateur posing experience – the evident sexual attraction of the artist to them (occasionally the primary goal) – as an interesting and even stimulating fringe benefit. The reasons for this apparent acceptance of the sexual dimension in a supposedly elevated artistic pursuit are complex, varied, and not readily understood by the models themselves. But two factors or conditions are present in most cases: first, the requirement that the situation feel safe, that nothing untoward will occur. Second, that the desire be unidirectional. All the models maintain that they were (are) not sexually interested in the artists for whom they posed. Yet each was well aware of, even seemed to relish, the sexual attention directed to her. Several respondents, including photographer (sometime model) Judy Dater, who will be introduced later, and Sam's Kelly, asserted that they would feel uncomfortable posing for a man (or woman) to whom *they* were physically attracted.

With this awareness comes a redefinition of the power dynamic in the artist– model relationship. To desire is to lose power. When asked directly about the issue of power and control, few seem to have considered posing in such terms. Their stories, nonetheless, invariably indicate awareness of the effect they had on the artists who, at least in part, invited them to pose because of personal attraction. Back in Sam's studio, Ann's experience is a case in point. She knew that Sam was attracted to her sexually and, as she confided in her survey response, he demonstrated his interest during at least two studio sessions. What this involved, several exploratory kissing episodes,[5] for her did not nullify the basic contract between artist and model. In fact, this apparently was accepted as part and parcel of their special relationship within the studio, one that allowed her to return to pose regularly over a period of at least six or seven years and several times thereafter. Clearly Ann and the other models did not feel vulnerable or threatened in Sam's studio, despite the presence of Eros. The balance of control, and trust, was maintained. Ann's experience with another artist friend turned out to be something quite different, finally constituting a violation of that requisite balance.

This Los Angeles conceptual artist, also a skilled draftsman, visited an aerobic dance class near his Venice studio that was also attended by Ann in the early 1970s. He requested and was granted permission to sketch as the women exercised, his stated interest being the study of motion. After several such sessions he asked Ann, with whom he was already acquainted, if she would pose for him privately and she agreed, understanding that it was to be in the nude. She recalls that in their first session he directed her into acrobatic positions that he would photograph.[6] Despite the difficulty of these poses, she was flattered that he found her body interesting in a variety of unusual positions and, convinced of his seriousness, she cooperated to the best of her ability as he photographed.

The model chose to interpret the artist's interest in her and the session in terms of his need for an inspiring life-drawing subject. Nonetheless, she was aware of his attraction to her, and during the second or third session (like so many details of these experiences, she has difficulty in recalling) his primary motive became unequivocally apparent. Returning from a bathroom break she found him waiting for her naked himself, ready to resume the work. Her memory of this unexpected event is not clear and has shifted over the years.[7] She is not entirely sure if the session ended at that point (either due to his behavior or because time was up), but she believes so. Although she found the incident in retrospect "rather funny," it angered her at the time. It spoiled the experience for her and made her determined to find other reasons not to pose. She even believes it possible that she agreed to one additional session (probably clothed, although on this point she is also unsure) to avoid creating an unpleasantness. By then all high-art muse ideals were shattered, and the only reason to continue would be frankly sexual, a series of erotic encounters in the guise of art making. The delicate balance maintained in her other modeling experiences had been destroyed.[8]

One way to interpret this event, the most generous but unlikely one, is that the artist himself was willing to reverse the gaze, allowing his model the intimate view that her posing afforded him. But the fact is that under the circumstances his nudity amounted to an aggressive declaration of intention. The unexpected introduction of his own body into the proceedings underlined the basic instability of the situation in terms of power relationship. Ann understood that the goal was seduction and, ultimately, physical as well as visual possession. His effort to control her was evident, as she later came to understand, when he choreographed the first session. And in light of his perceived motives, she is resigned to the fact that the photographs are out in the world, beyond her control. Her own agency had effectively been removed, making her no longer an equal participant in the studio negotiation. She and all the other models with whom I have spoken readily acknowledge the erotic tension in some private studio encounters. But to a woman, they insist that its actual indulgence be consensual, the result of *their* own choice acted out on *their* terms.

* * *

I've been gifted with the thing that you want. Who's better than who?
Never underestimate a woman like me.

> Chrissie Hynde, "Money Talk" from Pretenders *Last of the
> Independents* (1994 Warner Music UK Ltd)

California photographer **Judy Dater** challenged, or at least cautioned regarding, the implications of this study. She rightly points out that without reversing the gaze no generalizations at all may be authoritatively made. That is true. So, to provide

134

Figure 7.5 Judy Dater, *Imogen and Twinka*, 1974. Courtesy of the photographer.

a measure of correction, I interviewed her on the subject. The results, including similar discussions with other female artists and models, are interesting in ways that maybe she herself did not anticipate. Dater read the original version of this chapter and therefore had the opportunity to respond to it in her interview. With that background she reflected upon the differences in male and female response and the issues of power and control. She herself had been a model and posed for photographers Imogen Cunningham, Wynn Bullock, and her former husband Jack Welpott. She also became known for her nude studies, including the famous image of model Twinka Thiebaud being photographed by Cunningham in a summer workshop in Yosemite (Figure 7.5).

In the interview Dater recalls erotic nude photo sessions with Welpott, just before and shortly after they married. These sessions always involved attractive female

Figure 7.6 Judy Dater, Untitled (seated nude), 1972. Courtesy of the photographer.

models. When Dater suggested using a male, her husband was not at all interested.[9] She characterized these collaborations in a way that was clearly divided along gender lines: both were interested in seduction, Welpott as a form of sexualized interaction and for her a way to get the models to do what she wanted. Two different forms of power, but power nonetheless. She describes this dynamic between husband and wife in terms of power, particularly involving his desire for women and her need to control it. For Dater both male and female carry erotic potential. She sees it as an identity issue for women, the projection of "self" onto others who then serve as mirrors for the viewer's sexuality and desire. During the early 1970s she did a series of erotic photographs. The nude self-portraits taken between 1980 and 1984 were not particularly erotic. In some cases she now expects that she may have misread motivation. Looking at a contact sheet from the earlier nude sessions, she encountered a female model who seemed to be "coming on" to her as she photographed. The model had voluntarily assumed an open pose and looks provocatively at the camera. Examining the image closely, the photographer finds it somewhat surprising that she was less aware of the possible sexual undercurrents than she seemed to have been. She was reminded of the presumption of mutual attraction that can emerge, especially in private sessions. The recognition of this apparent sexual overture from the past, the woman model using her body as if trying to arouse a man, led Dater to print the image recently for the first time (Figure 7.6).

Among the most interesting and thought-provoking anecdotes related by Dater involved her experience as a fellow at the Djerassi Foundation, an artists'

Figure 7.7 Judy Dater, Untitled (amorous couple al fresco, Djerassi Foundation), 1999. Courtesy of the photographer.

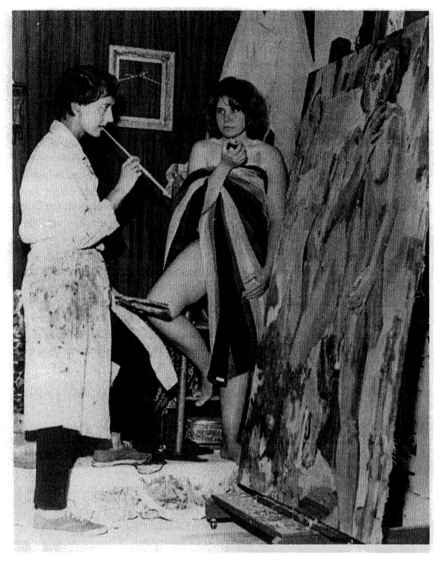

Figure 7.8 Ken McLaughlin, "Eleanor Dickinson and model Sandi Kazajian in Dickinson's studio," *c.*1962. Courtesy of the artist and the *San Francisco Chronicle.*

retreat south of San Francisco in 1999. She describes how she went into the hills with a man and woman, fellow artists not romantically involved, who had agreed to pose for a series of nudes. While Dater photographed, her models became increasingly aroused, eventually forgetting that she was there. She described the episode as emotionally overwhelming to the point where she almost put down her camera to join them. The photo session took place in a barn where the couple engaged in posed sexual foreplay (she asserts that they did not have intercourse) while

138

Dater watched and photographed (Figure 7.7). This led to a discussion of the artist as facilitator for sexual encounters, raising issues of power and just who is in control.[10]

The art-facilitated activity described by Dater is not unique and it is definitely not limited to male artists. San Francisco artist **Eleanor Dickinson**, a long-time life-drawing teacher at California College of Arts and Crafts, not only conducted figure-drawing sessions with models at the California Palace of the Legion of Honor in 1975, but also on one occasion videotaped models having sex in her studio.[11] The reasons behind this extension of traditional life-drawing practice to what amounts to performance art are interesting from the standpoint of 1960s social ideas and bohemian sexual liberation (Figure 7.8). The transformative efficacy of life lived (and art practiced) without boundaries and limits appealed to many. Dickinson was not alone among those women, generally feminists, who saw social and artistic license as a useful and appropriate means to answer patriarchal oppression and to create a community of self-possessed, sexually liberated women. Among Sam's models, Anita and Kristina fit especially well in the company of those women who took charge of their sexuality as part of a personal quest for autonomous existence.

Painter **Joan Semmel** made creating a sexual vocabulary for women the main goal of her pioneering feminist imagery of the 1970s (Figure 7.9). Implicit in her project was the rejection of all traditional treatments of the nude in which female models were exploited and objectified by male artists. In the 1970s she initiated a practice that would seem to up the ante in the game of power poker with male artists. She reportedly would engage the services of a male model who would bring sex partners with him to her studio where their activity would be filmed, drawn, photographed by a group of artist-voyeurs.[12]

I use the term "voyeur" intentionally because it has been deployed to stigmatize male artists who have been accused of setting up modeling situations where they can sexually observe and enjoy women in the name of art. One wonders how their practice differs from that of Joan Semmel or Eleanor Dickinson. Perhaps the difference, if there is one, lies in the ability of the women artists – themselves veterans of the dehumanizing effect of male objectification and power – to empathize with the models whom they are observing and recording. In a recent interview, Dickinson told me that she identifies fully with her subjects: "I become the person I am drawing" (see note 11). And she further acknowledged that, as a visual person, she was herself aroused while videotaping the artist couple making love in her studio. However, despite the goal of parity and equal opportunity to sexualize the content of works of art, many women may in fact bring a fundamentally different approach to representation of the nude human figure than do most men. This then raises the big question – a fundamental one in discussions of gender – as to whether or not women artists view their subjects, men or women, as objects of desire. Is Eros in the studio a shared, cross-gender experience? Do women artists enjoy the benefits of visual access to nude models to the same degree their male colleagues do and have done throughout the history of western art?

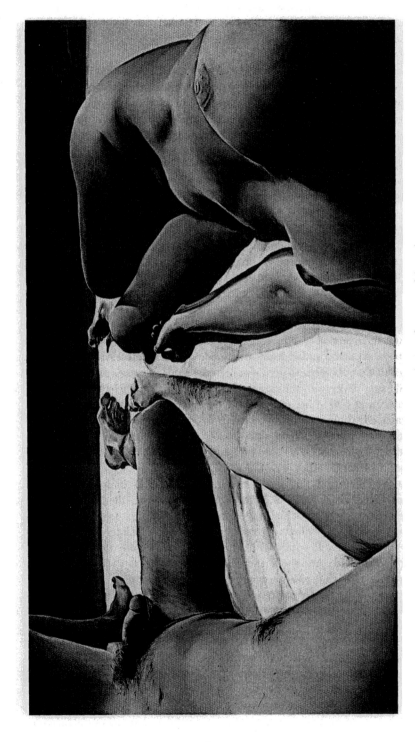

Figure 7.9 Joan Semmel, *Intimacy/Autonomy*, 1974, oil on canvas, 50 × 98 inches. Courtesy of the artist.

This is a key issue in recent feminist consideration of the male gaze, whether in the studio or outside. But for women it seems to be less a matter of model "object" in sexual terms and more a question of power in the social, professional, and political arenas.[13] Many heterosexual men would argue that their enjoyment of a nude female is a natural, biological phenomenon, limited to their sexuality and desire. The women I interviewed, it would seem, disagree. They would argue that without the power to negotiate the terms of the use of one's body, there is no freedom to operate effectively in society.[14] For those who are interested in such matters, art becomes the theater (or laboratory) where power relationships are examined and investigated. At stake for these individuals – artists, models, observers – is nothing less than sexual autonomy.

But just who is in charge in these situations? There seems to be some disagreement even among feminists about what constitutes "empowerment" in the artist–model relationship. The debate is largely between generations. Many women, artists and models among them, are perfectly willing to encourage the deployment of female sexuality as one arrow in their quiver as they negotiate their positions in the world. The story behind the famous photograph of writer **Eve Babitz** playing chess with Marcel Duchamp during his 1963 retrospective at the Pasadena Art Museum provides a marvelous case in point. What has entered into art history as a quintessential Duchampian image involving chess, this time with a naked woman as opponent, turns out to be a set piece devised by 20-year-old Babitz and photographer Julian Wasser. Her motivation as the nude model had nothing to do with Duchamp or, for that matter, fine art. She agreed to the unusual assignment as a means to get the attention of Walter Hopps, organizer of the exhibition, with whom she was angry because Hopps had neglected to invite her to the several parties held in conjunction with the historic event. She knew little about Duchamp and, in any event, "found him too old" for her.[15] No matter how it would be construed later, her nudity was not about the famous French artist. It was about her and the deployment of her youthful sexual powers in obtaining what she wanted. Apparently the strategy worked, because after Hopps discovered her, to his great surprise, naked in the museum gallery, he began returning her calls. Her "act of vengeance" had been successful as she "threw [her] body into the art game." Like the pre-feminist that she was, Babitz viewed her naked body as an instrument to advance her cause.

This expediency was, and generally remains, anathema to an earlier generation of feminists, among them Joan Semmel. While acknowledging the powerful presence of sex in human interaction, she is dismayed by what she views as a retreat into seductive passivity masquerading, in her view, as empowerment.[16] A younger generation of artists might argue that the power of the female body as sexual metaphor, and widely recognized emblem of desire, is useful in their work. They see it as a legitimate motif that effectively invokes cross-gender human experience, whether they wish to make a cultural critique or not. The nude self-portraits of British painter Jenny Saville, or the exaggerated female bibelots of Lisa Yuskavage, in their different ways offer compelling examples of this contemporary tendency. Feminism of the 1970s seems to be pushed to the background by a generation of media consumers sexualized to an unprecedented degree. For them, commodification is not only (or even necessarily) a moral question but also a defining feature of contemporary life characterized by a global economy in which images and experiences are increasingly homogenized. Under such circumstances, personal sexuality and desire – no matter how caricatured, obsessive, or regressive their treatment – are among the few themes available for the assertion of individual separateness.

Semmel herself underscores complications and contradictions inherent in the issue of power and control in the use of the female nude in art. Despite her avowed objective of taking the use of the female body out of the hands of men, thereby restoring a self-determined sexuality, it is not entirely clear how her practice and imagery are consistent with this goal. This is especially true in her studio sessions involving live sex acts by the models. She acknowledges that "things have changed since the 1970s" when she began her series of nudes, including self-portraits in sexual situations. Nonetheless, she defends her original goal of constructing "another model of sexuality." She continues to believe that women remain (sexually) vulnerable, and have difficulty in positioning themselves in other areas, as long as the terms are set by men.[17]

The problem, however, may partly be due to the distinct ways the male and female body is seen.[18] The male gaze is not easily reversed. As Linda Nochlin has argued, writing at the height of feminist art activism, in our society the male nude simply has not carried the same erotic charge as does the female.[19] Despite the efforts of prominent feminist artists of the period, among them Joan Semmel, Judy Chicago, and Sylvia Sleigh, the attempt at "turning the tables" on male-dominated art history by eroticizing the male nude, the results are seldom effective from the standpoint of sexually arousing imagery. The "parity project," representation of male subjects based on erotic female images, may even appear ludicrous, as in Nochlin's famous photograph of a nude man holding a tray of bananas over which his penis dangles, visually ready to join its symbolic analogues. The image is intended as an experimental (female) response to a familiar erotic nineteenth-century convention of women displaying their breasts on trays of apples, grapefruits, or melons. But in her own caption to *Buy Some Bananas* Nochlin asks, "What happens when traditional erotic symbols change sex?"[20]

As Nochlin and others have pointed out, ideas of beauty and sexuality typically have taken up residence in the female form. Whatever one's gender or even sexual orientation, in our culture the imagery of women overwhelmingly connotes ideas about sex. The obvious exceptions to this admitted generalization are homosexual men, for whom the eroticized (young and muscular) male body is omnipresent and apparently omnipotent. The nude male as sex object forcefully informs gay imagery, from popularly consumed pornographic magazines and videos to the sexually focused (frequently explicit) work of well-known artists. Among those who are identified to one degree or another with homo-erotic motifs are David Hockney, Lucien Freud, Francis Bacon, Robert Mapplethorpe, and Jerome Caja, as well as American masters Thomas Eakins, Paul Cadmus, Charles Demuth, and Marsden Hartley. Much of the imagery involved emphasizes male sexual apparatus as erotic focal point, emblem of potency, and actual individual/group identity (Figure 7.10).[21]

Figure 7.10 Unknown photographer, Charles Sexton (left) and Jerome Caja, San Francisco
Art Institute, *c.*1986. Courtesy of Smithsonian Institution Archives of American
Art, Charles Sexton Papers.

Genital focus as the means of establishing identity beyond the biological is, of course, a contribution to 1970s feminist social and political awareness provided by visual artists such as Judy Chicago with her provocative but controversial "centralized-core imagery."[22] The quintessential central image, or open pose, however, remains Gustave Courbet's masterpiece of erotica, *L'Origine du monde* (*The Origin of the World*, 1866). This work still has the ability to shock – or at least startle – the viewer who encounters it unexpectedly on a museum wall or reproduced in an art book. It is around potent images of unabashed, and unapologetic, male desire such as this that the feminist debate about dehumanization (the model's head is not shown; her identity resides solely in her sexual attributes) of women and ownership of one's body is conducted. In American photographic art, Alfred Stieglitz's 1918 portrait of Georgia O'Keeffe's nude torso provides the closest analog to Courbet's notorious image with which I am familiar. But in this case, the model, herself an artist, stares directly at the camera, challenging the photographer's gaze. There seems to be little question that a true collaboration was involved.[23]

In my recent interviews with artists and models in which we discussed representation of the nude and the theme of the eroticized studio, I was particularly eager to hear what they had to say about the differences between men and women in these situations and particularly reversal of the male gaze. California painter **D. J. Hall**, whose realist work is almost exclusively devoted to women, acknowledged that she "understands the concept" of reversing the male gaze but "never saw it happen."[24] Furthermore, she suggests that – based upon her experience teaching life-drawing and photographing models for her paintings – women are simply more interesting subjects than men, whom she finds emotionally "blank." In part she attributes this to erotic energy as learned behavior and a cultural "dichotomy" in which women are allowed more individuality in terms of expressive freedom, at least on the superficial level. Herself married and avowedly heterosexual, she nonetheless prefers women models with whom she often becomes friends and finds more to "get involved with when drawing."[25] In talking with Hall and other women artists, not to mention the models, the very strong impression emerges that the whole process of making art, and the images that result, have really to do with themselves and their own individual needs, desires, and experiences. And these are more often than not felt, understood, and expressed in female form (as, ironically, is so often the case with heterosexual male artists). For women, artist or model, drawing and painting involve the projection of a gendered self onto receptive, blank paper or canvas.

Artist **Leta Ramos**, herself the model for many of her husband Mel's well-known Pop Art pin-ups presenting voluptuous nude women in conjunction with animals, produce, candy, has little interest in doing male nudes. Mel Ramos describes his controversial use of the female body, roundly criticized by feminists, as a critical but humorous commentary on American eroticized consumer society: "I am careful that my work isn't overly erotic, that it always just turns towards humor."[26] The conceit is extended in his various contemporary riffs on art history, among them *You Get More Salami with Modigliani, No. 4* (1976), for which wife Leta was the model (Figure 7.11). Like Anita working with Sam, Leta enjoyed this collaboration, providing the face and body, and often specific body parts such as hands he needed as elements in his compositions. She also seems to have enjoyed being the "object" of her husband's attention and the material for sexy female images that she described as "celebrations of women." She was especially proud of her breasts and pleased that they often appear in the paintings.[27] But this awareness of personal sexuality and delight in the deployment of her body in image making did not appear to cross over into her own work, at least in depicting the male figure which she finds less attractive than the female.[28] There is, for her, no reversal of the male gaze in terms of sexual objectification of the model. Even her husband's efforts to introduce himself into the depiction of a nude couple seems somehow forced and self-conscious (Figure 7.12).

The apparent exception to this pattern, as seen in the handling of the male nude in the marvelous allegorical canvases of the late Los Angeles painter **Joyce Treiman**, is really not an exception at all. Turning the tables on the great American realist painter Thomas Eakins, Treiman places her hero on an elevated model's stand where he poses in the nude for Treiman and a number of her readily identifiable friends and family members (Figure 7.13). Among the group is art historian E. Maurice Bloch, at the time on the faculty at the University of California, Los Angeles (UCLA) where he taught American art. He also directed the Grunwald Center that housed the university's distinguished collection of prints and drawings. The presence of Bloch is a key to the meaning of the painting that otherwise could easily be interpreted in terms of subjecting a famous male artist, one intimately connected with the study of the nude, to the scrutiny he brought to his own subjects. In fact, Treiman was almost reverentially inviting Eakins into her own world, where he was already in the form of the artist's shared interest with Bloch in art history and collecting museum quality objects from the past. She knew that Eakin's dedication to observation and the "truth" of looking, a devotion that she shared, led to his famous life-drawing classes at the Philadelphia Academy from which he was dismissed for, among other transgressions, introducing his female students to the particulars of male anatomy.[29] She also was familiar with the photographs Eakins and his male students took of one another, with homo-erotic implications that have received considerable attention from scholars over recent years.

Treiman's wonderful group portrait is a tribute to Eakins and the principled rigor of his art. It is also in the most thorough and penetrating way a representation of her life, values, and interests. Finally, it is a complex and remarkably revealing *self*-portrait, devoid of the erotic (or any political statement) other than the Eros that may accompany the invitation of others into one's intimate life. I hesitate to make a general statement about gender drawn from this one example. But it does reinforce the observation that, at least for the women with whom I spoke, the nude figure often takes on a role as surrogate for one's being in the world. In a sense, Eros is indeed domesticated. The elements in Trieman's painting, including the nude male, are familiar and therefore reassuring, indicating that the artist has been able to surround herself with what is most meaningful to her as she brings order to her world through

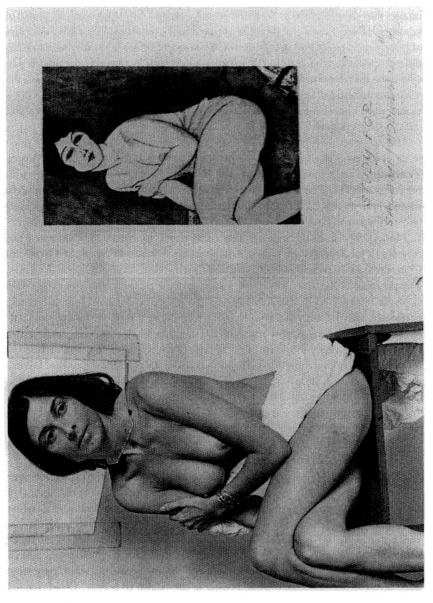

Figure 7.11 Mel Ramos, collage study for *You Get More Salami with Modigliani, No. 4*, 1976. Courtesy of Smithsonian Institution Archives of American Art, Mel Ramos Papers.

Figure 7.12 Mel Ramos, *David's Duo*, 1973, oil on canvas, 70 × 96 inches. Courtesy of the artist.

Figure 7.13 Joyce Treiman, *Thomas Eakins Modeling in California*, 1974, oil on canvas, 70 × 70 inches. Courtesy of the Joyce Treiman Estate.

the creation of art. All is well in her world, at least as she has created it within the familiar confines of her studio. Once again, the true subject is the artist herself.

This inclination to tame Eros appears elsewhere in the stories of women artists and models. From the model's standpoint, the desexualizing of the studio seems not only reasonable but also prudent. Again, this is especially the case with women who are far more vulnerable to professional lapses on the part of the artists who engage them. This dilemma appears throughout a fascinating narrative account written by professional model **Pegi Taylor**. Entitled *Full View*, the book has the avowed purpose to counter the common tendency, at least in popular imagination, to sexualize her profession.[30] The base of the problem, she seems to assert, is that nudity is too often mistakenly equated with sex. While she wisely acknowledges that this can indeed be the case, she insists that the studio ambience need be no more erotic than any other workplace. This is no doubt true in most art school life-drawing

148

situations. The students are there to learn, the instructors to teach, and the models to facilitate education.

True, Eros is also generally kept at bay in private studios where models are engaged by one or more artists. However, it does not follow that sex is never present in these situations – skulking in the background, hiding in the corners, waiting for the opportunity to pounce. This despite the protestations of those who would "sanitize" the activity for popular consumption by a fascinated, titillated, and potentially judgmental public. A divergent view is offered by Los Angeles sculptor Guy Dill as he recalled his years at Chouinard Art Institute (late 1960s). In a recent interview he described the atmosphere of the school as "sexually charged, with the smell of turpentine and naked forms all around."[31] He recalls that the excitement was shared by male and female students, no doubt amplified by the liberated social behavior of the period.

It is around this issue that Pegi Taylor's narrative becomes somewhat confused or at least confusing, betraying an ambivalence that may well be not only endemic but entirely unavoidable. A number of incidents described report what can only be characterized as situational relaxation, if not abrogation, of the professional reserve and standards of behavior expected from both sides of the easel. Taylor is probably representative of many female models, and probably a few males, who find themselves in situations where the line between sex and art is not as clear as they would like, and have every right to expect, it to be. But throughout this very candid account, Taylor's own vacillation about how to respond and when to get up, get dressed, and walk out the door is evident. In fact, it becomes one of the themes, a subversive one, in the book.

Her experience with Walter in 1994, published recently on a web periodical, puts both the dilemma and the model's ambivalence unambiguously front and center. It is Pegi Taylor's story to tell, which she did on the internet, but the gist of it is that she agreed to pose for a former fashion photographer, a widower whose work had appeared in *Vogue* and similar publications during the 1950s. As the after-noon session progressed, Walter in his conversation and requests for poses indicated that his interests in his model's body went beyond a subject for his drawing efforts. He commented on her "big" or "pink" nipples, she could not tell which due to his heavy accent. Later, when she adopted a revealing (open) pose, he said that her vagina "looks just like a flower." Despite these developments, the model continued to do her job, and even for the final pose she "would make sure Walter had my crotch in all its red-winged glory." She proceeded to display herself as if she was "at the gynecologist's office."[32] The session ended abruptly when Walter began to comb her thick pubic hair to improve the view and told her she was "prettier than a tulip." Taylor finally left, her patience exhausted. But she surprised herself by an interest in learning more about Walter, talked with him on the phone, and even accepted a luncheon invitation (but not a request to pose again). He explained that he "found it curious that great artists, like Picasso and Matisse, had 'pretty dirty minds and painted dirty pictures.'"[33] Pegi, it would seem, had to come to terms with an obsession that, as a model, she could either accommodate as acceptable within an expanded idea of limits or invoke as a legitimate reason to withhold professional services. It would appear that she was willing to keep both the contract and pose open as long as the observer maintained a modicum of decorum and, more important, remained interesting and amusing. And, of course, demonstrated interest in her as an individual. Walter failed in these requirements, as did Ann's conceptualist admirer in Los Angeles.

In conclusion, I would like to suggest that there are many forces at work when Eros leaps to the center of the studio. Two of them seem especially present in this

Figure 7.14 Fritz Scholder, *Passion No. 1*, 1999, oil/acrylic on canvas, 80 × 68 inches. Courtesy of the artist.

story. They also take us back to Sam's studio and some of his models, recapitulating what have emerged and established themselves as central themes that invite far less speculative investigation than they have received here. One key idea commences from the observation that many artists, certainly including but not limited to Walter, confuse visual possession (intimately seeing) with touch and even penetration, as painter Fritz Scholder recently conveyed using a self-revelatory vampiric metaphor (Figure 7.14). Scholder himself has acknowledged that the artist as vampire is both a general statement about the creative process and a specific self-portrait.[34] The model's poses can become a response to this kind of control through obsessive looking. Pegi's open pose may have been more than a gift to Walter. It could be seen as an assertion of self, in effect locating her "being" in her genitalia. This strategy, a refusal to separate mind from body, was learned by Anita in Sam's studio and led to an epiphany that made possible a kind of self-integration. Part of this process, and its salubrious result for Anita, was full participation in the creative process. Herein lies an important twentieth-century attitude, that the self is necessary to art. Both Pegi and Anita deny the traditional subject–object paradigm, with a resounding demand that their full identity be recognized. Sexuality becomes an important part of identity, an indivisible component of self-hood.

Another, equally important, factor is the negotiation of Eros and how it enters into works of art. I have discussed this primarily in terms of a "dance" that takes place in the studio, a conversation in which competing needs and desire are reconciled. At this point of reconciliation the viewer enters the studio through the window, so to speak, provided by the artwork. The viewer is manipulated by the artist, with the complicity of the model, to participate in the studio dance and confront his or her own erotic feelings. Implicit is a bargain struck between artist and model that has the potential to evoke a sense of the erotic self in others. In the end, the viewer recognizes in these images an aspect of personal sexuality that emanates from the studio and is shared with those who have negotiated their own erotic contract. Mind and body are united through imagination and desire in a way that points the direction for proceeding yet further on the open-ended journey of self-discovery.

Notes

1 This chapter incorporates and expands upon my original response to Sam Clayberger's invitation. That essay, also entitled "Eros in the Studio," appeared in a limited (85 copies), letterpress portfolio published by Andre Chaves of Klinker Press, Pasadena, California, 1999. A number of individuals, especially Sam and his models, helped me develop the ideas presented here. Numerous others seemed eager to be interviewed or simply chat about the subject. Among colleagues, Richard Cándida Smith carefully read the manuscript and offered informed insights throughout the process of writing, as did Peter Selz, Leo Mazow, Whitney Chadwick, Barry Menikoff, Mark Johnson, and Frances Velasco. Leo Holub and Eleanor Dickinson also have provided valuable assistance based on their own work with models. But my chief collaborator in this project was my wife, Ann Heath Karlstrom, who has generously shared her own experience as a model and with whom I have discussed this intriguing topic for over thirty years. This is a case where

 ˙ quite literally the chapter could not have been written without her, both her "career" as an artist's model and her patient indulgence of my considerable interest in the subject.

2 Kelly has posed for Sam a number of times since answering the survey questions. Invited to invent her own poses for his sketchbook dedicated to the models' ideas of what constitutes the erotic, she responded with open poses, indicating an evident male–female consensus. Conversation with Clayberger, October 16, 2000. In a taped interview (February 15, 2000, Archives of American Art, Smithsonian Institution) (hereafter AAA), she reflected upon the evolving studio relationship with Sam. She also described an earlier private modeling experience in which the artist's romantic attachment to her (encouraged, Kelly believes, by his wife) complicated the situation (11, 13–15). The erotic sketchbook was actually initiated by Kristina Faragher, who describes herself as a sensualist and reports that "I actually wanted to experiment with erotic poses and I was the one to take them with his [Sam's] request" (email to author, November 29, 2000).

3 Nathan Oliveira interviewed by the author, December 29, 1981 (AAA, 23, 24).

4 Ibid. In this interview devoted to artists and models, Oliveira described at some length the group drawing sessions, funded by a Carnegie Foundation grant, in which he and fellow Stanford faculty members Frank Lobdell and Keith Boyle participated in the mid-1960s (see especially AAA, 13–21). Leo Holub, who photographed sessions in Lobdell's Palo Alto (Hamilton Street) studio, recalls that on several occasions two female graduate student models were encouraged to interact in ways that were calculated to enhance the sexuality of the poses. The proof sheets bear out this account. Author's conversation with Leo Holub, September 18, 2000. In a recent interview Camille (née Falk) Feinberg described posing for Richard Diebenkorn in his Ocean Park studio, where he was sometimes joined by James Weeks and William Theophilus Brown. She characterized their treatment of her as very respectful, but also that revealing poses were nonetheless subtly encouraged. This interest was much more evident in private sessions with John Altoon, Jirayr Zorthian, physicist Richard Feynman, and other Los Angeles artists of the 1960s. Camille Feinberg interviewed by the author, June 27, 2000 (AAA, 22–23, 42, 43, 47).

5 Ann's survey response indicated only that Sam had demonstrated that "he liked her" during working sessions. In subsequent separate conversations artist (readily) and model (reluctantly) agreed that he had kissed her in the studio. Neither initially recalled the exact circumstances, or even whether she was nude at the time. When asked recently to clarify this relevant point, Ann acknowledged that one episode took place during a posing rest break, with her nude "sitting [together] somewhere – on a bench or something" (email, September 21, 2000). Sam confirms that his model was indeed nude. He recalls that he kissed her on the navel and that she gently pushed him away. She has no memory of this incident. The artist's memory, in this instance, may trump that of his model. Although Sam is unable to remember the episode in detail, he believes they were seated, matching Ann's recollection in that respect (see p. 123).

6 Interview conducted by Betsy Currie with Ann Karlstrom, March 4, 1982 (AAA, 10–11). This basic account appears in the interview that was among the first in the artist and models series that was revived in connection with the present project. Some of the recollections are based on more recent conversations with the author.

7 It seems possible that many of these memories have been adjusted or even blocked. The same is true of Sam in his review of the models' questionnaires. He seemed genuinely surprised, if not taken aback, by reports of intimate physical contact by Sandi and particularly Anita, who writes of dozing while lying on her back in an open pose and awakening to the "sensation of tongue licking my inner thigh." She recalls the essence of their polite exchange. Sam: "Do you mind?" Anita: "Yes, I mind." (Anne Nickerson model questionnaire, October 5, 1999). Sam has no recollection of these incidents. Nonetheless, he allowed that his models' memories could be more accurate than his

own. This was especially true for Sandi, whose account included a description of a specific sensual practice involving a mouthful of hot coffee. Ann remembers surprisingly few details of her experience with her conceptualist artist, what she describes as one of those "small brain-explosion" moments. In retrospect, she reasons that she must have been nude as she returned from the bathroom to finish the posing session. She assumes that he intended for them to resume their work in a mutual state of undress. Artist and model stood together, both naked, as Ann considered how best to extricate herself "in my 'mannerly' way, trying not to make a big deal of it" (email to author, September 21, 2000).

8 In addition to posing in Los Angeles, Ann did so several times during the mid-1970s for the Bay Area drawing group that convened at the San Francisco studio of Mark Adams and Beth van Hoesen. The other participants were William Theophilus Brown, Gordon Cook, and Wayne Thiebaud. She recalls no studio Eros during these sessions.

9 Author's interview with Judy Dater, June 2, 2000 (AAA, 27). The following accounts come from the same interview.

10 Author's post-interview conversation, off tape, with Judy Dater, June 2, 2000. The anecdote brings to mind Dater's lifelong fascination with Thomas Hart Benton's *Persephone*, an image that "never left" her and that she found "tantalizing and titillating" in its voyeuristic focus (Dater interview, AAA, 2, 3).

11 Author's interview with Eleanor Dickinson, October 25, 2000 (AAA, 17–19). The videotape in question documents a one-time encounter during which two artist models, male and female, were moved to make love while posing. Dickinson taped them with their permission in a series of explicit embraces that Walter Hopps, upon viewing the edited video, described in a letter as "the most human and sensitive, literal depiction of sexual intercourse I have yet seen" (Hopps to Dickinson, November 18, 1976; Eleanor Dickinson Papers, AAA). The tape itself, along with a series of video interviews with models conducted by the artist, will also be deposited at AAA as part of her papers.

12 Described in Norma Broude and Mary D. Garrard (eds.), *The Power of Feminist Art* (New York: Harry N. Abrams, 1994). According to contributor Joanna Frueh, "The Body through Women's Eyes" (190–207), "Semmel would move around the couple with her camera, looking where *she* wanted, seeing with *her* desire, creating an imagery as different from standard porn shots as her single female figures are different from conventional nudes" (202).

13 The most dramatic reversal of the male gaze of which I am aware happens in fiction. In her novel *Spending: A Utopian Divertimento* (New York: Simon and Schuster, 1998), Mary Gordon tells the story of a middle-aged painter, Monica Szabo, whose muse, a commodities broker and art collector, provides her with all the benefits many male artists have traditionally enjoyed, including models as objects and sex partners. In this fantasy, the arrangement involves money, studio space, and time to work. She convinces her muse to pose for a series, based on Andrea Mantegna's *Dead Christ* (Brera, Milan), depicting Christ immediately after sexual climax (*le petit mort*). Aside from the transgressive sacrilege inherent in her creatively "emancipated" protagonist's choice of subject, the author seemed as interested in a woman's scrutiny of male sexual vulnerability and the negotiated control in this artist/model role reversal. Seemingly ill at ease with this "ideal" situation, the novel becomes as much Gordon's examination of the effect of power in relationships as a celebration of liberated self-discovery and of a woman "having it all."

14 This point was tellingly made by University of California, San Francisco epidemiologist Nancy Padian in an interview conducted by Claudia Dreifus ("Battling AIDS in Africa by Empowering Women," *New York Times*, Science, August 22, 2000, D3): "The bottom line, universally is, If you cannot negotiate what you are doing with your body, you will not be able to lead a healthy and long life." What appears on the surface to be a health

153

issue, removed from the discourse of art, is in fact a statement of the reality of what it means to be female and the fundamental difference between representation in the hands of men and women.

15 Interview with Eve Babitz conducted by the author, June 14, 2000 (AAA, 23, 24). Photographer Julian Wasser confirms the account. Both maintain that Marcel Duchamp knew nothing of their plan but accepted his nude opponent seated across the chessboard with gracious good humor. In effect, Babitz and Wasser were the collaborative conceptualists, and Duchamp was the model.

16 Phone interview with Joan Semmel, June 20, 2000. She views the contemporary sexualizing of the nude female, whether by men or by women themselves, as a return to the dehumanizing objectification typical of the male-dominated visual culture.

17 Phone interview with Semmel.

18 Among the numerous recent studies devoted to gender differences in response to male and female nudity and the cultural implications, Susan Bordo's *The Male Body: A New Look at Men in Public and Private* (New York: Farrar, Straus and Giroux, 1999) is particularly insightful and relevant to our discussion. This complicated territory is intelligently explored in chapters entitled "Beauty (Re)Discovers the Male Body" and "Beautiful Girls, from Both Sides Now."

19 Linda Nochlin, "Eroticism and Female Imagery in Nineteenth-Century Art," in Thomas B. Hess and Linda Nochlin (eds.) *Woman as Sex Object: Studies in Erotic Art, 1730–1970, Art New Annual 38* (1972): 9–15. In a more recent article, "Body Politics: Seurat's Poseuses" (*Art in America*, 82(3) (1994): 70–77, 121–123), Nochlin describes the famous painting of models – depicted as contemporary working women – in the studio as among the period's few desexualized renditions of the subject.

20 Nochlin, "Eroticism and Female Imagery," 13. In the same essay Nochlin makes the important point that "there really *is* no erotic art in the nineteenth century which does *not* involve the image of women, and precious little before and after" (9). However, in the later "Body Politic" she acknowledges that in "the history of the nude in art . . . the female subject did not always occupy such a central position" (72). The key point is that, historically, the *sexualized* nude was almost invariably female.

21 A fascinating article by David McCarthy discusses the effort among several artists in the 1960s "to find pictorial sources for a liberated male body" in nudist magazines. See "Social Nudism, Masculinity, and the Male Nude in the Work of William Theo Brown and Wynn Chamberlain in the 1960s," *Archives of American Art Journal* 38(1 and 2) (1998): 28–38. Focus on genitalia (and penis size) seems to be characteristic of both hetero- and homosexual erotic male imagery. This appears to be less the case for heterosexual females, except where politics enter the picture. Lesbian artists and writers do indeed introduce into their work breasts and vaginas as *loci* of sexual desire. What distinguishes this imagery from that of straight males is, of course, the erotic self-reference. The same may be seen in the nude self-portraits by William Theophilus Brown, who is seen working on this series in photographs preserved in his papers at the Archives of American Art, Smithsonian Institution. In some of the photos he appears to have a partial erection as he contemplates the blank sheet on the easel or studies his reflection in the mirror. William T. Brown Papers, microfilm reel 921, frames 344–351.

22 In addition to Broude and Garrard (especially "The Problem of Essentialism," 23–28), see Amelia Jones (ed.), *Judy Chicago's* Dinner Party *in Feminist Art History* (Los Angeles: UCLA Armand Hammer Museum Museum of Art and Cultural Center in association with University of California Press, 1996) and Judy Chicago, *Through the Flower: My Struggle as a Woman Artist* (Garden City, NY: Doubleday, 1993). Given Chicago's association with vaginal imagery, frequently referred to as "cunt art," it interested me that the image on display in her dining room – which I had the opportunity to study in 1998 as her and her husband's dinner guest in Belen, New Mexico – was a frontal depiction of a male

nude by New Mexican artist Delmas Howe. According to Chicago, Howe has "reinterpreted many of the classical themes of Greek art with a gay perspective" (email from Judy Chicago, November 6, 2000). Some of my friends were disappointed to learn that dinner was not served on plates from the *Dinner Party*, one of the icons of feminist art (currently stored in an adjoining building in large crates, waiting for a permanent museum home). It occurred to me that Chicago and other women artists, perhaps more so than men, seem to be able to separate political ideology from personal erotic interest.

23 The image is reproduced in *Georgia O'Keeffe, A Portrait by Alfred Stieglitz* (New York: Metropolitan Museum of Art, distributed by Viking, 1978), 28. Janet Malcolm's 1978 book review in *The New Yorker* describes the image in terms of "blunt sexuality" and as a feminist ideal – "fifty years before its time" – of the strong woman, "authentic, unselfconscious, independent of male approval." She sees in this frankly sexualized portrait the "full force of [O'Keeffe's] radical feminism."

24 D. J. Hall interviewed by the author, June 29, 2000 (AAA, 38, 39).

25 Ibid. The key here may be that more women seek in their models connection with an entire person than do most men, many of whom seem to be able to separate mind (and the evidence of individual experience) from body.

26 Mel Ramos interviewed by the author, May 15, 1981 (AAA, see especially 4–8). Ramos is among the many male artists (very few females) who readily acknowledge the erotic aspect of working with the female nude (in his case photographs) and believe that capturing that energy can be an important aspect of the creative process. According to Ramos, "it's more fun to paint a breast" (12). The text quote appears in *Mel Ramos: Pop Art Images* (essay by Robert Rosenblum, "Mel Ramos: How Venus Came to California"), (Cologne: Benedikt Taschen, 1994).

27 Leta Ramos interviewed by the author, June 23, 2000 (AAA, 21). She confided that she even disliked seeing her head attached to the body of another model whose breasts she judged aesthetically inferior.

28 Ibid., 34. Leta Ramos expressed a sentiment that I found to be shared by the majority of women (non-artists as well as artists) with whom I discussed the subject, including those who describe themselves as highly attracted to men. One might even say that the sexual correlation between image (male) and personal desire seems to be generally absent for many women artists, providing a marked contrast to the situation with their (again, heterosexual) male counterparts.

29 For one of the many accounts of this famous episode in the history of American art, and a thorough discussion of Eakins's teaching emphasis on the nude, see Lloyd Goodrich, *Thomas Eakins* (Cambridge, MA and London: Harvard University Press for the National Gallery of Art, Washington, 1982), vol. 1: 282–309.

30 Margaret E. (Pegi) Taylor generously shared her unpublished manuscript with me in 1998. We had numerous email conversations about the text and the subject of the eroticized artist–model relationship. Despite the fact that our approaches differ in ways that she found troublesome, I am grateful for the insights and experiences that she afforded me through our exchanges.

31 Guy Dill interviewed by the author, August 29, 2000 (AAA, 2, 11). He further reports that many of his models were girlfriends, a situation that heightened the sexual association. Now he describes drawing as a means to clarify a relationship, to provide a point of reference for understanding. He suspects that this emotional and psychological dimension may be part of the difficulty he encounters in trying to draw his wife of twenty-five years.

32 Pegi Taylor, "Artist at Work," *Salon.Com (Sex)*, July 10, 2000.

33 Ibid.

34 Fritz Scholder interviewed by the author, December 7, 2000 (AAA, untranscribed).

8

MUSCLE MEMORY

Performing embodied knowledge

Jeff Friedman

This exploratory chapter is an effort which links several bodies of thought in an attempt to theorize embodied knowledge through choreographic practice. The case study I use to focus attention on my concerns is a performance work I both choreographed and currently perform titled *Muscle Memory*. The title is not a coincidence; this chapter begins to explain how choreography and performance are modes of research which address questions about embodiment including the corporeal quality of oral speech and, subsequently, the role of oral history as a documentation methodology for dance as an art form.

I am supported by past and current theories of embodiment including cognitive scientist Jean Piaget, linguists George Lakoff and Mark Johnson, and anthropologist Pierre Bourdieu, who partner me as I lay down my path of thinking. I also stretch these theories to include new interpretations and deeper, more corporeal meaning. In particular, I intend to flex Bourdieu's concept of *habitus*, which assesses a cultural group's precognitive agreements on given frames of reference for mutual understanding based on embodied knowledge. This chapter expands Bourdieu's habitus to include a new intrapersonal constituency of elements translated into the choreographic interplay of movement and text in performance.

The extension of these theories provides the stage on which I introduce choreography as an embodied form of expression which highlights the corporeal elements of communication. I deploy linguist Gillian Brown's discussion of *deixis* in order to examine how these semantic codes frame space, time and the subject of discourse. Deixis points to context in speech with semantic text in order to anchor the subject in his or her spatio-temporal location: e.g. "this" person at "that" time in "those" spaces. Because the elements of time, space and the bodily subject are the basics of dance performance, I demonstrate with Brown's concept of deixis how they are transformed into choreographic "pointers" in *Muscle Memory*.

I expand the concept of semantic deixis to include choreographic tools in order to develop a particular relationship between the event of *Muscle Memory* and its audiences. This relationship is based on theater historian and theorist Bertolt Brecht's notion of *gestus*, the performance's "attitude" towards its content which develops a mutually understood metaperspective or standpoint in the theatrical event between performers and their audiences. Brecht's gestus is an ally to his alienation effect which purposefully detaches audiences from the unexamined pleasure of empathetic cathartic emotion and instead challenges them to deploy theatrical experiences towards social change. I flex Brecht's gestus in order to include a choreographic standpoint that focuses on the processes of memory and "re-membering" themselves through embodied knowledge.

ACT I, Scene 1: Interlude
Listen.
                       (pause -- I gesture with one hand to my ear,
bending slightly forward and to one side . . .)
Find a pulse. Listen to the pulse.
Inside muscle fibers,
       the fibers inside . . . twitch.
                 (spilling onto the floor;
I rise abruptly in quick motion to standing)
Twitch the switch to muscle memory
       and listen to the pulse down the spine.
Open the bones
       (I splay my body open from the hip joints)
       Listen to the pulse of muscle memory, in between the bones.
       Open the bones.
       Twitch the switch to muscle memory
              and listen to the pulse . . .
               (I touch a rising sequence of pulse points from
               femoral artery in my thigh,
                      the thin skin of my wrist,
to my heart,
my throat,
temple)
       Listen to the pulse of muscle,

                      memory,
                           bones.

I explore the expression of embodiment through movement. As a practicing choreographer and dancer, I have trained my own body and have directed other bodies towards diverse choreographic ends since the mid-1970s. While pursuing a dance career in San Francisco, in the late 1980s both I and my dance community experienced a sudden shift in the landscape of our social "body": the onset of AIDS and its vast repercussions for the survival of our own mortal bodies and the survival of our ephemeral work in dance. Anxieties stimulated by the epidemic-proportion illness and deaths of our friends and close colleagues were channeled into performances. The time-based art form of danc*ing*, in the gerund form (from the Latin *gerere*: to act) evokes the transient nature of both time and physical bodies. Our dancing became charged in two senses of the term. First, performances became a site for embodied expression intensified by the volatile emotions of rage and mourning. Second, choreography served as a performative act, mandated to speak out, to "Act Up" as a commentary on desperate times. My own participation in this evolving genre of performance was set in motion by the sudden death of Joah Lowe, a local performer, choreographer, and physical therapist, one of my own healers.

Joah didn't know he was HIV-positive; no one knew. He went home to Texas for Christmas and died within two weeks under an oxygen text, surrounded by his family and his lover. His family in Texas and his circle of friends and professional colleagues in the Bay Area were in a state of shock. My lasting recollection of Joah's memorial service is the flickering video images of his choreography on a lonely video monitor placed center stage at a local venue. "There must be something better than this," I thought. I didn't want to forget Joah's corporeal reality, so charismatic in his live stage performances. I also wanted to stay in touch with Joah's distinctive artistic process through which those performances came alive over time. While video served to remind me of *a* particular performance, it was a disembodied "product" deprived of any contextualization for his aesthetic statement. With Joah's death, a whole life in dance, a unique movement style, and a body of artistic work had disappeared. I decided to research alternative dance documentation methods that were more corporeal and also those that comprehensively reflected the developmental creative process and the lifetime of experience that informed that process.

During my investigations of alternative models for documenting dancers' lives and work, I discovered an oral history program at the New York City Public Library's Dance Collection at Lincoln Center. In discussion with director Leslie Farlow, I felt this methodology served my interests in both maintaining physical presence and expanding context of the performance product. A life-history gives artists a chance to articulate their own voice through personal insights into the process of dance. Opening the lens further to focus on professional career develop-ment coupled with a life review offers important contextual clues on the long-term influences of family and teachers. Interviews also situate dance practices in broader artistic and social movements over an individual's lifetime. As a result, the life-history format traces the trajectory of an individual's aesthetic development, particularly eliciting early childhood memories of body-based experience.

I am particularly interested in early childhood experience because Piagetian theories suggest that the preoperational cognitive stage (from approximately ages 4 through 7) relies almost entirely on embodiment for learning to process infor-mation and experience. For example, a preoperational child may watch the wheels of a bicycle rotate and imitate that movement by swaying his or her own body back and forth. This embodied action is eventually internalized and serves as kinesthetic stimuli for the creation of a mental symbol for physical action. From ages 4 to 7, the child retains this mode of concept development but internalizes movement more rapidly and applies more complex meanings to the resulting symbols.

I posit that these mental symbols are directly linked to verbal expression through embodied vocal expression. According to the theories of linguists George Lakoff and Mark Johnson, their sample population (western middle-class Americans) bases its verbal articulation of experience on embodied knowledge.[1] The authors suggest that metaphors, which frame culturally constructed references to up as "positive" and down as "negative" ("I feel up today"; "I was downgraded"), are based on the body's own verticality as a physical experience of space. These embodied experiences are part of what anthropologist Pierre Bourdieu calls "habitus," a culturally constructed nonverbal social agreement on a group's frames of reference, a complex interwoven fabric of behaviors preceding cognition.[2] Children, especially those in the preoperational Piagetian stage of learning which emphasizes motor learning, absorb the habitus of their local culture "early and often" in their lives so as to assimilate to their familial and social context. These embodied experiences frame worldviews and I suggest they support the development of a personal dance aesthetic.

For example, movement theorist Rudolf von Laban's father was a member of the Austrian Empire's military in the late nineteenth century. As a child, Laban both viewed and participated in drills which subsumed individuals into large group movements. Later, as an adult, Laban experimented with a form of non-professional experience he called *Laientanz*, large group movement "choirs" which emphasized the interplay between individual contributions and group experience. For a Laban movement choir, separate individuals create and then contribute a segment of movement to a group choreographic process. Incorporating (but not subsuming) that segment into a more complex design allows the individual to sustain a personal awareness within the choir's tapestry of movement. Laban's movement choir theory was then manipulated by Nazi leaders during the mid-1930s as a propaganda technique. The government forced Laban to generate distorted movement choirs, large-scale unison movement for the masses choreographed by a single authority and designed for the opening ceremonies of the 1936 Berlin Olympics. Laban eventually resisted, barely escaping with his life by fleeing to England prior to World War II.[3] This example, which links early childhood embodied experience to important historical events and the evolution of a major dance figure of the twentieth century, illustrates how a child's assimilation to the unique habitus of a culture can contribute a personal reference point for subsequent movement practice and theories. Surely habitus can be part of forging an important basis for the development of dance practices which articulate embodied knowledge into a more conscious aesthetic perspective. If so, then the role of dance as a lens through which to perceive and understand culture has been undervalued and deserves more attention. Beginning to document dance practices is a start towards the goal of interpreting how movement and gesture articulate social understanding. In particular, I was interested in using documentation methods which preserved and even highlighted embodied experience.

Casting my net for an embodied documentary strategy, I was also drawn to how oral interviews, as a methodology, reveal corporeality. From my own experience as a practicing dance artist, both the teaching and creative practices of the profession rely on orality during the transmission of kinesthetic knowledge. For example, young ballet students in Britain are required to pass the Royal Academy of Dance examinations by physically performing a teacher's purely oral speech of a formal French ballet vocabulary: (Try saying this phrase out loud with rhythmic accents that define the movement phrase: "*Tombé, pas de bourée, jeté, jeté, assemblé . . .* And begin . . .") The transmission of contemporary modern dance teaching and creative processes often uses speech, combining oral articulation of concepts or steps and a bodily demonstration of movement: For example: "Start here with that movement phrase (brief reference in my body of the first move of the sequence) we just made up, reverse it halfway, and add (demonstrating miniature version with hand gestures) the 'Baryshnikov' at the end."[4] These examples of oral and kinesthetic instruction, as opposed to print documents, also depend on multiple channels of expression of gestural and paralinguistic communication interweaving to provide the necessary contextualization to enact the semantic message.

In fact, the complex messages of orality resist print documentation. For example, oral/kinesthetic communication can be consciously ironic,[5] purposefully contradicting the semantic content with non-semantic coded signals. If I say: "Love that dress," I may be sincerely appreciating your fashion statement. However, in an oral expression that also includes full body, postural, hand and facial gestures as well as complex vocal delivery including pitch, tone, intonation and volume among others, I could speak the same words but express the opposite sentiment:

"***LOOOOVE*** . . ." (said overly <u>loud and drawn out</u> to reinforce my intended ironic tone, with a dramatic <u>hand gesture</u> to the forehead while <u>leaning back posturally</u> as if to indicate the virtual force of your bad taste) "**. . . that dress!**" (pause) [**<u>wink</u>**]. (The pause gives you time to interpret that I really don't love it; the wink indicates "Not to worry, we'll happily help you improve.")

An attempt to represent the comprehensive set of messages in this short example reveals how print documentation becomes unwieldy for representing high context oral communication.[6] In summary, it became increasingly clear to me that the corporeal quality of oral history interview methodology could provide a familiar format for dancers to articulate their life experiences and, in particular, the complexities of embodied knowledge.

Bodily movement is an important component of oral history since it has an important role in both the production and storage of memory. Subjective memories can be stimulated by referencing an indexical gesture that represents a larger and more complex movement sequence, a physical prop that evokes bodily experiences or the description of the space in which the event took place. Embodied channels of communication such as vocal production of speech and posture/gesture/facial expression combinations also provide elements of emphasis and repetition which generate mnemonic assistance for remembering the complete message (semantic plus non-semantic). In addition, embodied communication channels also provide important framing codes which, though often treated as subordinate, actually anchor memory of semantic messages. According to Gillian Brown, in her text *Speakers, Listeners, and Communication*, temporal, spatial and subject deixis specifically function as orientation, locating and specifying context. These "identifying features which are stable with respect to the character . . . have a good chance of being fixed in the memory."[7] However, Brown locates deixis in purely semantic terms, i.e. how we use language to "point" to which object we refer to in space or identify another object, event or person's temporal relationship to ourselves. I suggest that expanding deixis to include embodied gestures includes the tools of choreography as well.

Oral history would also be an especially effective documentary form for the dance community whose members already link many embodied identities: "always already" gendered, raced, and classed individuals working in an art form that foregrounds embodied expression. As previously noted, dance performances make conscious the underlying embodied habitus that permeates any culture's complex social agreements. The dance community's mission is to formulate performances of embodiment into a single nexus of physical expression for the theater. However, Brown notes:

> Every actual utterance is spatiotemporally unique, being spoken or written at a particular place and at a particular time, and provided that there is some standard system for identifying points in space and time, we can, in principle, specify the actual spatiotemporal situation of an utterance act.[8]

If one were to substitute "performance" for "utterance" (and "danced" for "written") it becomes clear that the spatial and temporal specificity of dance events prevents a glossing of difference between multiple identities within any one habitus. Each event must be "historical" in that it occupies a particular "spatio-temporality." As a result, performances are group events which choreographically "act out" the negotiations between (and *within*) specific individuals and their embodied identities as they adjust and change over time. As a result, choreography itself, as a representational exegesis for embodied knowledge(s) and the negotiations between/within the social identity and personal identities that emerge from knowledge, is a rich site for both documentation and future research analysis.

On the basis of oral history's contribution of longitudinal context to artistic expression, the corporeality of orality's vocal expression, its link to memory storage and retrieval, and orality and dance's mutually held values for kinesthetic expression, I created LEGACY in 1988 to collect, preserve, and make accessible oral histories of San Francisco Bay Area dance community members. Since 1988, I have collected over forty oral narratives of dance practitioners, administrators, and educators. LEGACY now constitutes a growing archive for present and future research on the Bay Area's dance community, which is second only to New York in size and scope.[9]

In 1994 I began performing excerpts from the collection in a solo performance work titled *Muscle Memory*. I had felt for a long time that the collected embodied knowledge of dancers in oral history format should eventually be returned to performance, the original site of their experiences.[10] *Muscle Memory* is one of LEGACY's most successful outreach projects. The small-scale intimacy of the solo form has allowed me to bring excerpts from LEGACY's collection to a hotel conference room in Reno, Nevada; a Rotary dinner in Stockton, California; a community center in Albuquerque; and the Chicago Public Library. More theatrical venues range from a visual arts gallery in Milwaukee, to full stage productions in Idaho and, of course, repeatedly all over the Bay Area.

Muscle Memory is a half-hour performance work that incorporates a variety of media. However, the emphasis is on choreographed gesture, with supplemental text in the form of edited excerpts from two transcripts in our collection. I intentionally juxtaposed two life-histories: 84-year-old Eve Gentry and 28-year-old Frank Everett. Eve's life experience reprises the classic period of modern dance, dating from the 1920s. Her reminiscence embraces a childhood in dusty rural San Bernardino, ballet lessons in the early heyday of Hollywood, her trek cross-country to become an artistic force in the Hanya Holm Dance Company in New York and eventually her own work.[11] Eve's long life is remembered in a rambling narrative style that alternately meanders and gels, spinning an interconnected web of people, place and experience.

In contrast to Eve's digressive style is Frank Everett, a young and brash dancer at age 28. He was a "snap queen," that is, someone who embodied the theatrical attitudes and "in-your-face" gestures of African American drag queens. Frank had AIDS and at the time of LEGACY's interview, he was in the throes of several opportunistic diseases.[12] His life-story incorporated growing up in a dysfunctional family, shuttling between parents, early independence, sexual promiscuity, and substance abuse. While I had never met Eve (she was interviewed by Mercy Sidbury, a LEGACY volunteer), I had spent years performing with Frank, touring the United States and internationally. I had spent late nights kept awake in distant hotels by his massive snoring habit. I knew this guy "up close and personal."

The choreographic form of *Muscle Memory* weaves these two life-histories together in a multilayered fabric of text and movement. I adapted excerpts from the oral history transcripts for two interwoven scripts. In some instances, I spoke while dancing, quoting carefully edited excerpts that moved each individual narrative forward. I also had an actress record excerpts from Eve's transcript. I also interwove those audiotaped speeches with choreographed movement and my own spoken text. In this way, I avoided impersonation; I maintained my own voice as a character in the performance (Jeff as "interlocutor"), even if occasionally shifting to a childlike skip or an adolescent pout while reporting Eve's narrative in text and gesture. At other times, a female voice spoke Eve's words. However, these audiotapes clearly used a young woman's voice speaking "as if" Eve were still 25 or 30 years of age. While I could have impersonated Frank more completely because of my intimate personal knowledge, I deliberately avoided this option. The interwoven format of the choreography inevitably made clear to the audience that I was performing "myself," as well as shifting between representations of both narrators throughout *Muscle Memory.*

I deliberately generated this choreographic interplay between mimesis and detachment in order to comment on an important aspect of oral interviews. From my own experience as an interviewer, when people begin to tell anecdotes from their past, they often shift their narrating voice between themselves as "reporter," to themselves as "a character in the anecdote" and also to "other character(s) in the anecdote." Sometimes, the narrator also impersonates the facial gesture, vocal intonations, bodily gestures, and posture of each voice. For example, while interviewing former Twyla Tharp company member Sara Rudner,[13] I observed Sara "become" Twyla by changing her posture to a vertical "wall," binding her flow, and speaking in a higher volume, rapid, monotonic vocal style. During this performance of "an other," Sara also performed herself as "Sara" in a dialog with "Twyla." I use this internal dialog format as a model for my performance of characters in *Muscle Memory.* However, these internal dialogs also reflect the overall dialogic format of oral history interviews as a methodology. I wanted to use this overall theme of dialog as a choreographic tool as well.

Mid-twentieth-century historians such as Alan Nevins at Columbia University considered oral history interviews a narrator's monolog, witnessed but not mutually shaped by the interviewer. However, more recent theorists such as Ronald Grele, in his collection *Envelopes of Sound,* note that narrators also perform this miniature theatrical event, by proxy, for future multiple audiences, those who would listen to the audiotapes, and many more who will page through the transcript held in archives.[14] Recently, oral historian Alessandro Portelli and others have refined and extended Grele's perspective towards an intersubjective relation in the production of oral narratives. Portelli posits that interviewers are also "performers," contributing their own script to the production. While much of that script may be silence, postural shifts or movement gestures, these too contribute to the dialogic production of the oral history.

Feminist viewpoints on oral history interviews suggest an even more extended analysis. Sociolinguist Kristine Minister notes that feminist frames for sociocommunication offer a more relevant and even foundational role for nonverbal communication and paralinguistics during oral history interviews. In addition to an intersubjective stance to reportage of *actions,* the feminist interview is considered, in and of itself, a *process* of self and gender construction which is dependent on the corporeality of gender and its expression through embodiment. Minister specifically observes that a multilayered (often simultaneous) two-way process of both verbal, paralinguistic and gestural interrogation between the two subjects develops into an emergent dialog.[15] I acknowledge both theories of intersubjectivity and corporeality, while extending Minister's analysis further into embodied performance as dance. In *Muscle Memory,* I have consciously framed the performances of both narrators by naming and acting as myself, an interviewer, editor, and choreographer in both a physical and vocal dialog with my interview subjects as theatrical characters:

ACT I, Scene 2: Interlude

Listen. (pause)

What is it like to listen? Deep inside my body.

I will take your pulse and press it onto this magnetic tape.

Will you wander? I will hold you lightly in my arms, with my voice.

  Until you rest, assured.

Or not. I await your nervous laughter, a shift in your seat,

  away from me,

  away from what we are here for.

I.

. . . I will reel you in. With my eyes, my voice,

  my unwavering will to listen.

  To what is unsaid – what <u>must</u> be said – what <u>is</u> said

    In that taut muscle, that viral eye.

Trust me.

  Trust me.

    Who <u>are</u> you?

      Who *are you?*

        Who <u>you</u> are.

I link this shift from subject:object to subject:subject relations in oral discourse to Bakhtin's theories of dialogic formation of knowledge. For Bakhtin, every utterance is formed in relation to the social situation in which it occurs. Previous speech by others and also the anticipated audience reception helps form a subject's oral speech. Embedding every utterance in social relations provides a frame for my interest in how choreography functions as a tool in performances of *Muscle Memory*. For example, Bakhtin's ideas combine with Brecht's theories of the *gestus* and his dialectic theater to expand the conceptualization of communication channels in theater to go beyond speech to include a more complete and integrated total gestus of music, gesture, movement and choreography in performance. According to Brecht, all communication must contribute a metaperspective to the theatrical event. This metaperspective, often pedagogical in purpose, is achieved from a point of view of alienation, detachment from the empathetic perspective usually associated with dramatic action. Getting audiences to identify with the characters on stage and achieve an emotional catharsis drains them of their responsibility to engage the pedagogic metalevel, subverting the learning process. To prevent the audience from treating the performance as "those characters' story, over there," the actors themselves model that detached stance from their character. This Brechtian "standpoint" encourages audiences to note that, rather than a wash of emotions that drain them of engagement, theater is a constructed experience in which they may actively participate in order to understand themselves and their social situation.[16] To foster this perspective, Brecht wants the actor to listen as hard as the audience listens:

ACT I, Scene 2: Reprise
Listen. (pause)
What is it like to listen? Deep inside my body.

In this way, a mutually created event (between audience and actor, actor and character, character and audience) occurs in the theater.

Because of the corporeality of oral speech, I believe oral history interviews can operate this way. Listening and responding from "*deep inside my body*" from a Bakhtinian dialogic position was a necessity for honoring the contemporary oral history subject. For me, it was important to represent this perspective in the staging of *Muscle Memory*. My first priority was to explicitly name myself as a listener, on stage, to create a detached *gestus* that generated a dialogic relationship in performance. I hoped that audiences would begin to resist a purely empathetic response to the characters on stage, including myself, and access a metalevel of discourse that addressed my additional concerns regarding dialogics.

Even though I wanted to perform authentically, honoring both Frank and Eve (and myself), I used several devices to subvert a full empathetic response. First, on a structural level, I began by alternating between each character, while staying in the role of "myself." I then increased the rate of alternation between each character's narrative, gradually producing a cross-referencing of similar shared experiences. This device of rapid alternation eventually generated a Bakhtinian "conversation" in text and movement between Frank and Eve which never occurred in reality. For example, both Frank's and Eve's families had rejected their interest in dance. Both left home at an early age and had found training in spite of that fact. Both Frank and Eve moved to San Francisco, hoping to find their own vision of a dance career and both found something completely different which changed their lives.

ACT II, Scene 1: Dialog
EVE: "*[My sister] Charlotte will teach me to be a dental assistant . . .*"
FRANK: "*. . . I worked as a hustler to eat. I'd trick, get up and go to class . . .*"
EVE: "*. . . with Ann Mundstock, who taught the German modern dance. Five girls, with bare midriffs and bare feet. And Welland Lathrop, the only boy, in a jockstrap . . .*
EVE: *. . . I was shocked.*"   FRANK: "*. . . I was shocked . . . I had never been in a Nutcracker before I joined the Oakland Ballet. I just faked my way through it . . .*"

Conjoining these shared experiences across a gap of over fifty years' time, I eventually developed enough cross-references between their narratives to generate a context that would support, from the audience's perspective, a mutually understood dialog. My reason for creating this dialog was to begin detaching audience identification with either character, generating instead a focus on the dialogic relation between them. Last, by including text of my own that pointed to myself as the listening agent in the oral history process, I also wanted to keep the role of "listener" explicitly present in *Muscle Memory*. Through all these devices, I wanted to set the stage for another, more transcendent perspective to emerge.

The Bakhtinian concepts of dialog keep alive the Brechtian *gestus* I was intent on creating in this work. On the level of constructing the theatrical event, I wanted to maintain a dialogic relation to the audience that mirrored the same format in both the original interview process and the dialog on stage. Ultimately, the metadialog between the choreography and the audience needed to address the issues of embodied memory, of muscle memory itself *as* the subject. To achieve this goal, I wanted to amplify the role of embodied gesture as a foundation for the construction of choreography. In this next section, I want to describe the choices I made that foregrounded bodily and spatial gestures to express the concept of "muscle memory," i.e. how it is that we store and then elicit kinesthetic knowledge of experience.

I chose to represent Eve choreographically in a movement style that reflected her life experience. To do that, I recounted her story using gestures that represented her early modernist dance experiences, a more mimetic gestural vocabulary. For example, when Eve reminisces about her early romantic ballet training, I kinesthetically cite Anna Pavlova's romantic performance of *The Dying Swan*. My body performs Eve as she mimes an indexical excerpt from *The Dying Swan* (hands and arms fluttering over the classic kneeling stance). In this brief moment, I engage the audience on several levels. First, I sustain my male-gendered body in relation to a performance of a prototypically female role ("ballerina as swan"). In this way, I keep my "self" visible within the performance of an other, expressing a physical counterpart to the internal dialog speech genre discussed in the previous section. Second, in order to address the more rural and less sophisticated context in which Eve received her first training, I cite my imagined version of Eve's recollection of Pavlova as the most famous contemporary ballerina of her time. In this way, the audience recognizes a well-tarnished "vulgarization" often found in vaudevillian imitators of the probably exquisite performance by Pavlova herself. The combinatory effect of both these projects is to, first, keep detachment present in the audience's experience of this moment (wrong gender) while also giving them an opportunity to retrieve their own cultural stereotypes of Pavlova's *Dying Swan* (or maybe a Disney version of it from *Fantasia* and the dancing hippos) and compare it with the performance on stage. This exercise in memory storage and retrieval of kinesthetic experience is one of the most explicit examples of several instances where I employed indexical gestures within *Muscle Memory* to evoke muscle memory as a *subject* of the choreography.

To link these diverse kinesthetic expressions into a narrative whole, I devised a spatial "gesture," a floor pattern across the stage, indexing Eve's "path" through life that mimed the meandering narrative style of her memoir. I occupy virtually every zone of the stage space in a rather random sequence, linked to the length and breadth of her varied life experience. However, halfway through Eve's rambling *narrative*, I carefully repeated the entire *spatial floor pattern*, now to be overlaid with new text and movement sequences as her life-history continued to unfold. The purpose of this repetitive spatial "gesture" was to bring the audience into a more conscious dialog with the muscle memory inside *Muscle Memory*.

Typically, audience reception of most choreographic form is attenuated. Grasping, remembering, and then interpreting formal choreographic choices (while also attending to the ephemeral performance of a charismatic live body) is a difficult task for audiences. More likely, the audience's awareness of corporealized form is limited to a vague suspicion of familiarity. However, *Muscle Memory's* repetitive spatial gestures challenge audience ability to perceive the formal intentions of the choreographer. To remedy the forgetting of form, repetition provides an opportunity for audience recognition of my choreographic choices. In this case, spatial floor pattern and iconic gestures repeat while the sequence of verbalized memories continue to flow over time. Audiences who can perceive the repetition of these patterns begin to consciously address their own process of remembering within the container of the performance itself. The initial juxtaposition of familiar spatial path/gestural movement and new text provides audiences with a didactic experience of the memory process. Audiences then interpret their embodied "re-membering" process while new text is overlaid onto the now familiar spatial design. For example, when I reintroduce the mimetic performance of *The Dying Swan* the second time, I am now quoting Eve's new text. Here, she tells us that she deliberately avoided calling her parents to ask permission when she stayed over in Los Angeles to continue training the next day:

ACT II, Scene 2: Excerpt
EVE: *"I didn't call long-distance.*
Someone had to die . . . (repeat fluttering hand and arms over the classic kneeling swan's pose) . . . *to use the phone that way."*

In this case, I laid the first and second texts over the same indexical movement to purposefully link the ephemerality of the dying swan and our own bodily mortality, both described in Eve's text. My intention was pointing to the audience's conscious production of memory through the stimuli of an embodied gesture, and the subsequent reinterpretation of those memories: muscle memory *as* subject. Once audience engagement is stimulated, the dialog continues to renew itself, in response to a dynamic and temporal movement process that provides new images as a screen upon which the audience projects new memories.

The process of "re-membering" and interpretation through the retrieval of memories from both cognitive and kinesthetic sources is the core intent of an oral history interview. All channels of communication come into play, including my emphasis on embodied experience in both the source memories themselves and the mode of expression of those memories through vocal and bodily gesture. In this way, the original oral history source material for my performance is supported by the choreographic form, as perceived in a dialogic relation between the choreographer's intent and audiences' reception. In other words, I wanted the work to perform not only the presentation of Eve and Frank's stories, but to perform the meta-*gestus* of "re-membering" as well. Like Brecht, I hoped to perform the telling of a story, referencing the process of memory retrieval and interpretation as well as the contents of memories themselves.

Frank's compact and tightly knit musculature embodied a personal style that was direct, quick and to the point. Because I was close to Frank and had my own strong internal "muscle memory" of his movement style, I used a different approach from Eve's story to produce the movement vocabulary for his narrative.

I was able to appropriate his familiar repertoire of finger snap gestures to punctuate verbal expression. These gestures act as a "leitmotif" for presenting Frank's style of embodiment in *Muscle Memory*. I consciously chose to deploy the finger snap gesture in different contexts to express multiple states of being within the dense introductory section to Frank's life-story. I included a single vertical snap to signify his insouciant arrogance:

ACT III, Scenes 1, 2, and 3: Excerpts
FRANK: *I don't remember which I saw first: "Fame" or "All That Jazz," but I saw them pretty close together and I thought to myself: "I can do that!* (**SNAP!**)*"*

Later, a series of arrhythmic snaps are performed compulsively behind his back to represent Frank's sublimated anxiety while angrily confronting his father's threats to commit suicide:

FRANK: *"Go ahead,* (snap) *do it.* (snap, snap) *Do it. You're* (snap) *an awful man* (snap). *Just do it."*

A softer replay of the vertical snap is also used to punctuate his poignant reflections on life's end:

FRANK: *"It's over.* (pause) *I don't want it to end --* (snap)*."*

This slippery gestural sign linked to multiple significations provides audiences with insight into Frank's ability to evoke multiple identities to cope with his numerous internal conflicts Audiences begin to perceive an accumulation of different gestural effects that accrue into a kinesthetic portrait of Frank, the eponymous "Angry Young Man."

Both my use of spatial floor pattern and the multiple significations of a single gesture can be thought of as deictic in nature. Deixis in language is a reference to context, an encoding process in communication process which links the speaker to specific objects including other people, places in space and events in time and expresses this contextualization to the listener. As such, time, space and subject are the elements which inform the listener as to the situation which surrounds every speech utterance. Because time, space and the human subject are also the primary elements of dance performance, I propose an analog between deixis in speech to choreographic deixis. In a performance of *Muscle Memory*, the performer and audience are also enmeshed in a dialogic formation of knowledge, through the dance equivalent of a speaker describing "a complex series of events of embedded time domains."[17] With this analogy in mind, I am interested in the functions of deixis not only in verbal language, but also in the kinesthetic and choreographic choices described above. For example, Eve's repeated floor pattern refers to a spatial context that is already shared by the speaker and listener. As cited in Gillian Brown's text on discourse analysis, Eve's theatrical spaces become "locations which have just recently been mutually agreed between the two participants . . . as part of their common ground." The choreographic floor pattern which was recently performed is referenced again through repetition. This repetition frames context as "context," pointing to the process of contextualization by eliciting the process of memory.

What about Frank's gestures? Spatial deixis references a more restricted location of the self in relation to some internally "pictured landscape."[18] When Frank verbalizes an arrogant statement, he snaps in a wide circle, into far reach space, away from his body's center, literally pointing to an expansion and definition of his kinesphere to support an expression of "can-do" attitude. When he compulsively and arrhythmically snaps his fingers behind his back in regards to his father's threats, Frank is deictically pointing with his snap gesture into the near reach space of his back kinesphere's sagittal zone, but close into his body's center, shrinking his personal location into a smaller target for his father's wrath. When he snaps at "the end of his life," it is a vertical gesture directly overhead, pointing the spatial direction of his presumed ascendance towards the vertical axis. Taken together as a category, these snap gestures function to articulate Frank's location within space over time and in different emotional "locations." These embodied gestures generate important data for the audience regarding both a spatial and psychological orientation process.

These orientation processes are also an important part of the oral history interview as narrators reflect on their past and use a number of different methods to "place" themselves in the past, both in a spatial and psychological landscape. This ability to kinesthetically "place" oneself strengthens the link between the remembering self and the prior selves that are reviewed for memory recovery. While many verbal questioning techniques are used to elicit this "placement" process, why not begin to articulate the efficacy of kinesthetic embodiment as a tool for reminiscence? Performances of *Muscle Memory* provide a laboratory for exploring such techniques.

My goal so far in this chapter is to link the language of verbal communication specifically to kinesthetic performance of embodied gestures. I created a vocabulary of gesture in *Muscle Memory* which opens up consciousness to the articulation of embodied knowledge. One of the possible effects of such an expanded vocabulary of communication is the expression of embodied knowing in historical documentation and analysis. If concepts of language can be expanded to include movement and gesture as suggested by Lakoff and Johnson, the documentation of human experience can encompass a wider range of those experiences through additional media such as kinesthetic expression.

As I noted at the beginning of the chapter, George Lakoff and Mark Johnson have proposed a cognitive model for such an expansion of language. They state that

Box 8.1 Expanding Lakoff

Expanding Lakoff and Johnson's spatial image schemas, author Peggy Hackney asks, "How large is the mover's Kinesphere <u>and</u> how is it approached/revealed?" Lakoff and Johnson's image schema of "Near/Far" can be interpreted in Labanalysis as Central Spatial Tension, which reveals a Kinesphere with movement radiating out from and coming back into the center. ♂

Labanalysts also include two additional approaches to the Kinesphere including Peripheral Spatial Tension, which reveals the edge of the Kinesphere: ☉
and Transverse Spatial Tension in which a kinesphere is created with movement that cuts or sweeps through, revealing space between center and the edge: ⊘

Lakoff and Johnson also suggest a spatial image schema based on the embodied concept of "Up/Down." Labanalysis identifies this reference as the one-dimensional vertical axis: ‑|‑

However, Labanalysis also includes the Sagittal 1-D axis which reveals the embodied concept of "Forward/Backward": ‑⁄‑ as well as the 1-D Horizontal axis which reveals "Left/Right" spatial pulls: ⟋

However, Labanalysis also compounds the simple one-dimensional axes together to create a series of three two-dimensional spatial planes: the 2-D Vertical Plane, including both Up/Down and Left/Right spatial pulls: ‑⊬‑

The 2-D Horizontal Plane: ⊁ and the 2-D Sagittal Plane: ‑⊁‑

Movements can be *phrased* over time using both the 1-D axes and 2-D planes in contribution with all three spatial tensions. Try for yourself: moving towards the vertical axis above your head, radiating out from your core using Central Spatial Tension and then adding a right side pull during your move to become part of a Vertical Plane, using a sweeping movement that cuts through your Kinesphere in Traverse Spatial Tension.

All quotations and diagrams are cited from Peggy Hackney's text *Making Connections: Total Body Integration Through Bartenieff Fundamentals*, illustrated by Mary Konrad Weeks (Amsterdam: Gordon and Breach Publishers, 1998), 219–225. These figures are a truncated discussion of Labanalysis at best, especially as it excludes Bartenieff's Developmental Body Patterns. I take responsibility for how I have linked these concepts and diagrams in a particular manner to illustrate the points in my chapter.

image schemas, those precognitive experiences which involve embodied consciousness (near/far; up/down, etc.) provide the foundation for metaphorical cognitive schemas. These metaphors then channel communicative verbal language as expressions of embodied knowledge. My work has emerged from the assumption that holders of specialized embodied knowledge, such as dance community members, provide a research sample which supports expanded research in this direction. Lakoff and Johnson have begun to identify a rich but largely untapped domain of image schemas. For example, Laban-based methods of movement analysis expand the options that the authors previously identified. Labanalysis gives

Box 8.2 Effort

Effort

Labanalysis also addresses new aspects of movement as an expressive process of change beyond Lakoff and Johnson's spatial image schemas. For example, author Peggy Hackney asks, "What is the dynamic quality of the movement?" Effort reveals the mover's attitude toward investing energy in four basic factors: Flow/Time/Space/Weight:

Flow: ⟋   Time: _ ′_ Space: ⌐ indirect ⌡

free ⟍   ⟋ bound   sustained _ ′ sudden ′_   direct ⌐

Weight: Hackney describes how weight has a complex effort dynamic with two variations including Active Weight: ⌐ light   and Passive Weight: ⌐ limp

⌐

⌐ strong   ⌐ heavy

In addition, rather than actively using or passively giving up Weight, you can also move as you experience Weight Sensing: rarefy your weight
with lightness

⌐

yield into the earth and push away with strength

These effort qualities also combine in both two quality effort compounds called "States" and three quality effort compounds called "Drives." For example, combining Sudden Time and Active Strong Weight, you create "Rhythm State." ⌐
   Try it out for yourself. In another example, if you were to add Indirect Space and Bound Flow together, you create "Remote State." If you were to add Strong Active Weight to your Remote State, you would combine three effort qualities called "Spell Drive," ⌐ a combination which has strong roots to the earth, while maintaining a controlled bound flow movement which has simultaneous awareness of multiple space around you. Try this out for yourself; it helps to think of a situation where you might do this drive, so think of yourself as one of the witches in Macbeth, stirring the pot, while casting a spell of earthy weighted control of the whole world.

---

us the opportunity to apply additional concepts of effort dynamics and shape change to the development of linguistic categories and oral expression, in addition to expanding their existing interest in spatial concepts. On a more sophisticated level, I suggest that the integrated systemic interrelationships between effort, shape and space in Laban Movement Analysis can also provide a kind of kinesthetic syntactical "grammar" (Boxes 8.1, 8.2 and 8.3).

This grammar can stimulate new image schemas that reference, not just individual semantic content, but also the transcendent (and dynamic) narrative structure

Box 8.3 Shape qualities

Shape qualities

Labanalysis also addresses Shape. Hackney asks, "How is the Shape changing, as an expressive process?" Every movement is an action of Shape Change, specifically in terms of answering the question, "Towards where" is the shape changing?

Rising   Spreading

                Advancing   Retreating

    Sinking   Enclosing

You can also combine each of these into two and three quality compounds, for example:

Rising and Advancing, like a swimmer coming to the surface:

Sinking, Spreading and Retreating, as if tumbling back and down onto your hands and feet:

All of these movement qualities provide new material for the production of an expanded array of embodied images schemas. In addition, each of these concepts can be combined into compounds which can phrase over time, interwoven with each other. In fact, almost all movement is completely phrased, using all three qualities of Space, Effort and Shape. (For space reasons, I have not explored all the possibilities within each category.)

Here is an example of how movement phrases:

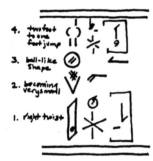

Do a twisting action to the right, emphasizing the horizontal plane and performed in sustained time and effort and light delicacy weight effort (one version of Rhythm State). You will be holding the edge of your kinesphere steady in peripheral spatial tension.

At the end of your twist, become very small, as your shape changes by enclosing into a ball-like still form using controlled bound flow effort.

From this still shape, use active strong weight sensing to jump from two feet to one foot, retreating and rising simultaneously in a backwards sagittal one-dimensional spatial direction, radiating from your core in central spatial tension.

Read this notation from the bottom to top:

These illustrations show how movement itself is complexly phrased and how many possibilities of phrased movement patterns can emerge to support more complex embodied image schemas. In turn, these schemas will generate linguistic expressions of both first and second order of dynamism.

that configures semantics into what we automatically recognize as "story." These new possibilities provide a depth and breadth to the image schema categories, and generate ramifications in the development of both new metaphors and means for verbal expression. In this embodied metareference to narrative through the phrased interplay of multiple categories of movement observation, I return to my interest in oral history. If my thesis proves justified, dance-trained people may produce oral narratives of breath-taking sophistication based on their refined somatic experience.

While we consider the expansion and development of Lakoff and Johnson's contribution, there can also be a reconsideration of the vocal category itself as gesture, regarding William Stokoe and David Armstrong's research in the deaf communities. When the oral transmission of embodied knowledge of dancers is examined from this perspective, the way that bodily expression is interactive with verbal expression becomes clearer. I suggest that the vocal production process, oral voicing as a bodily gesture, becomes the vibratory link between somatics and narrative. For example, my recent research project involving oral history interviews with Sara Rudner, a choreographer and performer respected for her sense of embodied expression, suggests the vocal production of sound in and of itself is a possible linking mechanism between bodily gesture and semantic expression.[19] I worked for an intensive in-depth Labanalysis of a very short video sample from Sara's oral history which beautifully integrated changes in posture, her bodily and vocal gestures and semantic word content. This phrase included both a singular semantic statement and a singular gestural phrase. While both are simultaneously occurring, there is a complex layered interaction between them. For example, the body changes to an alert posture just prior to beginning to vocalize; the gesture phrase amplifies and then diminishes while the vocal statement emerges into more and more clarity, arriving at a substantial philosophical declaration. Within this twelve-second richly layered communication complex, I have been able to identify a through-line of dynamic "bound" effort that began in Sara's body, which then passed into the vocal quality of her voice, and was finally expressed in the semantic expression of her vocabulary. This project suggests that vocal expression is defined not only by the auditory nature of its reception, but also by the embodied nature of its production.[20] As such, vocal production may provide a foundational link between our body's vocal/physical gestures and our semantic expression. As for *Muscle Memory*, the choreographic process reinscribes personal style, writ large, as it were, in more explicitly interwoven patterns of movement, gesture and vocal expression. The clipped vocal production of Frank's speech is directly linked to his finger snap gestures and the semantic message to his Dad: "Go ahead, kill yourself, get it over with, quick."

However, I am conscious to avoid idealizing an ever-congruent relationship between somatic experience and narrative production. In the historical "guild," oral narratives were not always considered valid evidence for the purposes of historiography. However, the discourses of postmodernism suggest that production of history is a construction which must be considered a situated "interpretation of what happened" rather than "what happened" itself.[21] As a result, the congruence between memory and distanced events in the past in and of itself is not always an

JEFF FRIEDMAN

appropriate test of the oral interview's validity as an historical document. For example, Italian oral historian and theorist Alessandro Portelli reminds us that individual reminiscence is nested within a social world with many levels of influences which require negotiation in the production of narratives. Tracking those influences is a form of valuable historical analysis which reveals how memory is constructed within constraints. In other words, a lack of "congruence" is a form of information in and of itself.[22] I suggest applying Portelli's important contribution on *inter*personal social interaction between subjects and their social worlds to the *intra*personal internal congruence among multiple communication channels, within a single subject.

For example, returning to Sara Rudner's interview, I have been able to identify "stray" body movements which suggest a lack of congruence between semantic content and bodily/vocal gesture. Similar to the use of irony introduced earlier ("**LOOOOOVE** that dress [pause] (wink)"), the body of an oral history subject may provide clues to understated or even subconscious messages that convey important information to the interviewer and eventually the researcher. In my study of what Rudolf von Laban calls "shadow movements" during oral interviews, I have found patterns that suggest that small and seemingly unrelated movements, especially of the distal edges of the body (feet, hands, facial gestures), provide clues to a strong emotional charge in verbal statements. For example, drumming the fingers on a knee, or tapping the toes on the floor indicate impatience or frustration. Laban might describe these movements as "mobile state," with an emphasis on quick time and free flow (see Box 8.4). In contrast to their more obvious weighted and stable sitting posture, is this narrator, in fact, eager to leave this line of questioning? The room? The interview?

A sensitized interviewer is forewarned by their awareness of the kinesthetic communication channel. There may also be a pattern of presaging, i.e. a predictive function, for shadow movements. Those movements, which suggest contradictory information to what is currently said, may, in fact, provide a clue to what is being considered in the narrator's conscious or subconscious mind. For example, Sara Rudner's narration of her career trajectory away from Twyla Tharp's company and towards a commitment to her own choreography was presaged in body movement. During a discussion of touring experiences and *before* telling me that she was considering leaving the company, Sara actually "walked" two of her fingers down her leg away from her weighted and centered torso. Noting these movement expressions can lead the interviewer and researcher towards new lines of questioning based on an analysis of the congruence among several intrapersonal modes of communication.

Inspired by Bourdieu's concept of social (interpersonal) habitus, which predates cognitive expression of social congruence within a culture group, I analyze somatic modes of behavior in an *intra*personal relation to the cognized wording of experience. This analysis offers a new source of understanding for the ongoing dynamic negotiation between forms of cultural knowing and expression. Additionally, this analysis offers new research opportunities to link embodied knowledge to their social

174

Box 8.4 Shadow movements

Shadow movements in distal body parts such as hands and feet suggest simultaneous multiple "non-congruent" intrapersonal embodied communicative messages:

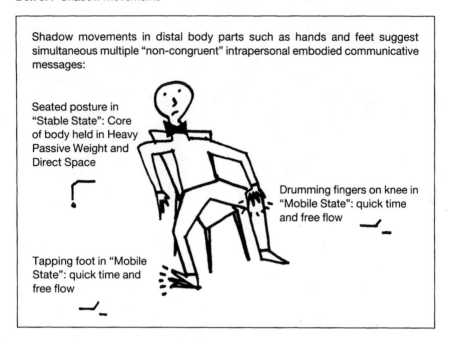

Seated posture in "Stable State": Core of body held in Heavy Passive Weight and Direct Space

Drumming fingers on knee in "Mobile State": quick time and free flow

Tapping foot in "Mobile State": quick time and free flow

context. Through Portelli's work, I have begun to understand the roles of external family, community and national identity on the production and negotiation of oral narratives. My theories of the relationships between intrasubjective embodied channels of communication may also become helpful sources of interpretative research into the effects of the social world on narrative production and historical representation.

Performances of *Muscle Memory* are also a tapestry of spoken and recorded word, gesture and full-body dancing. Audiences have the opportunity to move along continua of both kinesthetic and semantic expression with the performer. As choreographer, I have consciously taken advantage of theatrical performance to tease apart these expressive channels, creating overlapping events in both media, or even purposefully disjunctive events which contrast one against the other. As a result, each channel of communication can be more easily individually tracked. For example, I may perform a "noncongruent" relation between gesture and vocal production. Frank's insouciant delivery of his words is accompanied by an angry gesture. I represented Eve's patient trek across the United States to New York with the elderly Miss Burnett, driving under forty miles an hour in her Chevrolet, by a silent movement interlude that progresses in a Noh-like state of timelessness. This slow motion "miniworld" is belied by the accompanying recorded text where Eve's semantic expression reveals a sublimated impatience to move into the next phase of her young life. The richness of choreographic representation is augmented through fine-tuning the balance and contrast between communication channels: kinesthetic, verbal, and semantic. The theatrical production of oral history narratives offers an opportunity to explore the subject's performance of embodied knowledge, including the negotiations between social influences and intrasubjective modes of expression.

LEGACY has a very small part-time staff: myself and a production manager. In order to sustain the annual production of new oral history interviews, in 1996 I created an oral history training program for local community members. Since then, LEGACY has trained over fifty volunteer interviewers not only to produce research quality documents but also to recognize the role of embodied knowledge in oral history interviewing. As I begin my lecture on interviewing, I encourage my students to open themselves to the possibilities of embodied knowledge in oral histories. To help create a container for these possibilities, I lead them in a visualization that emphasizes the sense of flow in oral interviewing.[23] I help them visualize for themselves that the oral interview is a mutually created event that mediates a flow between interviewer and narrator that exists in both the kinesthetic and verbal channels of communication.

In this visualization, I describe a situationally constructed historical narrative through a sense of "flow" between a streambed and the stream, with the oral historian's questions appearing as obstacles to flow around, over and below. The generative force for this flow refers to Portelli's suggestion regarding the source of all research investigation: difference.[24] Each interviewer and narrator is different enough from one another to generate a mutual flow of information between them, through all communication channels. For the interviewer, this pedagogical visualization can become more elaborated over time and provides a useful anchoring conceptualization for both the interviewer and narrator, prior to an interview. The sense of flow also purposefully elicits an appreciation and awareness for the kinesthetic aspects of embodied experience. Retaining a sense of flow in the interviewer's own body and recognizing this dynamic effort in other bodies can give an embodied anchor for the intellectual flow of the interview.

During interview training, I also encourage the narrator to become aware of their own gestures. Ideally, a skillful interviewer encourages the narrator to describe salient gestures in their own words, which often deepens the narrator's awareness of their own intentions. As Frank's character in *Muscle Memory* might gesture angrily while expressing his *joie de vivre*, a narrator may find new sources of motivation for their verbal expression in their own gestures. Those movements that elude the narrator's awareness often provide important clues to the interviewer.

Folklorist Dennis Tedlock's work has established beyond a doubt the importance of the poetics of orality. Tedlock suggests that print transcripts should provide ample representation to the poetics of orality.[25] Silence, repetition, vocal pitch, and volume all provide important clues to the context of producing oral communication in dialog. In addition to the recognition of these vocal gestures, I would add a responsibility to represent body movements or the lack of movement in the form of notes on posture, conscious gesture and shadow movements (I have given several short examples in this chapter bracketed by "performative" text cues, e.g. "ACT I,

Scene 1", that designate them as theatrical events within this text). As the examples shift reader attention to the performance aspects of orality, I encourage the reader to also recognize themselves in the oral history transcript at a conversational level. We communicate with our whole bodies; these additional channels are important means for transmitting nonverbal embodied knowledges. *Muscle Memory* is a theatrical presentation of transcripted oral narratives. While edited for dramatic purposes, the integrity of the narrator's intentions and statements is maintained. As choreographer, I wanted to deploy these oral narratives to further an artistic goal of both representing diverse lives in dance to new audiences while enlivening the transcripts through embodied performances.

I have performed *Muscle Memory* in several different settings for many different audiences. I have often linked performances to oral history training workshops in which elders, students and other community members learn cognitive skills about interview and editing techniques. However, when audiences attend a performance of *Muscle Memory*, they often note how the process of oral history comes alive. The narrators seem to "leap" off the page and enter their hearts; audiences come to know these narrators in a way that cannot be substituted in transcripts or even the original audio recordings. These comments reveal that my objective has been furthered. Representation of these narrators has been enlivened through embodied performance through the processes of distillation, clarification and projection. Vocal production and physical gestures, and through choreographic form itself, audiences both "re-member" the subject, and experience a metacommentary on the act of remembering, achieved through communication at several levels, from my mindful body to the shared audience's social body.

ACT IV, Scene 1: Postlude reprise
Listen.
(pause . . . relax . . . take a breath. you can gesture with one hand to your ear, bending slightly forward and to one side . . .)
Find a pulse. Listen to the pulse.
> *Listen to the pulse of muscle memory, in between the bones.*
> *Twitch the switch to muscle memory*
> > *and listen to the pulse . . .*
> > > *of muscle*

> > > > *memory*

> > > > > *bones*

Notes

1 George Lakoff and Mark Johnson, *Metaphors We Live By* (Chicago and London: University of Chicago Press, 1980), 14–19. Lakoff and Johnson's text introduces their theories on embodiment, cognition and verbal expression, supplemented by Johnson's later text *The Body in the Mind*.

2 Pierre Bourdieu, *The Logic of Practice* (Stanford, CA: Stanford University Press), 66–79.

3 Martin Gleisner, "Movement Choirs," *LIMS News* (Laban/Bartenieff Institute of Movement Studies) 6(3) (1984): 10. Martin Gleisner (1897–1983), a student of Laban's during the early development of movement choir and theory, suggests

> [movement choir] does not suppress individuality rather, it encourages it. The possibility for [i]ndividuality is given through cooperation of the different types of mover, each in his own group . . . continuously allowing the individual personality to be aware of itself within the wider form . . . [i]ndeed it is satisfying to see how the diversity of the individual remains, although retaining the common expression of the whole group . . . personal characteristics are brought to consciousness. They also provide the supplementation necessary for the extension of the individual as well as of the group.

4 The reference to dancer Mikhail Baryshnikov comes from choreography created by the Oberlin Dance Collective (ODC), a contemporary performance group based in San Francisco. As a member from 1980 to 1989, I participated in the reconstruction of a dance work titled *The Red Shoes*, in which numerous ironic references to iconic dancers and dance practices were inserted into the choreography. The "Baryshnikov" movement reference was an overly flashy virtuosic move which functioned as a "button," punctuating the overall pedestrian movement vocabulary with an overstatement something like a "Look, Ma! I'm *dancing*" exclamation point in movement.

5 Linguist William Stokoe, who worked with the deaf communities for several years, suggested that sign language which is received kinesthetically and visually is not necessarily opposed to oral speech, which is received aurally. This contrast had been the basis of ongoing conflict about "main-streaming" efforts in education for deaf communities. Instead, Stokoe reframed the conflict by reminding us that both oral speech and sign language are *produced* through embodied action. This perspective places vocal production in a new role as kinesthetic gesture, rather than only a vehicle for semantic content.

6 Elizabeth Fine's *The Folklore Text: From Performance to Print* (Bloomington, IN: Indiana University Press, 1984) provides a detailed discussion on the limits of both "natural language" and graphic symbolic systems for comprehensive representation of oral communication in print (113–148).

7 Gillian Brown, *Speakers, Listeners, and Communication: Explorations in Discourse Analysis* (Cambridge: Cambridge University Press, 1995), 166.

8 Ibid., 51.

9 LEGACY's collection is held at the San Francisco Performing Arts Library and Museum, located at the Civic Center. Please contact SF PALM at 401 Van Ness Avenue, Room 402, San Francisco, CA 94102 or by phone at 415-255-4800 for more information on research access to LEGACY's collection.

10 Fine, *Folklore Text*, offers a useful argument for this intention regarding the dangers of the "appropriative comprehension of analysis" which the author intends to disrupt through a counterbalancing gesture that embodies the "integral presence" of the original performance through a "second, interpretive performance" (148, 163).

11 In addition to her artistic contributions to dance, Eve Gentry (formerly known, at that time, as Henrietta Greenhood) was also one of four founders of the Dance Notation Bureau in New York City in 1940. DNB focuses on the development and dissemination of Labanotation graphic notation scores which represent an increasingly diverse archive of choreographic documentation.

12 One of Frank's physical problems included a localized paralysis of his tongue and other muscles in his mouth. Our first interview began with his slurred speech but, according to Frank, by the end of the session, his drive to record a life-history seemed to gradually renew the necessary neurological connections to heal his short-term paralysis. This

experience brings Dr. Oliver Sack's work with Parkinson's patients to mind. Many of these patients depended on what Sacks calls "flow" to keep movement sequences integrated and restart them if they become frozen in place as a symptom of their neurological deficit.

13 Sara Rudner. Videotaped oral history interview, May 6, 1998 (Side A: pp. 2, 3, 5, 7–9; Side B: p. 16). Choreographer and performer Sara Rudner was the narrator in four life-history interviews conducted between May 5 and May 7, 1998 by Ph.D. students Patrick Alcedo, Jeff Friedman, Yatin Lin, and Janet O'Shea, interviewer/editors. The interviews comprised a practicum exercise for a graduate seminar in oral history methods taught by Associate Professor Sally A. Ness. For more information regarding Dance Department oral history archive holdings and research access, contact: Department Secretary, Ph.D. graduate program in Dance History and Theory, University of California, Riverside, CA 92521; phone: 909-787-5424.

14 Ronald Grele, "Movement without Aim: Methodological and Theoretical Problems in Oral History," *Envelopes of Sound: The Art of Oral History*, ed. Ronald Grele (Chicago: Precedent, 1985), 127–154.

15 Kristine Minister, "A Feminist Frame for the Oral History Interview," *Women's Words: The Feminist Practice of Oral History*, eds. Sherna Berger Gluck and Daphne Patai (New York and London: Routledge, 1991), 27–41.

16 In John Willet's text *Brecht on Theatre*, the editor cites several examples over a chronological period from 1918 to 1948 where Brecht discusses the role of emotion and empathy in theater. Brecht's writings make a clear trajectory from a stance against the use of emotion to a reconsideration of the place of emotion in his theories and their application to theater performance. At first, Brecht states in texts written between 1918 and 1932 that "[t]he essential point of the epic theatre is perhaps that it appeals less to the feelings than the spectator's reason. Instead of sharing an experience, the spectator must come to grip with things" (23). However, later on, Brecht notes that the alienation effect of detachment in acting does not absent emotion, but that "the form of emotion need not correspond to those of the character portrayed" (94). He cautions that the rejection of empathy is not the rejection of emotion, but a necessity to enjoin a critical stance to that emotion in order to historicize it, from a class-based ideology. In 1948, Brecht's *Short Organum for the Theatre* allows that his theater has made mistakes in regards to emotion: "our [actors] show too little of the real thing. Aiming to avoid artificial heat, we fall short in natural warmth" (248). However, Brecht continues to reject what he calls an "aristotleian dramaturgy" which demands catharsis only from the point of view of empathy. Instead, he calls for "a type of theatre which not only releases feeling . . . within the particular historical field of human relations, but employs and encourages those thoughts and feelings which help transform the field itself" (190).

17 Brown, *Speakers, Listeners, and Communication*, 169.

18 Ibid., 109. Brown also suggests that spatial deixis in speech directly references "the body parts of the speaker" (109).

19 Jeff Friedman, "Verbal and Non-Verbal Expression in Oral Interviews with a Dance Subject: A Labanalysis of Verbal Semantic, Verbal Production and Postural/Gestural Movement Phrasing." Unpublished project for certification as a Laban/Bartenieff movement analyst from the Integrated Movement Studies Program, University of Utah, 1999. Peggy Hackney and Ed Groff, advisors.

20 I am indebted to authors David Armstrong, William Stokoe and Sherman Wilcox's text, *Gesture and the Nature of Language* (Cambridge: Cambridge University Press, 1995). These researchers at Gallaudet University, the United States' first university for the deaf communities, have conducted vanguard research in this area.

21 I am indebted to Haitian historian Michel-Rolph Trouillot for further articulating the difference between "what happened" and "what we say happened" and for naming

the "historical guild" to reference the "uninitiated" populations who produce history yet who are silenced as outsiders to guild membership. Michel-Rolph Trouillot, *Silencing the Past: Power and the Production of History* (Boston, MA: Beacon Press, 1995), 2, 56.

22 I am indebted to Italian historian Alessandro Portelli's theories regarding Luigi Trastulli's alleged death in a labor riot in 1940s Italy as they relate to my hypothesis regarding lack of "congruence" among intrapersonal communication channels. Portelli suggests individual, social, and nationalist affiliations influence the production of oral interviews of observers of "what happened." His theories codify how we negotiate the production of our personal oral narratives in relation to a hierarchy of external social milieux. This negotiation provides a new and highly useful model for interpreting the interpersonal relationships between oral sources and the social construction of history and suggests further refinement on the intra-personal level. Alessandro Portelli, *The Death of Luigi Trastulli and Other Stories: Form and Meaning in Oral History* (Albany, NY: State University of New York Press, 1991), 1–26.

23 The use of flow as an image to establish access to kinesthetic embodiment can be linked to Rudolf von Laban and his successors' theories regarding flow as a baseline effort dynamic for human movement. Flow is also an important sociological concept explored in Mihaly Czikszentmihalyi's work.

24 Portelli, *Death of Luigi Trastulli*, 55–58.

25 Dennis Tedlock, "Learning to Listen: Oral History as Poetry," *Envelopes of Sound: The Art of Oral History*, ed. Ronald Grele (Chicago: Precedent, 1985), 108–125. See also Tedlock, "On the Translation of Style in Oral Narrative," in *Towards New Perspectives in Folklore*, eds. Américo Paredes and Richard Bauman (Austin, TX: University of Texas Press, 1972), 114–133.

9

"HOPE . . . TEACH, YAKNOWHATI'MSAYIN"

Freestylin knowledge through Detroit hiphop

Ryan Snyder Ananat

This chapter follows the Breakfast Club -- a Detroit hiphop cooperative made up of Hodgepodge aka Montana aka Big Tone (Hodge for short), Lacksi-daisy-cal aka Tarach (Lacks for short), and Elzhi (El for short) – as they start the process of making names for themselves as professional musicians. When we met, both Lacks and Hodge had put out homemade tapes of their material with tracks featuring Elzhi as a guest artist. Later, they began dropping singles on Antidote – the hiphop imprint of a local electronic music label that Angela, their unofficial manager and full-time supporter, helps to run – with EPs (extended plays) and full-lengths on deck. While tracing this artistic growth, my work here also tells the story of me on a mission to strike an agreement between the senses I have of myself as a hiphop head and as a scholar. To be successful means doing scholarship that's not just about hiphop, but is hiphop. In other words, I'm hoping for a day when hiphop will be acknowledged as a way of being a scholar and scholarship is considered an official – that is, popularly recognized – element of hiphop. To these ends, I'd like to share my experiences of getting to know and staying in touch with the Breakfast Club.

RYAN: So what do you think needs to *change?*

LACKS: Thinkin! [Hodge laughs]

RYAN: Howdoyouhowdowehowdoyou go about c h a n g i n g t h i n k i n? Or do you just assume that it's going to change? [Hodge laughs]

LACKS: Hope . . . teach. Teach through like bein an example, yaknowhati'msayin, it's . . . it'sit's just a lack of diligence, yaknowhati'msayin, it's like too deep for em, they don't know, they don't understand . . . they don't understand certain things, and then what they do understand, they're like: yeah, well, but . . . it'sit's like always an *excuse* for everything, always an excuse.

Who am *I?*

I met Lacks on a Thursday, January 14, 1999. At the time, he was organizing and hosting an open mic night and working part time at Café Mahogany in Harmonie

Park, one of the few sections of downtown affected in a positive way by Detroit's "urban renewal." In other words, the infrastructure's been invested in to the extent that there are restaurants and whatnot for people from the suburbs to frequent on the weekends. I was one of these people, in my first year of graduate school at the University of Michigan in Ann Arbor, beginning my career as a hiphop scholar, trying to figure out exactly what that means.

In my efforts to do so, I'd discovered ethnomusicology and was taking a class on field methods, learning about the history of ethnography and thinking about it as a way of studying music.[1] Our project for the term was to put what we were learning into practice by doing short-term fieldwork on a musical topic of interest in the Detroit Metro area and writing a paper about what we'd learned. Around the time we were supposed to start doing our fieldwork, my friend Carla – who was also taking the class and doing a project on Detroit techno – showed me a column about local hiphop spots. She and I headed down to Mahogany, which sounded like the coolest place. It was somewhere we knew we could find and close to another spot in case we wanted to bounce before the night was over.

We got there early. Lacks was warming up the room on the turntables, setting the mood by spinning bouncy underground joints with just enough mass appeal. The crowd began to build – mostly black people with three or four white people, including myself. Mahogany is a meeting ground for the overlapping hiphop, boho, and black working-class communities in Detroit. When I asked Lacks why he decided to devote his time and energy to putting on his Thursday night open mic there he said that nothing else was going on, that "nobody else does *hiphop*," and that Mahogany "has a certain *vibe*." "So I'm like, damn, yaknowhati'msayin, it needs to happen *some . . . where*."[2]

The host that night was a female MC (master of ceremonies) named N'jeri, who was definitely in charge of the crowd, commanding us to get on the dance floor and regulating the open mic with finesse. Her freestyles were the highlight of an otherwise lackluster open mic session. She invited all the aspiring MCs to step to the mic to begin the performance and soon there was a crowd – mostly men, with one or two women – clamoring at the skirt of the stage (really just a short platform) waiting for N'jeri to pass them the mic. One by one they kicked their freestyles – or at least what were supposed to be freestyles, since many of the rhymes had a prewritten flavor. They seemed uncomfortable in front of the crowd, not knowing how to carry *themselves* much less carry a musical conversation with either the audience or the DJ (disc jockey). In short, they were unpracticed – they just couldn't flow. What's worse, many of them didn't seem to know it. Instead of considering the open mic an opportunity to learn and hone their skills, they considered it a chance to show everyone how dope they are.

This behavior provoked a couple of indirect lyrical tongue-lashings from N'jeri and a straight up, in-your-face freestyle from Lacks hilariously educating fools on the proper methods of holding the mic . . . literally. I could tell by his demeanor at the time that he considered this a last-ditch effort to get people to take this event seriously. Although I sympathized with him, I perhaps didn't take the open mic as seriously as I could have. But making that mistake, in fact, proved to be an important learning experience. It was crucial that it wasn't until later, when I was writing my paper, that I realized that during that open mic session *I* was in the midst of learning the first in a series of lessons on how to go about doing my work as a hiphop scholar. If I'd been able to realize my errors at the time rather than in retrospect, I never would have made the same sort of well-meaning blunders later that allowed Lacks to "teach through bein an example" and I would have missed gems of knowledge like the one recorded in the sample that starts off this section and provides the inspiration for this entire chapter. It's accidental occurrences like these that allow us to imagine and attempt to actualize new possibilities for ourselves, our communities, and the world we live in. I was painfully embarrassed by each misstep I took at the time, but I can say that making these mistakes was key to learning what I did about hiphop. Otherwise I'd never know just how deep "hope . . . teach, yaknowhati'msayin" really is and I wouldn't be continuously reminded how much growing up I still have to do. In other words, I wouldn't have learned how to freestyle.

What am I *talking* about?

Popular wisdom tells us that hiphop is a youth culture – made up of "four elements": DJing, MCing, breakdancing, and graffiti writing – collaboratively developed by African Americans, Jamaicans, and Latinos in New York City during the 1970s and centered around live musical performances involving a DJ who spun popular records of the day, often isolating and repeating the percussive breaks, while an MC rapped over the beat, performing many of the duties N'Jeri or Lacks did while hosting the open mic at Mahogany: getting people on the dance floor, creating a sense of community by communicating local knowledge, and in the process demonstrating their skills on the mic. The media industry soon discovered that "rap music" could be lucrative to record, market, and distribute. Hiphop subsequently developed into a big business and popular culture with global influence during the course of the 1980s and 1990s.[3]

This account isn't inaccurate, but in getting to know the Breakfast Club I began to recognize how it departed from common sense. Such an approach to studying hiphop not only overlooks the process of translating expertise in live performance into unique studio-crafted methods of recording – hiphop lyricism and sampling technique as we know them today – but also fails in general to give an accurate sense of what the lives of professional hiphop artists are actually like.[4] In other words, it undervalues the learning process aspiring artists continuously work through. Acknowledging and understanding this apprenticeship and self-schooling requires that hiphop scholars work to find out what professional hiphop artists do and think about on an everyday basis. In part, this means recognizing that today's established artists were yesterday's wishful listeners.

As hiphop heads proceed on their artistic education and witness their favorite artists getting jerked by the major labels, getting no airplay on the radio or MTV, getting ignored or dissed by the magazines, and being unable to book venues for their live shows they get more and more wary of the media industry's representations of hiphop and move further into what some call underground, hardcore, streetlevel – but what I call *independent* hiphop, not in order to claim that it's in any way independent of the media industry but to emphasize that it insists on being understood on its own terms and thus suggests alternative ways for artists to relate to the music industry. Heads enter a world where information is exchanged by hearing what a select few DJs spin and put on their mixtapes, by checking out websites and small-circulation publications, by watching the shelves at local record stores, and most importantly by listening to what they hear word of mouth. So it's a place where it's important who you know – people who can up you on what new artists to check out, what magazines are worth reading, where the websites are, when shows are going on, where cool regular spots are.

It's also important to get to know the artists themselves on a personal basis because music-wise a lot of them are putting out their own tapes and have limited supplies or distribution, and local heads are always reliant on bombers and breakers for information on where and when to see the best of what they do. The learning process never stops, because independent hiphop isn't a specific *thing* or even a stable set of beliefs – it's an inclusive way of envisioning the future and working to make what we imagine a reality. Through studying how and why hiphop artists do what they do and writing about it I hope to help shape what I learn into a common language for talking about hiphop that will simultaneously respect the independence and originality of the artists I talk to and encourage broad lines of communication that can be used to discover new possibilities for cooperation among members of various local hiphop communities.

In particular, through this ethnographic work I'm striving to balance the demands of art and the responsibilities of scholarship. My first night at Mahogany was definitely a new experience for me. I'd been to open mics before, but not *as a scholar*. Going to a live hiphop event as research rather than just for fun, you're not just there to enjoy yourself, you're there to learn something. This feeling is especially intense when you go to a new event. Not knowing anyone, you're at a loss for what to do with yourself. It was also my first go at doing ethnography. I'd done some music journalism for my college newspaper, but my experiences getting to know hiphop artists didn't extend beyond press kits and formal interviews. It was important for me to know hiphop not just as it's represented, but as it's *lived*.

Like Ingrid Monson I believe that, as she writes in her study of jazz improvisation, "musicians themselves are the most authoritative sources of knowledge about music."[5] For a scholar, putting this belief into practice entails "an obligation to document actively the everyday life experiences, histories, opinions, self-representations, and practices of real people" (Monson, 212). In other words, wanting to be involved in and contribute to the music that I identify with and that has shaped the ways in which I think, it was important to me to talk to hiphop artists in order to understand the incredible things people do with mics, turntables, samplers, spraypaint, and their bodies and thus the ideas, feelings, and identities these practices make possible. Sitting there that night and strolling around the café *observing*, I was eager to become a *participant*, to be *known*. But being a newcomer and at times feeling like a complete outsider, I was shy about introducing myself to either N'jeri or Lacks. Putting myself in the loop, so to speak, would take the skills of a tightrope walker and I was unsure whether I had that much *tact* – which, as Michel de Certeau describes it, "requires that one maintain a balance that is never permanently acquired . . . because in fact the practitioner himself is part of the equilibrium."[6] The reason I was even contemplating such a feat was because it sounded like the practical consequence of what William James described way back in the day as *reasoning* – "the mere play of the mind comparing its conceptions" through which "arises a perception of relations between things so naturally separate that we should otherwise never have compared them together at all."[7]

As a professional student, I definitely had a lot of practice at reasoning. But tact is a matter of putting the results of reasoning into action, working to actualize the relationships you imagine. In essence, what I was considering was the transition from hiphop head to b-boy – that is, from someone who knows what they're talking about to someone who both knows and *does* what they're talking about. Making such a change required that I be willing to let my understanding of hiphop – and thus my understanding of myself – be transformed. In fact, I would have to come to a new understanding of what to *know* means. Such an undertaking calls for the "artistic poise" Paul Berliner shows being demonstrated through skillful improvisation – an "instant response to the musical turn of events and agile handling of vocabulary," a "tolerance for ambiguity and courage in the face of risk," keeping one's cool while experiencing "the intensity of struggling with creative processes under the pressure of a steady beat."[8] "When great artists explore ideas with the force of conviction," he explains, "they mesmerize the audience by moving toward goals with such determination and logic that their direction seems inevitable, their final creations compelling" (Berliner, 262).

Such virtuosity seemed out of my reach. My experience that night was so dense and quick it was overwhelming, and making sense of it meant thinking back on things, realizing where I went wrong, and imagining how I could do things better in the future. What I didn't realize at the time was that this is exactly the sort of learning process and artistic growth that jazz musicians – and, I would find out later, hiphop artists – go through during their careers, particularly at the beginning. "There is, in fact," Berliner writes, "a lifetime of preparation and knowledge behind every idea an improviser performs," and "this preparation begins long before prospective performers seize upon music as the central focus of their lives" (17). Being that the vocation of musical performance asks jazz improvisers to bring with them parts of themselves that exist prior to their careers, it makes sense that improvisation, involving a person's whole self, becomes "not merely a process by which musicians create a record album or an evening's performance," but in fact "a particular artistic way of going through life" (486).

Berliner's descriptions of jazz improvisation here provide a guide for beginning to understand freestylin, the art that an open mic like the one Lacks put on at

Mahogany provides a stage for. I'm hoping that thinking about hiphop as an "artistic way of life" will help us to begin imagining the ways in which scholars and musicians, although we do different kinds of work, can share common ways of going about doing our respective works and thereby learn from one another as we increase our expertise in our chosen professions.

What did I *learn*?

Hiphop lyricism is a dynamic art that consists of interwoven acts of thought, speech, and music. Lyrical skills, then, are as much a matter of making transitions and conjunctures as they are a matter of developing a special aptitude at thinking, speaking, or making music. Writing, recording, and live performance are all ways in which MCs practice synthesizing thoughts, words, and sounds into effective combinations. Although there are similarities between these three methods of lyrical composition, each constitutes a distinct process that results in emphasizing some of the components of lyricism more than others.

Hiphop lyricism is composed of three major elements. First, *content* – which can be understood simply as having to do with the literal or figurative meanings of the language used in the rhymes as well as their poetic and narrative structures. The second major element is *flow*. When talking about flow most people focus on it as a matter of *rhythm*, the ability to keep a beat. But I want to emphasize that flow involves *percussion* as well, which is subtly different from rhythm. Percussion, as I'm using it here, is the ability to produce at the right times and intensities those *breaks* in a steady beat, most often through vocal stress and hard consonant sounds, that not only make the beat interesting but in doing so keep it going and, in fact, make it possible.

An attention to these breaks can contribute to our understanding of hiphop lyricism in much the same way Roland Barthes's attention to still images enhanced his interpretation of modern films. Percussion can be considered the sonic equivalent of what he designates as "the founding act of the filmic," "the transition from language to *signifying*" – that is, from what analysis or criticism can say about art to the surplus meanings of art that at present "my intellection cannot quite grasp."[9] In this sense, the percussive quality of an MC's flow overlaps in effect with the third and central element of hiphop lyricism: *style*. It is also the most complicated, and thus hard to get our minds around. Style isn't a problem to be solved, but a body of inconclusive evidence that nevertheless insists on being kept in mind. Our under-standing of it, then, will be "less an answer to a question than a proposal concerning the continuation of a story which is just unfolding."[10]

Most obviously, style is an expression of self-awareness through a distinctive sound, which requires MCs to both make use of the most resonant timbral qualities of their voice and expertly – almost implicitly – harmonize this personal timbre with the musical qualities of the instrumental tracks over which they rhyme, putting their own sound in the mix of which the beat is composed.[11] In doing so it not only synchronizes the poetic and narrative coherence of content with the rhythmic cadence and percussive force of flow but also produces along with this synthesis

186

the most compelling aspects of hiphop lyricism. Being mostly a matter of sound dynamics – that is, a kind of *music* – style puts in effect what Stephen Blum calls "musical syntax," a technique for "'detaching' sounds" from what we consider their normal functions "and manipulating them in altered contexts."[12]

In terms of hiphop lyricism, what this musical syntax amounts to is the ability to use words in innovative ways that communicate meaning beyond the significance that we normally attach to them by foregrounding the *actual sounds* we can produce through creatively uttering these words and emphasizing the feelings these sounds evoke. In other words, style produces the sonic equivalent of what Barthes calls the third – or "obtuse" – meaning he found in film images. He defines this third meaning as "an *accent*" made possible through " a complex, very intricate arrangement" (Barthes, 56, 48). He calls it "obtuse" because by "extend[ing] beyond culture, knowledge, information it can seem limited in the eyes of analytic reason" (44). Taken out of context – that is, interpreted according to an established set of values – "the obtuse meaning inevitably appears as a luxury, an expenditure without exhange" (56). So, judged according to established political and economic standards, "there is something ridiculous about it" (44).

But the style of hiphop lyricism, like Barthes's third meaning, demands that we draw our aesthetic values not from an abstract realm of reason but from actually existing social relations. In addition, its emphasis on sonic dynamics challenges our present political and economic beliefs by insisting on an unorthodox standard of judgment. The sounds of independent hiphop, in the words of Barthes, "carr[y] a certain *emotion*" – that is, "emotion-as-value, an evaluation" (49) that insists that feeling and thinking are complementary moments of the same process rather than positions that refuse to come to an agreement. In this way, they grant a certain substance to our thoughts and language by suggesting the weight they hold in the context of our changing world. The experience of hearing these sounds allows us to feel what we think and mean vibrating through and altering material reality, reminding us that our ideas and beliefs can be sensible as well as reasonable, context-specific in addition to logically consistent.

Shaping our actions and behaviors according to such an inclusive and adaptable system of values allows us to accept – and therefore make use of – the consequences of a recent history characterized by rapid technological innovation. Recognizing that what we can think is a gauge of what we can do – and vice versa – allows us to realize that this historical change entails not only faster and more complicated modes of production that lead to a proliferation of resources but also broader and more complex routes of communication that can be used to increase rather than limit the availability of these resources.[13] The politics of independent hiphop, then, should be understood as a matter of method rather than content – of following, as Barthes puts it, "a certain way of reading 'life' and hence 'reality'" (54) through to its practical conclusions rather than insisting on the priority of an established set of values regardless of their effect in real life. This commitment to resist abstracting the present by remaining open to the future and conscious of the past is fundamental to hiphop's ethos of diligent improvisation.

Style, an aesthetic idiom of this ethos, is the primary resource put into circulation through successful freestylin. The degree to which MCs have succeeded composing such a distinctive and compelling sound for themselves is a gauge not only of "the degree to which old models are transformed and new ideas created" but also of the degree to which MCs are able to organize and sustain "the dynamic conditions and precise processes underlying their transformation and creation" (Berliner, 221). Understood in this way, style also aids MCs in the type of "suspenseful development of ideas [through] the dramatic shaping of sound" that Berliner and the jazz musicians he interviewed call storytelling (262). In the case of hiphop, these stories of style in sound not only complement the narratives crafted through content, but are in fact what is ultimately coherent and compelling. Freestylin, then, can be understood as a form of what anthropologist Elizabeth Tonkin calls "oracy." Such "skilled orality" foregrounds the extent to which "narrations always exist through a web of social relations,"[14] by using the shared, yet unspoken, knowledge of a social group as the frame of reference for an often very personal story. At the same time, hiphop lyricism grants this social context a certain poignancy by allowing it to be experienced in the form of a personal relationship.

Practiced MCs, like the West African oral historians Tonkin interviewed, develop the ability to "convey the accumulative power of narrative through purely oral means" (Tonkin, 63). For Tonkin, "the oral" designates certain "[f]eatures of delivery": "voice quality, chanting or singing, accompanying music or dancing, the type of occasion on which a performance occurs and the place, the status of the performer and nature of the audience itself" (51). In other words, orality is made up of those uses of speech that emphasize its sonic, musical, sensory, and social qualities. MCs – especially when they're freestylin – make use of the sonic dynamics of style to "build up delayed climaxes by the pitch, pause and tempo of vocal delivery, and also by clustering evocative suggestions whose implications the knowing audience themselves link together as powerfully conclusive" (63). It's in this way that successful freestyles or compelling written rhymes "prepare the audience to respond in certain ways" (51) and therefore shape stories that facilitate "people's transmission of experience" (114).

For the Breakfast Club, this ability to, as Lacks put it, "be *sayin* shit without *sayin* shit" (BC 4/1/99) distinguishes dope storytellers and allows them to make the stories they imagine seem more real – that is, *sound better* – than the stories someone who actually lived through similar experiences would tell. In the end, Lacks said, the question "is he telling a story or did he really feel that shit?" is a moot one since what constitutes the art of storytelling is the ability to tell "a story from a perspective of what actually happened to [you]" (BC 4/1/99). What MCs do in telling a dope story is to imagine, based on their actual experiences, what they would do in a fictional situation and in the process create a persona that is a combination of their actual and imaginary selves and therefore more compelling than any "real" person. The effect is an intensified sense of reality, the full force of which it's impossible to understand unless we recognize that the MC is a storyteller. "There are certain things," Lacks said, "that certain cats *say* in they *rhymes* that you know they're not bullshittin what they sayin. You know they're not bullshittin *certain things*" (BC 4/1/99).

These "certain things" are believable not because they refer to experiences an MC has actually lived through but because that artist has thought about his or her actual everyday experiences deeply enough to effectively imagine living through a fictional and extraordinary experience and make it feel real. This compelling feeling is all about how an MC *sounds*. But, as Tonkin argues, it takes a "knowing audience" to pick up on these "evocative suggestions" and realize their outcome. In other words, what makes freestylin effective – what allows it to tell convincing stories – is the extent to which it's embedded in a specific social context. The style that allows hiphop lyricism to serve as a vehicle to transmit experience in the present and imagine experiences in the future draws upon and is shaped by a fund of common past experiences, a shared history. Emphasizing these sonic dynamics, freestylin addresses the challenge of adequately portraying and sharing these historical experiences through words by reminding us that, as Tonkin writes, "[p]eople do not need discursive accounts to represent themselves as historical entities" (Tonkin, 111) or "to communicate to one another their sense of being in a community with the past" (126). The style of independent hiphop can add to standard historical narratives by emphasizing the sonic, musical, sensory, and social qualities of speech. As Tonkin puts it, these "purely oral means" can be used to "re-enact, modify, deny and conserve 'pastness' as both lived experience and mode of understanding" (111).

In this sense, a dope MC lives up to the task Walter Benjamin outlined for his ideal storyteller. After following out an apprenticeship and course of self-schooling in independent hiphop's ethos of diligent improvisation that call for equal parts of introspection and understanding of one's social context, MCs are able to, in Benjamin's words, "reach back to a whole lifetime . . . that comprises not only [their] own experience but no little of the experience of others" (Benjamin, 108). By drawing on shared experiences and realizing common values, freestylin personalizes history and historicizes personality in much the same way jazz musicians do through the process that Monson calls "saying something." As in instrumental improvisation, the actualization of lyrical style through hiphop storytelling occurs "[w]hen a musician successfully reaches a discerning audience, moves its members to applaud or shout praises, raises the energy to dramatic proportions, and leaves a sonorous memory that lingers long after." Being able to create this "moment of community" means that the musician "has moved beyond technical competence" by making "the collaborative and communicative quality of improvisation" a matter of habit (Monson, 1–2).

An open mic provides opportunities for aspiring MCs to learn and practice telling stories structured as meaningful patterns of sound that model, in the words of Christopher Small, "ideal relationships as the participants in the performance imagine them to be."[15] It remains for people to figure out how to actualize these imaginary relationships outside the event in the real world in order to prove that music-making can be in this way, as Small claims, an effective "way of knowing the world" (*M*, 50). Freestylin, because it makes music and the stories it tells both memorable and memorizable, is one possible means for addressing this problem. Such memorizations, as Tonkin writes, "create a sense of the past – even where there is no coherent stream of narrative but only of disparate individual recollections – [that] contribute[s] to the experience of group identity *now*." Insofar as freestylin emphasizes the sensible sounds of independent hiphop, it "help[s] to constitute the social" (Tonkin, 111) through the composition and transmission of models for making an ideal community a reality. In the process, imaginary relationships become tangible in the form of shared experiences. We can understand hiphop lyricism, then, as a music-based poetry that inspires political activities shaped by both an understanding of ourselves and an understanding of our social context. These politics materialize as independent hiphop culture – if by culture we mean dynamic ways of life shaped by a distinctive system of values, specific processes of living, making, thinking and doing as well as their products and end results. Freestylin is foundational to this culture because it allows MCs to narrate and re-enact a shared history that allows us to grasp our present and envision our future.

During my first weeks seeing and hearing the open mics at Mahogany I was beginning to think about what it is exactly that freestylin *means*. In trying to answer this question, I paid attention to interactions during open mic sessions.[16] I sketched out the ways in which the skills involved in freestylin demonstrate artistic virtuosity while shaping social processes on and off the stage. From this perspective, I began to consider Lack's open mics as workshops in freestylin that he put on for potential artists and community-building events for independent hiphop in Detroit rather than just opportunities for aspiring MCs to show how dope they are. The way Lacks regulated the open mic sessions, especially when participants were out to pad their egos or were lazy about freestylin, demonstrated that he had a similar notion of what Thursday nights at Mahogany were all about.

Open mics are formal events – taking place within venues that have stages, mics, turntables, and amplification, not to mention an audience – based on the informal practice of rhyming in ciphers. A cipher takes place when a group of MCs, most of whom usually know one another, circle-up and take turns kicking verses a capella, with a human beatbox, over prerecorded instrumentals, or to the accompaniment of any form of percussion that's close at hand (bangin on lunchroom tables). These events are characterized by being egalitarian and inclusive. "Participants," as Dawn Norfleet writes, "can range from professional to beginner, and participation is an act of equalization of all players." Also, she notes, ciphers "can be formed on a sidewalk, subway station, or park – anywhere there are people who rhyme."[17] Some of the open mics at Mahogany stuck close to the cipher flavor, with MCs taking turns and passing the mic in an orderly fashion.

But often, in order to encourage participation and add structure to what otherwise could have been a chaotic process, Lacks ran the open mic as a low-key battle. Lacks chose two MCs from the crowd and they stepped to the stage. Each kicked a verse, sometimes addressing the other in a competitive fashion, and the champ was determined by the audience based on how much applause each MC received. Then a new challenger stepped to the mic and the process was repeated. Pulling this off required Lacks, and the people who helped him run each session, to balance the competitive energy generated through style wars with the democratic spirit that is the legacy of the cipher – the ideas that anyone can take part and that everyone deserves their time on the mic. Their job was made easier when MCs followed their lead and participated in the rhyme battles in ways that flexed their individual styles, but also reinforced the cooperative ethos on which the open mic is based.

Striking this delicate balance between competition and cooperation depends a lot on the expectations that the aspiring MCs bring to the event. If someone comes to an open mic session willing to fight or unwilling to accept a truce in good graces – to smile when they know they're being beat by some clever disses and the dope freestylin skills of their opponent – there's a good chance that they'll be kicked out. One night, well into a battle, a new challenger stepped up to a champ who had been on stage since the beginning of the session, just straight rippin fools. The challenger kicked an all right verse, during which the champ did some kung fu moves and athletic stretches, demonstrating both his competitive spirit and his nonchalance regarding competition and then came right back with a dope freestyle dissing the challenger's Bad Boy jacket. The audience made its choice, and the champ prevailed. The MCs hugged, exchanged pounds, and everything seemed cool. A new challenger stepped to the mic and started kicking a verse, but the recently defeated MC refused to get off the stage, dancing and getting in the way. The new challenger directed his battle rhymes in the perpetrator's direction, dissin him off the stage in his freestyle with a punchline about how he'd "only been to New York once," referring again to the cat's Bad Boy jacket – a symbol of Puff Daddy's influence, which is the epitome of everything independent hiphop heads despise, from commercialization to lack of creativity.

There was a sense that a fight was in the air, as Bad Boy held his ground while some of the other MCs got in his face. Obi Wan, a local MC who Lacks had convinced to host the battle that night, took the mic back and dissolved the conflict, telling all involved that they were fools for "scrapin over a damn rap." He brought the battle to an unofficial close by making a break in the flow of the event by calling for two new MCs to finish things off. The first kicked a competent verse about squashing beef, ending on a note of onelove – a common hiphop reference to Bob Marley's music and beliefs. Lacks, who grabbed the mic to be the last MC of the evening, made it a point to give props – mentioning other artists in a rhyme as a sign of respect – to all the MCs who took part in the battle.

Using the spirit of the cipher to structure his open mics led Lacks to value the art of freestylin and to emphasize its practice during the hiphop nights at Mahogany. Freestylin is, as Los Angeles-based b-girl T-Love puts it, "the ability to rhyme straight from the top of the head,"[18] and is contrasted with, as Norfleet learned through her fieldwork in New York City, kicking "writtens" – that is, "memorized and/or pre-rehearsed materials" – "for the sake of repeated performances and audience recognition as a composition" (Norfleet, 245). But many of the MCs who participated in the open mics at Mahogany relied on written raps for their verses and were unwilling to take the risks involved in the diligent improvisation of freestylin. T-Love emphasizes the role competition plays in inspiring creative change in hiphop, but she also points out that "in order for an MC to be considered a worthy competitor, he or she must practise and freestylin is just that: drills for skills." Freestylin "opens the mind, and helps to keep fresh and new ideas flowing, which improves the competition amongst MCs, therefore upgrading the quality of true hiphop flavour." "As long as there are MCs . . . striving to be the best as well as the most diverse and staying in tune with everyday changes," she concludes, "hiphop music will continue to evolve and breathe" (T-Love, 306).

"Freestylin *is* the expression of your heart," Lacks explained. "Without having to confine yourself to *content. Any* sorta content." This sort of lyrical freedom not only allows MCs to take certain liberties as far as content goes, but constitutes a decisive test for their skills down to their foundations. "It's gonna expose what your style is," he said. "What your *personality* is" (BC 3/17/00). On an aesthetic level, freestylin brings style to the fore, pushes both poetry and narration into the realm of music, frees style by detaching word sounds from their conventional content in everyday language use. As such, it's a form of free improvisation through which, as Small writes elsewhere, "musicians rely on their own experience to create the idiom, the syntax, through which they establish their relationships."[19] Through freestylin MCs lay the foundation for the personas that allow them to synthesize the imaginary and the actual through powerful storytelling in sound. The practice of freestylin allows MCs to actualize the expressions of their hearts by revealing style and transforming it into *personality*, how MCs identify themselves. Through acts of lyrical freedom, MCs reach an awareness of personality as a continuous process of identi-fication and harmonizing of different sonic, social, and intellectual styles.

An MC like Elzhi provides an extreme example of the high value b-boys and b-girls place on this sort of lyrical freedom. When I asked him what the writing process was like, he told me that even his writtens were mentally composed:

> The first time I wrote a rhyme, yo, is in my head . . . I felt kinda like: AH! Cause everybody was writin em on paper and I'm like: naw, man, this ain't the way to do it. And then I start lookin at it like: well, I don't need no paper, yaknowhati'msayin . . . the more I do it, the more I work at it, man . . . the more I learn, yaknowhati'msayin, the more I remember . . . that's my style. I don't even write nowhere. And *will* write nowhere, yaknowhati'msayin. The words look funny to me on paper. I mean, it's crazy. The words look funny to me.
>
> (BC 4/1/99)

The freedom that Elzhi experienced when he realized he could compose his lyrics in his head led him to find actually *writing* lyrics to be inhibiting, to the point of being unnatural. From this perspective, we can consider writing as a way for an artist to focus his or her attention on developing the mental skills required for freestylin until such diligent improvisation becomes a matter of habit and she or he is able to spontaneously compose and actualize in performance memorable patterns of thought. These patterns can consist of either memorized verses or just abstract feelings of the general direction in which one's thinking tends to go that enables an MC to string words and sounds together in meaningful ways off the top of the dome.

Ultimately, learning how to freestyle is essential for learning how to write quality rhymes, rather than vice versa, since the quality of rhymes is judged primarily as an ability to strongly express a personal style through sound, what Mtume ya Salaam describes as "a celebration of self through inventive wordplay[,] a fascinating exercise in the usage of language and sound [that is] an art form in and of itself."[20] Skillful arrangement of words and lines into tight poetic or narrative forms is a secondary, if important, consideration. Like a jazz soloist, a hiphop lyricist, as Berliner writes, "typically favors inconsistency in the service of spontaneous, creative exploration over consistency in less extemporaneous invention" (Berliner, 273). After Elzhi related how he composed in his head, Hodge talked about his experiences trying and not being able to and then humorously expressed his amazement at his friend's ability. "You're crazy!" Hodge replied after Elzhi insisted on his ability to compose spontaneously, "I don't understand how you can do that though, there's something *wrong* with you, psychologically messed up to be able to do that" (BC 4/1/99), and we all laughed at the joke. In order to catch Hodge's irony and admiration, it's important to understand that within independent hiphop it's often a *good* thing not to be psychologically "normal," to challenge accepted conventions, to be able to do things that most practicing professionals aren't able to.

In effect, the ability of these innovative artists to create a distinctive personal style through diligent improvisation allows them to change what we accept as reality. As Hodge put it, "[i]t don't make no sense for you to be that incredible" (BC 4/1/99). But as hiphop heads we push ourselves to likewise master the incredible until we can compel it to make sense for *us*. B-boys and b-girls make it a habit to bend the rules and be spontaneous. "If one thing we do, man," Lacks explained, "we concentrate too hard. It's like we overdo shit, yaknowhati'msayin. We're like writin contemplatin writin contemplate. We been doin this for *years*. We should just get the beat, go into the studio, and drop it" (BC 4/1/99). Striking this balance of contemplation and action is key, but actualizing it in performance requires years of practice and a high degree of mental discipline.

Lacks's point in arguing for spontaneity isn't that artists shouldn't concentrate on learning the conventions of independent hiphop, but that they should make this concentration *habitual*. As Hodge put it, being an artist means hiphop "took a part in you" (BC 4/1/99), shapes who you are and what you do on an everyday basis. Lacks suggests that the fact that people develop such habits can lead to change as well as continuity, and so can be a means to expand and realize our potentials rather than limit the realm of possibility. Rather than considering conventions as inherently constraining and bemoaning their very existence, then, we should accept their inevitability and in doing so work to make our habitual activities as diverse, inclusive, and flexible as possible. As William James wrote, "*we must make automatic and habitual, as early as possible, as many useful actions as we can*, and guard against the growing into ways that are likely to be disadvantageous to us." The Breakfast Club suggest that recognizing these *"ethical implications of the law of habit"* are fundamental to an independent hiphop education,[21] and that doing hiphop for a living means, in part, putting these beliefs into practice. Practicing hiphop professionals, always aware that the balance between concentration and spontaneity is never permanent, work to continuously develop their skills and are willing to put themselves on the spot at a moment's notice. Of course, for MCs like El, Lacks, and Hodge the ramifications of this commitment stretch beyond the creation and performance of their music. And it's in this sense that independent hiphop is a way of life as well as an art form.

In balancing consistency and transformation, the improvisational personality actualized through freestylin composes a sense of agency that grants oneself and one's community a meaningful presence in the overwhelmingly vast and often hostile world of our contemporary global society. In hiphop terms, freestylin allows MCs to make the sort of diligent improvisations required to maintain a balance between independence and cooperation a matter of habit. In the process, they develop both the degree of mental discipline to spontaneously organize immense and continuous streams of thought into memorizable patterns and the compelling style required to immediately express these patterns in sound so expertly that even thoughts they seem to exclude are in fact evoked. Through freestylin MCs remember the roots of hiphop, and thus the foundations of their own personalities. These acts of remembrance allow them to memorably communicate to their listeners the beliefs of independent hiphop and in doing so inspires us to work together to actualize these memories through musical and social structures, to take the risks involved in the process of striking agreements between what we imagine to be possible and what we know is real, between what we think and what we do.

By focusing on freestylin in this chapter, I'm tracing one idiom of hiphop's complex conventional language of diligent improvisation. Such a shared system of values involves, in the words of sociologist Howard Becker, "a multimedia collaboration" that creates "one big art world."[22] This hiphop art world is composed of the interwoven practices of lyricism, turntablism, production, breaking, bombing as well as uncountable other activities that have yet to be actualized as official "elements" of hiphop but that share the same common ways of making, doing, thinking, and living. Open mics – and by association other local events – provide opportunities for hiphop heads to "see and hear [such] new element[s] in a variety of contexts" (Becker, 64). In the process, artists like Lacks teach us about the possibilities of these innovative conventions: what they mean, how they work, and how we ourselves can experience them through creating our own improvisational performances.

What am I *doing*?

It was actually Lacks – not me – who brought up the possibility of doing an interview. In doing so, he was giving me pointers on how to go about doing my work, helpful suggestions that I was slow to pick up on but that I'd finally start getting when I began transcribing and remembering the interview that finally took place. Doing so would lead me to think about how this experience was similar to the open mic sessions at Mahogany – how this conversation was a test for me like an open mic is a test for an aspiring MC, an opportunity to practice freestylin and build my skills. Since I was, to a large extent, at the very beginning of a learning process, I was often unsure about what I was supposed to be learning and uncertain about how I should go about learning it.

As far as the interview went at least, I was working with an inappropriate idea of what it was supposed to be. At first, I was looking forward to an opportunity to gather a wealth of information that I could use to shape the ideas I was formulating about hiphop music and the social networks built through its production and performance into a legitimate argument.[23] But after a few weeks of watching and listening to the open mics at Mahogany, my basic views had been transformed to the point that it became difficult to distinguish between what I thought and what I had picked up along the way. It was only as I thought back on these experiences, often during the early morning car rides back to Ann Arbor, that I realized that what I was learning was not merely "data" to be filtered through my "previously acquired . . . conceptual framework" (Gourlay, 22) but a system of lived beliefs that changed the way I thought about the work I was doing as a hiphop scholar. Therefore, I think that even theoretically segmenting learning and fieldwork, as well as drawing a distinction between "researchers" and "performers," is counterproductive.

It's not only that research forms a considerable part of a scholar's learning process, but that an account of fieldwork, like K. A. Gourlay's, that focuses on "the ethnomusicologist's role in research" leaves itself open to the danger of underemphasizing the musician's role. According to his model, the only outcome of the learning/research process is a "presentation process" in which the scholar shares his or her work with other academics, presumably on academic terms (22). For someone like myself who is interested not only in changing academic conventions but also in doing so making my work relevant to hiphop heads and b-boys and b-girls this outcome is disappointing to say the least. Not accounting for the individuality of each musician a scholar learns from, the relationships that this model suggests aren't on equal terms. I agree that it's important to remain aware of the differences between scholars and musicians in order to do an adequate job of tracing our similarities, but since I'm interested in the feedback of the hiphop artists I learn from – as well as other participants in independent hiphop – it's important for me to find an alternative to the strict distinction Gourlay draws. In part this means finding a way to present the outcomes of my work that resonate with both the expectations of academic writing and hiphop's conventions of diligent improvisation and thereby appeals to a broad and diverse audience without smudging the clarity of my argument.

It was only by first going through the standard ethnomusicological process and figuring out where it went wrong, however, that I realized the necessity of such an alternative and began to imagine new possibilities. To be more specific, it was by initially thinking of the conversations I would have with the Breakfast Club in terms of formal interviews that I realized this assumption was hindering my ability to do the sort of work I wanted to do by causing me to commit what Charles Briggs calls "communicative blunders." My unexamined insistence on a formal interview led to "the imposition of one set of communicative norms . . . on a speech community that organized talk along opposing lines."[24] Resulting from incorrect assumptions about what an "important conversation" amounted to, these sorts of impositions – as Briggs points out – led me to miss a lot of information I could have more quickly picked up on if I'd been more open-minded about when and where such interactions can take place at the outset. In retrospect, I think my initial unwillingness to insist on an interview, or even mention the possibility, was a result not only of my shyness but also of an intuitive sense that acting on my initial assumptions would be tactless.

During the three months I was a regular at Mahogany, sharing experiences with the people I was learning from and beginning to understand exactly how busy their lives were, I began to realize not only that a formal interview was impractical but also that it wasn't the type of interaction through which I'd learn what I needed to know in order to do good work as a hiphop scholar. Gaining this knowledge would involve, as Jeff Todd Titon writes, learning to place "emphasis on human relationships rather than on collecting information."[25] I started to imagine the important conversations I'd have with the Breakfast Club, not as "structured interviews," but as the sharing of "those life stories told to sympathetic listeners or friends in a 'real life' situation" that serve as "a means toward understanding" (Titon, 89). But in order to make this possibility a reality, I would have put in more work getting to know them, and thereby learning what they had to teach me about the conventions of independent hiphop. This learning process began by accident, but it was through making these mistakes and reflecting on them that I discovered the sense of purpose I was searching for, the confidence to practice the skills of a hiphop scholar with expertise.

After Lacks mentioned the interview, we made a series of appointments to get together and talk, but each time one of us either got the time or place wrong, or we just plain missed each other. When it came to be the first of April and I still didn't have an interview I brought my hand-held tape recorder along with me to Mahogany, remembering that when we missed our first appointment Lacks suggested that we could hang out sometime after an open mic. That night, fortunately, he was down to do the interview, and so were Angela, Hodge, and Elzhi. The five of us headed over to Café Mediterraneo in Greek Town – the Detroit hiphop community's regular late-night eatery, just a short way from Mahogany.

After grabbing a booth and ordering, we talked and ate from 2:30 till 4:30 in the morning. I had come with a list of some basic questions and asked some of them at the beginning to get the conversation started. But soon Lacks and his colleagues were guiding the conversation to places that I couldn't have imagined beforehand and that proved to be more fruitful than any of the directions I had expected. During most of the discussion, I just sat back listening to them talk to me and among themselves. I'd ask a question to push them to say more or see if I could spin the topic in a slightly different direction. As the interview went on I became more skilled at making these cues and spins, but in the beginning more often than not my prepared questions were heading me in the wrong direction and either Lacks or Hodge would steer me back to the right path. I tried to respect, as well as I possibly could, the directions in which they wanted to take the interview, to hear what they wanted to say. Fittingly, I started to get the hang of it as they told me about their own learning experiences.

After asking easy questions about where they were from, where they met, and when they got into hiphop, I swerved towards what I thought was the heart of the matter and asked what made them decide to be artists. Hodge seemed to be confused by the question, half like the answer was obvious and half like it was impossible to know for sure. "Artist?" he asked in response, making me wonder if I'd used the right word, if he would describe himself as an artist. "I don't know, I just . . . I think it was subconsciously done. I don't know, it just took a part in me, man. Kept listenin to it all the time, wanting to rhyme."[26] Hodge had no problem considering himself an artist, it just wasn't something he had consciously thought about. Still conceiving the decision to become an artist as something that had to be conscious, I asked Hodge what kept him going, why he kept rhyming. "Cause it's too late now, brother!" Hodge said and everyone laughed. "Too far in it, too late now, too far in it. You quit now, you ain't got nothin. What the fuck I been doin for the past five years? It's a part of me now, it's too late, it's a part of me." His answer to my questions was not only articulate, it was packed with unspoken meaning, giving me just enough to keep working to figure out what it meant. In effect, Hodge was encouraging me to go through the same work he'd gone through in figuring out what it meant to be a hiphop artist.

Lacks's answer to the question of what inspired him to become an artist was more forthcoming, but surprising in a different way. He told me it was Hodge's example that made him want to be an MC. "So I started writin," Lacks explained. "I was into Hammer, though." He went on to tell me about how he emulated his idol, but then realized he needed to create his own identity when other students at his high school began to make fun of him. "I just had to distance myself," Lacks said. "So I found something inside of me." It's not that he stopped admiring the work of other MCs. Rather, he learned to draw the line between influence and imitation and thereby broadened his frame of reference in his chosen field of work. As MCs begin to find their voice they become more critical, partly because it's through the critical activity of continuously comparing different artists and themselves that they develop their styles. Remembering imitating early idols is part of knowing oneself and therefore evidence of the introspection it takes to be a dope MC, the foundation of the divergent and improvisational thinking manifested through freestylin.

Listening and relistening to the tape of the interview as I worked to transcribe it, and as I read and reread the transcription, I began to realize that in telling me these kinds of stories the Breakfast Club weren't just sharing information with me, they were teaching me how knowledgable interactions go down in the Detroit hiphop community. To paraphrase the title of Briggs's study, I learned how to ask questions in ways that would evoke relatively unguarded answers. In order to do so, however, I first had to recognize that hiphop conventions shape not only ways of asking but also ways of answering. This required that I put what I'd learned about freestylin by observing the open mics at Mahogany into practice, both in listening and in talking.

The pattern that quickly developed during the course of the interview was that I'd ask a question and whoever answered would launch into what seemed to me at first a tangent. But as my consultants kept leading me through this routine, I began to realize that these divergences from the obvious topic were in essence freestyles on the content of the question providing meaningful leads to a clear and powerful answer. In order for this response to be voiced I had to improvise on the content of their stories, respond with a freestyle of my own in the form of a line of context-specific questions. Contextualizing these questions was a matter of both sensing the cues my consultants gave me about themselves and working my own style into the flow of the conversation, composing ways of asking that were also a means for answering the questions they had about me. In order to get to know the Breakfast Club, I not only had to accept the ways in which what they said confounded my expectations of what it means to be a hiphop artist. I also had to be open to how our interactions could transform my preconceptions about who I myself am and willing to act on what I learned by taking part in a process of collective freestylin.

Thinking back on my fieldwork, I realized that this work of contextualization is the aim of my project in Detroit. In order for my work to adequately represent local hiphop artists and the community they work to build, it has to be in part structured and understood according to their conventions. What Lacks had taught me about freestylin opened my eyes and ears to these habits of diligent improvisation. My interview with the Breakfast Club – the event, the tape, the transcription – was a series of drills pushing me to follow his lead, to find my own style, working up to the challenge that this chapter presents: finding a way of doing scholarship that teaches through being an example, that acts as an element of independent hiphop at the same time it manifests as a piece of academic writing spreading the lessons hiphop has to teach to a broader audience. This challenge, however, is itself an exercise for a more general project: to make the resources available through privileged institutions like the academy open to a wider population.

During the course of our conversation that night I quickly noticed how frequently the people I was talking to said "yaknowhati'msayin." At the time, I sensed that it was a way for Lacks, Hodge, and El to both make sure I caught their drift and to evoke a common understanding among all the participants in the discussion. It's not a question, it's a statement. As I began transcribing and reading through my transcription, however, I began to realize that "yaknowhati'msayin" was also a way for them to tell me to make sure I paid attention to what they were saying, to put their weight down on it, marking it with their personal style in order to make it compelling. "Yaknowhati'msayin" is an example of what Briggs calls "metacommunication" – statements that "root speech events in a particular social situation and imbue them with force and meaning" (Briggs, 2) by "simultaneously commenting on communicative processes (including the interaction itself) and indicating a referent" (106). This act of reference is "a creative and powerful act" in which "[o]ne or more entities, processes, imaginative constructions, and so on are selected by the speaker from an infinitude of referential possibilities and are recreated in the mind of the hearer" (51).

This process of metacommunication not only, as Briggs writes, "provides an ongoing interpretation of its own significance[,] conveyed mainly in stylistic terms" (106) but in doing so evokes "an adequate sense as to how the information" it communicates "fits into broader patterns of thinking, feeling, and speaking" (2) – in this case the beliefs and conventions of independent hiphop. As time went on, every time I heard "yaknowhati'msayin" running through my head the open mic sessions at Mahogany came to mind. It's in this way that I began to think of it as a manifestation of the habits of diligent improvisation that these events fostered, an analog to the art of freestylin. "Yaknowhati'msayin," like the streams of interwoven thought, words, and sounds that MCs create on the mic, is a way to actualize hoping through teaching, to harmonize thinking and acting with style. In droppin it on me, the Breakfast Club weren't just organizing a one-time event where they could school me on the arts of hiphop, they were creating a vibe, giving me material to continue to work through and make my own. I was inspired by their diligence and wanted to live up to the example. Consequently, in writing this chapter, I'm beginning the process of figuring out how I can translate the art of freestylin that Hodge, El, and Lacks worked to teach me into ways of going about my own work as a scholar and teacher.

Notes

1   Thanks to Professor Travis Jackson and the other students in this class for helping me on my way and always being there with support.

2   Interview with the Breakfast Club at Café Mediterraneo in the Greek Town section of Detroit, April 1, 1999. Further references will be cited parenthetically as BC 4/1/99.

3   For examples of this popular account check out Steven Hager's *Hip-Hop* (New York: St. Martin's Press, 1984), David Toop's *Rap Attack 3* (London: Serpent's Tail, 2000), S. H. Fernando, Jr.'s *The New Beats: Exploring the Music, Culture, and Attitudes of Hip-Hop* (New York: Anchor, 1994), or Nelson George's *Hip Hop America* (New York: Viking, 1998). For academic work in this vein see Tricia Rose's *Black Noise: Rap Music and Black Culture in Contemporary America* (Hanover, NH: Wesleyan University Press, 1994) and the essays collected in William Eric Perkins (ed.), *Droppin' Science: Critical Essays on Rap Music and Hip Hop Culture* (Philadelphia, PA: Temple University Press, 1996) and Jon Michael Spencer (ed.) *The Emergency of Black and the Emergence of Rap* (Durham, NC: Duke University Press, 1991).

4   My understanding of hiphop as a recorded music, as well as my commitment to ethnography as a research method, is indebted to the work of Joe Schloss. See his "Making Beats: The Art of Sample-Based Hip-Hop" (dissertation, University of Washington, 2000).

5   Ingrid Monson, *Saying Something: Jazz Improvisation and Interaction* (Chicago: University of Chicago Press, 1996), 4. Further references to Monson's work will be cited parenthetically.

6   Michel de Certeau, *The Practice of Everyday Life* (Berkeley, CA: University of California Press, 1984), 73.

7   William James, *The Principles of Psychology* (New York: Dover, 1950), vol. 2, 659.

8 Paul Berliner, *Thinking in Jazz: The Infinite Art of Improvisation* (Chicago: University of Chicago Press, 1994), 218–219. Further references to Berliner's work will be cited parenthetically.

9 Roland Barthes, "The Third Meaning: Research Notes on Several Eisenstein Stills," in *The Responsibility of Forms* (Berkeley, CA: University of California Press, 1985), 58–59, 44. Further references to this work will be cited parenthetically.

10 Walter Benjamin, "The Storyteller," in *Illuminations* (New York: Schocken, 1968), 86. Further references to this work will be cited parenthetically. Benjamin uses this phrase to describe *counsel* – a form of knowledge, characterized by "[a]n orientation toward practical interests" and made possible by "the communicability of experience," that he argues is fundamental to the art of storytelling.

11 Style, then, is similar to what linguist Geneva Smitherman, in her work on African American Vernacular English, calls "tonal semantics." In employing tonal semantics, she writes, "the rapper gets meaning and rhetorical mileage by triggering a familiar sound chord in the listener's ear. The words may or not make sense; what is crucial is the rapper's ability to make the words *sound* good." To that effect, "the voice is employed like a musical instrument with improvisations, riffs, and all kinds of playing between the notes." See Smitherman's *Talkin and Testifyin: The Language of Black America* (Detroit, MI: Wayne State University Press, 1977), 100, 134. But since hiphop lyricism, strictly speaking, is of limited tonal range (part of what makes an MC dope, in fact, is the ability to make slight, subtle, and swift changes in tone mean a lot), especially when compared to the melodic loops that are often part of the musical ensemble making up a hiphop track, it is distinguished by timbre, specifically, rather than tone, generally. So while Smitherman's Toast-tellers have "their verbal ingenuity taxed to the limit in trying to sustain the melodic structure" of their raps, MCs focus their energy on harmonizing the quality of their voice with those of the other MCs they're rhyming with as well as the instrumental elements of each particular track in order to create a compelling overall sound. This relative importance of timbre compared to tone is what distinguishes hiphop lyricism from singing (obviously) and, I would argue, spoken word poetry.

12 Stephen Blum, "Towards a Social History of Musicological Technique," *Ethnomusicology* 19(2) (1975), 214.

13 In addition to Barthes's work, my thinking here is indebted to the interpretation of twentieth-century United States history James Livingston offers in his *Pragmatism and the Political Economy of Cultural Revolution, 1850–1940* (Chapel Hill, NC: University of North Carolina Press, 1994).

14 Elizabeth Tonkin, *Narrating our Pasts: The Social Construction of Oral History* (Cambridge: Cambridge University Press, 1992), 3, 38. Further references to Tonkin's work will be cited parenthetically.

15 Christopher Small, *Musicking: The Meanings of Performing and Listening* (Hanover, NH: Weslayan University Press, 1998), 13. Further references to this work will be cited parenthetically as *M*.

16 By "interactions" I mean, as Anthony Seeger writes, "how sounds are conceived, made, appreciated and influence other individuals, groups, and social and musical processes." See his "Ethnography of Music," in Helen Meyers (ed.), *Ethnomusicology: An Introduction* (New York: Norton, 1992), 89.

17 Dawn Michaelle Norfleet, "'Hip-Hop Culture' in New York City: The Role of Verbal Musical Performance in Defining a Community" (dissertation, Columbia University, 1997), 139. Further references to Norfleet's work will be cited parenthetically.

18 T-Love, "The Freestyle," in Brian Cross, *It's Not About a Salary . . .: Rap, Race and Resistance in Los Angeles* (London: Verso, 1993).

19 Christopher Small, *Music of the Common Tongue: Survival and Celebration in African American Music* (Hanover, NH: Wesleyan University Press, 1987), 308.

20 Mtume ya Salaam, "The Aesthetics of Rap," *African American Review* 29(2) (1995): 308.
21 James, *Principles of Psychology*, vol. 1, 122, 120.
22 Howard S. Becker, *Art Worlds* (Berkeley, CA: University of California Press, 1982), 163. Further references to Becker's work will be cited parenthetically.
23 Coming into the project, my fieldwork methods were guided by the "ethnomusicological process" K. A. Gourlay suggests. In this model, scholars and musicians each go through their own courses of education and develop their "appropriate 'world views.'" Only after this "preparatory period" is completed, according to Gourlay, can the "research process" take place, "during which ethnomusicologist and performers are brought together." See his "Towards a Reassessment of the Ethnomusicologist's Role in Research," *Ethnomusicology* 22 (1978): 22. Further references will be cited parenthetically. My experience, however, led me to question the usefulness of drawing a clear line between "preparation" and "research."
24 Charles L. Briggs, *Learning How to Ask: A Sociolinguistic Appraisal of the Role of the Interview in Social Science Research* (Cambridge: Cambridge University Press, 1986), xiv. Further references to this work will be cited parenthetically.
25 Jeff Todd Titon, "Knowing Fieldwork," in Gregory F. Barz and Timothy J. Cooley (eds), *Shadows in the Field: New Perspectives for Fieldwork in Ethnomusicology* (New York: Oxford University Press, 1997), 92. Further references to Titon's work will be cited parenthetically.
26 This and the rest of the quotes of the Breakfast Club in this section are from BC 4/1/99.

10

LES GAMMES

Making visible the representative modern man

Richard Cándida Smith

In his lectures of 1864, "Philosophy of Art," philosopher and art historian Hippolyte Taine told his audience that the mathematical laws of sensation provided the basis of a truly modern art that the age demanded but which did not yet exist. Practitioners in any medium would break free of both tired convention and novelty for its own sake by discovering the "scales" that would assure them more formalized control over the conditions of experience.[1] I have used the English word "scales" to translate his term *gamme* as he based his discussion on music before he addressed other media. However, *gamme* is a word with broader usage. It can refer as readily to the painter's palette, the light spectrum, or any organized arrangement of sensations, for which English uses the less technical cognate "gamut." This word *gamme* shifted attention from individual signs and the referents they invoked to a process of meaning formation grounded in the systematic relationships linking sensations.

Taine's concept of the scale related to new ideas about language gaining ground in France in the 1860s. The noted linguist Michel Bréal, holder of the chair in comparative grammar at the Collège de France, introduced the concept of value to describe how words gained their meaning in any given statement primarily from association with other words, both those actually used and those conspicuous by their absence. Communication of complex ideas was possible only because every sign had multiple significations. Speakers highlighted some associations over others in order to limit possible interpretations to those values relevant to the exchange of purposes and feelings that motivated their acts of expression. Predication or the assignation of attributes was the fundamental characteristic of language, not signification. Words pointed to possible meanings but they failed to specify anything until they were placed into propositions that stated one's response to the phenomena in question.[2]

For painters, a corollary of Taine's foregrounding of the *gamme* as the nexus of a scientific approach to sensation would be a startling reversal of the step-by-step progression from line to volume to color in the construction of a painterly reality. This method had long been taught as the basis of art in French painting schools, including the Ecole des Beaux Arts, where Taine had just become professor of aesthetics and art history at the time of his lectures. Instead of starting with a goal of rendering mimetic solidity to represented objects, Taine's emphasis might suggest to artists that they begin by identifying the sensational ranges relevant to their painting, for in that range lay the reason why human vision interpreted some sensory inputs as solid. Careful contrast of highlights and shadows gave way to color modeling based on the construction of a color key that established for any given painting the relationships of the hues used.[3] Whether sensory gamuts in painting reproduced what an artist perceived directly in nature or expressed interpretative states of mind was a question that quickly arose and divided the impressionists from the postimpressionists.[4] In neither case, if we follow the lead of Taine, is the subjective state distinct from a modern commitment to understanding the processes governing sensation. Indeed for Taine, the problem with the culture of the first part of the nineteenth century had been its romantically subjective character. It failed in expressing the nature of the modern age because it separated sensation from reason, response from description, through an emphasis on spectacular effects.

The view that modern art was a form of knowledge and thus performs a sober social role informs the appreciation of Claude Monet that Georges Clemenceau published in 1928 during the installation of the *Nymphéas* at the Orangerie two years after the painter's death. Clemenceau had been prime minister of France from 1906 to 1909, when he earned the nickname the "Tiger" for his fierce repression of strikes. In 1917, he returned to lead the nation in its war with Germany with an uncompromising program of total mobilization and sacrifice. He was also a man of letters who was an intimate friend of poets and painters. During the war, Clemenceau ensured that Monet had supplies and materials to continue his work unimpeded, and he even secured train space for transporting Monet's canvases. When the war ended in November 1918, the painter promised to donate two large panels of water lilies to the nation as an act of thanksgiving for France's victory.[5] For Clemenceau the donated paintings assumed a sacred status. They expressed the values that the nation had defended in the war and exhibited in particularly clear form the state of mind that gave modern democratic societies their special character.[6]

Monet's accomplishment, Clemenceau said of his deceased friend, had been to give his fellow citizens a "representation of a state of emotive perception that permitted us to assimilate new aspects of universal energies, allowing an improved comprehension of the world and of ourselves along with it."[7] Monet surpassed "everyday vision" by leaping past the objects of vision to see vision itself. Clemenceau affirmed the scientific detachment that Monet had made the basis of his life in a famous anecdote that describes the painter's response at seeing his first wife Camille lying on her death bed. Clemenceau reported that Monet told him that as his eyes fixed on her, he began mechanically to examine the new colors that death had brought to her face. His attention focused on the ranges of blues, grays, and yellows he saw emerging. It would be natural to make a final image of the woman he had loved, but the color changes sparked an "organic automatism" deep within him. His reflexes took over and he threw himself into an "unconscious operation" to capture the novel experience before him. Thus, Monet concluded, he was "the beast that turns his millstone."[8]

Monet's self-characterization is not simply pathetic modesty, at least not as Clemenceau will develop his theses on the role of modern art in the republic. From the juxtaposition of brute labor and refined scientific sensibility flows Clemenceau's declaration that Monet had exemplified a new type of "superior man."[9] In the modesty that the anecdote inscribes is the morality of the new era, a morality of sacrifice – extending even to the acceptance of a personal mediocrity that still can miraculously be transcended through mastery of one's métier. In search of a knowledge that will liberate productive capacity, one must subordinate personal sorrow into a hierarchy that establishes the superiority of dedication to one's work.

The completed painting *Camille Monet on her Deathbed* (1879, Musée d'Orsay) reduced Camille into an object of Claude's passion for knowledge. The painting enacts as well an objectification of the painter into a machine. Monet's eye had become nothing less than the entire man. "Retinal sensibilities" captured all his intelligence and hopes and took control of his hands. This does not mean that the sorrow he felt had been suppressed. It united with reason and transformed into a higher mental state what Clemenceau called "un ordre sensationnel," a structure governing sensation.[10]

For Clemenceau, Monet's submission to the ethos of work revealed the play of supreme harmony "in which we find an interpretation of universal correspondences." The emotional vibrations that Monet captured corresponded to the underlying order of the external world.[11] His yoking of emotion to rational curiosity allowed a body of work to appear that helps viewers reorganize their own sensational responses into an emotional state consistent with what modern science had revealed about the structure of the cosmos. His work prepared their viewers to live in harmony with science. To uneducated sensibilities, the universe appears as a "storm of waves that crash against each other and intensify . . . through the perpetual retreat of lost hopes."[12] Ignorance reinforces despair, but modern art promoted *disponibilité*, another key word, that signifies openness and availability because one is disengaged. Science is not a dogma that replaces superstition. It puts the mind in a state of readiness by subordinating the flux of emotion to reason and productivity. Intelligence and discipline do not efface but refine and deepen emotion. Personal feelings are heightened through their redirection into a harmony with reason and will. Monet had shocked all those locked in the habits of previous eras, but as far as Clemenceau was concerned his friend had allowed a new personality to emerge that was responsive to the "truth of movement." Those who accepted the message that the nation preserved in the sanctuary it had created for the *Nymphéas* experienced the beauty of form and color as a spiritual liberation.[13]

Clemenceau's interpretation is speculative and problematic, as he himself recognized. Nothing that Monet said in extant private correspondence or in public statements suggests that he had these intentions.[14] Clemenceau acknowledged that Monet was not a philosopher and that he did not generalize about the import of what he did.[15] Monet had limited his discussion of painting to the technical problems he faced. He was indeed the beast at his millstone, mutely performing the labor that made him a superior man, that is to say, a representative citizen of the modern, republican world.

Monet's refusal of theoretical speculation sets him apart from and above other painters.[16] It is precisely his apparent mediocrity as a theoretical thinker that makes him a paragon, the representative man for modern France. The grandeur of his accomplishment demonstrates that it is labor and labor alone that establishes what might be called a secular form of grace. Correspondence of self and cosmos is possible. It is known, both analytically and sentimentally, through the fruits of one's sweat and the value they provide to one's fellow citizens. The celebration of Monet as the representative modern man enunciated a central value of a republican liberalism already implicit in Taine, but which could not become dominant until after 1871 and the foundation of the Third Republic. Democratic ideology is grounded in a faith that there need be no inherent contradiction between universal law and individuality, provided that science, labor, and a sense of duty are in balance. If individual psychology is universal, democracy is possible because all people share the same capacities for self-government. What society must ensure if it is to be just and stable is to draw people away from the particular and reinforce the universal aspects of their being. Through a union of science and labor they can transcend the local. Each individual can achieve a discipline that allows for an outflowing of cosmic harmony through their efforts. Democracy as the organization of humankind's universal attributes would prove through its stunning successes that it was the most perfect form of society.

For Clemenceau, Monet's paintings were practical demonstrations that such a balance could be achieved, while the paintings themselves have the virtue of revealing to those appropriately disengaged from ancient prejudices and in a state of readiness for a "true experience" the necessary link between individual, social, and cosmological states. Monet's single-minded focus on his métier and his refusal to philosophize offered convincing proof that it is the average citizen, not the romantic hero, who can be the ideal human.

Clemenceau asserted that sacrifice is the ultimate test of every citizen's integration into the harmonies that govern all natural processes, social as well as cosmological. He quoted Brutus's farewell to his soldiers as they depart for battle: "It is necessary that we all go forward to the enemy; I cannot say that we will all return together." Contemporaries reading this knew well that Clemenceau had been an absolutely unforgiving war leader. He assumed leadership of the nation at a point during World War I when it was not clear how much longer France could endure. Hundreds of thousands of casualties had failed to turn back the Germans. Mutinies were spreading along the front, unrest and strikes plagued munitions factories, and defeatist attitudes appeared at the highest levels of government. Clemenceau had long been critical of the army's emphasis on machinery and bureaucracy, which he argued inevitably led to demoralization as long as the opposing sides in the war were in stalemate. In his first address to the nation as war leader, Clemenceau asked France, "Is it through the superiority of our arms that we will attain the final decision?" No, he replied, "what is the most marvelous machine worth if man is not at the lever? We shall conquer because it is our will to conquer, our will to the very end, whatever may happen." Clemenceau refocused the nation onto a program of total war until victory or defeat, and quieted growing popular opposition to the war by prosecuting and imprisoning national leaders who had vacillated.[17] The republican serves the common good with his life, or the republic succumbs to the ever-present dangers of demagoguery, corruption, absolutism, and despotism. War is the ultimate test of the virtue of a republic's citizens, but victory depends upon a taming and organization of individual will into a collective power capable of every sacrifice required to prevail.

Mastery of one's craft also involves sacrifice, and it is Clemenceau's duty to insist that his fellow citizens recognize their obligation to submit. Modern geniuses do not develop all of their talents. They select their area of work and subordinate all their faculties and skills, every aspect of their life's conduct, to "incessant labor" in one field and one field alone. They develop an "interpretative intelligence" and a "tension of will" that is honed by the unique challenges of their discipline. Monet's life achievement vindicated the people who had engendered him by reclaiming their right to dignity. Monet, "despite the mediocrity of his cosmic condition," proved himself and "the average man, by virtue of his labor," to be the genuine advanced guard of the modern age precisely because he tended to his work without moralizing and let the products of his labor speak for him.[18]

Let us return to 1864 and Hippolyte Taine's *Philosophy of Art*, which posed a number of incomplete, general propositions about the functions of art in modern societies. Though he called for a modern art, he could not describe what it would look like. Over the succeeding twenty years that he served as professor of aesthetics and art history at the Ecole des Beaux Arts, he converted his course lectures into lengthy books on the art of ancient Greece, the Italian Renaissance, and on Netherlandish painting. His most famous book on culture was a history of English literature, where he developed his perhaps still widely held if mechanistic position that art was a product of geography, social relationships, and political conditions.[19] When he turned to the art of his own day, his imagination faltered. In "Philosophy of Art," he could do no more than proffer a few general specifications. First, a modern conception of art would be "historic," rather than "dogmatic." By this he meant that art ought to reopen human sensibilities clogged by metaphysical perspectives to a fuller range of immediate experience, what he called "le sentiment vrai," which his American translator rendered as "natural feeling."[20]

Two obstacles stood in the way of a "true feeling." These obstacles are really one and the same process with corresponding effects in the life-cycle of the artist and in the historical development of social taste. In the first phase of his career, an artist "sees things as they are" and studies them "minutely and earnestly."[21] He overcomes blocks built into existing available artistic languages and provides his viewers with a thrill of renewed sensation. But with public acclamation, the artist thinks he understands his media of expression thoroughly. He has developed personal rules in the course of successfully penetrating pre-existing rules to reattain the valid experience that lay at their origin. These practical communicative measures become more and more important until the experience transmitted is no longer "true" but "clever." This is the period of mannerism and decline that every great artist endures after he has developed his own idiom. His interest shifts from sensation to his own system of representation, containing a handful of forms which he uses entirely conventionally.[22]

The same curve appears across generations in the histories of nations. France had achieved the most perfect forms of expression in all of its arts during the reign of Louis XIV following the formation of the academies earlier in the seventeenth century that succeeded in establishing rule books governing every art.[23] Convention readily replaced experience, because as his later book *On Intelligence* argues, thought-through systems of representation provide a supple and predictable set of signs that can effectively guide action provided nothing changes.[24] For the following two centuries, French artists struggled to express themselves honestly in formal languages that alienated them from nature. Since art, like every science (that is formalization of sensation into an abstracted system of representation), drew its strength from nature, such a state of affairs had to break down. In all previous epochs when convention had dominated, a "great school" emerged that swept away ancient rules with the power of the emotions they unleashed – these revolutions in the representation of sensation would provide the focus for Taine's subsequent writings in cultural history. French culture in the mid-nineteenth century had reached a similar breaking point – a revolution in the arts had to occur so that hearts and minds could regain a grounding in a "true sensation" liberating the senses with a flood of knowledge about the world and freeing the will to act appropriately.[25]

Taine's celebration of a revolution in the arts coincided with official policies of his government and was not supportive of the experimental cultural movements forming all around him. "Philosophy of Art" served as his inaugural lectures when he assumed his appointment as a professor at the Ecole des Beaux Arts. He joined the school's faculty a year after the ministry of education had revoked the school's charter, taken direct control of the institution, and initiated a series of reforms in its practices and teaching methods. The decree that instituted these reforms specifically attacked the classicism that the school had long promoted. Instead of offering restatements of established truisms, art, the decree's authors stated, should be geared to the practical tasks of society. Instead of aiming at developing genius, the curriculum should provide basic instruction in techniques that anyone could learn with profit. In the course of this upheaval, Taine's predecessor, Viollet-le-Duc, was dismissed, and the minister of education personally chose Taine to take his place. Taine's use of the word *gamme* to highlight what he considered distinctive about a modern approach to art pointed to simplified, mathematically based languages of design that would make the arts more serviceable for an industrializing society.[26]

Taine's series of lectures on the scientific basis of art was part of a larger official effort to transform the practice of art and make it more "modern," a word that Taine used frequently but refrained from defining until the very conclusion of his book. His emphasis on such aspects of sensation as the *gamme* underscored the conventionality of academic rules by opposing to them another convention based in a positive conception of science. His explication made clear that he did not think that the new art he was assisting in promoting would simply be a photographic or stenographic reproduction of possible experiences. The totality of experience is chaotic, he noted, which is why society needed artists: they provide a shared conceptual framework for experience. That framework ought to be based on direct observation of the world and ought to transmit to the public greater understanding of the forces shaping social action. Responsibility to living society rather than to a dead heritage would guide the choices a modern artist made.

The artist presents only a "portion" of the object of his knowledge: "the relationships and mutual dependence of parts."[27] Recognition of these relationships and the structures or *gammes* upon which they rest provided a commonly shared practical experience that unified a nation. An effective aesthetic representation clarifies the "essential condition of being in the object," that is the quality from which all other, or at least most other, qualities are derived.[28] The successful work of art provides a sensation that feels fresh, the logic of which is revealed through the inscription of value (contrast with possible pairs), organized in a systematic hierarchy, the *gamme* that makes sensible (un vrai sentiment) the priority of causal factors in an experience. Hierarchy tells one what to do, value explains why, and sensation establishes the validity of an interpretation.

This schematic system corresponds to the fundamental schema of nineteenth-century psychology in both the French- and English-speaking worlds, a framework that Taine reproduced without dissent in *On Intelligence*. The human mind has three overarching faculties: sensation, reason, and will. All three need to be aligned for effective interaction with the world. "Freedom" (*volonté*, a word that elides with will or agency) is dependent upon the ability of the mind to draw logical conclusions from its experiences. Should any one of the three faculties become too prominent, effective action becomes increasingly impossible.

In Taine's terms, the power that classical representational systems had achieved stifled a fresh experience of the world and hence froze the will in its ability to interact with the continuous challenges that sprang forth in a world under constant evolutionary development. Everything that stood outside modes governing experience appeared unreal, no matter how palpable. This stimulated an unhealthy fascination with fantasy, which was simply a suppressed reality reasserting itself as phantasm; or, equally pernicious, the quest to refresh experience led to an excessive attention to the will, as if the blockage derived from an imbalance of sensation and rational framework could be overcome through impulsive action or emotional discharge. Taine thus characterized the world in which he lived as under the spell of Faust and the "insatiable and sad" Werther. Taine repudiated equally the dead hand of academic classicism with its blind respect for the glories of the *ancien régime* and the subjective excesses that had emerged in response. The literature and art that the first part of the nineteenth century had produced had been effusive reactions against control rather than a rethinking of standards appropriate to an era that had gained the benefits of science and industry.[29]

Taine's observations on Goethe's two most famous heroes appear as the book outlines the essential character of art, that single attribute that governs all aspects of its production, distribution, and reception. Art in all times and all places serves to align sensation, reason, and will in forms that exemplify the "representative character" of a society.[30] The artist brings forward the sounds, the forms, the colors that make this personage sensible and an object for imitation. The alignment of inclinations and faculties is clear and reinforces through the power of recognition of an ideal self what individuals' aspirations ought to be and how they ought to behave naturally to be in harmony with the structures of their place and time.

In Greece, this ideal was found in the naked youth of physical and mental alertness. In the Middle Ages, the representative man appeared in the contrasting forms of the ecstatic monk or the amorous knight. In the perfection of Louis XIV's day that still hung over mid-nineteenth-century France, the ideal took shape as a courtier atune to the minutest variations of expression, honor, and policy. Imitation Fausts and Werthers expressed decadent forms of previous ideals. They had not yet captured the modern mind emerging all around them.

The three attributes that Taine argued characterized the ideal modern man corresponded to the then-scientific conception of the three fundamental mental faculties:

- In the modern man, sensation was governed by positive science; this led to a more profound investigation of and accounting for the facts of experience, promoting daily discoveries and an infinite growth of experience.
- The modern man was a worker disciplined by reason; submission to scientific method led to increased productivity, as well as the spread of communication and transport.
- The will of the modern man was directed by a sense of personal limitation that inculcated a rational and humane approach to political life that protected talent, favored order, and succoured the feeble and poor.

In short the modern representative man embodied science, labor, and humanitarian morality. Taine concluded his celebration of the established order with a prediction: this new modern man had finally found a stage for effective deployment of his talents as a result of the revolution of 1830.[31] The second phase of the revolution had not yet begun, but would as young artists awoke to the new beauties and truths emerging from the triumph of modernity — when the arts worked to propagate a sensibility appropriate for scientifically trained, productive, engaged citizens who knew how to subordinate their sensations and emotions to an ethos governed by labor.[32]

Clemenceau's apotheosis of the stolidly middle-class hero Claude Monet was a continuation of Taine's charge and effected a reconciliation of official and avant-garde art. Taine had no intention of promoting the trajectory of cultural experimentation that flowed through the impressionists and postimpressionists into the modern art movements of the twentieth century. But his prescriptions established criteria for what modern art should do as well as the character traits of the ideal modern artist. Clemenceau found in Monet a figure who fit those specifications, with the added twist that the ideal representative modern man was the artist himself, provided he was no bohemian fabulizer.

Monet's movement from self-taught outcast to ideal modern man was no sudden development. The steady growth of interest in his work made him a likely candidate to reconcile experimental and official culture. After the temporary setbacks of the late 1870s and his retreat to Vétheuil, Monet enjoyed a steady, unbroken rise in fame, income, and popularity.[33] The changes in working method taking shape in the paintings he created in 1880–1881 consolidated his language and established working methods that allowed him to work on several canvases simultaneously, thus preserving the vital experiential link between the canvas and his observation. We might say that he had entered into what Taine defined as the mature phase of an artist's career: he had standardized a language that could convey a predictable, semantic understanding of the world that reordered sensations.

Critics drawn to Monet in the 1880s used two words in particular to characterize what set him apart from other painters, either academic or experimental. *Instantanéité* (of the instant, the moment) and *enveloppe* (envelope or covering) defined Monet by his ability to make accessible for contemplation the overall spectral qualities bathing a scene usually only for very brief periods of time.[34] Octave Mirbeau's catalog essay for Monet's 1889 exhibition at the Georges Petit gallery defined *l'instantanéité* as a method for identifying the light scales that allowed one to make sense of a scene. The values that constituted the scale of a scene were "seeded here and there." They changed so frequently that one was seldom aware of the role they played in determining one's emotional reaction. Monet's careful observation and selection allowed him to fix the values he found "in their exact form" so that an otherwise "fleeting" design might become available to all for observation. Monet understood, Mirbeau assured his readers, that in order to arrive at an interpretation of nature that was at once both more exact and more emotionally moving, one had to pierce the passing effects of time and make visible the movement of harmonic values.[35]

Nature's actions have powerful effects on the human soul, but they appear mysterious to those who have not learned how to perceive in the "instant." In his series *Les Débâcles*, documenting the severe winter of 1880 and the ice floes that filled the Seine near his home at Vétheuil, Monet vanquished terror as an inevitable response to natural disaster by concentrating on the shapes and colors the floods and ice floes presented him.[36] The question, What is the form of disaster?, tames the emotional tides that danger releases and directs the troubled soul to the peace that generates an effective response. What is peace? Clemenceau asked and replied that it never meant the absence of conflict. Peace sprang from an ability to confront nature's capricious actions with the conviction that humans are after all conscious and capable of intelligent replies to disaster.[37]

Taine had identified modernity with careful observation of contemporary life refined by knowledge of the mathematical laws of sensation. His lectures directed painters to apply their formidable technical skills to a presentation of the world they saw around them. In so doing he reinforced the power of anecdote and sentiment in academic painting. The impressionists pointed to another conception of modernity, one that was cognitive and revelatory of the lasting, underlying processes at play in sensation. Monet's practice remained grounded in Taine's conception of the modern because it united careful observation with a scientific conception of sensation. He could satisfy Taine's specifications of "modern art" more effectively than the reformed academy because his work demonstrated that there was no need for reproduction of what everybody lived with. What the public needed to become themselves "modern" was retraining in how to see what surrounded them. Reportage of the everyday scene reproduced the confusing emotions that the phenomenal had triggered. The visual screen, Clemenceau noted, was always in perpetual change, but Monet's paintings were invaluable because they transformed "the unseizable relays of Infinity" into forms that could be thought so that "the emotion of nature and its interpretation will be what it ought to be."[38]

The unabated appeal of the impressionists have deeper foundations than their ability to associate the modern with a spectacle of consumption, as T. J. Clark powerfully argued in *The Painting of Modern Life*. The urban scene reorganized around street life, shop windows, and café entertainment provided a ready subject matter for a painting linking a study of atmosphere that foregrounded the ephemerality of mood. So did the summer pleasures of boating and bathing. Modern life stimulated and fulfilled desires in a dance of seductive images for which impressionist paintings remain ever popular exemplars.[39] Alongside images that celebrate fashion, recreation, and the transformation of the human environment, was another strand of paintings that critics claimed rendered visible the unceasing flux underlying natural process. The capricious play of light, water, and vegetation provided a stable matrix within which the flutter of human practices assumed new meaning. The quietude essential to much of Monet's work points to a conception inseparably ideological and metaphysical that adds dignity to the valences surrounding consumption – and sets aside a special place of honor for those self-governed men who perform their jobs and accept the personal limitations that appear to undergird material and moral progress.[40] Images of the city evoked the female figure displaying as Baudelaire had described in "The Painter of Modern Life" the innate power of the soul to escape nature into a realm of pure beauty. The modern masculine subject did not need to appear directly for his ideal self-image was displayed in the creative intelligence that forced nature to reveal its secrets. What allowed (and continues to allow) impressionist "style" to read as ideology independent of any given painting's specific content was an enactment of the modern self through appreciation of underlying method rather than identification with the scene. The artist emerged as the representative modern man to the degree that he mediated creative intelligence through a process of disciplined labor, to the degree that he transcended the romantic Faustian image of technical skill transformed into burning genius.

The pleasures of modern entertainment are inseparable from the capabilities for productive excess inherent to modern social relations, but leisure stands as a point of conflict within a bourgeois self-image that predicates the right to enjoy wealth upon hard work and sacrifice. Monet's work provided a more stoic self-image that encased the capacity for both work and fun within an aura of scientific responsibility.[41] Despite the undeniable finitude of personal existence and the mediocrity of immediate circumstances, the austere pleasures of Monet's painting provided a comforting reassurance that the individual and the universal can synchronize. When they do the modern citizen may not have found paradise, but he or she achieves an imaginary of the present day that they can affirm as the best of all possible sublunar worlds. God remains in His Heaven, but His children behold themselves tending to His garden with modest dignity.

Acknowledgments

This chapter was commissioned initially for the Symposium "Monet and the Cultural and Social Milieu of Impressionism," held at University of Michigan Art Museum, February 7, 1998, in conjunction with the museum's exhibit "Monet at Vétheuil: The Turning Point." I would like to thank Annette Dixon and Carole McNamara for their support and advice.

Notes

1 Hippolyte Taine, *Philosophie de l'Art*, 2nd edn (Paris: Librairie Germer Baillière, 1872), 68.

2 Michel Bréal, "The Latent Concepts of Language," in *The Beginnings of Semantics: Essays, Lectures, and Reviews* (Stanford, CA: Stanford University Press, 1991), 83–84. On Bréal, see George Wolf, "Translator's Introduction: The Emergence of the Concept of Semantics," in *Beginnings of Semantics*, 3–17; Hans Aarsleff, *From Locke to Saussure: Essays on the Study of Language and Intellectual History* (Minneapolis, MN: University of Minnesota Press, 1982); and Brigitte Nerlich, *Change in Language: Whitney, Bréal, and Wegener* (New York: Routledge, 1990). See also Paul Ricoeur, *The Rule of Metaphor: Multidisciplinary Studies of the Creation of Meaning in Language* (Toronto: University of Toronto Press, 1977), 44.

3 For the importance of this method to impressionist work, see Steven Z. Levine, *Monet and his Critics* (New York: Garland, 1976), 103.

4 Signac identifies this difference in *De Delacroix au néo-impressionnisme* (Paris: Hermann, 1964; first published 1899), 70.

5 Charles F. Stuckey, *Monet: Water Lilies* (New York: Hugh Lauter Levin, 1988), 19–21.

6 On Clemenceau see Gregor Dallas, *At the Heart of a Tiger: Clemenceau and his World* (New York: Carroll and Graf, 1993); David Robin Watson, *Georges Clemenceau: A Political Biography* (New York: David McKay, 1974); Wythe Williams, *The Tiger of France: Conversations with Clemenceau* (New York: Duell, Sloan, and Pearce, 1949); and Georges Lecomte, *Georges Clemenceau: The Tiger of France* (New York: D. Appleton, 1919).

7 Clemenceau, *Claude Monet* (Paris: Librairie Plon, 1928), 11.

8 Ibid., 19–20.

9 Ibid., 7, 9.

10 Ibid., 19–20.

11 Ibid., 36. Clemenceau followed nineteenth-century conceptions in stating that emotions are responses to underlying vibrations, the phenomenal form of which take shape in visual, auditory, or other sensory stimuli.

12 Clemenceau, *Claude Monet*, 20.

13 Ibid., 80.

14 See Daniel Wildenstein, *Claude Monet: Biographie et Catalogue Raisonné* (Lausanne: Bibliothèque des Arts, 1974) for a complete edition of Monet's correspondence in relation to his paintings and background interpretation.

15 Clemenceau, *Claude Monet*, 111, 116.

16 This particular marker was also significant to Paul Cézanne's reputation and is a factor in Kahnweiler's advice to Picasso and Braque that they strictly refuse to theorize verbally about their cubist paintings or engage in disputations with other painters over the functions of art.

17 Clemenceau quoted in Dallas, *At the Heart of a Tiger*, 452; full text in Clemenceau, *Discours de guerre* (Paris: Librairie Plon, 1934), 157–182.

18 Clemenceau, *Claude Monet*, 115.

19 On Taine, see François Aulard, *Taine, historien de la révolution française* (Paris: A. Colin, 1928), Thomas H. Goetz, *Taine and the Fine Arts* (Madrid: Playor, 1973), and John Morley, *Biographical Studies* (London: Macmillan, 1923).

20 Taine, *Philosophie de l'Art*, 19, 23–24, 26.

21 American translation by John Durand, *The Philosophy of Art* (New York: Holt and Williams, 1873), 41. In the French original: "il regarde les choses elles-même, il les étudie minutieusement et anxieusement" (26).

22 Taine, *Philosophie de l'Art*, 27–28.

23 Taine's characterization of French classicism was overstated and developed in full in the first volume of his later book *Les Origines de la France contemporaine* (Paris: Hachette, 1876), in which he stated "There is nothing alive in the eighteenth century" (258). His contemporaries were well aware that his view completely ignored the revolutionary changes in literary expression that Rousseau and Diderot, among others, had effected.

24 Taine, *De l'Intelligence* (Paris: Librairie Germer Baillière, 1869), 23, 35–37, 73.

25 Taine, *Philosophie de l'Art*, 60–61.

26 The reforms are discussed in detail in Albert Boime, "The Teaching Reforms of 1863 and the Origins of Modernism in France," *Art Quarterly* 1 (n.s.) (1977): 1–39. In *The Academy and French Painting in the Nineteenth Century* (London: Phaidon, 1971), Boime outlines in greater detail the continuities linking academic and independent painting in the second half of the century.

27 Taine, *Philosophie de l'Art*, 42–43.

28 Ibid., 51.

29 Ibid., 154.

30 Ibid., 155–156.

31 Taine's reference cites the unity of nation and crown that had supposedly been achieved by the parliamentary monarchy of Louis Philippe and consolidated through Napoleon III's restoration of the French Empire in his coup d'état of 1851. The revolution of 1789 would not be celebrated nationally until 1879 when the leaders of the Third Republic turned to the first revolution to validate their regime.

32 Taine, *Philosophie de l'Art*, 158–161.

33 Charles Stuckey, "Love, Money, and Monet's *Débâcle* Paintings of 1880," in Annette Dixon *et al.*, *Monet at Vétheuil: The Turning Point* (Ann Arbor, MI: University of Michigan Museum of Art, 1998), 59–62; John House, *Monet: Nature into Art* (New Haven, CT: Yale University Press, 1986), 11.

34 See House, *Monet*, 220, and Steven Z. Levine, "The 'Instant' of Criticism and Monet's Critical Instant," *Arts Magazine* (March 1981).

35 Octave Mirbeau, *Claude Monet* (Paris: Galerie Georges Petit, 1889), 11–12, 14–15.

36 On these paintings, see Carole McNamara, "Monet's Vétheuil Paintings: Site, Subject, and *Débâcles*," in Dixon *et al.*, *Monet at Vétheuil*, 65–89.

37 This aspect of Clemenceau's thought is explored in Dallas, *At the Heart of the Tiger*, 194.

38 Clemenceau, *Claude Monet*, 53–54, 79.

39 See T. J. Clark, *The Painting of Modern Life: Paris in the Art of Manet and his Followers* (New York: Alfred A. Knopf, 1985). See especially 3–22, 47–49, 248–258.

40 On the division of the impressionists into two camps, one focusing on landscape and the other exploring the urban scene see John Rewald, *History of Impressionism* (New York:

Museum of Modern Art, 1973), Chapters 12–13, and Joel Isaacson, *The Crisis of Impressionism, 1878–1882* (Ann Arbor, MI: University of Michigan Museum of Art, 1979).

41 See C. Wright Mills, "Diagnosis of our Moral Uneasiness" and "The Unity of Work and Leisure," in *People, Power, Politics: The Collected Essays of C. Wright Mills* (New York: Oxford University Press, 1963), 330–338, 347–352, for more regarding the dilemmas of leisure in capitalist societies.

11

COMPOSITE PAST

Photography and family memories in Brazil
(1850–1950)

Ana Maria Mauad

This chapter focuses on the historian's use of photographs and oral sources. What is not shown by images created as testaments to what humans have experienced, what images alone might not allow us to see, can often be inferred from other texts. My research has included conducting interviews with the keepers of family photograph collections, with those who have served as practical guardians of family memory. In examining the relation of photographs and oral sources, I discuss two Brazilian families and the place of photography in their daily lives. The chapter treats photography as a "place of memories" that each family developed in forms distinctive of social situation and historical period.[1]

Photography has, without doubt, shaped the understanding of the past 150 years. The technology has instilled a sense that one can readily enter into and become an eyewitness to the past as a tangible reality. It seems to promise as well that the present can be transformed into a lasting experience in the form of a memory record created for the future. Photographs, as elements of collective memory, function as monuments, that, far from describing what "really happened," commemorate values, ideas, traditions, and forms of behavior. They present images that those in the past wanted to preserve for the future.[2] The cultural level of information that photographic representations provide evidence of the lifestyles of different social groups, as well as suggesting how representations of the past can be an element of social cohesion for their descendants. Historians are developing new critical methods to work with the distinctive qualities of sources such as photographs.

In this chapter, I will use the concept of *intertextuality* to bring image-texts such as photographs and word-texts such as oral history interviews into a dialogical relationship. Both types of historical evidence are understood as autonomous but linked segments of a larger cultural frame generating representations of the past. Every act of interpreting a text is based on interpretation of other, related texts. Historical research utilizing photographs as sources must consider the whole process of producing, consuming, compiling, and preserving images, a set of relationships elucidated through consideration of written accounts, chronicles, advertising, and oral testimonies. In order to cover both the visual and verbal aspects of the subject, I first look at the relationship of oral and visual sources in the process of building memory. Second, I consider the more general relationship between words and images. Finally, I evaluate the role the photographic genre played in Brazilian daily life by looking at two families from Rio de Janeiro's social elite in two different periods, the second half of the nineteenth century and the first half of the twentieth century.

The narrativity of memory

Works on the concept of memory often note that visual and oral sources have been important sites for preserving and recovering group memories, as if a group's experience of the past were hidden in these simulations. Efforts to recover, recuperate or even redeem memories are seldom concerned with the intertextual construction of memory. Each type of source is addressed separately. I have been working with photography as a historical source since the late 1980s. At every opportunity, I have combined oral accounts and photography. In two projects where I worked with family albums, interviews with the owners proved central to the process of reconstructing the chronological sequences of photographs that the families had saved. At the same time, the owners' accounts helped me to understand the photographs as forming a meaningful text, as forming a message that had succeeded in traveling through time.

In my first research project, conducted for my doctoral thesis, I compared two different photographic series: first, photographs that a Lebanese family that had immigrated to Brazil at the beginning of the twentieth century had taken and kept; second, photographs from three popular illustrated periodicals published in Rio de Janeiro between 1900 and 1950. My goal was to uncover codes of behavior and social representation important for the Brazilian upper classes. By comparing private and public image-making, I hoped to describe and evaluate the introduction of a bourgeois way of life into Brazil. Organizing the family photographs into a chronological series was central to my larger historical investigation.[3]

Old photographs belonging to my grandmother, Mrs. Mariana Jabour, had been sitting in a chest for many years. My grandmother and I cleaned the pictures and organized them into an album. She identified and dated the pictures. She recognized the various people and places caught by the camera lens, and she helped me place the photographs into distinct periods. I recorded our talks about the photographs, including the stories that our viewing the photographs together had revived. Her stories helped identify what could be seen immediately in each image, but she also reconstructed the circumstances surrounding the taking of each picture. In the process of organizing a photographic album, her impressions of the time when a photograph was taken provided traces of the historically defined cultural competencies of those who built this memory record. The album composed a narrative in dialogue with both the past and the present, bringing up to date the task of the collection keeper as a guardian of shared memories.

My second research project examined the *social circuit* of photography in the nineteenth century. I worked with a collection of family portraits from the second half of the century that had belonged to a wealthy family from Bananal, a small city in the state of São Paulo. The collection had been maintained by a family descendant.[4] In this project, the process of recovering family memory was completely different. A possessor of a prodigious personal memory, the descendant had recorded every story that his grandmother had told him into a notebook. He engaged in genealogical studies, as well as research into the history of the Brazilian Empire. One man's personal life project to preserve and expand his family's past created an extensive discursive frame for the photographs his family had saved.

I discovered the existence and relation of these other texts only in the process of analyzing the photos. When organizing the photographs, he had found an antique album from the nineteenth century that he used to illustrate his genealogical text. Captions on the back of the photos identified the photographers with a detail of commentary revealing my informant's deep knowledge of the history of social relationships of upper-class Brazilians. The historical text he created was found in his precise and critical analysis of aristocratic Brazilian society in the century. A family text emerged in his personal remarks identifying relatives.

For both projects, family photographs and the oral accounts I recorded established a dialogical relationship that proved fundamental to conceiving each photographic collection as a set of historical and cultural texts. At the same time, my experience raised methodological questions about the relation of words and images that required more theoretical consideration on my part.

Words and images

The simple question "Is an image worth more than a thousand words?" contains hidden within it a complicated problem. Both words and images play a very important and special role in the communication process and in the framing of social memories. Usually, the interpretation of images involves a translation of visual impressions into words. Words and images however involve messages based in autonomous production processes. Words and images are autonomous texts produced within a common historical context but with different perceptual, semiotic, and institutional constraints.

A word can be emitted through either oral or written discourse where the control one has on the final product of either type of discourse depends on:

- the genre context of the verbal discourse (biographical narrative, interview, public speech, etc.)
- the reception possibilities (dialog, identified large public, unidentified large public, etc.)
- the place where the discourse is being given (private circle, domestic environment, from an institution, street, etc.)

- the topic of discourse (special themes, spontaneous recollection, interview prepared for a specific project, etc.)
- the type of discourse support (alive, recorded by video cassette recorder (VCR), tape recorder, transcription, etc.)

All these elements have an influence on the interpretation of words organized in discourses conceived as texts. The same thing happens to images. In this case, important variables are:

- type of apparatus (photography camera, film camera, digital camera)
- relationship between subjects (producer and consumer of images)
- stages of activity (production, circulation and consumption of images)
- storage type (family albums, RAM memory, shoe boxes, public archives, private archives, etc.)
- image topics (daily memories, fictional narrative, evidence, public issues, etc.)

The realization of the communication process requires the production of texts, which can be considered as a macroscopic unity of the communication process.[5] The specific shape of a text involves combining a system of meanings with a system, or medium, of communication. In this way the process of interpreting texts must be concerned with variables such as conditions of production, circumstances of transmission, the position of the speaker, the channels of transmission, and so on.

However autonomous image-texts and verbal-texts might be in terms of their production and communication contexts, both can be analyzed in a dialogical relationship. Texts do not have a meaning independent of the social and cultural context that produced them.[6] As analytic categories, *text*, *context*, and *production of meaning* share a framework of reference that understands culture as a result of the social practices of communication. In daily life, there are several codes referencing cultural and historical contexts, the practice of which are expressed through objects, thoughts, behavior, words, gestures, and so on, that assume a great variety of sign functions in the endless process of social semiosis.[7]

Photographs, movies, architectural devices, oral sources, and so on can all equally be conceived as texts. The plurality of texts across media is a necessary precondition for applying the concept of intertextuality and understanding historical textual analysis as a social practice building upon previous social practices. Each text relates to previous texts, and interpretation involves reconstructing that connection. The cultural competence of message-receivers determines how they understand the meaning of a message. Cultural competence rests on taking for granted the repertoire of preceding texts that provide a shared social-cultural experience necessary for understanding the messages new texts might convey.

Within this theoretical perspective, taking pictures is a social practice for the composition of memories into image-texts. In order to understand how families build their memories through photographs, I will evaluate the relationship between collective genre principles and the ways in which the two Brazilian families I have studied each conceived the functions of photography in a manner meaningful for their social contexts.

Family photographs as places of memory, Brazil, 1850–1950

In the twentieth century, taking pictures has almost become an obligation on certain occasions: vacations, parties, and other celebrations. Snapshots have become one way for families and other social groups to build a memory record. Analysis of photographs as monuments with the charge of memory creation raises several methodological questions: How can we understand daily life in the past through photographic images? In what way has the technical development of photography influenced the nature of family memories? How can we evaluate differences in photographic representation of social relations between the nineteenth and twentieth centuries? What has remained the same and what has changed in the photographic process? What has motivated people to keep on taking pictures through the years? I found some of the answers to these questions in the history of the two families I studied.

Pedro Ramos Nogueira was born in 1823 on a farm in Bananal County in the state of São Paulo, Brazil. He attended the Pedro II School, an aristocratic boarding school attached to the imperial court in Rio de Janeiro, before enrolling as a student at the medicine faculty. From his first days at school, Nogueira, known usually by his aristocratic title, the Baron of Joatinga, was interested in politics. He participated as a leader of student demonstrations for liberal causes. Nonetheless, even if a liberal by principle and by temperament, the Baron of Joatinga accepted the conservative politics of the rest of his family. In 1868 he broke with the liberal party to take a position in a conservative government. The power of family tradition obliged him to join the conservative party, and as a result, he became an important local politician.

The baron then married the daughter of a rich farmer from Bananal. For their honeymoon, Pedro and his new wife went to Paris. There the baron was photographed by Eugène Disderi, a famous French photographer who promoted the use of the "carte-de-visite," a fashionable portrait format widely used in the nineteenth century. In the Baron's carte-de-visite, we see the signs of social distinction appropriate for a world of splendor and sumptuousness (Figure 11.1). The image as well has connotations of elegance and intellectuality. With pensive eyes, Pedro rests his head on one hand, as he stands with an open book. The image represents its subject in profound moral and philosophical reflection on some political principle. Above all, the photograph with its highly artificial conventions presented a personal self-image that he wanted eternalized for the future.

The Baron of Joatinga, his wife, and family were exemplary clients for a style of portraiture found in photography studios all over the world in the second half of the nineteenth century (Figures 11.2 and 11.3). The carte-de-visite was inevitably associated with a representation of wealth and social distinction important to the

Figure 11.1 Pedro Ramos Nogueira, Baron of Joatinga, Paris, carte-de-visite, albumen, *c.*1880. Courtesy of the Resgate Collection.

Figure 11.2 The Baron of Aguiar Vallim as a child, Rio de Janeiro, carte-de-visite, albumen, J.F. Guimarães, 1880. Courtesy of the Resgate Collection.

Figure 11.3 "Aunt Cadinha, Aunt Amelia, Daddy, and Uncle Eduardo at the photographer's studio," Rio de Janeiro, cabinet size, albumen, 1879. Courtesy of the Resgate Collection.

creation, transmission, and preservation of family traditions for São Paulo's agrarian elite, who were possessors of slaves, large landed estates, capital, and political influence.[8]

Several decades later, in a very different social and political context, Elias Elias Jabour, his wife, and sons arrived in Rio de Janeiro at the beginning of the twentieth century, along with many other immigrants from Lebanon. The family settled in Providencia, a small city in the state of Minas Gerais where there was a Lebanese colony of merchants selling clothes, food, furniture, and often even offering photographic services. The family prospered and when he was 15, Elias's son Abraão left home to open a rice-processing business with his father's friend and his own godfather, Jorge Mauad, in a near-by city. The venture provided a new direction for the family's fortunes (Figure 11.4).

By the 1930s, Abraão Jabour had moved to Rio de Janeiro, where he was a successful coffee exporter. His family followed him, and they assumed an upper-class status, with all the outward signs of bourgeois distinction, including numerous photographs of family celebrations and rituals (Figures 11.5, 11.6 and 11.7). The images the family saved present fifty years of memories fixed in time by the camera lens, illustrating the growing wealth of the family and their conquest of a distinctive place in the city. For each change, a photograph, the emblem of a new time.[9]

Photographs, biographical accounts, diaries, and interviews provided me with the materials for reconstructing the contrasting histories of a Lebanese immigrant family that prospers in the first half of the twentieth century in Rio de Janeiro and of an aristocratic family integral to São Paulo's agrarian elite during the golden age of the coffee plantation. A central question for both projects was how to relate oral texts and family photographic images intertextually to develop a fuller understanding of family identity and experience. There were no straightforward models for relating oral sources and photographs. Given the very different contexts for family photography in the two time periods, I needed two different approaches.

For my study of a nineteenth-century aristocratic family, I combined genealogical, historical, and family texts in order to develop an interpretation of the meanings the family had placed in photographs taken of themselves. An oral interview with the descendant responsible for preserving the photographs conducted while reviewing the archive he had created played a small but important role in identifying connections linking surviving written documents and the photographs. As I worked through the archive and studied each document, my interviewee answered questions, clarified obscure topics, identified individuals appearing in photographs, and retraced the family genealogical tree for me. His explanations helped me to reconstruct the cultural competence needed to see clearly the network of relationships represented in the album.

My informant was not a regular interviewee, nor even a professional archivist, though he was, in fact, the guardian of family memory. My interviews with him did not follow the usual procedures for an oral history recording first-hand testimony of past events and people. He and I discussed individual documents and photographs

Figure 11.4 João Jorge Mauad, Providencia, 1928. Author's collection.

Figure 11.5 Abraão Jabour and his brothers at the Jockey Club, Rio de Janeiro, 1928. Author's collection.

Figure 11.6 Business meeting at the Coffee Trade Center, Rio de Janeiro, 1927. Author's collection.

Figure 11.7 Friends at 5 o'clock tea, Copacabana Palace Hotel, Rio de Janeiro, 1930. Author's collection.

created long before he was born. I typed up a record of these conversations, which I then showed to him for further comment and revision. He responded with his own understanding of his family's trajectory constructed through filters of genealogical research and personal self-reflection. Every file he had compiled into a family archive contributed to the historical interpretation I made of the social circuit of family photographs in nineteenth-century Brazil. This interpretation then made possible a deeper intertextual understanding of the relation of oral and written testimonies to the images in the family's photo album which laid the basis for the narrative I developed of the family's history.

In my earlier project reconstructing the trajectory of a Lebanese family in Brazil during the first half of the twentieth century, oral testimony played a more important role in the interpretation of family photographs. Family pictures were not already organized in an album. Instead, they had been kept in a box, stored away in a chest with many other things. As the owner of the photographs and I organized the pictures into an album, I recorded her commentary on what she thought was happening in the picture as well as her identifications of individuals and locations. At every stage of the research, her oral account provided information important for a more thorough understanding of what the photographs had meant for family memory and identity.

The interviewee was my grandmother, and the relationship as interviewer and interviewee was based in the confidence we felt for each other long before the

Figure 11.8 Abraão Jabour, his mother Said Jabour, and his sister Joana Jabour, Tripoli, Lebanon, early twentieth century; the last photograph taken before the family left Lebanon for Brazil. Author's collection.

research process had begun. I interviewed her twice. The first time, we sat together with the photographs, and I recorded what she had to say about them without any structured agenda. I then listened to the tapes and wrote a draft family history organized around the memories my grandmother's photographs had stimulated. Finally, I returned to my grandmother for a second set of interviews, this time organized around a set of questions about what had happened to the family. In the second set of sessions, we did not look at or refer to the photographs.

The result of this process was an analytic narrative reconstructing the meaning these photographs had carried for my family. I started with the oldest photograph, taken when the family was still in Lebanon. With this photograph in her hands, my grandmother told me what she had heard from her mother about the decision for leaving home. The location of the studio had been written on the reverse side of the photo, which provided evidence I used to determine that, prior to emigrating to Brazil, the family had left their home town of Troblus and had lived for a while in the city of Tripoli, where the picture was taken. As we identified each of the people photographed, my grandmother and I began to build a genealogical tree for our family, starting with the pioneers who first came to Brazil (Figure 11.8).

In another photograph of the whole family when they lived in Minas Gerais, I learned about the members of the family before Abraão Jabour made his fortune. My grandmother's description of this photograph provided insight into what it was like for Lebanese to live in this small, remote community. The storyteller reconnected to her past through the images we reviewed. Each image related to another through accounts of new characters and places. I, as a historian, used her stories inspired by the photographic images to interpret the historical significance of why the family moved from one region to another, why it chose to live in a particular district of Rio de Janeiro, why it went on holidays in particular, fashionable places, or why children were always photographed with women. At the same time we were both building a shared family memory and identity (Figure 11.9).

The social circuit of photography in Brazil, 1850–1950

When a family decides to keep special objects, to take photographs, to retell particular anecdotes, it is determining what ought to be remembered and preserved from the action of forgetting. No social group can be sure that it will continue. It has to work to preserve its existence. From this effort comes a preoccupation to preserve an identity of the group through the conservation and transmission of its memories. The family is a site for the recollection of the past precisely because it is also the very object of remembrance.

As vehicles of collective memory, families build self-representations that last through time and are reaffirmed every moment when individuals invoke their shared identity through the invocation of familiar reminiscences. Objects are saved, accounts are repeated, and the social space of the family is reformed in the present for another generation of descendants. Photography provides an ideal source to evaluate how relatively spontaneous representations of daily activity became an expected part of a process of family remembering, replacing more formal, rigid images of family members. Advertising of photographic services and products is a primary source available to historians for reconstructing the consumers of photographic imagery and the expectations they brought to the photographic act.

In 1870, there were thirty-eight photographers working in Rio de Janeiro, then the capital of the country. They sought their clients through advertisements for their

Figure 11.9 The Jabour family at Providencia, 1925. Author's collection.

services published in Brazil's most important social almanac. These photographers promised a variety of services, but their advertisements stressed studio location. The closer to Rua Ouvidor, the fashionable street where wealthy families shopped, the more exclusive and distinguished the studio was. To be a client of a very exclusive photographic studio was a mark of distinction. Such patronage linked the inhabitant of Rio to the inhabitants of Paris, and the Rua Ouvidor to the Boulevard des Italiens, integrating the Brazilian city into the larger circuit of occidental civilization.[10]

For members of the Brazilian aristocracy of the twentieth century, such as the family I studied, going to the photographic studio and allowing oneself to be photographed, having images fixed on a silver plate or on other kinds of precious materials, was part of a ritual of conspicuous consumption. Other elements in a series of rituals defining aristocracy in this historical period included strolling at five o'clock down the Rua Ouvidor; taking cakes and tarts at Castelões, an exclusive pâtisserie; engaging in political gossip at the Café do Rio; and attending parties in the ballrooms of the aristocratic families or at the castles of the Brazilian imperial family. Joined to these symbols performative of social status were photographic rituals that preserved for the future memories of participation in "high society."

At the beginning of the twentieth century, the Kodak slogan "You press the button and we do the rest" arrived. Freed from the stress of the pose, by the shortening of the time of exposure, photographers and their subjects were able to catch the instantaneous moment, multiplying the possibilities of images. In 1904, the Rio newspaper, *O Jornal do Brasil*, published a cartoon on the front page of one Sunday edition. The drawing presented a crowded beach scene, typical of Sunday morning in Rio, with all of the adults and children holding a small camera, with the following caption:

> Photography and the beaches – a few days ago a respectable lady that used to go to the beach for bathing and swimming exclaimed. "It is a plague! Nobody swims but everyone takes pictures! If someone stands up, a 'click' is heard; if they sit down, here comes another 'click', we must be concerned with a more convenient way to sit, because, from now on, we are completely surrounded by cameras."

Kodak's advertising was designed to educate the larger public as potential consumers of photographic products. Beginning in the 1920s, Kodak published advertisements in the most important Brazilian illustrated magazines with lessons on how use the camera to record the best moments of daily life in its great variety. The target of this publicity was the amateur photographer, but almost all of the figures depicted taking pictures in the advertisements were female, while the subjects of the images were both male and female. The shift in advertising focus from studio service to do-it-yourself photography involved a vital change in who in the family carried the responsibility for the work of creating memories. In the nineteenth century, the person controlling photographic activity, the person in charge of building memories through images, was the head of the family. In the following century, the father had to share this role with the mother, who had long been responsible for the domestic realm. As preserving moments of domestic life became the great theme of family snapshots, women in the household assumed responsibility for keeping these fragments of daily life from being forgotten. The spread of the photographic habit throughout the world and among different social groups has contributed to a change in the nature of the twentieth century's family memories, as well as a shift in who might well be the keepers of family memory.

The Jabour family took pictures of themselves in order to build a narrative of its daily life. In the first half of the twentieth century, when the process of popularization of photography remained incomplete, taking pictures and participating in a photograph helped to compose a catalog of self-representations and social practices considered ideal to an ascendant bourgeoisie. Vacations, leisure, study time, raising children, carnival – all these moments were recorded as photographic images that helped to construct memories of prosperity and success.

Photographic albums of the nineteenth century created a family narrative built around rigidly posed portraits and the mise-en-scène of the studio. Traces of the changes produced by time are shown in signs of aging, in children growing up, in a succession of fashions, in hair-styling, and in the use of make-up. Simultaneously, preferred studio backgrounds changed with the passage of time as well. Shifting preferences, such as from the column to the bicycle, a tendency that illustrated the gradual relaxation of behavior, reveal the self-images of each decade. In a narrative constructed from studio portraits, family life is seen only through a sequence of special occasions when the father took all the family to the studio. Taking a photograph typically was a special moment requiring expense and effort, and photographic conventions combined with other signs of social distinction to stress the ceremonial dimension the photographic act involved. Family memories in the nineteenth century were thus largely structured with a high degree of artificiality. Itinerant photographers traveling through the countryside and visiting families at their country homes provided a possibility for more relaxed pictures, with informal clothes, taken on the grounds of the family or in improvised studios in the farmhouse yard. Even in these relatively familiar situations, the photographers tried by all means possible to imitate the conventions of exclusive studios in the capital. As the time of exposure diminished, the grade of artificiality fell, however, and the capacity of photography to represent a broader range of family activities increased.

The narrative composed by family photographic collections from the first half of the twentieth century varies both in time and space. Time is measured by the rites of family as well as by changes in daily life. Marriages, births, baptisms, birthdays, graduation parties, together with journeys, vacations, balls, lunch-parties, children growing up, and so on, provided narratives recreating daily life through the combination of special events with records of daily life. With the movement from the portrait to the snapshot a whole new universe of themes and subjects opened up for family photographers, whether amateur or professional. The faster registration of images redefined the structure of family memories in contemporary society. Getting closer to the intimacy of the home, bourgeois family memories introduced many subjects into the frame that had been forbidden to the nineteenth century. It had been unthinkable, for example, that barefoot children – unless they were family slaves – be portrayed in a nineteenth-century studio "mise-en-scène." Further, due to technical limitations, snapshots of the family on the street, say on shopping expeditions, were unusual.

After the turn of the century, family members often created their own photographic documents, but professional photographers remained important for special occasions. They provided official records of marriages and other big celebrations. The photographer was responsible for delivering a high quality image that fit precise patterns for marking social distinction. It is only the very recent past that the informality of family imagery has grown to the degree that locations that were before almost forbidden territories, such as bathrooms and kitchens, are now acceptable.

Although the photographs of the Baron of Joatinga's family in the nineteenth century are stylistically different from those of the Jabour family in the twentieth century, both collections developed in the work of building family memories. In both cases, the families took or had taken photographs for a future time when the family could come together around records of a past it could remember, recall, or celebrate. The necessity to recognize and identify shared remembrances and images is intimately linked to the processes of building social identities. Photography, whether registering family scenes or social conflicts, updates social memory with images from a renewed collective history.

In conclusion, let us go back to our first problem: the relationship between oral sources and photographic images. Reflecting on the meaning of family photographs Julia Hirsh points out the difference between a written reference and an oral one:

> The caption on the back of a picture, or in an album may simply read: *Mom and Dad, Brighton, August, 1893*, and offer only a record of time and place. A personal, oral account usually has more texture and complexity, reaching far beyond the scope of picture itself. *That's aunt Sadie and Uncle George*, a loving niece might say. *She made the best oatmeal cookies you'd ever want to eat. And he just loved fishing.* Their prodigal son, viewing the same shot, might speak of a doting mother and a tyrannical father . . . Family photographs themselves do not change, only the stories we tell about them do.[11]

In the accounts provided me by guardians of family memories, I learned how to follow the clues their stories gave. After cross-referencing different historical records such as advertisements, newspaper chronicles, news in the illustrated magazines, family photographs, etc., I came to understand more fully how groups develop historically situated photographic and storytelling conventions that together build a social identity as part of the activity of building shared memories.

Notes

1 Nora, Pierre, *Les Lieux de mémoire* (Paris: Gallimard, 1984), xviii–xlii.
2 Le Goff, Jacques, "Monumento/documento," in *Enciclopédia Einaudi*, vol. 1 (Lisbon: Imp. Nacional, Casa da Moeda, 1985).
3 Mauad, Ana Maria, "Sob o signo da imagem: a produção da fotografia e o controle dos códigos de representação social da classe dominante, no Rio de Janeiro, na primeira metade do século XX." Niterói, UFF, CEG, ICHF, History Ph.D. thesis, 1990.
4 Mauad, Ana Maria, "Resgate de Memórias," in *Resgate: uma janela para o oitocentos*, eds. H. Mattos and E. Schnoor (Rio de Janeiro: Top Books, 1995).
5 Vilches, Lorenzo, *La lectura de la imagen: prensa, cine, televisión* (Buenos Aires: Paidós-comunicación, 11, 1992), Chapter 2.
6 Eco, Umberto, *Conceito de texto* (São Paulo: Edusp, 1984).
7 Rossi-Landi, F., *Linguagem como trabalho e como mercado* (São Paulo: Difel, 1985).
8 Mauad, "Resgate de Memórias."
9 Mauad, "Sob o signo da imagem."
10 Mauad, Ana Maria, "Imagem e Auto Imagem do Segundo Império," in *História da Vida Privada no Brasil Império*, ed. L. F. Alencastro (São Paulo, 1997).
11 Hirsch, Julia, *Family Photographs: Content, Meaning, and Effect* (New York: Oxford University Press, 1981), 5.

12

MEMORIES OF MAMMY

Lizzetta LeFalle-Collins

If there is any word that arouses emotion in the heart of a true Southerner, it is the word, Mammy. His mind goes back to the tender embraces, the watchful eyes, the crooning melodies which lulled him to rest, the sweet old black face. What a memory! he exclaims.[1]

I am a Negro woman, and I was born and reared in the South. I am now past forty years of age and am the mother of three children. My husband died nearly fifteen years ago . . . For more than thirty years – or since I was ten years old – I have been a servant . . . in white families . . . During the last ten years I have been a nurse . . . More than two-thirds of the Negroes of the town where I live are menial servants of one kind or another . . . The condition . . . of poor colored people is just as bad as, if not worse than it was during the days of slavery. Tho today we are enjoying nominal freedom, we are literally slaves.

Anonymous[2]

The popularized image of mammy by whites was one of the most defining popular images of black women from the slavery period into the first two decades of the twentieth century. With few exceptions these white interpretations of black women were demeaning, depicting African American women as the antithesis of womanhood according to Euro-American standards of beauty.[3] The image of mammy was so deeply rooted in the portrayal of black women in the United States that while originating in the South, it became the icon that was adopted by writers and artists alike when they sought to evoke an image of black motherhood.

Whites often characterized mammies as wet nurses, whose sole joy in life was to serve the needs of the white family. Her signifiers became her size, skin color, white apron and especially her red and white bandana, popularized in song during the 1930s.[4] Her physical characteristics dictated a large and full-bosomed statue to cradle and nurse the children of the household, but it also positioned her to be sexually exploited in a more devious plot by the males of the household.[5] K. Sue Jewell writes:

Two of mammy's most endowed features are her breasts and buttocks. This should not be surprising as these two qualities are considered desirable, particularly by males, in the United States; and it is a known fact that males who occupy positions of power in our society control societal institutions and influence ideas. Thus, it is fairly obvious why this group has carefully included physical features that it finds appealing in all women. Both breasts and buttocks are enlarged in all images that symbolize womanhood. However, in mammy these features are extremely exaggerated. The unusually large buttocks and embellished breasts place mammy outside the sphere of sexual desirability and into the realm of maternal nurturance. In so doing, it allows the males who constructed this image, and those who accept it, to disavow their sexual interests in African American women. Therefore, when the slave owners were sexually involved with female slaves, the implication was that it was the result of the sexual advances of the overweight female slave and not the slave owner.[6]

Verta Mae, who finds similarities between mammy's bosom and the breast of the Gibson Girl or Jayne Mansfield, has also discussed the bosom as a safe haven (a comfortable place for men to lay their heads) and as a symbol of nurturance. Mammy as "pin-up" girl she contends is there for the gratification of the men who construct these images of women. But the most powerful image that Verta Mae calls forth is that from Gyland Kain's poem "The Blue Gorilla" in which he says, "The big ample bosom of mammy is as American as apple pie. And that everybody wants to rest in the big, soft, warm haven of mammy's black bosom."[7] Equating mammy's bosom with apple pie so thoroughly branded the image of mammy in American culture that most black domestics, even if slightly overweight, and almost all obese black women have been viewed in that context. As the embodiment of black motherhood, mammy could therefore evoke both fantasy and erotic passion in the eyes of her white creators, but as the domestic (even the mammy) she also influenced how some black writers and artists portrayed nurturing black women in their works.

This chapter interrogates the archetype of a mammyesque form created by Sargent Claude Johnson, the San Francisco artist, who won recognition in the 1930s for his sculptures of African American women. The sculpture that is most endearing is *Forever Free*, the full and stout woman who also closely resembles a popularized image of the black domestic and even the black mammy, pictured with little chocolate brown children at her side (Figure 12.1). Johnson was like many blacks who had been privileged due to their light skin color and class standing. He realized that were it not for those two things, he would suffer extreme marginalization like other blacks. The color class dilemma caused some blacks to empathize with their brethren who were held back by skin color and class position. Additionally, many artists felt that within this group of blacks rested the foundation of black culture.[8] Johnson turned the mammy image on its head, redefining it and subverting its meaning among whites and blacks. His mammy embodied the attitude of a resistant

Figure 12.1 Sargent Johnson, *Forever Free*, wood with lacquer on cloth, 1933. Courtesy of San Francisco Museum of Modern Art.

black woman. But the mother in *Forever Free* closely resembled the mammy character in popular cinema and press and for the white viewers who could not penetrate the black self-conscious, misreading the figure caused them to embrace her as the old subservient mammy, a victim rather than survivor.

For Johnson, his archetype for black motherhood was embodied in his definition of "Negro Art." He articulated this characterization of her in the now well referenced statement from the "San Francisco Artists" column in the *San Francisco Chronicle*, October 6, 1935.

> I aim at producing a strictly Negro Art . . . studying not the culturally mixed Negro of the cities, but the more primitive slave type as it existed in this country during the period of slave importation . . . It is the pure American Negro I am concerned with, aiming to show the natural beauty and dignity in that characteristic lip, that characteristic hair, bearing and manner.[9]

With limited critical evaluation from the art press, Johnson himself shaped the critical reading for his works. In the *Chronicle* article, Johnson encouraged African American artists to go South (where he traveled once) to find the characteristic "primitive slave type." He stated,

> The slogan for the Negro artist should be "go South, young man." Unfortunately for too many of us it is "go East, young man." Too many Negro artists go to Europe and come back imitators of Cézanne, Matisse, or Picasso. And this attitude is not only a weakness of the artists, but of their racial public.

Dedicated to this ideal, he memorialized black women in the terracotta *Standing Figure* (1934), the chalk drawing *Mother and Child* (1934), the conte crayon *Defiant*, and the polychrome *Forever Free* (1933) and *Negro Woman* (c.1935), signature works that attest to Johnson's preoccupation with this archetype of black motherhood (Figure 12.2).

By the time Johnson sought training at the A. W. Best School of Art in 1915, American sculptors trained in academic realism were retiring and instructors who were more interested in a non-realistic approach to sculpture were replacing them.[10] It may have also been at the Best School where he first explored African sculpture. It was the sculptural form most frequently cited in support of the non-realistic approach to sculpture due to its plastic qualities and emphasis on essentials.[11]

His experimentation with materials and a desire to interrogate the primitive slave-type accounted in part for how Johnson represented his woman in *Forever Free*. Johnson liked color and employed an Egyptian technique of polychrome enamel over a linen-covered wood, which he then painted. Sculpture in the twentieth century returned to direct carving to exploit fully the surface possibilities of the

237

Figure 12.2 Sargent Johnson, *Standing Figure*, painted terracotta, 1934. Courtesy of Fine Arts
   Museums of San Francisco.

medium. Johnson's simple carved shapes and minimal line textures reflected a
post-World War I newfound respect for materials developed in the field of American
design.

   Johnson's *Forever Free* stands in uniform-like attire, bare foot suggesting her
domestic/slave status. She protects her two nude toddlers who are incised into the
skirt of her dress. Her embrace is not only one of nurturing but also protecting

238

against an unseen element as she gazes sternly in its direction. Her touch on her children cannot be interpreted any other way. *Forever Free* so closely resembles the black mammy figure in American popular culture, that her declared freedom in the title of the work is somewhat undercut by her domestic servitude.

In 1934, Johnson sculpted *Standing Figure* when all of the United States, including the artist, was steeped in a widening depression filled with many images of despair. He almost decided to give up his career as an artist when he was accepted into the Works Progress Administration Federal Art Project (FAP). As artists groped with how the United States should represent itself, they gazed across the country and portrayed what they felt were "true" images of the American people. In the FAP, some directors of government programs dictated control over their teams of artists as to what types of images were acceptable. For example, Roy Stryker, head of the Farm Security Administration (FSA) Photographic project, wished to protect the dignity "of the poor."[12] He wrote that "To my knowledge, there is no [FSA] picture . . . that . . . represents an attempt by a photographer to ridicule his subject, to be cute with him, to violate his privacy, or to do something to make a cliche."[13] To achieve this Stryker told his photographers to "emphasize the idea of abundance – the 'horn of plenty' – and pour maple syrup over it . . . I know your damned photographer's soul writhes . . . Do you think I give a damn about a photographer's soul with Hitler at our doorsteps?"[14] While Johnson's *Standing Figure* was not emaciated and did not show physical signs of poverty, her spirit unlike his *Forever Free* seemed broken. With gaze upward, *Forever Free* stands in defense of her freedom and children, but *Standing Figure* is humble and with a downward gaze, this woman seems resigned to her fate as a domestic. Yet, for his part in this grand scheme to promote American images in art, Johnson seemed determined to insert black women in the visual dialog.

At a time when American artists were encouraged to create an art that reflected the American experience and character, some artists seemed wedded to a sense of geographical regionalism in their portrayals. In Johnson's narrowly conceived view for his black subjects, he located the archetype for the women in the southern United States. Even as the great migration to the North, Midwest and West had dispersed the domestic mother, Johnson thought that her purest form resided in the South. Johnson's image of his slave type quite probably could have been influenced by the countless incarnations of images of mammy in popular culture as well as descriptions found in literature by African Americans from the 1920s into the 1940s. Alain Locke wrote of stereotyping of blacks in literature indicating how blacks were characterized in specific categories that included the comic peasant, scapegoat, pariah, savage stranger and bogeyman. In 1933, the year that *Forever Free* was created, Sterling Brown delineated categories for blacks in literature such as the contented slave, comic Negro, exotic primitive, tragic mulatto and the brute nigger.[15] While these were favorite characterizations by white writers, some black writers tried to redefine the archetypes with alternative interpretations. The poem by James Weldon Johnson entitled "Go Down Death: A Funeral Sermon" contains a passage which seems to describe the character and physical form of Johnson's mammyesque women, especially *Standing Figure*. It follows:

And God said: Go down, Death, go down,
Go down to Savannah, Georgia,
And Find Sister Caroline.
She's borne the burden and heat of the day,
She's labored long in my vineyard,
And she's tired –
She's weary –
Go down, Death, and bring her to me.[16]

Here Johnson (the author) locates a region, a small rural town in the South; defines the type of fieldwork in *His* vineyard (probably cotton); indicates her physical state, she is tired and weary; and suggests her reward, life in *His* arms.

Standing Figure is the visualization of Sister Caroline a humble, pious black mother who has to work in the homes of whites to make a living for herself and her family. Her breasts are sunken and sagging which suggests her part as a wet-nurse, nursing her children as well as the children of wealthy white families. Her hands are clasped which presents a sense of restraint, subjugation, and repressed anger. Johnson stated that he was portraying a slave-type. This high cheek-boned, full-lipped, "pure" black woman was the true personification of the American black female for him. She also fits the classic characterization of the black mammy.

Johnson did not view his women of servitude as degrading to the race because they were a reality for so many black women. It is more likely that he sought to pay homage to her in his work. As workers, these women were partners in labor with men. Not spared the indecencies of the auction block during slavery, they were bought and sold like men based on their physical attributes in association with labor. Separated from their families just as the men, women lost children who were sold from them without consideration of maternal bonds. Their sole purpose on earth was to work like the black men, at the will of others. This equality in labor with black men accounted for the number of women within the struggle for human rights due to their vested interest in labor issues.

Johnson's women should be read not only as domestics, but also as providers and a symbol of black women laborers, for it was often easier for women to gain employment than their male partners. This is precisely where Johnson subverts the popular image of mammy. While women at work were often portrayed separate from men, it was understood that their labor was in partnership with them. In the United States as early as 1903, at the convention of the National Negro Business League, one member made a point that he owed his success as a businessman to his wife and told other members that he "could truthfully say that they owed more to their wives than to any other one thing for their achievements as businessmen."[17] At the 1904 convention, Fannie Barrier Williams spoke of the women as "silent partners" who were always concealed from the public eye; she said that it was the wives who stood "between the businessman and bankruptcy."[18] She also asked that black women "become more important in those larger affairs of life where character and achievements count for more than prejudices and suspicions," and encouraged black men to help to make black womanhood a part of "all that is best and most beautiful in the world's conception of an ideal woman."[19] Because so many women were initially in the workforce as "silent partners" that supplemented their partner's income, it became easier for them to move into a place of domination within the workforce and in a position of sole supporter. While this labor role reversal is by no means complete, it should be acknowledged that the expectation and reality of black women in the workforce is the norm rather than the exception. By the 1920s, black women shared the responsibility as partners with their husbands in business as they had in labor. "In 1929, Negro women showed the highest rate of employment of any racial group."[20]

As laborers whites also stereotyped black women as asexual, opposing another popularized image of the black woman as seductress who was usually found in fine art in a nightlife environment.[21] Black domestics garnered respect from other blacks because of their willingness to work to support their families, but because of their class status, like other unskilled workers, they were subjected to other more lurid stereotypes. Middle-class black women viewed domestic work as undignified and dangerous, something that well-bred women avoided. Most times, there was also a division of labor based on physiognomy, specifically color where lighter skin color often connoted privilege and freedom from domestic assignments. In general, those black women who most closely resembled white women, with light skin, straighter hair, and smaller physical frames were more desirable by black men and thus found it easier to marry into wealth and position that protected them from entering into the domestic labor arena. Dividing women based on skin color, and texture and length of hair helped to strengthen the dichotomy among black women in a color conscious society and to perpetuate the caricature of the mammy.

One of the most vivid portrayals of color preferences documented in art is found in Palmer Hayden's *Beale Street Blues* and *The Dress She Wore Was Blue* (Figure 12.3), both from the John Henry Series (1943). In the latter work a white writer, Louis Chappell, influenced the characterization of John Henry's woman. He described her as either "white" or "almost white." In response to an inquiry by Hayden to Chappell about the John Henry legend, Chappell cautioned Hayden, "If you have occasion to include this woman in your paintings, I hope she will look something fit to go home to when the day's work is over and the night's work is ready to begin, and such a woman is not altogether a matter of clothes."[22] Hayden complied with what he felt was "fit to go home to" and thus fit for male consumption. Chappell also suggests that a working man deserves a specific type of woman. In the same painting, the "fit" woman who approximates the mulatto characterization, stands next to a head-wrapped mammy character, so that the viewer can make his own comparison and make up his own mind as to which woman is preferable.

There were few options open to unskilled or uneducated black women, except domestic work in white households; many middle-class women were forbidden by their parents from most types of work because they might be subjected to sexual advances from their white employers. Those uniformed (and those not) domestics who had to work were still subject to harassment by the male members of the household as the anonymous writer explains:

Figure 12.3 Palmer Hayden, *The Dress She Wore was Blue*, oil on canvas, 1943. Courtesy of Museum of African American Art, Los Angeles.

I remember very well the first and last work place from which I was dismissed. I lost my place because I refused to let the madam's husband kiss me. He must have been accustomed to undue familiarity with his servants, or else he took it as a matter of course, because without any love-making at all, soon after I was installed as cook, he walked up to me, threw his arms around me, and was in the act of kissing me, when I demanded to know what he meant, and shoved him away . . . I believe nearly all white men take, and expect to take, undue liberties with their colored female servants – not only the fathers, but in many cases the sons also.[23]

Employers also felt that their domestic workers could do all manner of work. In the mammy context, she was viewed as a superhuman laborer and given a multiplicity of tasks to complete from sun up to sun down. An anonymous writer stated:

I'm not permitted to rest. It's "Mammy, do this," or "Mammy, do that," or "Mammy, do the other," from my mistress all the time. So it is not strange to see "Mammy" watering the lawn in front with the garden hose, sweeping the sidewalk, mopping the porch and halls, dusting around the house, helping the cook, or darning stockings. Not only so, but I have to put the other three children to bed each night as well as the baby, and I have to wash them and dress them each morning. I don't know what it is to go to church; I don't know what it is to go to a lecture or entertainment or anything of the kind; I live a treadmill life and I see my own children only when they happen to see me on the streets when I am out with the children, or when my children come to the "yard" to see me, which isn't often. Because my white folks don't like to see their servants' children hanging around their premises. You might as well say that I'm on duty all the time – from sunrise to sunrise, every day in the week. I am the slave, body and soul, of this family. And what do I get for this work . . . The pitiful sum of ten dollars a month![24]

As this domestic worker attests, the white family, especially the wife and children "live in the bosom" of her goodness. Her size also signified the strength that she needed to cook and clean the house. She was expected to lend an open ear, hearing and consoling family members in times of crisis and giving the God-given good advice that seemed to be innate to her character. She had "mother wit" because of the spirituality that she possessed. Johnson's mammyesque figure was also found in protest novels such as Ann Petry's *The Street* that spoke to the issues of the destruction of the family.[25]

While Johnson chose to depict darker-skinned women in the 1930s, he himself was very light skinned and came from a family of light-skinned women, with some of his sisters choosing to pass for white once relocating to Chicago. Johnson's wife was a very fair woman from New Orleans and his daughter was also very fair. Johnson's investigation of the black domestic was a portrayal of "the Other," outside of his personal experience. Even though Johnson had little money, he had been associated with the black middle class as a youth in Washington, DC, and Oakland, California, as an adult, prior to his move to the North Beach area of San Francisco. As a part of an educated middle class, Johnson, as well as others of that class, felt that they had adequately distanced themselves from lower-class blacks and could take a more objective look at them. By the 1920s, they sought to define this group, and they glorified their strength in the face of poverty and child rearing with little resources. His portrayal of mammyesque domestics was a part of the larger movement of American artists who sought to define the American experience through their artwork. In most cases, they focused on the underclasses.

Black artists were faced with a dilemma of portraying their interpretation of black people without condescension and without veering too close to negative caricature. Palmer Hayden and to a lesser degree Archibald Motley, Jr., did not escape the wrath of some black intellectuals when their figures became too close to buffoonery. Many of their caricaturist portrayals of blacks did in fact resemble those that had been made by whites to make fun of the race and suggesting inferiority to whites in physical appearance and intellect. For instance, Hayden's *Mid-Summer's Night in Harlem*, in which Harlemites flood the streets and stoops smiling and laughing, strutting and congregating with a type of gaiety that seems boisterous and "southern" offended some of the more conservative black middle class. Scenes of drinking and gambling were often a part of Motley's scenes. *Chicken Shack* showed the wealthy and the wino sharing the same street in which the neighborhood store advertised pig feet and chitterlings, and *The Liar* (1936) gave an inside view of a social gathering of men drinking whisky, playing pool and lying, all associated with the black underclass. In *Chicken Shack* the well-to-do were not moved far enough away from the less fortunate and *The Liar* privileged the scoundrels and con men. This type of portrayal of black people was one that the black middle class would have rather kept under wraps.[26] Johnson was saved from the ridicule of Hayden and Motley because his women were not comic. As sculptures, they were read without the trappings of context and could be both celebrated by whites and acceptable for black middle-class tastes.

After Johnson's parents died, a teenage Johnson with his siblings moved to a middle-class household in Washington, DC, to live with his uncle, a school principal and his aunt, May Howard Jackson, an accomplished sculptor and a part of the Howard University community arts community. In California, Johnson and his wife purchased a home across from San Pablo Park, then the up-and-coming middle-class neighborhood in Berkeley where blacks flocked to once they had enough resources to move out of West Oakland. Yet, did whites always have the privilege of defining black images? James Weldon Johnson wrote in *Autobiography of an Ex-Colored Man*,

> No matter how well we may portray the deeper passions [of black people], the public is loath to give him, the American Negro, up in his old character; they even conspire to make him a failure in serious work, in order to force him into comedy.[27]

Johnson's stoic black woman exuded a sense of pious struggle that was very appealing to educated blacks and white patrons. By presenting this image of African American motherhood, Johnson could subvert the prevailing negative archetype into a positive dignified icon. Johnson sought to promote the motherly qualities of this mammyesque form and her quiet dignity, thereby making her humane. Dignity, pride, and humanity were high morals of both blacks and whites and the characteristic of Johnson's women – striking a blow against the humorous beast-like inhumane mammy of popular culture. This seemed to be Johnson's intentions because of his statement in the *San Francisco Chronicle*. He said that he wanted to study "not the culturally mixed Negro of the cities, but the more primitive slave type that existed in this country during the period of slave importation." He viewed with scorn the artists who went to Europe or who inserted African masks and other African objects of art into their compositions to signify their adherence to a modernist acceptance of non-European forms, which was presently in vogue. Johnson's focus was on New World blacks and felt that their brush with Africa and the incorporation of African objects in their work was superficial. He felt that they should learn techniques from the study of African sculpture, rather than simply place images of it in their compositions. As a sculptor, Johnson must have seen these superficial renderings of highly structured three-dimensional objects as travesties in technique, for it was the structure of the African masks and statues that first captured the attention of the world.

Johnson used symbolic color on sculptures in order to "heighten the racial character" of his black subjects.[28] Explaining this, he stated,

> I am interested in applying color to sculpture as the Egyptians, Greeks, and other ancient peoples did. I try to apply color without destroying the natural expression of sculpture, putting it on pure, in large masses, without breaking up the surfaces of the form, respecting the planes and contours of sculpturesque expression. I am concerned with color not solely as a technical problem, but also as a means of heightening the racial character of my work. The Negroes are a colorful race. They call for an art as colorful as it can be made.[29]

In the ever color-conscious black middle and upper class, wearing bright colors was often shunned for more pastel combinations. Because bright reds had signified big red lips and red bandanas in popular negative imagery, many in the black privileged class avoided bright colors because of their negative associations. Therefore, the color of the skin and/or the color of one's clothing could often signify one's social class. Bright colors accentuated dark skin; subdued colors muted it.[30] But Johnson's black women of the 1930s had larger and broader implications on how black people were defined and how they defined themselves in the modern American context. As many New Negroes viewed themselves as moderns, their white supporters continued to contextualize them as primitives. While the educated black middle class pursued the same values as the white upper and middle classes, many of their artists focused on what Langston Hughes termed "the low-down folks." Like other artists of the era, Johnson created images of the black American experience that he thought were more authentic than his own.

Johnson's black women were well received by both black and white viewers, but for decidedly different reasons that are based on cultural memory. In San Francisco, with its large white population and in the white circle of friends and patrons of Johnson, they knew black women as mammies and domestics working in their homes. But for the black people who have viewed Johnson's sculptures, his female figures have translated as a nurturing mother/provider. Rather than negative portrayals of mammy, they played as positive representations of black womanhood. As for the racially conscious Johnson, he looked beyond the popular mammy image and chose to see the proud, dignified, nurturing black mother. Yet, when one considers the many mammy images permeating the popular press and cinema during the 1930s, Johnson's figures of women come dangerously close to those more negative representations. Johnson's technical facility in sculpture allowed him to explore the mammyesque form without creating the comic mammy, thereby subverting how whites had characterized her and revealing how she was known to and remembered by blacks.

Johnson, although left of center, denounced politicism in his work. Known as an easy-going person, he navigated his way through a white art world focusing on blacks until the 1940s when he began to de-ethnicize his work. While his mammy figures reached backward, that is, concentrating on supplication and servitude and not forward and upward focusing on upward mobility among blacks, their presence in the 1930s was political.

Most blacks saw few other works by Johnson until the late 1960s and early 1970s, when museums across the United States, responding to protest by black artists, organized "black art" exhibitions. Often a black artist/curator was asked to organize these exhibitions. Artists that had been published in books on black artists such as Alain Locke's *The New Negro*, James Porter's *Modern Negro Art*, or Cedric Dover's *American Negro Art* were invited to exhibit as more interest grew in the serious study of work by black artists. Most black curators felt compelled to "prove" to whites who had long held that there had been no innovative black artists that there had in fact been hundreds. From the mid-1960s to the mid-1970s there was an outpouring of black art shows, from major museums to minor ones, galleries to corporate multinational headquarters. During this period, a more revolutionary mammy emerged as overt subversions of mammy appeared in the work of Betye Saar, Murry de Pillars, and others. Saar's *Liberation of Aunt Jemima* (1972) is the most important subversion of mammy of this period because Saar did not recreate the mammy; she appropriated an existing popularized image and manipulated it into a female resistance fighter (Figure 12.4). Her mammy deflated the notion that mammies were docile and submissive. In recent years research on resistance among slave women makes Saar's *Liberation of Aunt Jemima* and Johnson's *Forever Free* even more significant because they both visually underscore a truth in American history, the resistance of blacks to slavery and servitude, which had been suppressed and ignored in the American psyche.

246

Figure 12.4 Betye Saar, *Liberation of Aunt Jemima*, mixed media, 1972. Courtesy of University Art Museum, University of California, Berkeley.

Notes

1 Charlotte Hawkins Brown, *"Mammy" The Correct Things To Do – To Say – To Wear* (Boston, MA: The Pilgrim Press, 1919), reprinted General Editor, Henry Louis Gates, Jr. (New York: G. K. Hall, 1995), 9.

2 "I Live a Treadmill Life," Anonymous (1912), in *Black Women in White America: A Documentary History*, ed. Gerda Lerner (New York: Vintage, 1973), 227.

3 K. Sue Jewell, *From Mammy to Miss America and Beyond: Cultural Images and the Shaping of US Social Policy* (London and New York: Routledge, 1993), 36.

4 Marlon Riggs, *Ethnic Notions* (Berkeley, CA: California Newsreel, 1989), video, 52 min.

5 The bosom is considered the anatomical center of secret thoughts and emotions. See *Webster's New Collegiate Dictionary* (Springfield, IL: G. & C. Merriam, 1977), 129.

6 Jewell, *From Mammy*, 40.

7 Ibid., 41. Also see Verta Mae, *Thursdays and Every Other Sunday Off: A Domestic Rap* (New York: Doubleday, 1972).

8 This was best articulated in the poems of Langston Hughes and a case for the "authentic black artist" is supported in the artistic career of the late Jacob Lawrence. The dark-skinned Lawrence came from very humble beginnings, painted what he knew best, the lives and environs of urban black people, in a style that was called both primitive and modern.

9 "San Francisco Artists," *San Francisco Chronicle*, October 6, 1935: D-3.

10 Jacques Schnier, *Sculpture in Modern America* (Berkeley, CA: University of California Press, 1948), 44.

11 Ibid., 47.

12 Maurice Berger, *How Art Becomes History: Essays on Art, Society, and Culture in Post-New Deal America* (New York: Icon Editions (HarperCollins), 1992), 4. Also see Roy Emerson Stryker and Nancy Wood, *In This Proud Land: America, 1935–1943, As Seen in the FSA Photographs* (Greenwich, CT: New York Graphic Society), 1973.

13 Ibid.

14 Ibid.

15 Seymour L. Gross and John E. Hardy (eds.), *Images of the Negro in American Literature* (Chicago: University of Chicago Press, 1966), 10.

16 James Weldon Johnson, "Go Down Death: A Funeral Sermon," *God's Trombones: Seven Negro Sermons in Verse* (New York: Viking, 1927), 27.

17 Jeanne Moutoussamy-Ashe, *Viewfinders: Black Women Photographers* (New York: Dood, Mead, 1986), 31.

18 Ibid., 31–32.

19 Ibid., 32.

20 Ibid.

21 Granted, Williams was often addressing middle-class women, but as noted in the anonymous statement from the domestic, she rarely saw her children or went to church, a lecture or entertainment, sharing similar values of black middle-class women.

22 Allan M. Gordon, *Echoes of our Past: the Narrative Artistry of Palmer C. Hayden* (Los Angeles: Museum of African American Art, 1988), 24. The letter from Chappell is dated April 8, 1944.

23 "We Are Little More than Slaves," in Lerner, *Black Women in White America*, 156.

24 In Lerner, from "I Live a Treadmill Life," 228, in "More Slavery at the South, by a Negro Nurse," *The Independent* 71(3295) (January 25, 1912), 196–200.

25 Issues of race and class are highlighted through a screen of black female sexuality in both Nella Larson's *Quicksand* (published in 1928) and in Zora Neale Hurston's (1946) *Their Eyes Were Watching God* (London: Virago, 1986), but in a rural setting.

26 During the 1930s when *The Liar* was painted, there were ongoing debates in journals such as *Opportunity* and *Crisis* on how African Americans should represent themselves. Many

writers in the journals (there were also reader surveys) objected to portrayals of blacks drinking and playing craps. They also objected to a focus on the underclass in literature rather than the middle class.

27 James Weldon Johnson, *Autobiography of an Ex-Colored Man*, reprinted in *Three Negro Classics*, ed. John Hope Franklin (New York: Avon, 1975), 486. Originally published anonymously (1912).

28 *San Francisco Chronicle*, October 6, 1935: D-3.

29 Ibid.

30 Relating color of clothing to skin color and class is among one of many beliefs transmitted by oral tradition in black communities. Others include pinching one's nose to make it pointed, braiding one's hair to make it longer, not drinking straight coffee because it will darken a person's skin color.

13

OFFICIAL ART, OFFICIAL PUBLICS

Public sculpture under the Federal Art-in-Architecture Program since 1972

Ivy Schroeder

In 1972, the US government launched the Art-in-Architecture Program under the aegis of the General Services Administration (GSA), the department of the federal government that oversees and maintains federal buildings and facilities. Since its inauguration, the program has generated commissions for hundreds of public artworks, including many high-profile outdoor sculptures by well-known artists, at federal buildings across the country. However, with the exception of a few controversial cases, such as Richard Serra's *Tilted Arc* in New York City (which was removed in 1989 after an extended, well-publicized debate), the sculptures commissioned by the program have received very little attention in the scholarly literature on contemporary public art in the United States.

If one considers the aesthetic merits of most of these sculptures, this critical oversight seems justifiable – a kindness, even. Some of the program's commissions from the 1970s look like the sculptural analogs of a big, faceless bureaucracy, while others from the 1980s and 1990s look like panicked attempts to counter that image with decidedly more cheerful, "populist" works. Aesthetically, few of the sculptures warrant individual consideration at all. By contrast, however, if we consider these sculptures as a group, and within their federal context, they become very interesting indeed. They comprise a remarkable historical survey of how an "official art" has been defined in contemporary culture since the 1970s. Likewise, since the Art-in-Architecture Program funds artworks that are by every definition "public," its commissions also reveal striking things about how "official publics" are defined in the United States.

As one might expect, neither the "official art", nor the "official public" has remained a static construction during this period. Both are negotiated and renegotiated according to the federal government's own interests, and according to the government's dialectical relationship to contemporary cultural debates. This chapter will use the sculpture commissioned by the Art-in-Architecture Program as a means to understanding the processes of cultural negotiation that take place as the federal government shapes its ideals of official art and official publics in contemporary culture.

To understand the central role that the Art-in-Architecture Program has played in these processes, we need to attend to the program's genesis. The program was originally implemented in 1963 as a result of the Kennedy administration's renewed interest in and encouragement of public art. It was suspended three years later due, officials claimed, to cost-cutting measurements in the federal government; the real reason for its suspension was probably due to controversy arising from some of the program's early commissions.[1] The program lay dormant for six full years.

In 1971, President Nixon issued a strongly worded call for more government support for the arts in his "Memorandum about the Federal Government and the Arts" (May 26, 1971).[2] In it, the president pledged his present and future support for federal art programs on the basis of art's importance in the lives of the American people:

> Americans in all walks of life are becoming increasingly aware of the importance of the arts as a key factor in the quality of the Nation's life, and of their individual lives . . . It is my urgent desire that the growing partnership between Government and the arts continue to be developed to the benefit of both, and more particularly to the benefit of the people of America.[3]

In these broadly drawn terms, a cultural mandate was born under the Nixon administration. The Art-in-Architecture Program, revived in 1972, was a direct outgrowth of this mandate. Some of its better-known early commissions include Alexander Calder's *Flamingo* (1973) for the Chicago federal building, and Claes Oldenburg's *Batcolumn* (1977) for Chicago's Social Security Administration building.

If we look beyond these two high-profile, somewhat idiosyncratic works, to the dozens of other program commissions from the 1970s, something of a pattern emerges. Tony Smith's *She Who Must be Obeyed* (1976), at the Department of Labor in Washington, DC, and Duayne Hatchett's *Equilateral Six* (1975) at the federal building in Rochester, New York, are typical of the types of sculpture commissioned in that decade – completely abstract, large enough to be visible from long distances but still accessible to pedestrians, with designs and scales appropriate to the modern architecture of the federal buildings. The program also encouraged sculptors to design works in response to the building and the site, rather than using pre-existing designs.

What could account for this pattern, this consistent favoring in the 1970s of large-scale, abstract, and, frankly, quite difficult sculpture? While the Art-in-Architecture Program itself published no stylistic guidelines that would explain this pattern, it did consistently stress that the art it commissioned should complement the building and become an integral part of the federal architecture; and that the art should activate and "humanize" the federal buildings for the public.

251

Since the architectural style of most of the federal buildings constructed during the 1970s is "bureaucratic-modern," featuring exposed steel and glass, concrete cladding and no ornamentation, it is not surprising that the program, which wanted sculpture to complement the building, would select modernist works of the same ilk – sleek, abstract, large in scale and made of industrial materials. What is less clear is how the program imagined that this type of sculpture would activate or humanize the buildings for the public. To understand this requires that we look at how these sculptures actually communicate with and engage their public; and, more specifically, what kind of "public" is being imagined as the audience for this sculpture.

Barbara Neijna's sculpture, *Right Turn on White* (1979), located at the Strom Thurmond Federal Building and Courthouse in Columbia, South Carolina, serves as an ideal example for the purposes of this chapter (Figure 13.1). The sculpture stands on the building's forecourt, a blank white metal wall with one segment at the top "peeling" back slightly toward the forecourt. It contains no figural suggestions, no legible narrative. However, in the most abstract manner, it fulfills the program's directives to complement the modern architecture. It was designed site-specifically, in response to physical cues from the building and its situation. It was meant to engage the viewers' visual and perceptual faculties, to heighten the awareness of the character of the site.

Figure 13.1 Barbara Neijna, *Right Turn on White*, 1978, Strom Thurmond Federal Building and Courthouse, Columbia, South Carolina. Commissioned by the Art-in-Architecture Program, Public Buildings Service, General Services Administration.

Figure 13.2 Beverly Pepper, *Excalibur*, 1976, Federal Building and Courthouse, San Diego, California. Commissioned by the Art-in-Architecture Program, Public Buildings Service, General Services Administration.

Right Turn on White, like most of the sculptures commissioned by the program during the 1970s, was designed to be "experienced," not "read" in the manner of more traditional, narrative sculpture. Barbara Neijna's own words about her work bear this out:

> I chose to involve my viewer on the lower level, and visually, as well as psychologically, to tie in the spaces . . . My intention was to create a structure for behavioral experience – to create an awareness of space through new relationships. I wanted to involve people on the ground level in the process of integrating their minds and bodies while traversing both real and implied limits.[4]

Sculptor Beverly Pepper used similar rhetoric to describe her 1976 work, *Excalibur*, a two-part, large-scale, boldly angular steel sculpture at the San Diego, California federal building (Figure 13.2):

> [T]he sculpture should invite the participation of the public . . . [It should] make possible a dialogue between the people and the site itself. The need to participate is more than physical: it is also to enter a shared space consciousness.[5]

253

In both of these cases, the viewing public is discussed in terms of experience, both visual and physical. This kind of sculpture appears to be designed to engage its public on the formal and perceptual levels only. It doesn't require any particular intellectual preparation or instruction to understand it – rather, it validates anyone's experience of it, as aesthetic experience is the primary value to which it appeals.

In one analysis, this is a very democratic model of public sculpture (and, by extension, a democratic model of the public itself): it appeals to anyone, regardless of who they are or what they know about sculpture; to understand it, they simply have to "be there." Regardless of who you are, regardless of your race, age, education, or gender, you are a member of the public being addressed by this artwork.

Stylistically, this kind of work might at first appear to be a daring choice for the federal governmental this time – boldly abstract and modernist, many of the sculptures were related to minimalism, a style that remains one of the most challenging and least popular in the history of art. However, the stylistic choice makes more sense if we consider its "democratic" qualities, as described above. This "democratizing" sculpture – abstract, formalist, "engaging" – conforms rather nicely to the broad criteria of Nixon's cultural mandate as outlined in his 1971 memo. It defines its public in the broadest possible terms, appealing to viewers from "all walks of life," containing no particular message but legitimized by the general acceptance of the salutary effects of art.

Nixon's memo continues: "I believe that we all can find that the arts have a great deal more to contribute to what we in government are seeking to accomplish – and that this will be good for the arts and good for the country."[6] In 1971, one of the things Nixon and the US government were seeking to accomplish was the creation of a kind of national consensus, or at least the image of one, that might counter the country's fractured identity that emerged from the 1960s. Public art had a role to play in the construction of that consensus. The art commissioned by the Art-in-Architecture Program for federal buildings, like all public art commissioned by the government, inevitably becomes "official art," embodying to some degree the image of the government itself. The more consistent, inclusive, and democratic that official art could be, the better for the image of the government. The Art-in-Architecture Program upheld this "democratizing" model of official art through three presidential administrations in the 1970s.

The persistence of this model of official art should not imply that it was totally successful. It has distinct limitations in practice, an observation which is borne out by two facts: it has gone completely out of style; and even during the 1970s, it did not achieve any kind of public popularity. On the contrary, many of the program's sculptural commissions from that period elicited numerous letters of complaint from the public. Interestingly, many viewers did interpret the sculpture as an embodiment of the federal presence – not, however, its democratic ideals, but rather its arrogance and misuse of public funds. Regarding Pepper's *Excalibur* in San Diego, one person wrote:

> This $90,000 monstrosity is an affront to taxpayers. Which particular bureaucrat is responsible for this extravagance – and will he be held

Figure 13.3 Nancy Holt, *Annual Rings*, 1981, Federal Building and Courthouse, Saginaw, Michigan. Commissioned by the Art-in-Architecture Program, Public Buildings Service, General Services Administration.

responsible for it in any way? Or is the blame to be shared by a group of irresponsible committees? The only useful purpose [the sculpture] can serve is to be symbolic of the shafting we are getting from the Federal government. When will you people start representing the workers who support you?[7]

The limitations of this sculptural model also stem from the idealized public it imagines as its audience, which is ultimately at odds with the actual public, that is, the specific experiences of viewers who encounter the work. A case in point is Nancy Holt's sculpture for the federal building in Saginaw, Michigan. Holt was selected to produce a site-specific work for this solar energy building on the basis of her previous sculpture, much of which is designed around solar paths and constellation patterns. The sculpture she produced for the Art-in-Architecture Program, *Annual Rings* (1981), was designed for the landscaped public roof plaza (Figure 13.3). On the north side of the sculpture is a circular opening which aligns with the North Star; openings on the east and west sides frame the rising and setting sun on the equinoxes. Several trees on the plaza were removed to ensure the sculpture's exposure to the sun and its physical accessibility.

By linking the site and viewers to various astral configurations, *Annual Rings* literally universalizes them. The sculpture's disregard for the *specific* composition of the public, and for how the site was *actually* used, bristled several members of

Saginaw's public. One federal worker complained that without the trees that were removed to accommodate the work, the blazing sun during the day made the roof terrace all but unusable. This writer continues:

> [T]his building sits smack in the middle of one of the worst neighborhoods in the state. Year after year, it is the derelicts and the wine-oes who frequent the roof after dark. Who in their right mind is going to go up there at night to view the north star? The idea is ludicrous, to say the least. Those of us who work in this building and are aware of the "summer residents" would not consider it. Do you think that the general public will?[8]

This writer makes clear that the revised function of the space – it is now a place to view the north star at night – ignores the actual uses of the site, even as it reveals the tensions among those members of the public who use it.

Put another way, this type of sculpture fails to account for history itself – which inevitably assures that history itself will be unkind to it. Witness the example of Ronald Bladen's *Host of the Ellipse* (1981) for Baltimore's Metro West Social Security Administration Building. In 1977, when art for this building was being considered, it was thought that a monumental sculpture at this high-visibility site could become

Figure 13.4 Ronald Bladen, *Host of the Ellipse*, 1981, Metro West Social Security Administration Building, Baltimore, Maryland. Commissioned by the Art-in-Architecture Program, Public Buildings Service, General Services Administration. This photograph shows the sculpture in its original situation, on an open lot with the building behind it.

Figure 13.5 Ronald Bladen, *Host of the Ellipse*, 1981. This photograph shows the sculpture in its original situation, with public housing units nearby.

a positive icon for both the building and the city. City officials expressed the hopes that the sculpture might improve the view and the quality of life for the residents in the nearby public housing.

Ronald Bladen's *Host of the Ellipse* consists of two black painted angular steel elements, one rising to a height of 63 feet, the other to a height of 35 feet. The sculpture was designed to stand on an open grassy lot accessible to pedestrians and visible to cars entering and leaving the city from the interstate (Figure 13.4). Local traffic passes the sculpture as it travels under the building's elevated pedestrian bridge. In this original situation, on the open lot with the building as backdrop, the sculpture did complement the architecture, drawing out the sculptural quality of the building. And the open character of the grassy lot did allow viewers to interact with the work if they chose to (Figure 13.5).

But the circumstances of this site have changed dramatically over time. Now, a high steel fence surrounds the lot where Bladen's work stands (Figure 13.6). A parking lot and fenced playground were constructed on the formerly open lot, and both virtually butt up against the work. Though the sculpture is still technically accessible by foot, to reach it a viewer now has to enter the parking area through the guarded gate, circumnavigate the playground, and walk across the (now) heavily landscaped patch of land to come near it. Interaction with the sculpture now feels like a transgressive act. Hopes that the sculpture would improve the quality of life

Figure 13.6 Ronald Bladen, *Host of the Ellipse*, 1981. This photograph shows the sculpture in its current situation, surrounded by the steel fence.

for people in the nearby public housing have come to nothing. With the addition of the parking lot and the fence surrounding the sculpture, the view from these housing units was obscured. It mattered little in any case: by 1996, the public housing units had been evacuated, and they have since been demolished.

Host of the Ellipse suffered so dramatically from the development of the site because its original design, and the original expectations for the sculpture, in no way accounted for this specific site, this specific public, or the fact that historical transformations naturally occur in both. The image of *Host of the Ellipse* behind bars serves to illustrate the demise of this ahistorical model of public art.

The ultimate symbol of this demise remains the removal of Richard Serra's *Tilted Arc*, a 1981 Art-in-Architecture Program commission for the Jacob K. Javits Federal Plaza in lower Manhattan. But while it stood, *Tilted Arc* represented the apogee of the 1970s model of public art upheld by the Art-in-Architecture Program. It was designed for its specific site, made to engage the viewers in a series of dramatic perceptual shifts that occur as they moved around the work on the plaza. Its bold, exposed steel surfaces – for better or worse – complemented the somewhat cold concrete, steel and glass facade of the federal buildings at the plaza.

However, these more subtle formal and perceptual effects were largely ignored in the discussions that attended this controversial work throughout the 1980s. At the 1987 public hearing on the sculpture, which was organized by William Diamond, the GSA regional administrator in New York City, a number of artists and arts professionals came to *Tilted Arc*'s defense, citing Serra's international reputation and his success with other public projects, and giving mini-lessons in the modernist sculptural tradition to which Serra's work belongs. Critics of the work tended to be harsher. Some read the work as a symbol of oppressive authority:

> [M]any of those who visit [the buildings] only occasionally are those who visit the Immigration and Naturalization Service in order to apply for citizenship . . . Yet when they enter the building from which they hope to emerge with hope and promise for a freer and better future for themselves and their families, they cannot help but be painfully reminded by *Tilted Arc* of the iron curtains from which they escape. Seeing the ominous rusty steel barriers which imprisoned them, minds as well as bodies, they seek the spiritual light, air, and space of America . . . They should not be compelled to circumvent a rusty reminder of totalitarianism.[9]

Other critics complained of the "authoritarian" or "bullying" nature of the work, and its tendency to dictate walking patterns rather than invite easygoing participation with the work:

> The sculpture cuts a huge swath across the center of the plaza, dividing it in two, and acting as a barrier to the building's main doorways. Access to the building is awkward and confusing, and the normal walking patterns of those who enter and exit the building are disrupted.[10]

Some opponents claimed that *Tilted Arc* was not a work of art at all, but just an insulting, rusty hunk of steel. Much of the critical commentary sounds glib and even philistine, but it does address one of the central problems with the sculpture: while *Tilted Arc* presumed to engage all viewers, in what could be described as a democratic way, it didn't actually address the public in any particular way. *Tilted Arc* contained no narrative, no content, nothing familiar or specific to a viewer's experience. Lacking this, it is not surprising that viewers insisted on reading symbols (of authoritarianism, of aggression) *into* the sculpture, symbols that Serra clearly never intended. This ultimately may have been the sculpture's undoing, and the undoing of the model of "official art" upheld throughout the 1970s and into the early 1980s by the Art-in-Architecture Program.

Tilted Arc was removed from Federal Plaza in 1989, the same year that the Art-in-Architecture Program finalized major revisions in its selection and commissioning procedures. Program administrators devoted the entire decade of the 1980s to designing these revisions and reconsidering the program's mission. The sculptural commissions of the 1970s had too often generated negative -- and sometimes hostile -- responses from the viewing public. Program administrators and a handful of members of Congress decided that changes had to be made. The major target of their attack was not the Art-in-Architecture Program itself, but, more specifically, the cooperative alliance between it and the National Endowment for the Arts (NEA), which, since 1973, had organized the program's selection panels and made artist recommendations to the program administration. The Art-in-Architecture Program originally sought the participation of the NEA because the GSA had no internal department experienced with commissioning art.

Throughout the 1970s, the artists and the types of art recommended by the NEA remained remarkably consistent: the artists typically had national reputations, without necessarily having any connection to the region where their art would be placed; and the sculpture, as we have seen, was of a consistent stylistic type – abstract, modernist, with no narrative content or regional specificity. This, it was decided, was the problem.

The first step in the long overhaul process of the Art-in-Architecture Program came in 1979, when Senators Moynihan and Chafee introduced a bill to Congress that would establish standard procedures for acquisition and installation of works of art in public buildings. Though the bill would have affected all federal arts programs, it was clearly written with an eye to the Art-in-Architecture Program, whose commissions had generated the largest amount of negative public reception. The bill specifically proposed that federally funded public art "recognize regional character" and should "provide for more local participation through the utilization of the advice and assistance of the states arts councils and create a broader base of artists through the recognition of lesser known artists."[11] This bill can be read not only as an attack on the NEA's selection procedures, but more specifically as an attack on the kind of artists – and, by extension, the kind of art – that had historically been commissioned.

The bill was not passed, but it did bring about the formation of a "Joint GSA–NEA Task Force" in late 1979, which was responsible for "seeking ways to maximize community support for and involvement in the Art-in-Architecture program, while continuing to provide for works of art in Federal buildings which are of the highest quality and highly appropriate to the site."[12] Throughout the 1980s, the relationship between the GSA and the NEA became more strained. The thrust of the disagreement lay in the matter of the art: the NEA continually emphasized the importance of building a collection of public art that would be national in character, while the GSA increasingly saw the need for selection panels to attend to specific regional characteristics, and to commission art and artists with some recognizable regional ties. The NEA continued to participate in the Art-in-Architecture Program's selection procedures on an interim basis throughout the 1980s, but the working relationship between the NEA and the GSA was officially broken off in 1989.

Thus, the 1980s were essentially spent decentralizing the Art-in-Architecture Program, and the results can be seen in the sculptures that were commissioned. While most of the sculpture commissioned by the program in the 1970s was large-scale, abstract, non-figurative and non-narrative, the years between 1981 and 1989 saw a dramatic rise in the number of figurative sculptures or works that emphasize local or regional character. A handful of examples will suffice to make this point: in 1987, Maria Alquilar, an Hispanic artist from the Southwest, created *Bien Venida y Vaya con Dios*, a figural sculpture incorporating Mexican folk art forms, for the main border station in San Luis, Arizona; Robert Graham, a California native, created a figural fountain sculpture for the federal building in San José, California; and Manuel Neri created *Ventana al Pacífico*, a figural relief work, for the federal courthouse in Portland, Oregon, in 1989. Since 1989, virtually every sculpture commissioned by the Art-in-Architecture Program has contained content directly relating to local populations and/or histories, and most of the artists chosen live in the region where their sculpture is placed.

The Art-in-Architecture Program's shift away from the abstract, modernist, non-narrative sculpture in the 1980s paralleled a general trend in the field of public art, toward a model that is often loosely characterized as "postmodernist." This new model of public art employs popular (or at least legible) visual language, acknowledging the diversity inherent in populations and histories, and freely using and combining familiar historical symbols. This broad stylistic description applies to a wide spectrum of recent examples of public art. It includes the recent conservative return to traditional realism in sculpture, as seen in Frederick Hart's *Three Fighting Men* (1984), erected as a counterpart to Maya Lin's abstract Vietnam Veterans' Memorial in Washington, DC, as well as Glenna Goodacre's bathetic, *Pietá*-inspired Vietnam Women's Memorial (1993), placed nearby. The Art-in-Architecture Program has also commissioned its share of this kind of work, such as Nizette Brennan's *Knoxville Flag* (1992) for Knoxville, Tennessee, a stylized version of the American flag carved in stone; and Raymond Kaskey's *Justice* (1994), a traditional-looking female allegorical figure in bronze, for the federal courthouse at Shreveport, Louisiana.

But the "postmodernist" or "populist" public art of the 1980s and 1990s has also taken less conservative forms. This is evident if we simply review some of the scholarly literature published in recent years on public art. Books such as *Culture in Action* (1995), a document of the activist public art program "Sculpture Chicago," and *Mapping the Terrain: New Genre Public Art* (1995), edited by Suzanne Lacy, both define a new ideal for public art, one that arises from and addresses localized interests, reflects particular publics, and seeks to engage viewers, not on some vague "experiential" level, but on a more explicitly informative and activist level.

This model of public art has also found its way into the Art-in-Architecture Program. Many of its recent commissions are figural and narrative, with familiar content and recognizable imagery. While these sculptures manage to avoid the criticism that dogged the program's commissions of the 1970s, they nevertheless come with their own set of complications that invariably attend any effort to represent particular cultural groups, experiences, histories and memories.

I will conclude with a discussion of two recent examples of the Art-in-Architecture Program's revised model of official art: Luis Jiménez's *Fiesta Jarabe* and Bob Haozous's *Spirit of the Earth*, both of which were commissioned in the 1990s for the Otay Mesa Federal Border Crossing Station outside of San Diego, California. Both of these works depict specific public histories, of the Mexican American and Native American culture within and without the parameters of the United States. It is perhaps appropriate that these contested histories are represented on the rather contested terrain of the border crossing.

When the Art-in-Architecture Program commissioned Luis Jiménez to produce a sculpture for Otay Mesa, he was already well known for his figurative fiberglass sculptures representing Southwestern and Mexican American characters and stories. Jiménez himself is a resident of the region, living in New Mexico and Arizona, and he seemed a logical choice for a commission dealing explicitly with themes of Mexican American cultural history. *Fiesta Jarabe* (1991) depicts a couple in traditional Mexican dress, dancing the Jarabe, or Hat Dance. Jiménez claims that his design specifically addresses both the Mexican and American cultures, both the past and the present: his figures are contemporary, but dressed in traditional costume; they represent the people who live in the United States but practice Mexican traditions. In his typical fashion, Jiménez has exaggerated the features of the figures and the colors of their costumes, and while the work has generated some negative response, it has been generally well received. The finished sculpture is playful and engaging, but its placement at the decidedly unplayful border crossing underscores the tension that persists at sites of cultural and political division.

Not far from *Fiesta Jarabe* at Otay Mesa station stands the steel billboard-style sculpture by Bob Haozous, called Spirit of the Earth (1994). The finished work, like *Fiesta Jarabe*, speaks volumes about the tensions that arise at borders, and about the often uneasy rifts between tradition and progress. But in Haozous's case, the process of negotiating a design that would be acceptable to the Art-in-Architecture Program administrators was itself very revealing. It serves as a lesson in the complex process

Figure 13.7 Bob Haozous, first part of the original design for *Spirit of the Earth*, 1994.

Figure 13.8 Bob Haozous, second part of the original design for *Spirit of the Earth*, 1994.

of cultural negotiation involved in the construction of official art today, and it warrants a close look.

Haozous received the commission from the Art-in-Architecture Program to create a new work for Otay Mesa in 1992. He was chosen, like Jiménez, for his artistic reputation but also for his cultural ties to the region. His original proposal for the border crossing station was for a steel billboard sculpture, divided into two parts, with one part addressing the Native cultures of Mexico, and the other addressing culture "across the border," that is, the culture of the United States (Figure 13.7).

While Haozous's original design for the Native half of his work was apparently acceptable, administrators for the Art-in-Architecture Program had reservations about his design for the American half (Figure 13.8). In a telephone conference with program administrators in 1993, Haozous was asked to reconsider "the dominance of the commercial aspects [of the American side], which is very extreme."[13] Haozous answers: "But I have traveled around the world and these are the symbols that you find representing the United States – McDonald's, etc." The program administrator answers back: "Well, if you look at the image you propose, the range of the cultural imagery on the Mexican side is just more dense. It contains a stronger sense of design, whereas the U.S. side appears geared toward commercialization." At this point another administrator offers a suggestion: "Perhaps you can integrate the two [sides] more, so it doesn't appear to be such a dichotomy or rigid division between the borders."

This interesting discussion reveals the process of negotiation involved in giving shape to an official artistic statement that would satisfy the needs of the federal government and still speak the "truth" of the border situation as Haozous saw it. For Haozous, the division between the sides of his work corresponded to the division between the cultures; for the federal government, that division was too strong – or, at least, Haozous's particular representation of that division was objectionable. *Spirit of the Earth* reveals how actual historical forces and cultural divisions now find their way into the public art being commissioned by the Art-in-Architecture Program.

In the end, Haozous abandoned the idea of a divided artwork. The final design features the native *kokopello* figure in the center, surrounded by trucks, cars, and airplanes (Figure 13.9). But his work is not a fiction of harmonious, unproblematic assimilation. Haozous insisted that barbed wire be strung across the top of the steel construction, above the puffy clouds in his sculpture, glinting in the hot sun. With this final gesture, which was not part of his original design scheme, Haozous managed to retain the prickly resonance of the contested, conflicted process of defining official art and official publics in the United States.

Figure 13.9 Bob Haozous, *Spirit of the Earth*, 1994, Otay Mesa Federal Border Crossing Station, San Diego, California. Commissioned by the Art-in-Architecture Program, Public Buildings Service, General Services Administration.

Notes

1 The early, somewhat embattled history of the Art-in-Architecture Program in the 1960s is related more fully in Donald Thalacker, *The Place of Art in the World of Architecture* (New York: Chelsea House, 1980), xii.

2 Richard Nixon, "Memorandum about the Federal Government and the Arts," dated May 26, 1971. In United States President, *Public Papers of the Presidents: Richard Nixon, 1971*, Washington, DC: Federal Register Division, National Archives and Records Service, General Services Administration, 681.

3 Ibid.

4 Barbara Neijna, quoted in Thalacker, *Place of Art in the World of Architecture*, 200.

5 Beverly Pepper, quoted in ibid., 158.

6 Nixon, "Memorandum about the Federal Government and the Arts," 681.

7 Duncan Curry, in a letter to Senator Cranston, dated August 16, 1976. The letter is located in the artist file on Beverly Pepper in the Art-in-Architecture Program archives, housed in the program offices in the GSA building, Washington, DC.

8 Karen Crawford, in a letter to the GSA, dated May 29, 1981. Located in the artist file on Nancy Holt in the Art-in-Architecture Program archives.

9 Collected testimonies from the March 1987 hearing appear in Clara Weyergraf-Serra and Martha Buskirk (eds.), *The Destruction of Tilted Arc: Documents* (Cambridge, MA: MIT Press, 1991). This excerpt appears on p. 126.

10 Ibid., 115.

11 This summary of the bill, S. 1791 (H.R. 5545) is taken from a letter from Sens. Moynihan and Chafee to Rowland G. Freeman, GSA Administrator, dated September 27, 1979. Located in the history file in the Art-in-Architecture Program archives.

12 From the "Report of the Joint GSA–NEA Task Force on the Art-in-Architecture Program," submitted on January 22, 1980, n.p. Located in the history file in the Art-in-Architecture Program archives.

13 This and the following quotes appear in the transcripts of a conference call between Haozous and Dale Lanzone and Cynthia Gould, Art-in-Architecture Program administrators, dated August 10, 1993. The written transcripts are located in the artist file on Bob Haozous in the Art-in-Architecture Program archives.

14

PRIVATE REFLECTIONS/ PUBLIC MATTERS

Public art in the city

Iain Borden and Jane Rendell

Although there has been a massive increase in the number and diversity of works of public art in recent years, this has not been met with a concomitant intensity of thought over what might constitute the "public" aspects of this "public" art, and in particular its dialectical relation to the "private." Here we offer some new operative and interpretive strategies as to how works of public art represent, or might represent, the collective nature of the city and its residents. In doing so, we consider the urban and public nature of the artist, the site, the audience, and the critic. Strategies and tactics considered include the everyday life of the metropolis, public art as fragment, the dialectical image, the detail, displacement and montage, thought-images, the experiencing subject, use values, and the gift economy. In this we are particularly concerned with the notions of time and memory in public art, and how these conditions may be addressed through such concepts as frozen time, erased time, discontinuous time, collective memory, the event, motility, narrativity, and spatial stories.

In what follows, most of what we say is conceptual. The chapter intersects with the writings of, among others, Walter Benjamin, Michel de Certeau, Luce Irigaray, Henri Lefebvre, and Maurice Merleau Ponty. In the imagery, which has equal status as the text, particular reference is made to city-based works in New York and Los Angeles, but also to other cities in the United States and worldwide. We also refer to urban imagery which has not been made by artists, but which nonetheless, we believe, is a form of public art.

This chapter is not, therefore, constructed in the manner of a conventional academic paper. It hovers between the conceptual and the observational, the theoretical and empirical, between subject and object, and between word and image. It is a dialectic of poetics and politics.

PRIVATE REFLECTIONS/PUBLIC MATTERS

I think this sense of what it means to be a social persona and the fact that every social person has a private person inside is vital to the sense of community and to any meaningful sense of "public" – of public service. The way to get to those issues sometimes is organizational and structural, but often it has to do with compassion with play, with touching the inner self in every individual who recognizes that the next individual has a similar self. And it is that community, whether the literal or metaphorical, that is in fact the real public that we as artists might address.

Allan Kaprow[1]

The terms *public* and *private* are cultural constructions whose definitions change both historically and depending on context. These two words are not neutral descriptive categories. They denote specific value systems. The words mean different things in everyday language, in theoretical discussion, and according to discipline – as social and spatial metaphors in geography, anthropology, and sociology, as terms of ownership in economics, as political spheres in political philosophy and law.

In public art discourse, "public" refers to "site" both in its physical state, as it is represented, and as it is understood conceptually as a terrain for interventions. A public site might be defined in terms of morphology (outdoors), in terms of activity (out of the art gallery). However, this "public site" is rarely taken apart to reveal problems of ownership and accessibility. In public art discourse, "public" also refers to "the public" as audience, viewer, and user – that idealized group of people whom public artists aim to understand, represent, and communicate with. However, this public audience is rarely considered in terms of difference or heterogeneity, passive and active, initiated and coming-in cold, viewer and user, or in terms of the public's various class, gender, race, age, and so on.

In order to understand "public" it is necessary to place it in dialectical relation to private, to see how one informs the other. For example, public art outside the private institute of art housed inside the gallery may still be within the corporate world of private property and finance, and further still inside the private world of the elite group of artists who get the commissions. Alternatively, public art may

267

bridge the private worlds of those who create it and the private lives of those who view it, or it may render public themes into matters of personal concern.

THE POSSIBILITIES MACHINE

Space is broad, teeming with possibilities, positions, intersections, passages, detours, U-turns, dead ends, one-way streets. Too many possibilities indeed.

Walter Benjamin[2]

At the turn of the millennium, we find a noticeable increase in the funding of public art projects. But despite the increase in quantity, qualitatively much of the work is reductive, both in terms of its production and its reception. Public art requires critical re-siting – theoretically and practically – within the context of everyday city life and at the intersection of critical debates concerning spatial and urban culture and critical and gender studies. This dialog sets in motion possibilities for rethinking "public art" as possibilities, that is, public art that works against, within and for the whole range of possibilities that the modern metropolis can offer.

FRAGMENTS

In any case, what is delightful here is the dissimilarity itself between the object wished for and the object found. Thus trouvaille, whether it be artistic, scientific, philosophic, or as useless as anything, is enough to undo the beauty of everything beside it. In it alone we recognize the marvellous precipitate of desire.

André Breton[3]

The idea of the fragment offers multiple possibilities for public art. It can provide the inspiration for public art. It can become a component of the work, or indeed, it can become the work itself. Or it can provide, as we suggest here, a way of understanding not only public art but also the whole urban fabric as a kind of art.

In this way, an urban fragment, either as everyday object or as an everyday description of that object, reveals philosophical or historical ideas. Indeed, if the city can be understood in this way, then we might ask what is the need for art as made by artists, when urban fragments say it all. All we need is Walter Benjamin to see the world as it already is – afresh. "Every fact is already theory." And if existing public art is understood as an urban fragment, and if the urban fragment is understood as public art, then the monumental gesture has no more resonance than the microscopic accident. Debris is sculpture and sculpture is debris.

DIALECTICAL IMAGE

The eternal is in every case far more the ruffle on a dress than an idea.

Walter Benjamin[4]

An urban fragment, in Walter Benjamin's work, can be a dialectical image, that is, at once material and ideational. A dialectical image is a thought. Whether arcade, fashion, flâneur or dust, it occupies a threshold position in space, time and consciousness. The dialectical image is a constellation of antiquity and modernity, dream and awakening.

THE DETAIL

Finding in each of life's details the totality of its meaning.

Georg Simmel[5]

The detail is that small part or fragment – of an artwork or of human life – which speaks of a larger whole as an entire artwork or a whole city. These details dwell on "the smallest things, meaningful yet covert enough to find a hiding place in waking dreams,"[6] thus displacing significance of the work away from pure form or theory. Benjamin even considers that such dialectical images as details can capture the original subject in ways indiscernible to the natural eye.[7] Either way, the detail helps to re-live the work, re-produce the urban, re-create history.

DISPLACEMENT

Could montage as the formal principle of the new technology be used to reconstruct an experiential world so that it provided a coherence of vision necessary for philosophical reflection?

Susan Buck-Morss[8]

At its crudest, dialectical imagery can mean rendering pairs of images, out of juxtaposed material in the city, or it can mean the placing of the work of art in the city in such a way that the site and meaning are recontextualized. This technique allows the conventional periodizations and causal explanations of historians to be destabilized and displaced. Meaning is then produced not by logical interpretation of facts and documents, but from a collision of politics, events, and ideas, shocked out from objects through their displacement in time and space.

TEXT IMAGE

Antique spoon – One thing is reserved to the greatest epic writers: the capacity to feed their heroes.

Walter Benjamin[9]

In *One-Way Street*, as in this quotation, Benjamin plays on the contradiction between subtitle (here "antique spoon") and the content of each prose piece.

Similarly, where artwork and text come together, meaning is displaced into the ambiguous state that hovers among or in-between matter and script. This can occur, for example, whenever we focus on scripts in the urban terrain as a way of rethinking and rereading that terrain, or whenever an artist uses words to displace the existing or perceived meaning of site and/or to reinscribe new meanings. In Benjamin's terms it is the "optical unconscious" where "a space informed by human consciousness gives way to a space informed by the unconscious."[10] The meaning of the work with both matter and text is an indefinable supplement, deliberately unknowable and ambiguous but present nonetheless.

CALM AND ADVENTUROUS TRAVEL

By close-ups of the things around us, by focusing on hidden details of familiar objects, by exploring commonplace milieus under the ingenious guidance of the camera, the film, on the one hand, extends our comprehension of the necessities which rule our lives; on the other hand, it manages to assure us of an immense and unexpected field of action. Our taverns and our metropolitan streets, our offices and furnished rooms, our railroad stations and our factories appeared to have us locked up hopelessly. Then came the film and burst the prison-world asunder by the dynamite of the tenth of a second, so that now, in the midst of its far-flung ruins and debris, we calmly and adventurously go travelling.

Walter Benjamin[11]

So far we have moved from considering public artwork in its everyday context to rethinking this relation in two ways: either by considering the everyday context as artwork in and of itself, or by considering particular pieces of work which intervene in the built environment of the city, thus transforming it. We now move on to consider dialectical imagery in relation to temporality.

FREEZING TIME   ERASING TIME

Dialectical imagery tends to destabilize time, making it discontinuous, pushing it outside of historical, periodized time. How then might we pursue this clue and further consider the issue of temporality in works of public art?

An image of a work does two things to time. First, it can freeze time, rendering the work prisoner of a particular historical moment. Second, it can erase time altogether, such that the work of art is without any historical period.

EVENT

To live is to leave traces.
Walter Benjamin[12]

Yet works of art are neither fixed in time, nor are they atemporal things. Rather they are part of social reproduction, part of the way people live their lives, part of the way cities evolve, part of the way art itself changes. Works of art can therefore be temporal in two ways: event and motility.

This pair of images shows a piece of sign-writing in the sky over Washington Square. Clearly this is an event and therefore temporal. The work is in motion and there is a sense of time even within the photograph of the event. But beyond this very short temporality, there is also a much longer one being alluded to, and this, curiously, is made explicit by the moment of erasure. As the white vapour disperses, as you can already see happening here in the second image of the pair, the work ceases to have ontological meaning in terms of its presence, and so becomes a work of art whose meaning comes from its temporary presence demarcated most explicitly through the ending of the materiality of the work and its onward existence as trace, memory, record, documentation, and so forth. Furthermore, the very fact that the photographer has chosen to record the moment of creation and simultaneous dispersal suggests that the event is significant, that something has happened that is significant and meaningful.

MOTILITY

Because movement is not limited to submitting passively to space and time, it actively assumes them.
Maurice Merleau-Ponty[13]

Another response to the problem of time in public art is to consider a sense of movement and passage around and through a work, showing its spaces not as isolated spaces and surfaces but as relational entities, encountered in differing sequences, glances, and memories. The aim here is frequently to concentrate on the moving subject's experience, showing how different parts of the work and of the city are encountered, how they emerge and present themselves to the motile subject.[14]

SPATIAL STORIES

In wide arcs of wandering through the city
I saw to either side of what is seen,
and noticed treasures where it was thought there were none.
I passed through a more fluid city.
I broke up the imprint of all familiar places,
shutting my eyes to the boredom of modern contours.

Aidan Andrew Dunn[15]

Urban fragments and dialectical images locate us physically and conceptually in both space and time. They allow us to make momentary sense of the world. Such fragments and images are an intrinsic element of spatial storytelling – for exploring city and self. In contemporary urban and architectural discourse, we are increasingly obsessed by figures which traverse space: the flâneur, the spy, the detective, the prostitute, the rambler, the cyprian. These urban figures are metaphors of our quest for knowledge, they are voyages of exploration, passages of revelation, journeys of discovery in, and of, the city, in and of the self. They are "spatial stories."[16] Between public and private, outer and inner, past and future, real and imagined, we all tell spatial stories, we exchange narratives in and of the city. Narrative is then a form of space and time, an unfolding of space through time and vice versa, an unfolding of time in space.

Another issue raised through time is the temporality of the everyday, that is as normal, routine encounters of works of various kinds as might happen day in and day out. With regards to architecture, this is a point that we have made in the Strangely Familiar programme showing how architecture is not just the product of architects, planners, and built environment professionals, but is also the product of users, subjects, and metropolitan dwellers of all kinds.[17] The same is true for public art. Art is not just produced by artists, but is reproduced by viewers and audiences.

278

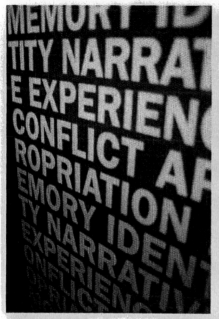

BIRTH OF THE USER

Use value, subordinated for centuries to exchange value, can now come first again. How? By and in urban society, from this reality which still resists and preserves for us use value, the city. A weakened but true vision of this truth is an urban reality for "users" and not for capitalist speculators, builders and technicians.

Henri Lefebvre[18]

By considering works in use, we can suggest that they are embedded within common human history – and thus that works of art are not static art objects. This can occur in three ways.

First, by fabricating the work through a process which involves the public. This may tend toward the choreographic, where the public works within a framework set out by the artist.

Second, by making the work as something which exists through its transformative interaction with a participant audience. This tends toward the aleatory, the accidental where the work is manifest less as on object and more as an event.

Third, by considering the way that works are experienced. This can involve any object or space in the city, whereby the artistic element is provided the user who may also operate intentionally or unintentionally as critic.

279

BIRTH OF THE CRITIC

The problem arises of knowing whether the unity of a discourse is based not so much on the permanence and uniqueness of an object as on the space in which various objects emerge and are continuously transformed.

Michel Foucault[19]

Once we start to consider the user, the meaning of the work of art shifts inexorably away from the artist and the object toward the reception of the work. What, in this light, is the role of the critic? To what degree do critics' opinions and observations determine the meaning of the work? Does the role of the critic amount to that of the pedagog, subverting critical dialog, or are they an intermediary who might help provoke a response from those who experience public art? Or if we follow Foucault in seeing all objects and events being constituted by discourse, we might even posit that the notion that works of art are not the cause or the origin of debates about art, but are the effect or trace of such debates conducted between critic, artist, and user. The preceding two images, for example, intimate at two very different critical positions on the work, thus in effect making two different pieces of work.

GIFT ECONOMY

Participating in your economy, I did not know what I could have desired.

Luce Irigaray[20]

Another way of thinking about this is then to posit the act of theory as a work of art in its own right, or rather to consider that theory is in itself a form of practice. This is not to deny the practice of the artist, nor that the artist operates as critic, but to complexify the ways in which we understand the relation of art and criticism, practice and theory, private and public.

We began this chapter by stating the public and the private need to be understood dialectically. Public art may bridge the private worlds of those who create it and the private lives of those who view it. As such, it may render public themes private, and private themes public. Public art is then an economy of exchange, between artists, public, critics. The challenge here is to take this as an economy not of objects to be sold, bought, and received as possessions of individuals and corporations, but as an economy of giving, desiring, and pleasuring – an economy which is yet unknown.

Notes

1 Allan Kaprow, cited in *Mapping the Terrain: New Genre Public Art*, ed. Suzanne Lacy (Seattle, WA: Bay Press, 1995), 36.
2 Walter Benjamin, *One Way Street* (London: Verso, 1992).
3 André Breton, *Mad Love* (Lincoln, NE: University of Nebraska Press, 1987), 14–15.
4 Walter Benjamin, *Passagen-werk*, cited in Susan Buck-Morss, *The Dialectics of Seeing: Walter Benjamin and the Arcades Project* (Cambridge, MA: MIT Press, 1991), 23.
5 Georg Simmel, *The Philosophy of Money*, 2nd edn (London: Routledge, 1990), 55.
6 Walter Benjamin, "A Small History of Photography," in *One Way Street*, 243.
7 Walter Benjamin, "The Work of Art in the Age of Mechanical Reproduction," in *Illuminations* (New York: Schocken, 1969), 220, 236–237. See also Brian Mclaren, "Under the Sign of Reproduction," *Journal of Architectural Education* 45(2) (1992): 98–106.
8 Buck-Morss, *Dialectics of Seeing*, 23.
9 Benjamin, *One Way Street*, 75.
10 Benjamin, "Small History of Photography," 243.
11 Benjamin, "Work of Art in the Age of Mechanical Reproduction," 236.
12 Walter Benjamin, "Paris: Capital of the Nineteenth Century," cited in *Sexuality and Space*, ed. Beatriz Colomina (New York: Princeton Architectural Press, 1992), 74.
13 Maurice Merleau-Ponty, *Phenomenology of Perception* (London: Routledge and Kegan Paul, 1962), 104.
14 This is what Adolf Hildebrand called the kinesthetic image (*Bewegungsvorstellungen*). See Adolf Hildebrand, "The Problem of Form in the Fine Arts," in *Empathy, Form and Space: Problems in German Aesthetics, 1873–1893*, eds. Harry Francis Mallgrave and Eleftherios Ikonomou (Santa Monica, CA: Getty Center for the History of Art and Humanities 1994), 229. See also Martin Caiger-Smith, "Site Work," in *Site Work: Architecture in Photography since Early Modernism*, eds. Martin Caiger-Smith and David Chandler (London: Photographers' Gallery, 1991), 7.
15 Aidan Andrew Dunn, *Vale Royal* (Uppingham: Goldmark, 1995), 9.
16 For Michael de Certeau on spatial stories see *The Practice of Everyday Life* (Berkeley, CA: University of California Press, 1988), 115–122.
17 The Strangely Familiar program was started by Iain Borden, Joe Kerr, Alicia Pivaro, and Jane Rendell. Events included a touring exhibition and related symposia in the United Kingdom during 1995 and 1996, as well as two publications: *Strangely Familiar: Narratives of Architecture in the City*, eds. Iain Borden, Joe Kerr, Alicia Pivaro, and Jane Rendell (London: Routledge, 1995); and *The Unknown City: and Social Space*, eds. Iain Borden, Joe Kerr, and Jane Rendell, with Alicia Pivaro (Cambridge, MA: MIT, 2000).
18 Henri Lefebvre, "Right to the City," *Writings on Cities*, eds. Eleonore Kofman and Elizabeth Lebas (Oxford: Blackwell, 1996).
19 Michel Foucault, *The Archaeology of Knowledge* (New York: Pantheon, 1972), 314.
20 Luce Irigaray, *Elemental Passions* (London: Athlone Press, 1992), 61.

INDEX